China's New United Front Work in Hong Kong

Sonny Shiu-Hing Lo
Steven Chung-Fun Hung
Jeff Hai-Chi Loo

China's New United Front Work in Hong Kong

Penetrative Politics and Its Implications

Sonny Shiu-Hing Lo
University of Hong Kong, SPACE
North Point, Hong Kong

Steven Chung-Fun Hung
Education University of Hong Kong
New Territories, Hong Kong

Jeff Hai-Chi Loo
Lingnan University
Tuen Mun, Hong Kong

ISBN 978-981-13-8482-0   ISBN 978-981-13-8483-7 (eBook)
https://doi.org/10.1007/978-981-13-8483-7

© The Editor(s) (if applicable) and The Author(s), under exclusive licence to Springer Nature Singapore Pte Ltd. 2019
This work is subject to copyright. All rights are solely and exclusively licensed by the Publisher, whether the whole or part of the material is concerned, specifically the rights of translation, reprinting, reuse of illustrations, recitation, broadcasting, reproduction on microfilms or in any other physical way, and transmission or information storage and retrieval, electronic adaptation, computer software, or by similar or dissimilar methodology now known or hereafter developed.
The use of general descriptive names, registered names, trademarks, service marks, etc. in this publication does not imply, even in the absence of a specific statement, that such names are exempt from the relevant protective laws and regulations and therefore free for general use.
The publisher, the authors and the editors are safe to assume that the advice and information in this book are believed to be true and accurate at the date of publication. Neither the publisher nor the authors or the editors give a warranty, express or implied, with respect to the material contained herein or for any errors or omissions that may have been made. The publisher remains neutral with regard to jurisdictional claims in published maps and institutional affiliations.

This Palgrave Macmillan imprint is published by the registered company Springer Nature Singapore Pte Ltd.
The registered company address is: 152 Beach Road, #21-01/04 Gateway East, Singapore 189721, Singapore

Dedicated to the late Professor Ming Chan of Stanford University

Acknowledgment

This book originated from a presentation at the Hong Kong Foreign Correspondents Club on China's new united front work in Hong Kong in late June 2018. We have to thank James Pomfret and Gregory Torode for providing us with a golden opportunity to develop our important project and to share our preliminary observations. We are also grateful to one of our friends who does not want to be named, who listened attentively to our preliminary findings and who raised good questions to provoke our further thoughts.

The three authors of this book worked very hard to complete this book project by utilizing all the open sources. We hope that this book will benefit all those interested in the study of China in general and Hong Kong in particular.

We dedicate this book to the late Professor Ming Chan of Stanford University. We were saddened by his sudden departure in late 2018.

March 31, 2019

Sonny Shiu-Hing Lo
Steven Chung-Fun Hung
Jeff Hai-Chi Loo

Contents

1. A Comprehensive Framework of Understanding the Context and Content of China's New United Front Work on Hong Kong — 1

2. The Democratic Alliance for the Betterment and Progress of Hong Kong as Flagship of China's United Front Work — 43

3. Political Participation of Fujianese Interest Groups — 77

4. Inter-Union Rivalry Between Pro-Beijing Federation of Trade Unions and Pro-Democracy Confederation of Trade Unions — 107

5. United Front and Women Interest Groups from Pro-British to Pro-Beijing — 149

6. United Front Work on Six Religions — 189

7. Penetrative Politics from Neighborhood Associations to District Federations: Electoral Mobilization and Competition — 221

8	Youth Interest Groups from Pro-Beijing Front to Radical Resistance	255
9	Influencing Civil Society Through Mass Media, Education and Migration	289
10	Co-opting Individuals with External Implications: Business Elites, Democrats, Civil Servants, Educators and Taiwanese	337
11	Conclusion	365
Bibliography		381
Index		401

Abbreviations

AAF	Association for the Advancement of Feminism
ACFWHKDA	All-China Federation of Women Hong Kong Delegates Association
ACWF	All-China Women Federation
ACYF	All-China Youth Federation
ALP	Australia Labor Party
BPA	Business and Professionals Alliance for Hong Kong
CAHKMS	Chinese Association of Hong Kong and Macao Studies
CCP	Chinese Communist Party
CIC	Hong Kong Christian Industrial Committee
CIHK	Confucius Institute of Hong Kong
CLSGUF	Central Leading Small Group on United Front
CMCFA	The Chinese Muslim Cultural and Fraternal Association
CPCA	Chinese Patriotic Catholic Association
CPPCC	Chinese People's Political Consultative Conference
CPPCCYA	Hong Kong CPPCC Youth Association
CRC	Cooperative Resources Center
CSGU	Hong Kong Civil Servants General Union
CTU	Hong Kong Confederation of Trade Unions
DAB	Democratic Alliance for the Betterment and Progress of Hong Kong
DPP	Democratic Progressive Party
EDAA	Eastern District All-Sectors Association
EEGU	Education Employees General Union
EGSP	Education Bureau, Government, Grant-in-Aid, Subsidized and Private Junior Schools Junior Staff Union.
EKDRC	East Kowloon District Residents' Committee

ExCo	Executive Council
FCC	Fukien Chamber of Commerce
FCSU	Hong Kong Federation of Civil Service Unions
FLU	Federation of Hong Kong and Kowloon Labour Unions
FNTY	Federation of New Territories Youth
FTU	Federation of Trade Unions
GESU	Government Educational Staff Union
HKACA	Hong Kong Army Cadets Association
HKASTA	Hong Kong Aided School Teachers' Association
HKBA	The Hong Kong Buddhist Association
HKCWC	Hong Kong Chinese Women's Club
HKFEW	Hong Kong Federation of Education Workers
HKFFA	Hong Kong Federation of Fujian Associations
HKFW	Hong Kong Federation of Women
HKGU	Hong Kong Graziers Union
HKIF	Hong Kong Island Federation
HKIWA	Hong Kong Island Women Associations
HKKFPWGU	Hong Kong and Kowloon Flowers and Plants Workers General Union
HKMAO	Hong Kong and Macao Affairs Office
HKPA	Hong Kong Progressive Alliance
HKPTU	Hong Kong Professional Teachers' Union
HKSAR	Hong Kong Special Administrative Region
HKSWRA	Hong Kong Students War Relief Association
HKTA	Hong Kong Teachers' Association
HKTFA	The Hong Kong Taoist Federation of Associations
HKUYA	The Hong Kong United Youth Association
HKWDA	Hong Kong Women Development Association
ILO	International Labour Organization
JPC	Justice and Peace Commission
KA	Kaifong Associations
KCRA	Kowloon City Residents Association
KFA	Kowloon Federation of Associations
KMB	Kowloon Motor Bus
KMT	Kuomintang
KTRA	Kwun Tong Residents Association
KWND	Kowloon West New Dynamic
KWOF	Kowloon Women's Organization Federation
LDFHK	Liberal Democratic Federation of Hong Kong
LegCo	Legislative Council
LO	Liaison Office
LP	Liberal Party

LPA	Liberal Party of Australia
MAC	Mutual Aid Committees
MKA	Mongkok Kaifong Association
NCNA	New China News Agency
NPA	National Party of Australia
NPC	National People's Congress
NPP	New People's Party
NSC	National Security Commission
NTAS	New Territories Association of Societies
OC	Owners Corporations
OIWA	Hong Kong Outlying Islands Women Association
PLA	People's Liberation Army
PMWC	Provisional Minimum Wage Commission
POAS	Principal Officials Accountability System
PRC	People's Republic of China
PS	Positive Synergy
QFA	Quanzhou Federation of Associations
RC	Rural Committees
SARS	Severe Acute Respiratory Syndrome
SCNPC	Standing Committee of the National People's Congress
SDAA	Southern District All-Sectors Association
SRA	Shumshuipo Residents Association
TCSC	Taoist Cultural Study Center
TMFW	Tuen Mun Federation of Women
TSA	Territory-wide System Assessment
TSWWA	Tin Shui Wai Women Association
TUC	Hong Kong and Kowloon Trades Union Council
TWKTDWA	Tsuen Wan Kwai Tsing District Women Association
UDHK	United Democrats of Hong Kong
WDAA	Wanchai District All-Sectors Association
YEA	The Y Elites Association

List of Figures

Fig. 1.1	A comprehensive framework of understanding China's new united front work on Hong Kong	41
Fig. 2.1	The DAB organization chart. Source: "Organization Structure," in the website of the Democratic Alliance for the Betterment and Progress of Hong Kong, available in http://www.dab.org.hk/AboutUs.php?nid=234, access date: April 4, 2018	47
Fig. 2.2	Number of DAB district branches, 1992–2018. Sources: See the website of the Democratic Alliance for the Betterment and Progress of Hong Kong in http://www.dab.org.hk/branch.php, access date: April 4, 2018	48
Fig. 2.3	Comparison of the votes gained by DAB and pro-Beijing forces in Legislative Council elections, 1998–2016. Sources: Votes gained were calculated from the official statistics in the website of the Electoral Affairs Commission	52
Fig. 2.4	Comparison of the voters gained by DAB and pro-Beijing forces in District Council elections, 1994–2015. Sources: Votes gained were calculated from the official statistics in the website of the Electoral Affairs Commission	55
Fig. 2.5	Numbers of DAB legislators, district councilors and members, 1992–2018. Sources: Same as Table 2.6	57
Fig. 2.6	The political structure of China's united front work in Hong Kong	64
Fig. 2.7	Formation of united front groups against Occupy Central Movement. Sources: The data are collected and calculated from a website that showed a signature campaign mobilizing 1411 organizations to join the petition in 2014, available in: https://	

	www.sign4peacedemocracy.hk/index.php?r=index/support, access date: April 4, 2018	66
Fig. 2.8	Votes gained by the pro-Beijing and pro-democracy camps in Legislative Council elections in Hong Kong Islands, 1998–2018	73
Fig. 2.9	Votes gained by the pro-Beijing and pro-democracy camp in Legislative Council elections in Kowloon West, 1998–2018. Sources: Votes gained were calculated from the official statistics in the website of the Electoral Affairs Commission	74
Fig. 2.10	Votes gained by the pro-Beijing and pro-Democracy camp in Legislative Council elections in New Territories East, 1998–2018. Sources: Votes gained were calculated from the official statistics in the website of the Electoral Affairs Commission	75
Fig. 3.1	Types of HKFFA affiliated groups. Source: Hong Kong Federation of Fujian Associations, *Special Issues*, vol. 10 (Hong Kong: Meijia Publishing Limited, October 2015)	86
Fig. 4.1	Patterns of activities of the Federation of Trade Unions, 1945–2008. Source: Hong Kong Federation of Trade Unions (2008), *Passing the Torch with Glorious Years: Collective Memories of Hong Kong Labourers and the historical photos of the Federation of Trade Unions, 1948–2008*. Hong Kong: Xinhua Book Store	122
Fig. 4.2	The organization structure of the FTU. Sources: http://www.ftu.org.hk/en/about?id=13. *There are five mainland consultation services centers, location in Guangzhou, Shenzhen, Dongguan, Huizhou and Zhongshan, see the FTU website, in http://www.ftu.org.hk/en/participate?id=110, access date: April 28, 2018	123
Fig. 4.3	Workforce participation in trade unions, 1990–2016. Sources: Registry of Trade Unions, *Annual Statistical Report of Trade Unions in Hong Kong*, from 1991 to 2016 (Hong Kong: Registry of Trade Unions, Labour Department), and Hong Kong Government, *Hong Kong Annual Report*, from 1990 to 2016, Hong Kong: Hong Kong Government	126
Fig. 4.4	Memberships of different trade unions, 1984–2016. Sources: Registry of Trade Unions, *Annual Statistical Report of Trade Unions in Hong Kong*, from 1984 to 2016 (Hong Kong: Registry of Trade Unions, Labour Department of the HKSAR Government, from 1984 to 2016)	127
Fig. 5.1	Core and peripheral pro-Beijing women groups	161
Fig. 7.1	The organization chart of the Kowloon Federation of Associations. Source: See https://klnfas.hk/tc/, access date: February 8, 2018	241
Fig. 7.2	Penetrative politics at the district level	253
Fig. 8.1	Core and peripheral pro-Beijing youth groups	256
Fig. 8.2	The Values and Attitudes of Hong Kong Youths: Accepting or Resisting United Front Work	257

List of Tables

Table 2.1	The background of founding members of DAB and HKPA	45
Table 2.2	DAB chairpersons, 1992–2018	46
Table 2.3	Major political representation of DAB members in Hong Kong and China	50
Table 2.4	The direct election results of the Legislative Council, 1998–2016	51
Table 2.5	The results of the District Council elections, 1999–2015	53
Table 2.6	Numbers of DAB legislators, district councilors and members, 1992–2018	56
Table 2.7	Success rate of the DAB candidates elected at various districts	58
Table 2.8	The success rate of DAB candidates in District Council elections, 1994–2015	59
Table 2.9	The DAB training programs	60
Table 2.10	DAB's direction camp	62
Table 2.11	The DAB forums and conferences	63
Table 2.12	Number and percentage of votes for DAB in the 2016 legislative election and various by-elections	65
Table 2.13	The DAB's political stance and political realities	67
Table 2.14	The DAB's new policy suggestions and initiatives, 2017–2018	69
Table 2.15	Activities showing the alliance between the Liaison Office and the DAB in 2017	71
Table 3.1	The main Fujianese interest groups in Hong Kong	82
Table 3.2	Types of HKFFA affiliated groups	87
Table 3.3	Fujianese candidates and District Council election results in North Point District, 2007–2015	89
Table 3.4	Fujianese legislators, 1997–2018	92
Table 3.5	Key Fujianese representatives in political parties as of 2018	93

xviii   LIST OF TABLES

Table 3.6	The Fujianese participation in the leadership of the Democratic Alliance for the Betterment of Hong Kong	94
Table 3.7	Fujianese advisors in the Democratic Alliance for the Betterment and Progress of Hong Kong	95
Table 3.8	Fujianese participation in pro-Beijing district-based groups, 2018	96
Table 3.9	Participation of HKFFA members in the 2017 Chief Executive Election Committee	97
Table 3.10	The elected Fujianese in the PRC National People's Congress Election, 2017	98
Table 3.11	Fujianese community leaders appointed as members of the Chinese People's Political Consultative Conference in 2018	99
Table 3.12	Fujianese as Basic Law Committee members as of 2018	100
Table 3.13	Chinese official attending the HKFFA's activities	101
Table 3.14	Mobilization activities of HKFFA	104
Table 3.15	Fujianese participation and anti-occupy interest groups	105
Table 4.1	Labor Unions affiliated with the Federation of Trade Unions	114
Table 4.2	Summary of FTU's membership and number of labor unions, 1948–2016	115
Table 4.3	Unions and Membership of Hong Kong with the Hong Kong Federation of Trade Unions and the Hong Kong and Kowloon Trade Unions Council Affiliated Membership, 1967–1983	116
Table 4.4	Trade unions in Hong Kong, 1984–2016	119
Table 4.5	The largest four trade unions in Hong Kong: platform and ideology	121
Table 4.6	FTU, CTU and public-sector unions with more than 3000 members	124
Table 4.7	Civil servants' union membership	124
Table 4.8	The Hong Kong-based service centers under the Federation of Trade Unions	125
Table 4.9	Election results of the Legislative Council's labor functional constituency, 1985–2016	128
Table 4.10	The FTU's participation results in Legislative Council Direct Elections, 1998–2016	129
Table 4.11	Election Results of the pro-Beijing Candidates in District Council Functional Constituency under Legislative Council elections, 2012 and 2016	130
Table 4.12	FTU District Councils members, 1999–2015	131
Table 4.13	Election results of the Labour Advisory Board in November 2016	132
Table 4.14	FTU Participation in the Chief Executive Election Committee's subsector elections, 2016	133

LIST OF TABLES　　xix

Table 4.15	Higher-level political representations of the Federation Trade Unions members	134
Table 4.16	FTU members in China's National People's Congress	135
Table 4.17	The political position of trade unions in controversial cases	137
Table 4.18	Trade unions in the aviation industry	145
Table 5.1	The educational and social activities of the Hong Kong Chinese Women Club	151
Table 5.2	The main leaders of the Hong Kong Federation of Women	158
Table 5.3	The gender distribution of Executive Councilors	163
Table 5.4	The gender distribution of Legislative Councilors, 1966–1984	164
Table 5.5	The gender distribution of Urban Councilors	165
Table 5.6	Women political participation in Urban Council and Regional Council	166
Table 5.7	Women participation in Legislative Council elections	167
Table 5.8	Differences in women and men participation in District Council elections	168
Table 5.9	The success rate and seats occupation rate of women candidates in District Council elections	168
Table 5.10	Political mobilization of pro-Beijing women interest groups in denouncing the oath-taking behavior of pro-democracy legislators-elect	170
Table 5.11	Political representation of Hong Kong Women in China's and Hong Kong's political institutions, 2018	171
Table 5.12	Political background of female Hong Kong members of the Chinese People's Political Consultative Conference, 2018	172
Table 5.13	Women participation in the District Council elections in outlying islands	176
Table 5.14	United front women groups in opposition to the 2014 Occupy Central Movement	180
Table 5.15	Co-optation of leaders of the Kowloon Women's Organizations Federation into China's Political Institutions, 2011	181
Table 5.16	Ten affiliated groups shared by the Hong Kong Island Women's Association and the Hong Kong Federation of Women	183
Table 5.17	Financial situation of the Pro-Democracy Association for the advancement of feminism	186
Table 6.1	Religious leaders who were politically co-opted before July 1, 1997	216
Table 6.2	Hong Kong members of the Chinese People's Political Consultative Conference	216
Table 7.1	Participation of *kaifong* associations and rural committees in opposition to the 2014 Occupy Central Movement	226

Table 7.2	The evolution of Kwun Tong *kaifong* associations	227
Table 7.3	Leadership and organization of three main district-based federations, 2018	231
Table 7.4	Key overlapping membership between the DAB and three district federations	232
Table 7.5	Membership OF Agriculture-based Hong Kong Graziers Union and Hong Kong and Kowloon Flowers and Plants Workers General Union, 1973–2016	234
Table 7.6	Women interest groups absorbed by the NTAS in 1990	236
Table 7.7	The district distribution of interest groups affiliated with the NTAS	236
Table 7.8	Interest groups and individual membership of the NTAS	237
Table 7.9	Interest groups under the district committees of the Kowloon Federation of Associations	241
Table 7.10	The linkages between Kowloon Federation of Associations, Kowloon West New Dynamic, East Kowloon District Residents' Committee and Positive Synergy	243
Table 7.11	District-based interest groups under the Kowloon Federation of Associations	244
Table 7.12	A comparison of two by-elections held for Legislative Council in March and November 2018	248
Table 7.13	Some declared donors in Rebecca Chan's election campaign	249
Table 7.14	Rental expenditure of Rebecca Chan's election campaign	250
Table 8.1	Chairmen of Hong Kong United Youth Association, 1992–2018	259
Table 8.2	Education background of General Committee members of the Hong Kong United Youth Association, 2012–2015	261
Table 8.3	Participation of HKUYA members in the 12th All-China Youth Federation	261
Table 8.4	Participation of HKUYA members in the 12th Chinese Youth Federations at the provincial and municipal levels	262
Table 8.5	Participation of HKUYA members as Legislators, 1997–2018	264
Table 8.6	Chinese officials who attended the activities of the Y Elites Association	268
Table 8.7	Chinese officials attended the major events of the uniformed cadet groups	275
Table 8.8	Critical Marxist groups and their political platform	281
Table 8.9	Radical localist groups and their political platform	284
Table 9.1	Newspapers ownership and the political background of media proprietors, 2019	294
Table 9.2	The editorial position of media organizations on the 2014 Occupy Central Movement	296

Table 9.3	The editorial position of the mass media on the PRC formal support of the Hong Kong Government's action of banning the Hong Kong National Party	297
Table 9.4	The classification and number of media in Hong Kong, 2018	299
Table 9.5	Participation of Hong Kong and Taiwan actors in the mainland's three political films. 2009–2017	300
Table 9.6	Prominent Hong Kong and Taiwan actors and actresses "blacklisted" by the PRC authorities	302
Table 9.7	The evolution of the Sino United Publishing	303
Table 9.8	Internet media and popularity of their Facebook	307
Table 9.9	The transformation of the pro-Beijing schools in Hong Kong after 1997	313
Table 9.10	Electoral results of the education functional constituency in Legislative Council elections, 1985–2016	315
Table 9.11	Political background of candidates who competed with candidates from the Professional Teachers' Union	316
Table 9.12	Major teachers' trade unions in Hong Kong, 2017	318
Table 9.13	Educational interest groups that are not registered as Teachers' Unions	319
Table 9.14	Membership of Education Unions, 1955–2017	321
Table 9.15	Different trade unions at Hong Kong's tertiary institutions in 2017	323
Table 9.16	The elected representatives from educational interest groups in the education subsector elections of Chief Executive Election Committee in 2006, 2011 and 2016	325
Table 9.17	Hong Kong academics as the founding members of the Chinese Association of Hong Kong and Macao studies	326
Table 9.18	Demographic and social characteristics of one-way permit holders, 1998–2017	332
Table 10.1	Comparison between the Liberal Party and the Business and Professionals Alliance for Hong Kong, 2019	341
Table 10.2	The contributions of Hong Kong Business Elites to China's modernization	347
Table 10.3	Co-opting pro-democracy elites	348
Table 10.4	Co-opting Hong Kong civil servants	351
Table 10.5	Chronology of a joint statement of the principals of ten universities	355
Table 10.6	Major Taiwan political figures who met mainland Chinese officials	358
Table 10.7	The chronology of the Lu Li-an incident	360
Table 10.8	Huang Xiangmo's donation to Australian political parties	363
Table 11.1	Four types of elites	375

CHAPTER 1

A Comprehensive Framework of Understanding the Context and Content of China's New United Front Work on Hong Kong

Historically, united front work in the People's Republic of China (PRC) could be traced back to an alliance between the Chinese Communist Party (CCP) and the Kuomintang (KMT or Nationalist Party) first in 1922 under the influence of the Communist International and later in 1937 shortly after the 1936 Xian incident.[1] In 1939, Mao Zedong regarded united front work as an indispensable element, together with armed struggle and party-building, in the CCP's revolutionary victory over the KMT.[2] During the anti-Japanese war, the CCP's united front work targeted at the "workers, peasants, small and medium capitalist classes, capitalists from ethnic nationalities, large landlords and the big capitalist class."[3] In August 1940, the CCP adopted a so-called three-three system in governing its controlled areas, where one-third of the administrators came from the CCP, one-third from the "progressive elements" of non-CCP parties and the rest from non-party individuals.[4]

---

[1] Lyman P. Van Slyke, "The United Front in China," *Journal of Contemporary History*, Vol. 5, No. 3 (1970), pp. 119–135. Also see James C. F. Wang, *Contemporary Chinese Politics: An Introduction* (New Jersey: Pearson Education, 2002), pp. 15–19.

[2] Liu Rumei, "Discussion on the Origins and development of the United Front Work," *Journal of the Academy of Guizhou Socialism* (in Chinese), vol. 4 (2014), pp. 26–30.

[3] Zhang Suyun and Xu Jian, "The Anti-Japanese Ethnic Nationalities' United Front and War Victory," *Journal of Liaoning University (Philosophy and Social Sciences)* (in Chinese), vol. 33, no. 5 (2005), pp. 1–6.

[4] Wang Mingqian, "'Three-Three System' and 'Two Factions': Regime-Building and United Front in Anti-Japanese Bases in Central China," *Journal of Zhejiang Normal University* (in Chinese), vol. 40, no. 6 (2015), pp. 34–42.

© The Author(s) 2019
S. S.-H. Lo et al., *China's New United Front Work in Hong Kong*,
https://doi.org/10.1007/978-981-13-8483-7_1

After the PRC was established on October 1, 1949, the CCP has been utilizing the Chinese People's Political Consultative Conference (CPPCC) as a tool for conducting united front work on non-Communist and "democratic" political parties.[5] In the recent years, the CPPCC has become a platform for "democratic" parties not only to "reflect public opinion" but also to "maintain their loyalty" to the CCP and patriotism.[6] With the implementation of the open-door policy in China under the leadership of the late Deng Xiaoping, united front work has, since the mid-1970s, been expanding to the intellectuals, the business people, non-CCP individuals and religious and charity groups.[7] In short, the PRC's united front work has been implementing the concept of the "mass line," consolidating the CCP on the one hand and unifying the ordinary people on the other.[8]

In the case of Hong Kong, the CCP decided to "fully utilize Hong Kong's position" after the founding of the PRC so that China could develop external relations and trade.[9] Liao Chengzhi, the former director of the PRC's Hong Kong and Macao Affairs Office, which was set up in August 1978, had told the Hong Kong members of the CPPCC in March 1978 that the PRC government would like to unite those people who "support Hong Kong's sovereignty return to China" and who "maintain

---

[5] Shih Wen, "Political Parties in Communist China," *Asian Survey*, vol. 3. no. 3 (1963), pp. 157–164.

[6] Xu Zhongtao, "The Basic Viewpoints of the Democratic Parties in Publicizing Public Opinion and Maintaining Principles," *Journal of the Academy of Guizhou Socialism* (in Chinese), vol. 4 (2013), pp. 26–28.

[7] Zhang Jiaoxia, "Examining the Characteristics of Intellectuals in Private Tertiary Schools Outside the Party and United Front Work," *Science and Technology Innovation Herald* (in Chinese), no. 11 (2013), pp. 217–218. Sun Lizhen, "China's Private-Sector Business Groups and the Features of United Front," *Journal of Zhejiang Shuren University* (in Chinese), vol. 17, no. 1 (2017), pp. 105–108. Wang Xiaojin, "The Evolution of the United Front Theory and Practices of the Chinese Communist Party," *Research on the Chinese Communist Party's History and Building* (in Chinese), vol. 219, no. 2 (2013), pp. 99–103. Ming Shifa and Li Lin, "The United Front Path and Improvement in Developing the Religious Sector and Charity Organizations," *Journal of Yunnan Nationalities University (Social Science)* (in Chinese), vol. 29, no. 5 (2012), pp. 66–72.

[8] Luo Hai, "Discussion of the Party-Building and United Front Work Under the New Circumstances," *Journal of the Academy of Guizhou Socialism* (in Chinese), Vol. 4 (2013), pp. 40–43.

[9] Wu Bin, "Liao Chengzhi and New China's United Front on Hong Kong and Macao," *Journal of Fujian Institute of Socialism* (in Chinese), Vol. 89, No. 2 (2012), pp. 9–12.

Hong Kong's prosperity."[10] Liao repeated these remarks in his meeting with the business people from Hong Kong in November 1982, when the Sino-British negotiations over Hong Kong's future began. His remarks were in conformity with Deng Xiaoping's idea that the "one country, two systems" in which Hong Kong would maintain its existing lifestyle for 50 years after 1997 would have the ultimate objective of "reunifying the Taiwan comrades."[11] With the emergence of the pro-Taiwan independence movement in the 1990s and 2000s, the former PRC President Jiang Zemin asserted that united front work was the main instrument through which the CCP would reunify Taiwan in the long run.[12] The united front work in Hong Kong and Macao has focused on the attraction of "comrades" in the two territories to invest their capital in the mainland, to assist the PRC's economic modernization and to interact with mainland Chinese for the sake of "developing a centrifugal force among the Chinese and overseas Chinese toward their motherland."[13]

Shortly before the United Front Regulation was revised in September 2015, a leading small group on united front work was formed by the CCP and its head was a Politburo member, Sun Chunlan.[14] The leading small group's first meeting was chaired by the CCP Secretary-General Xi Jinping, emphasizing the need for the Party to consolidate the unity among ethnic minorities in mainland China and to implement the principles and policy of united front work. In view of the fact that many young students, intellectuals and democrats in Hong Kong severely opposed the national education policy of the local government in the summer of 2012, PRC authorities responsible for Hong Kong matters began deeply concerned about the lack of political and social unity in the HKSAR.[15] The anti-national education movement in the HKSAR was a "precursor" to

[10] Ibid.
[11] Zhang Hongyan and Zhang Xiaomin, "The Content, Impact and Implications of Deng Xiaoping's United front Theory," *Journal of Huzhou Teachers College*, Vol. 27, No. 5 (2005), pp. 51–55.
[12] Wen Qiaoshi, *Tongzhan Gongzuo (United Front Work)* (Beijing: Chinese Communist Party History Publisher, 2008), pp. 15–16.
[13] Ibid., pp. 180–182.
[14] *Jinghua Shibao*, July 31, 2015. Also see Gerry Groot, "The Expansion of the United Front Under Xi Jinping," in Gloria Davies, Jeremy Goldkorn, and Luigi Tomba, eds., *China Story Yearbook 2015* (Canberra: ANU Press, 2016), pp. 166–177.
[15] Paul Morris and Edward Vickers, "Schooling, Politics and the Construction of Identity in Hong Kong: The 2012 'Moral and National Education' Crisis in Historical Context," *Comparative Education*, Vol. 51, No. 3 (2015), pp. 305–326.

the Occupy Central Movement from September to December 2014, when more young people of Hong Kong were determined to clamor for a faster pace and broader scope of democratization in the HKSAR.[16] The Occupy Central Movement, however, failed to exert pressure on the PRC to yield to the demands of the protestors. In the summer of 2015, a political reform plan prepared by the HKSAR government and supported by Beijing failed to get the support of most members of the Legislative Council. In early 2016, some young people in the HKSAR felt politically frustrated and alienated by not only the lack of democratic progress but also the disappearance of several local publishers who published books critical of the mainland, culminating in a riot in Mongkok where localist protestors confronted the police violently.[17]

The PRC leaders were shocked by the occurrence of the anti-national education campaign, the Occupy Central Movement and the Mongkok riot, believing that united front work would have to be strengthened in the HKSAR. After the 19th Party Congress was held in Beijing in October 2017, the CCP was determined to expand the "patriotic forces" in Hong Kong and Macao by adopting a new united front strategy.[18] First, "a stronger sense of national consciousness" will have to be developed through "an increase in the Hong Kong and Macao people's collective memory of their national and emotional bonds," "the refutation of remarks and actions that violate the Basic Law" and "an enhancement of their historical and interactional linkages with the mainlanders."[19] Second, "national education will have to be promoted" through "an identity education of using the Chinese constitution and the Basic Law as the core systems," "an emphasis on history and national education" and "an integration of the psychological acceptability of Hong Kong and Macao youth."[20] The "refutation of remarks and actions that violate the Basic Law" of Hong Kong

---

[16] Klavier Jie Ying Wang, "Mobilizing Resources to the Square: Hong Kong's Anti-Moral and National Education Movement as Precursor to the Umbrella Movement," *International Journal of Cultural Studies*, Vol. 20, No. 2 (2017), pp. 127–145.

[17] Sonny Shiu-Hing Lo, *The Politics of Policing in Greater China* (London: Palgrave, 2016).

[18] No author, *Thirteen Lectures on the Spirit of the 19th Party Congress* (in Chinese) (Guangzhou: New Democracy Publisher, 2017), p. 172. The publisher is under the administration of the Hong Kong Commercial Press Bookstore and the mainland's published book is obviously a work that espouses pro-CCP or CCP views.

[19] Ibid.

[20] Ibid.

has become apparent since the Occupy Central Movement in late 2014, leading to a series of actions, including the November 2014 interpretation of the Basic Law by the Standing Committee of the PRC National People's Congress over the provocative actions of two legislators-elect in their oath-taking ceremony. The pro-Beijing media launched attacks and political campaigns against political activists, such as Benny Tai, who was one of the leaders of the Occupy Central Movement, and Andy Chan Ho-tin, who was deemed to be one of the advocates of the so-called Hong Kong independence.[21] The pro-Beijing media, such as *Ta Kung Pao* and *Wen Wei Po*, have sent reporters to dig out all the details of the PRC's political enemies, namely, the radical democrats and even some moderate democrats who have been regarded as cultivating relations with the pro-Taiwan independence activists. Therefore, another hallmark of China's united front work in the HKSAR is to isolate its political enemies and level severe verbal criticisms against them.

The Content of China's United Front: Objectives, Evolution, Agents and Penetrative Politics

The PRC's united front work in Hong Kong under the British rule was mostly carried out by the New China News Agency (NCNA), which started its work in the colony in 1944 when the PRC Premier Zhou Enlai extended the CCP work from Guangdong to Hong Kong.[22] In the late 1940s, the NCNA's united front work aimed at wooing the political and social support of the local industrial and commercial elites, followed later by a focus on both business people and intellectuals.[23] During the PRC's Cultural Revolution from 1966 to 1976, Beijing neglected the role of the NCNA in Hong Kong, allowing the Guangdong Military Committee to issue directives to the agency.[24] The radical Maoists took command of the NCNA, stimulating local left-wing supporters to confront the Hong Kong British government violently through the actions of planting bombs and

---

[21] Gary Cheung, Tony Cheung and Joyce Ng, "China's top body lays down law on Hong Kong's oath-taking," *South China Morning Post*, November 8, 2016 in http://www.scmp.com/news/hong-kong/politics/article/2043768/chinas-top-body-lays-down-law-hong-kong-oath-taking, access date: April 3, 2018.

[22] Cindy Chu Yik-yi, *Chinese Communists and Hong Kong Capitalists* (London: Palgrave Macmillan, 2010), pp. 42–43.

[23] Ibid., p. 43.

[24] Ibid., p. 48.

conducting suicidal attacks at some anti-CCP local people. There was virtually no need for any united front work on the people of Hong Kong, losing the political and social support of those Hongkongers who cherished socio-political stability. After the Cultural Revolution in mainland China, Beijing's pragmatic and moderate officials took command of Hong Kong affairs, including the late former director of the Hong Kong Macao Affairs Office Liao Chengzhi from 1978 to 1983 and the late former director of the NCNA Xu Jiatun from 1983 to 1990. From the 1970s to the 1980s, when the open-door policy of the late PRC leader Deng Xiaoping was implemented, Beijing adopted a more outreaching united front work on Hong Kong, expanding official interactions with the members of the capitalist class, middle class and working class. Nevertheless, Beijing's united front work in Hong Kong was dealt a severe blow in June 1989, when the Tiananmen incident erupted. Xu Jiatun sided with the late and deposed Premier Zhao Ziyang and he eventually escaped to the United States. Moreover, Xu was at loggerheads with Lu Ping, the former late director of the Hong Kong Macao Affairs Office (HKMAO).[25] Xu's successor Zhou Nan (1990–1997) failed to create an image of being a popular CCP official, partly because he confronted the popular late Governor Christopher Patten over the British-initiated political reform plan and partly because of Zhou's apparently hard-line and politically arrogant style.[26] In light of the criticism that Xu Jiatun had paid too much attention on the local business elites in his united front work, Zhou Nan reoriented his united front target at the working class.

The objectives of the PRC's united front work in the HKSAR are multiple. They include the need for the PRC (1) to win the hearts and minds of more Hong Kong people than ever before, (2) to secure most Hong Kong people's support of the central government's various policies toward the HKSAR, (3) to enhance the patriotism and Chinese national and polit-

[25] Sonny Shiu-Hing Lo, "The Chinese Communist Party Elite's Conflicts over Hong Kong, 1983–1990," *China Information*, vol. 8, no. 4 (Spring 1994), pp. 1–14.

[26] In June 2017, Zhou said the people of Hong Kong were "brainwashed" by the colonial British for so long that anyone who opposed the policy of national education was to "force the youth to return to the brainwashing-style of the colonial education." He added that, after the emergence of the 2014 Occupy Central Movement and the rise of the local independence movement, the enactment of Article 23 of the Basic Law to ban subversion, treason, sedition and secession should be implemented as soon as possible. See "Interview with Zhou Nan," June 19, 2017, in https://www.thestandnews.com/politics/, access date: February 5, 2019.

ico-cultural identity of the Hong Kong people, (4) to achieve Beijing's dominant control or "comprehensive jurisdiction" over Hong Kong, (5) to isolate and defeat political enemies and opposition, including the moderate democrats and radical ones, (6) to strengthen a coalition of "patriotic" elites governing Hong Kong and (7) to protect Beijing's interest of maintaining the supremacy of "one country," specifically its national security interest. All these objectives have become very prominent in the PRC policy toward the HKSAR since the onset of the Xi Jinping era in November 2012, when he was selected as the CCP Secretary-General. In March 2013, Xi became the President of the PRC, receiving 2952 votes, one vote against him, and three abstentions in the meeting of National People's Congress (NPC).[27] Since then, national security interest has become more prominent in the PRC's policy toward Hong Kong, especially after the establishment of the National Security Commission in November 2013.

Historically, from July 1, 1997, to June 2003, China's united front work in the HKSAR had no breakthrough. As with the 1990s when the NCNA focused on its united front work on the capitalist, middle and working classes, Beijing's officials responsible for Hong Kong affairs continued with this approach and reached out to every sector of the local society. Yet, the crux of the problem of China's united front work from 1997 to mid-2003 was its tendency to report to Beijing the positive aspects of the HKSAR rather than engaging in an objective assessment of public sentiments. In late 1999, the NCNA was renamed the Liaison Office. Gao Siren, the Liaison Office director from 2002 to 2009, was relatively inactive in the HKSAR, leaving the task of united front work to his subordinates, especially the deputy directors. Nevertheless, there was a tendency on the part of his subordinates to consolidate relationships with the already co-opted pro-Beijing Hong Kong elites. Some deputy directors made public remarks that were regarded as relatively hard-line.[28] For

---

[27] "Xi elected Chinese president, chairman of the PRC Central Military Commission," March 14, 2013, in http://www.npc.gov.cn/englishnpc/news/Appointments/2013-03/14/content_1783118.htm, access date: February 4, 2019. Also see Max Fisher, "Xi Jinping's election as president of China, as told in crazy statistics," *The Washington Post*, March 14, 2013, in https://www.washingtonpost.com/news/worldviews/wp/2013/03/14/xi-jinpings-election-as-president-of-china-as-told-in-crazy-statistics/?utm_term=.5c9bbcac3928, access date: February 4, 2019.

[28] Sonny Lo, Eilo Yu, Bruce Kwong and Benson Wong, "The 2004 Legislative Council Elections in Hong Kong: The Triumph of China's United Front Work After the 2003 and 2004 Protests," *Chinese Law and Government*, vol. 38, no. 1 (January/February 2005), pp. 3–29.

example, Wang Fengchao's criticisms of the Hong Kong Cable TV program that interviewed a pro-Taiwan independence leader Annette Lu in March 2000 raised the eyebrows of some Hong Kong critics. Another Liaison Office official, He Zhiping, even claimed that the Hong Kong business people should not have transactions with Taiwanese counterparts. The public image of the Liaison Office in the 2000s was that it did not hesitate to intervene in Hong Kong matters.

Political correctness and positive reporting were the two main characteristics of the Liaison Office from 1997 to mid-2003, thus leading to the gross miscalculation of the outbreak of the half a million people's protest on the streets of Hong Kong on July 1, 2003.[29] Excluding those critics of the PRC from consultation and dialogue, officials of the Liaison Office naturally developed a favorable and biased view of the HKSAR development. The huge public protest was a great embarrassment to the PRC's united front work, which appeared to fail to inform Beijing of what was happening in the HKSAR. Hence, after the July 1, 2003, protest, the Liaison Office and the HKMAO started to develop greater political sensitivity to Hong Kong's public opinion.[30] However, this did not mean that Beijing's intervention in Hong Kong affairs would be diluted. Intervention, from the PRC perspective, can be positive and conducive to the HKSAR's development. A turning point came in January 2008, when a researcher named Cao Erbao from the Liaison Office wrote a report, stressing the need for two governing forces in the HKSAR, namely, the HKSAR administrators and the mainland cadres and officials being sent to Hong Kong.[31] Cao wrote:

> Because our country took back Hong Kong according to the 'one country, two systems' policy under which 'Hong Kong people governing Hong Kong' with a high degree of autonomy is implemented, the governing power also changed from a single governing team, namely, the British Hong

---

[29] For the July 1, 2003 protest, see Sonny Lo, "Hong Kong, 1 July 2003: Half a Million Protestors," *Behind the Headlines*, vol. 60, no. 4 (2004), pp. 1–14.

[30] One of the authors of this book was contacted by mainland academics and observers who went down to the HKSAR to understand the "real sentiment" of the Hong Kong people after July 1, 2003. One of these mainlanders later became a research professor at a Hong Kong university.

[31] Cao Erbao, "Governing Hong Kong under the conditions of 'one country, two systems,'" in *Study Times*, No. 422, January 29, 2008, translated into English, in https://www.civicparty.hk/cp/media/pdf/090506_cao_eng.pdf, access date: January 26, 2019.

Kong Government ('British Hong Kong authorities') before Reunification to two governing teams under the conditions of 'one country, two systems' after Reunification. One is the 'Hong Kong SAR establishment team', which includes the Chief Executive, Principal Officials, members of the Executive Council and the civil service, the Judiciary and other personnel of the administration of justice system. This team exercises high degree of autonomy according to the Basic Law, by delegated authority delegated by the Central Authorities. The other team is 'the team of cadres of Central and Mainland Authorities carrying out Hong Kong work' which includes departments of the Central Government and their external organs with responsibilities in Hong Kong affairs or specializing on Hong Kong work: departments of the Central Government responsible for other national affairs and relevant policies; and cadres in the Government and CCP Committees of provinces, cities and districts closely related to the Hong Kong SAR, who handle matters involving Hong Kong. This team exercises constitutional powers to govern the SAR (including dealing with the relationship between the Central and Mainland authorities, and the HKSAR) in accordance with our Constitution and the Basic Law of the HKSAR, and [it] does not interfere with the affairs within the autonomy of the SAR.[32]

His report aroused the concern of some democrats and critics, who believed that the Liaison Office wanted to have a greater say and influence on Hong Kong matters. Cao's arguments were, strictly speaking, nothing new, for the Liaison Office had long intervened in the local elections by mobilizing its staff members to assist pro-Beijing political forces and candidates in various ways, such as election campaigning, strategic planning in elections and the provision of manpower and logistical support for pro-Beijing political parties and candidates. What was new was his attempt at openly legitimizing the participatory role of the Liaison Office in the Hong Kong affairs.

China's new united front work in the HKSAR witnessed a turning point in November 2013 when the National Security Commission (NSC) was established. The NSC formation was clearly a response to the growing domestic terrorist activities.[33] Little reports have been published on how the NSC has viewed the HKSAR. But the preparatory activities of the three pro-democracy leaders for the Occupy Central Movement, namely, legal expert Benny Tao, academic Chan Kin-man and religious priest Chu

[32] Ibid.
[33] See Sonny Shiu-Hing Lo, *The Politics of Controlling Organized Crime in Greater China* (London: Routledge, 2013).

Yiu-ming, in January 2003, did alarm the PRC national security apparatus.[34] As such, the NSC establishment in November 2013 could be seen as a move coping with not only terrorist activities in the mainland but also the potential socio-political turbulence in the HKSAR. China's deep concern over Hong Kong was revealed in June 2014, when the White Paper on the practice of "one country, two systems" policy in the HKSAR was published by the PRC's State Council. It reiterated:

> As a unitary state, China's central government has comprehensive jurisdiction over all local administrative regions, including the HKSAR. The high degree of autonomy of HKSAR is not an inherent power, but one that comes solely from the authorization by the central leadership. The high degree of autonomy of the HKSAR is not full autonomy, nor a decentralized power. It is the power to run local affairs as authorized by the central leadership. The high degree of autonomy of HKSAR is subject to the level of the central leadership's authorization. There is no such thing called "residual power." With China's Constitution stipulating in clear-cut terms that the country follows a fundamental system of socialism, the basic system, core leadership and guiding thought of the "one country" have been explicitly provided for. The most important thing to do in upholding the "one country" principle is to maintain China's sovereignty, security and development interests, and respect the country's fundamental system and other systems and principles.[35]

The White Paper was politically significant in emphasizing Beijing's "comprehensive jurisdiction" over the HKSAR, applying its brake over the scope and pace of democratic reform in Hong Kong and specifying its political veto power over the territory's affairs. It constituted a severe warning to the local pro-democracy activists, who however reacted to the White Paper negatively and saw it as a deeper intervention of Beijing in Hong Kong affairs.

In July 2015, Beijing set up the Central Leading Small Group on United Front (CLSGUF). The group's main objectives are to implement the central government's policy directives on united front, to study the progress of its policy implementation and to direct government depart-

---

[34] For the Occupy Central Movement leaders' declaration in January 2013, see http://oclp.hk/index.php?route=occupy/book, access date: January 26, 2029.

[35] "The Practice of the 'One Country, Two Systems' Policy in the Hong Kong Special Administrative Region," June 10, 2014, in http://www.fmcoprc.gov.hk/eng/xwdt/gsxw/t1164057.htm, access date: January 26, 2019.

ments and party units and cells on how to ensure the smooth implementation of such directives.[36] In fact, once Xi became the CCP Secretary-General, he emphasized the importance of consolidating united front work in the mainland from December 2012 to December 2014, when Sun Chunlan was appointed as the minister of the United Front Department. In September 2014, Xi delivered "an important speech" on united front in the 65th anniversary of the Chinese People's Political Consultative Conference (CPPCC), saying that "great unity and solidary are the nature of united front work," that "united front work was the key treasure for not only the CCP's revolutionary success and reform enterprises but also the Chinese national renaissance" and that we would have to deepen the process of "democratic deliberation" at "all levels of institutional development."[37] In April 2015, the director of the National Minorities Department, Wang Zhengwai, was appointed as the deputy director of the United Front Department, showing the PRC's move of combining united front work with the affairs of ethnic minorities. Given the apex of domestic terrorist attack in Urumqi in May 2014 when 43 people died, and given that many "terrorist" activities coincidentally involved members of some ethnic groups, Wang's co-appointment was clearly aimed at enhancing united front work targeted at ethnic groups.

On April 30, 2015, the CCP Politburo approved a work regulation on the CCP's united front work. According to Article 1 of the CCP United Front Work Regulation, united front work will have to be "consolidated and developed."[38] Article 2 emphasizes the need for a "patriotic coalition" composed of those people who love the Chinese nation and support its unification. Article 3 stresses the need to stick to President Xi's idea of having the Chinese national renaissance and to "maintain Hong Kong and Macao's long-term prosperity and stability, and to realize the unification service of the nation." By implication, the PRC's united front work on Hong Kong and Macao is a means to an end, namely, reunifying Taiwan in the long run. Article 4 clearly delineates the scope of united front work, including "(1) members of democratic parties, (2) non-party members, (3) intellectuals outside the CCP, (4) ethnic minorities, (5)

---

[36] See *The People's Daily*, July 31, 2015, in http://cpc.people.com.cn/xuexi/n/2015/0731/c385474-27391395.html, access date: January 26, 2019.

[37] Ibid.

[38] "The Chinese Communist Party's United Front Regulation," September 23, 2015 in http://cpc.people.com.cn/n/2015/0923/c64107-27622040.html, access date: January 26, 2019.

members of the religious sector, (6) those people not working in the state-owned economic sector, (7) members of new social strata, (8) those people who study overseas and who return to the mainland, (9) Hong Kong and Macao comrades, (10) Taiwan comrades and their relatives in the mainland, (11) overseas Chinese and their returnees and relatives in the mainland, and (12) those people who need to be contacted and united."[39] The last category—"those people who need to be contacted and united"—is very broad, showing that the PRC government aims at winning the hearts and minds of all the Chinese people, ethnic minorities and overseas Chinese in the world—a very ambitious task in the era of President Xi Jinping. Article 5 of the Regulation outlines all the leading actors of united front work, including the united front departments at and above the county level, designated persons at the township and street levels, and party secretaries at the levels of central government, provinces, higher educational institutes, scientific research agencies and state-owned enterprises. Moreover, "people's organizations" should have designated persons responsible for united front work, meaning that various interest groups are expected to operate as the CCP's effective "transmission belts" that can bridge the gap between the ruling party and the masses. Article 7 emphasizes the role of party secretaries in united front work, including the operation in Hong Kong, Macao, Taiwan and overseas, where "the related parties, groups and individuals are the targets of united front work and investigation." Article 8 stresses that united front departments have to coordinate with the CPPCC to consolidate the work on ethnic minorities, religious believers, the people of Hong Kong and Macao, the Taiwan people and overseas Chinese. Article 12 places much emphasis on the role of the CPPCC to engage members of "democratic parties" and those outside the CCP to engage in deliberative discussions for the sake of "democratically supervising" the ruling regime. Article 14 claims that the CCP and the non-parties and democratic parties play the role of mutual supervision through giving their opinions, criticisms and constructive suggestions. Article 16 focuses on the united front work targeted at intellectuals outside the CCP. Article 18 mentions the need for united front work on the students who study in Europe and America and other places by setting up overseas Chinese students associations at the levels of provinces, cities, universities and research institutes.

[39] Ibid.

Article 20 shifts to the united front emphasis on ethnic minorities so that they can develop their "identity" with "the Chinese nation, Chinese culture, CCP and socialism with Chinese characteristics." Article 21 vows to "oppose Hans chauvinism and narrow nationalism" but to respect the cultures and customs of ethnic minorities so as to "struggle against any attempt at splitting the nation." Article 22 asserts that the CCP respects "religious freedom" but opposes the action of using religion to "undermine social order," "harm the personal health of citizens," "create tensions among ethnic minorities" and "undermine the activities of national unification."[40] Article 23 says that "CCP members should unify religious believers and the masses, but they should not believe in religion." Finally, Article 29 to Article 32 focus on the united front work on Hong Kong, Macao and Taiwan people. Article 29 states the importance of supporting the policies of both the Hong Kong and Macao administrations and of "consolidating the national identity" of the Hong Kong and Macao comrades. Article 30 stipulates that the united front work on Taiwan aims at opposing Taiwan independence and realizing the important mission of reunifying Taiwan and achieving the Chinese renaissance. Article 31 declares the mobilization of overseas Chinese to oppose Taiwan independence and to support the goal of national reunification. Article 32 outlines the need for united front work targeted at the members of democratic parties, those outside the CCP, the people's groups and the associations in Hong Kong, Macao, Taiwan and overseas in support of unification. Article 36 to Article 44 are all concerned about the co-optation of members of democratic parties and those outside the CCP to participate in the work and affairs of the existing political institutions, such as the NPC, CPPCC, government departments and courts at all levels. Overall, the Regulation represents a comprehensive policy of the CCP to conduct united front work in depth and breadth not only in the mainland but also on the people of Hong Kong, Macao, Taiwan and overseas Chinese.

In October 2017, President Xi Jinping visited the HKSAR and emphasized Beijing's exercise of its "comprehensive jurisdiction" over Hong Kong "organically."[41] He added that there was no contradiction between Beijing's exercise of its "comprehensive jurisdiction" and Hong Kong's "high degree of autonomy." Adopting a dialectical Marxist perspective,

[40] Ibid.
[41] Tony Cheung, "All you need to know about Xi Jinping's remarks on Hong Kong in his report to the party congress," *South China Morning Post*, October 20, 2017.

Xi's comment pointed to the coexistence of Hong Kong's autonomy and Beijing's exercise of its control over the HKSAR.

In fact, united front work is a means by which Beijing exercises "comprehensive jurisdiction" over the HKSAR. At the level of Beijing, a number of institutions are responsible for Hong Kong policies, including the Leading Small Group on United Front Work, the Central Coordination Committee on Hong Kong and Macao, the CPPCC and the think tank named the Chinese Association for Hong Kong and Macao, which was set up by the State Council to co-opt intellectuals and academics. At the provincial level, the provincial CPPCC and united front departments interact with Hong Kong's interest groups and individuals intensively. At the territorial level of the HKSAR, the Liaison Office's social liaison department, coordination department and the social work department are responsible for interacting with local groups and individuals. At the district level of Hong Kong, the pro-Beijing political party, the Democratic Alliance for Betterment and Progress of Hong Kong (DAB) and other like-minded forces, such as the New People's Party led by former senior civil servant Regina Ip, the Federation of Trade Unions (FTU), the Fujianese clan groups, women groups, youth groups and district-level federations and neighborhood (*kaifong*) associations, are active in becoming the executors and the auxiliary arms of China's united front work. As this book will discuss, all these groups and organizations are extremely important for us to understand the dynamics of Beijing's new united front work in the HKSAR.

From 2012 to the present, the PRC's new united front work in the HKSAR has displayed several characteristics. First and foremost, pro-Beijing interest groups have been fully mobilized to support not only the HKSAR government policies but also the interpretation of the Basic Law by the Standing Committee of the National People's Congress (SCNPC), especially its interpretation over Article 104 of the Basic Law in November 2016 when radical localists Yau Wai-ching and Baggio Leung showed disrespect to the PRC during their oath-taking ceremony in the Legislative Council.[42] Arguably, this feature was not new, as similar phenomena could be seen whenever the SCNPC interpreted the Basic Law, such as the interpretation of the right of abode of the mainland Chinese in the HKSAR in mid-1999. However, it can be argued that a new phenomenon slightly

---

[42] "Interpretation of Article 104 of the Basic Law of the HKSAR of the PRC by the SCNPC," November 7, 2016, in https://www.basiclaw.gov.hk/en/basiclawtext/images/basiclawtext_doc25.pdf, access date: January 27, 2019.

different from the past was that the full mobilization of pro-Beijing groups and individuals in support of the SCNPC interpretation was accompanied by ferocious attacks on the political enemies, namely Yau and Leung. In this sense, China's new united front work in the HKSAR took on a new dimension.

Second, the PRC has formulated and implemented the Greater Bay Area plan in 2018 and 2019, respectively, to encourage Hong Kong people to move into the mainland and to integrate socially and economically with Southern China. The use of a large amount of economic incentives to lure the people of Hong Kong to increase their socio-economic interactions and cooperation with the mainland companies, individuals, institutes, start-up companies and research organizations is unprecedented. The objective is to deepen interactions and broaden human exchanges with the people of Hong Kong, whose identity would hopefully transform from having a very strong local Hong Kong identity to embracing a mainland Chinese socio-economic, if not political, identity. This identity agenda of China's new united front work in the HKSAR is arguably new and forceful.

Third, a new focus on the youth, ethnic minorities, women and scientists can be seen in the PRC united front drive in the HKSAR. Many youth groups have been created and encouraged to visit the Greater Bay Area. Interest groups composed of ethnic minorities, especially South Asians, are integrated into the umbrella of united front work conducted by pro-Beijing groups, notably the DAB, mainly because they constitute an increasingly important source of votes in Hong Kong's elections at the legislative and district levels. Women groups have been fully mobilized to enhance their status and sense of influences. Scientists have been encouraged to apply for the mainland research grants for funding support, which can be transferred to the HKSAR across the mainland border. Intellectuals and academics are increasingly under the target of the PRC's new united front work in Hong Kong.

Fourth, formerly inactive pro-Beijing interest groups have been reactivated, rejuvenated and remobilized to connect with other like-minded political forces. Better organization and intensive mobilization can be easily seen. The formerly pro-British neighborhood associations are now under the target of political co-optation. PRC officials from the Liaison Office have been reaching out intensively to interact with these *kaifong* associations to win the hearts and minds of more Hong Kong people.

Fifth, a new phenomenon of China's united front work in the HKSAR is to create a few pro-Beijing groups inside the mainland, notably Shenzhen, and to establish their headquarters in Hong Kong. For instance, a Fujianese-based Pingtan Federation of Associations was first established in Shenzhen in June 2018 with the participation of the officials from the Hong Kong Liaison Office and the Fujian United Front Department, followed later by its formal inauguration in the HKSAR in October with the attendance of party officials in Pingtan.[43] The inauguration appealed to the Pingtan Federation of Association for upholding its "patriotic" sentiment and to support the HKSAR government. The cross-border operation of pro-Beijing interest groups is noteworthy as PRC officials fully utilize the networks of clan associations and individuals so that maximal mobilization can be achieved.

Sixth, as this book will demonstrate, the new united front work relies on the core interest groups as the magnet expanding outwards to other peripheral and fringe interest groups, creating dense networks of groups that can be easily mobilized in election campaigns and on the voting day. These political networking activities are very significant in the victory, as this book will show, of Vincent Cheng of the DAB and pro-Beijing independent candidate Rebecca Chan Hoi-yan in the 2018 legislative by-elections.

One continuity of the PRC's united front work in Hong Kong is its utilization of the livelihood issues to keep close contacts with its constituents and voters. For instance, the DAB taught the elderly people how to apply for the government's caring subsidy of HK$4000 each for the poor and the needy. The mixture of livelihood issues with welfare services delivered by pro-Beijing interest groups remains a powerful weapon through which they grasp voters' support.

Another continuity is the use of pro-Beijing federations at the district level as umbrella organizations uniting and integrating all the smaller like-minded groups in a more professional and effective way. These federations include the Kowloon Federation of Associations, the New Territories Federation of Associations, the Hong Kong Island Federation of Associations and the Hong Kong Federation of Women Associations. Apparently, a tremendous amount of money has been spent on the organization, coordination and mobilization of all these interest groups. In other words, the expenditure of the PRC to maintain social stability in the HKSAR is huge.

[43] *Wen Wei Po*, June 20, 2018 and October 13, 2018.

The third continuity of China's united front work is the multiplicity of its agents. These agents embrace representatives and leaders of the capitalist class, middle class and working class. They also include all kinds of interest groups from various occupational sectors, reaching out to every corner of the society. These cross-class and cross-occupational features of united front work persists in the era of President Xi Jinping, whose political agenda of achieving the Chinese renaissance and Chinese dream means that the hearts and minds of more Hong Kong people have to be won over.

The final, and the most prominent, continuity of the PRC united front operation in Hong Kong is the communist style of penetrative politics. Penetrative politics require an organized, coordinated and long-term process of political infiltration into the civil society through the creation, utilization and mobilization of various kinds of interest groups, thereby shaping the society to support a ruling regime. In the case of Hong Kong, penetrative politics has dual purposes: supporting not only the HKSAR administration but also the central government in Beijing. This book will explore how united front work infiltrates the civil society and analyzes the constraints on the CCP style of penetrative politics in the HKSAR.

Twelve Perspectives on China's New United Front Work in the HKSAR

To understand the PRC's new united front work in the HKSAR, it is necessary to adopt a comprehensive approach to integrate various perspectives: (1) enhancing the legitimacy of both the central and local governments; (2) co-opting Hong Kong elites; (3) achieving politico-economic convergence and integration between the PRC and the HKSAR; (4) narrowing the elite-mass gap; (5) creating a pro-Beijing civil society through the mobilization of social capital and interest groups; (6) securitizing the HKSAR and the PRC regime; (7) curbing political opposition through electoral competition; (8) engaging in ideological struggles between China's paternalistic authoritarianism and Hong Kong's limited pluralism; (9) encountering the resistance from citizens and groups with not only relatively strong local Hong Kong identity but also a new form of citizenship; (10) facing the tensions between materialistic values held by most pro-Beijing Hongkongers and post-materialistic values cherished by most pro-democracy Hongkongers; (11) distributing extensive favors to Beijing's clients through patronage networks and (12) seeing Hong Kong as a potentially political threat to the mainland from the geopolitical perspective of a rising heartland versus a politically defiant borderland. These twelve perspectives, as will be discussed below, are important for us to understand the dynamics of China's new united front work in the HKSAR.

Legitimacy Perspective

The PRC has to consolidate not only its legitimacy over Hong Kong but also that of the HKSAR government by backing up their related policies. Legitimacy, as David Beetham argues, comprises the moral and/or normative aspects of power relationships.[44] He has stressed that any socioscientific analysis of legitimacy is concerned with the impacts it has on the people's behavior. As a matter of fact, legitimate power or authority has the right to expect the obedience from subordinates even though there may be disagreement with the content of a law or policy directive. Subordinates are expected to have an obligation to obey, and if they do not do so, the legitimizing power is undermined. Beetham contends that citizens obey the authority partly because of "acquired attitudes and characteristics, such as the internalization of a respect for authority."[45] Legitimacy is extremely important for the existence of power relations, for it produces compliance and cooperation. Beetham believes that legitimate power sets the limits to the powerful actors through the normative expectations and principles it embodies, and that an analysis of these norms and principles is crucial to our understanding of the distinctive character and institutions of a given system of power.[46]

In the context of the HKSAR, Beijing's moral and normative aspects of the power relations have been questioned by its critics, especially the local democrats who question the legitimacy of the CCP in using military force to suppress student democrats on the Tiananmen Square in June 1989. The Tiananmen legacy is still haunting the relations between Beijing and some Hong Kong people.[47] As such, Beijing's attempt at winning the hearts and minds of the people of Hong Kong through its united front work must encounter resistance, opposition and severe limitations, unless the official verdict on the Tiananmen were reversed.

---

[44] David Beetham, *The Legitimation of Power* (Basingstoke: Macmillan, 1991), pp. 25–26.
[45] Ibid., p. 26.
[46] Ibid., p. 38.
[47] See Sonny Shiu-Hing Lo, *Competing Chinese Political Visions: Hong Kong vs. Beijing on Democracy* (Westport: Praeger Security International, 2010).

On the other hand, the HKSAR leadership's legitimacy, especially the Chief Executive and his or her principal officials, is conferred upon by the central government in Beijing. With an Election Committee whose members are appointed by the PRC to select the Chief Executive, his or her legitimacy is bound to be questioned by some people of Hong Kong, especially the democrats. In Beetham's terms, the Chief Executive of the HKSAR is not elected by the consent of the governed. The people of Hong Kong have no say on who should be the candidates running in the Chief Executive election. Some of them even view the Chief Executive as an agent or a client of Beijing. As such, China's united front work directed at the people of Hong Kong is destined to encounter resistance, opposition and disagreement. While most pro-Beijing citizens regard themselves as having the "obligation," to use Beetham's term, to obey the HKSAR leadership, the pro-democracy critics do not share their norm at all.

The late Samuel Huntington argued that legitimacy has two main dimensions: performance and procedural.[48] In procedural terms, as mentioned before, the Hong Kong Chief Executive is elected by a small group of elites appointed by the PRC regime, and therefore, his or her procedural legitimacy is relatively weak in the eyes of most Hongkongers. In terms of performance, the HKSAR government is constantly under the scrutiny of the mass media and its critics, especially the pro-democracy forces. Under these circumstances, Beijing finds it imperative to utilize united front work for the sake of buttressing the legitimacy of the HKSAR regime, including its Chief Executive and principal officials.

Political Control and Co-optation

Communist regimes are characterized by the attempts of the ruling communist parties to exert political control over the society, including the elites. Such political and personnel control can be seen in the former Soviet Union, the PRC, Vietnam, Cuba and North Korea.[49] This control can be achieved through the process of co-optation, which according to Philip Selznick refers to "the process of absorbing new elements into the leadership or policy determining structure of an organization as a means

---

[48] Samuel P. Huntington, "Democracy's Third Wave," *Journal of Democracy*, vol. 2., no. 2 (Spring 1991), pp. 12–34.
[49] See, for example, Jerry F. Hough and Merle Fainsod, *How the Soviet Union is Governed* (Cambridge, Massachusetts, 1979), Chapter 14, "The Distribution of Power," pp. 518–555.

of averting threats to its stability or existence."[50] Formal co-optation occurs when there is a need to establish the legitimacy of an authority, while informal co-optation takes place when there is "a need of adjustment to the pressure of specific centres of power within the community."[51] Co-optation arise out of a situation in which the formal authority is "actually or potentially in a state of imbalance with respect to institutional environment."[52] United front work conducted by China combines the elements of political control, specifically personnel appointment and the infiltration of CCP agents, with co-optation in which, to borrow from Michael Seward, the "cooptees" are appointed into the policy-making or advisory bodies.[53]

In the context of Hong Kong before 1997, the PRC's web of political control was conducted partly through the CCP's nomenklatura system, which gives the party the authority to vet the appointment and to dismiss significant leaders of PRC-based organizations operating in Hong Kong.[54] During the 1980s, the CCP's nomenklatura contained leading positions in various government bodies that managed Hong Kong affairs directly and their party core groups in the territory. The scope of nomenklatura embraced the Hong Kong delegates to the provincial-level and central-level National People's Congress (NPC) and the CPPCC. Although delegates were nominally elected to their positions, they were first vetted by the relevant departments of the CCP. In the transition leading to July 1, 1997, the Hong Kong and Macao Work Committee under the CCP built up its nomenklatura system, which included positions like the leadership of the New China News Agency (NCNA), pro-Beijing mass media and business organizations and trade unions.[55] After the handover, there are strong grounds for believing that the CCP's nomenklatura has been expanding rapidly. Given that 150 mainland Chinese have arrived the HKSAR every day since July 1, 1997, at least a million mainlanders have

---

[50] Philip Selznick, *TVA and the Grass Roots: A Study in the Sociology of Formal Organization* (New York: Harper& Row, 1966), p. 13.

[51] Ibid., pp. 259–260.

[52] Ibid.

[53] Michael Seward, "Cooption and Power: Who Gets What from Formal Incorporation," *Political Studies*, vol. 38, no. 4 (December 1990), pp. 588–689. Seward uses the term "cooption" rather than "co-optation."

[54] John P. Burns, "The Structure of Communist Party Control in Hong Kong," *Asian Survey*, vol. 30, no. 8 (August 1990), pp. 757–759.

[55] Ibid.

become Hong Kong residents and an unknown portion of them may have already joined the CCP in the mainland. A member of the Democratic Party, Lee Wing-tat, claimed in March 2019 that 210,000 mainlanders out of these migrants are CCP members.[56] His remarks sparked immediate criticisms from the pro-Beijing media. Anyway, together with many mainland students and business people who study and work respectively in the HKSAR, the CCP's hidden or underground membership in Hong Kong is inevitably huge and much larger than any self-proclaimed political party in the territory.[57] As such, the party cells in the HKSAR could have reorganized some of these migrants who are CCP members in a better way. Moreover, many mainland state-owned enterprises and business firms have been operating in the HKSAR, including the inevitable formation and existence of CCP cells where members can discuss issues of their concerns easily. As such, the CCP's nomenklatura in the HKSAR is perhaps expanding silently but rapidly even though there are no concrete statistical figures on this trend.

POLITICO-ECONOMIC CONVERGENCE AND INTEGRATION

Scholars of comparative communism in the 1970s, notably Alfred Meyer, argued that the former Soviet Union would gradually converge with the United States economically and politically.[58] Nevertheless, the persistence of the CCP-led regime in the PRC in the 2000s means that it aspires to make capitalistic Hong Kong converge with the mainland politically, socially and economically in the long run. The "one country, two systems" is expected to preserve Hong Kong's capitalistic lifestyle for 50 years after 1997, but the PRC since the mid-1980s has been adopting capitalistic means to achieve its socialist modernization. Given China's rapid economic rise, Beijing naturally expects to not only catch up with Hong Kong's capitalistic system but also utilize the latter's economic strength to converge with the mainland, especially Southern China. As a socialist state that formulates and implements long-term developmental strategy, Beijing expects the HKSAR to integrate with the mainland's economic planning.

---

[56] *Apple Daily*, March 25, 2019, in https://hk.news.appledaily.com/local/realtime/article/20190325/59407438, access date: March 31, 2019.
[57] Hong Kong's political parties are registered under the Company Ordinance, and there is no political party law in the HKSAR.
[58] Alfred Meyer, "Theories of Convergence," in Chalmers Johnson, ed., *Change in Communist Systems* (Stanford: Stanford University Press, 1970), p. 337.

Through economic integration, the PRC hopes to shape and transform the identity of the Hong Kong people economically, socio-culturally and even politically.[59] From 1997 to the present, most Hong Kong people identify themselves as culturally Chinese, but they do not identify themselves with the CCP regime in the mainland. In mid-2018, when Beijing proposed the idea of the Greater Bay Area for the HKSAR to integrate with Guangdong and Macao, it was crystal clear that accelerated economic integration has become an instrument by which Beijing wishes to achieve economic and socio-political convergence between South China and the HKSAR in the long run. Economically, the HKSAR is expected to converge with the Greater Bay Area. Socially and culturally, the people of Hong Kong are expected to see the mainland "comrades" on equal terms, rather than discriminating against them from 2012 to 2015, when a minority of Hong Kong residents saw the influx of mainland tourists as a liability to Hong Kong's public health services and daily necessities, because many mainland pregnant women went to Hong Kong hospitals to give birth to their babies. Many mainland visitors bought excessive amount of baby formula, leading to a shortage of local supplies. Socio-politically, Beijing's planners hope that, through economic integration and convergence between Hong Kong and the Greater Bay Area, more Hong Kong people can and will develop patriotic sentiments toward their mainland comrades, leading to less social conflicts and more societal harmony. The more difficult challenge for Beijing is to change the identity of the Hong Kong people politically in the long run, meaning that we can expect many Hongkongers to remain politically autonomous and not easily identify themselves with the CCP regime in the PRC.

As a matter of fact, Alfred Meyer has long documented three forms of convergence theory: (1) the communist and democratic states would move toward a middle ground of democratic socialism; (2) both systems would drift toward the direction of a bureaucratized polity and (3) both East and West would move toward "a kind of apocalypse wherein regimes are malevolent and citizens depersonalized" and wherein social order and compliance would have "the highest value."[60] Communist states would see the failures of revolutionaries to implement an orthodox Marxist state

---

[59] Economic integration can be seen as a process of abolishing "discrimination between economic units belonging to different national states" and it is represented by "the absence of various forms of discrimination between national economies." See Bela Balassa, *The Theory of Economic Integration* (Westport, Connecticut: Greenwood Press, 1961), p. 174.

[60] Ibid.

and generate a new aristocratic regime with the vested interest.[61] According to Daniel Nelson, convergence implies a process in which institutions develop with a diversity of viewpoints and priorities.[62] This process would be paradoxical to the communist regimes which embark on an accelerated path of modernization and which drift away from the ideological unity and tight control imposed by the ruling party.[63] It is outside the scope of this book to discuss whether the PRC is converging with the West politically and economically. But it is important to note that the CCP regime in the PRC under President Xi Jinping faces the contradictions mentioned by Meyer: accelerating modernization in the era of globalization and yet reasserting its political control over the society and economy that have necessitated some degree of liberalization. As China exhibits internal economic and political contradictions, any attempt by the CCP to reassert its political and ideological control must have ramifications on its policy toward the HKSAR. In fact, since 2012, the PRC authorities have been reaffirming the importance of "one country" over "two systems." Such emphasis has pointed to the phenomenon that whenever China experiences a cyclical change from political liberalization to control, the HKSAR's political development is bound to be affected to some extent.[64]

If political integration between the HKSAR and the PRC is a long-term objective of China's united front work, identity transformation from a very strong local Hong Kong identity to Chinese nationalism is an ideal ultimate outcome. According to Claude Ake, political integration is punctuated by two problems: "how to elicit from subjects deference and devotion to the claims of the state," and "how to increase normative consensus governing political behaviour among members of the political system."[65] In other words, political integration, or convergence, is a process of "developing a political culture and of inducing commitment to it."[66] The crux of the problem is that Hong Kong under the British rule was marked by

---

[61] Daniel N. Nelson, "Political Convergence: An Empirical Assessment," *World Politics*, vol. 30, no. 3 (April 1978), p. 412.

[62] Ibid.

[63] Ibid., p. 414.

[64] For the rise of conservative nationalists in China and their policy toward Hong Kong, see Sonny Shiu-Hing Lo, "Ideologies and Factionalism in Beijing-Hong Kong Relations," *Asian Survey*, vol. 58, no. 3 (2018), pp. 392–415.

[65] Claude Ake, *A Theory of Political Integration* (Homewood, Illinois: The Dorsey Press, 1967), p. 1.

[66] Ibid.

depoliticization rather than politicization and by deemphasis on nationalism instead of territory-wide education to promote Chinese nationalism.[67] Hence, after the retrocession on July 1, 1997, the challenge of Beijing's united front work is to instill a greater sense of Chinese nationalism and patriotism in the psyche of the Hong Kong people. Patriotism is "an effort or readiness to promote the interests of all the persons born or living with the same *patria*, i.e., country, whereas nationalism aims at promoting the interests of all those of the same nation, i.e., literally a group of common descent and upbringing, that is to say, of complementary habits of communication."[68] Patriotism appeals to all residents of an ethnic group, regardless of their ethnic background.[69] Patriotism often appears at an earlier stage of economic and social mobilization, like Europe during the mercantilist era up to the middle of the nineteenth century.[70] As mobilization proceeds and embraces a large number of people who develop a strong sense of competition and yet insecurity, patriotism is replaced by nationalism which is based on the more intimate personal features and communication habits of each individual citizen.[71] Patriotism can strengthen "the passions of a particular people with a specific cultural and historical identity," and it can also "reinforce bonds" which can consolidate "the cultural tradition or the shared destiny of a people."[72] Patriotism can even compete with nationalism because it uses rhetorical rather than rational arguments.[73]

In the case of Hong Kong, the British colonial state depoliticized the society, but the post-colonial regime under Beijing's sovereignty has been expected to develop both Chinese patriotism and nationalism, a task that is bound to be difficult and remains to be fulfilled in the coming decades. After all, if political integration, as Ake observes, aims at transforming the political culture of citizens, the political culture of the Hong Kong people will have to be changed from a mix of political apathy and activism to being mostly politically patriotic toward the PRC.[74] Such change, how-

---

[67] Lo Shiu-Hing, "Decolonization and Political Development in Hong Kong: Citizen Participation," *Asian Survey*, vol. 28, no. 6 (June 1988), pp. 613–629.

[68] Maurizio Viroli, For Love of Country: An Essay on Patriotism and Nationalism (New York: Oxford University Press, 1995), p. 4.

[69] Ibid., p. 5.

[70] Ibid.

[71] Ibid.

[72] Ibid., p. 8.

[73] Ibid.

[74] Lam Wai-man, *Understanding the Political Culture of Hong Kong: The Paradox of Activism and Depoliticization* (New York: M. E. Sharpe, 2004).

ever, has to be natural and evolutionary rather than a coercive process initiated by the authorities of either the HKSAR administration or the central government in Beijing. Otherwise, the process of political convergence and integration is destined to be conflict-ridden.

Narrowing the Elite-Mass Gap

Robert Putnam has long alerted political scientists of the importance of narrowing the "elite-mass gap" in any political system.[75] In communist regimes, the ruling communist parties tend to use pro-government interest groups, such as trade unions and other mass organizations, as the "transmission belts" that could narrow the elite-mass gap, thereby consolidating regime legitimacy.[76] Communist regimes are keen to annihilate any political and social forces that challenge the central authority. As Daniel Nelson argues, communist governments "maintain links with the masses" and "have no room for particularistic interests connoted by the bases for local power accretion."[77] Communist regimes tend to exhibit features of authoritarian polities in which the power center is reluctant to devolve political and administrative power to not only the localities but also any social forces.

In Hong Kong under British colonial rule, the elite-mass gap was narrowed by a whole range of intermediary institutions, including pro-government business and professional groups, neighborhood associations and charity organizations. These groups and organizations worked for the colonial administration, although some began to shift their political allegiance gradually to Beijing during the final years of the British rule. After 1997, the post-colonial government and Beijing have sought to politically co-opt most of these social groups and organizations for the sake of winning the hearts and minds of most Hong Kong people. In other words, China's united front work has to broaden and deepen its relations with all

---

[75] Robert D. Putnam, *The Comparative Study of Political Elites* (New Jersey: Prentice-Hall, 1976), pp. 154–164.

[76] C. A, Hathaway, "On the Use of 'Transmission Belts' in Our Struggle for the Masses," *The Communist: A Magazine of the Theory and Practice of Marxism-Leninism*, vol. 10, no. 5 (May 1931), pp. 409–423. Also see Michael Waller, "Communist Politics and the Group Process: Some Comparative Conclusions," in David S. G. Goodman, ed., *Groups and Politics in the People's Republic of China* (Bristol: University of Cardiff Press, 1984), pp. 196–215.

[77] Daniel N. Nelson, *Elite-Mass Relations in Communist Systems* (London: Macmillan, 1998), pp. 33–34.

kinds of interest groups in the HKSAR, not only narrowing the elite-mass gap but also utilizing elite-mass linkages to consolidate the dual legitimacy of the HKSAR government and Beijing. As this book will discuss, many interest groups are under the new united front work of the PRC under President Xi Jinping, whose subordinates are determined to mobilize them as the "transmission belts" in Hong Kong to achieve "the Chinese dream" and "renaissance."

Creating Pro-Beijing Civil Society Through the Mobilization of Social Capital

The relatively pluralistic polity of Hong Kong is characterized by an autonomous civil society free from the influence and penetration of the post-colonial state. Yet, the PRC's authoritarian politics exhibits a different hallmark, namely, the ruling party's penetration into the civil society through its agents, including pro-CCP interest groups and mass organizations. Here, the concept of "social capital" articulated by Robert Putnam is useful for us to understand the political context and content of China's united front work in the HKSAR. According to Putnam, social capital refers to the features of social organizations, such as "trust, norms, and networks, that can improve the efficiency of society by facilitating coordinated actions."[78] Social capital facilitates "spontaneous cooperation."[79] It can bring about the formation of informal saving institutions like credit associations in some countries. Most importantly, social capital, to Putnam, can develop into a "public good" that is not only "undervalued and undersupplied by private agents" but also produced by other social activities unlike conventional capital as a "private good."[80]

China's united front work in the HKSAR galvanizes its social capital into a force that brings about a civil society supportive of the PRC's policies toward Hong Kong. In other words, the PRC wishes to recreate the civil society of the HKSAR, transforming it from an independent entity to one that is overwhelmingly pro-Beijing. This necessitates the political mobilization of the existing pro-Beijing interest groups and the transformation of other groups from political neutrality and moderation to politi-

---

[78] Robert D. Putnam, *Making Democracy Work: Civic Traditions in Modern Italy* (Princeton: Princeton University Press, 1998), p. 167.
[79] Ibid., p. 180.
[80] Ibid.

cally "patriotic" ones. To counter the local pro-democracy forces that have occupied a considerable segment of the civil society, the PRC has to penetrate into the local civil society extensively and intensively through its agents, namely, the "transmission belts" in the form of pro-Beijing interest groups. The pro-Beijing social capital has to be formed through the existing and newly generated networks, bonds and trustful relations between the PRC agents and all kinds of interest groups. Under these circumstances, Beijing's united front work will be able to achieve the ultimate objective of winning the hearts and minds of the majority of Hong Kong people.

SECURITIZATION PERSPECTIVE

Arguably, the PRC under President Xi Jinping has been emphasizing the significance of its national security in various areas, ranging from public health to environment, from food and industrial safety to economic production, from cultural heritage to regime longevity. Similarly, the PRC viewed Hong Kong's political reform as a national security issue, especially the question of whether and how the Chief Executive should be directly elected by citizens through universal suffrage in 2017.[81] As such, the theory of securitization is pertinent for us to comprehend the political context of China's new united front work in the HKSAR.

According to Michael Williams, security studies have been broadened in its agenda to include threats beyond the narrow confines of the state and military security to embrace "the security concerns of actors ranging from individuals and sub-state groups."[82] In the theory of securitization, "security" is treated "not as an objective condition but as the outcome of a specific social process: the social construction of security issues (who or what is being secured, and from what) is analyzed by examining the 'securitizing speech-acts' through which threats become represented and recognized."[83] Issues become "securitized" or are treated as security issues through these "speech-acts" which describe and represent successfully an existing security situation.[84] By uttering "security," a government official

[81] Lo, *Hong Kong's Indigenous Democracy*.
[82] Michael C. Williams, "Words, Images, Enemies: Securitization and International Politics," *International Studies Quarterly*, vol. 47, no. 4 (2003), pp. 511–512.
[83] Ibid., pp. 512–513.
[84] Ibid., pp. 512–513.

shifts a particular development to a specific area, claiming "a special right to use whatever means are necessary to block it."[85] Treating security as a speech-act can enlarge possible threats and exaggerate the actors and objects that are threatened, according to Williams. In the political realm, what is at stake is the legitimacy of a governmental authority, and therefore "the relevant threats can be ideological and sub-state, leading to security situations in which state authorities are threatened by elements of their own societies, and where states can become the primary threat to their own societies."[86]

According to the Copenhagen School, security is "not just any kind of speech-act, not just any form of social construction or accomplishment," but it is an "existential threat" calling for "extraordinary measures beyond the routines and norms of everyday politics."[87] In security discourse, an issue is "dramatized and presented as an issue of supreme priority; thus by labelling it as security an agent claims a need for and a right to treat it by extraordinary means."[88] Assertions on security and threats are made politically through the authoritative declaration of an "existential threat" to the object concerned, and through the acceptance as "security issues" by the audience.[89]

These discussions of securitization are pertinent to the HKSAR under the PRC rule. In January 2015, following the former Chief Executive C.Y. Leung's high-profile criticism of a tiny minority of Hong Kong youngsters who advocated the "independence" for Hong Kong, the pro-Beijing local media added fuel to the fire and kept on scolding some localist students.[90] From an objective perspective, the concept of "independence" was ambiguous, and some localists merely called for Hong Kong's maximal political autonomy and institutional independence vis-à-vis Beijing. However, the official criticism from the HKSAR government stimulated the rise of the "independence" thinking, which could perhaps be traced to a thought-provoking work by an intellectual Horace Chin Wan. Chin argued in his

---

[85] O. Waever, "Securitization and De-securitization," in R. Lipschutz, ed., On Security (New York: Columbia University Press, 1995), p. 55.

[86] Williams, "Words, Images, Enemies: Securitization and International Politics," pp. 513–514.

[87] B. Buzan, O. Waever and J. de Wilde, *Security: A New Framework for Analysis* (Boulder, Colorado: Lynne Rienner, 1998), p. 32.

[88] Ibid., p. 26.

[89] Ibid.

[90] *Apple Daily* January 2015, p. A01.

work that Hong Kong's core values like civil liberties represented a "genuine *huaxia* culture" in Greater China.[91] But Chin was not really advocating for Hong Kong's "independence"; instead, he called for the cultural penetration of Hong Kong values into the entire Greater China region. Hence, he was not really a "father" of Hong Kong nationalism,[92] but his beliefs stimulated other localists to turn more radical and to contend that Hong Kong should be culturally, socially and politically secluded from the PRC. The parochial attitudes of some Hong Kong youth were arguably misinterpreted, or deliberately interpreted by PRC authorities as supportive of "independence," thus immediately generating "an existential threat" to the security of the central government in Beijing. Indeed, in October 2016, when two young radical localists, Yau Wai-ching and Baggio Leung of the Youngspiration, showed their disrespect to the PRC government as they participated in the oath-taking ceremony at the Legislative Council shortly after they had been directly elected, the PRC authorities elevated the "existential threat" of "independence" to the highest level. Yau and Leung's behavior, to Beijing, necessitated the interpretation of the Basic Law's oath-taking stipulation by the Standing Committee of the National People's Congress (SCNPC) in November 2016. In September 2018, the HKSAR government officially banned the Hong Kong National Party (HKNP), which was founded by youngster Andy Chan Ho-tin, on the grounds that its "pro-independence" calls could not be viewed as a "political rhetoric" and that the HKNP did motivate its followers to "cause violence and public disorder."[93] These events from late 2016 to late 2018 witnessed a gradual and continuous escalation of the "existential" threat to Hong Kong and the PRC.

From early 2015 to 2018, the concern about "Hong Kong independence" was first triggered by a fear on the part of the HKSAR leadership, then stimulated by an emergence of the call for "independence" by a minority of young people, culminating in the ban on the HKNP. The

---

[91] Chin Wan, *A Discussion of Hong Kong as a City-State* (Hong Kong: Enrich Publishing Company, 2011).

[92] See Tommy Cheung, "'Father' of Hong Kong Nationalism: A Critical Review of Chin Wan's City-State Theory," *Asian Education and Development Studies*, vol. 4, no. 4 (2015), pp. 460–470.

[93] Tony Cheung and Jeffie Lam, "Ban on Hong Kong National Party over 'armed revolution' call met with both cheers and fear," *South China Morning Post*, September 24, 2018, in https://www.scmp.com/news/hong-kong/politics/article/2165439/hong-kong-issues-unprecedented-ban-separatist-party, access date: February 6, 2019.

entire development was a testimony to a successful process of, to borrow from Williams, "securitizing speech-acts" through which the threats of "Hong Kong independence" was recognized, represented and controlled. Under the political context of "securitization," PRC authorities feel it imperative to enforce its united front work on the people of Hong Kong, ensuring that Beijing's security interest is protected, that the "Hong Kong independence" is to be eliminated and that the Hong Kong comrades are educated to understand the central government's national security concern. After the ban on the National Party, Hong Kong has so far not envisaged youth discussion of this taboo topic, showing the success of China's new united front work.

Curbing Political Opposition through Electoral Competition

The study of political opposition is pertinent to our examination of China's united front work in the HKSAR. In many Asian states, political oppositions emerged in the 1980s and 1990s as industrialization brought about the rise of middle class and the emergence of civil society.[94] In Hong Kong under British rule, political opposition grew from a similar process of modernization that unleashed social forces supportive of democratic reforms. The emergence of a nascent middle class in Hong Kong led to the growth of local democracy movement, pushing the colonial regime to liberalize and democratize the political system.[95] After Hong Kong's sovereignty return from Britain to the PRC, the civil society is relatively autonomous from Beijing and the political opposition has remained resilient. The eruption of the half a million protestors on the streets of Hong Kong on July 1, 2003, was marked by not only the coordinated efforts made by pro-democracy and pro-human rights groups but also the spontaneous action from many individual citizens.

From the PRC's united front perspective, the July 1, 2003 protest was a political watershed because it undermined the legitimacy of the HKSAR government led by Chief Executive Tung Chee-hwa. It also tarnished the image of united front work, which appeared to fail miserably in the eyes of top PRC leaders. Moreover, the mass protests in July 2003 was triggered, organized and led by a strong political opposition in Hong Kong. As such,

---

[94] Garry Rodan, ed., *Political Oppositions in Industrializing Asia* (London: Routledge, 1996).
[95] Lo Shiu-Hing, *The Politics of Democratization in Hong Kong* (London: Macmillan, 1997), Chapters 4 and 5, pp. 137–206.

PRC authorities were forced to reassert themselves through a revamped united front strategy in the territory. If "democratic centralism" is a principle held by the CCP to govern the mainland, and if it refers to the efforts made by the Party to reach closer to the masses,[96] then curbing the political opposition is the foremost task of the CCP's united front work in Hong Kong. If the democrats can capture half of the elected seats, including both directly elected and those seats returned from functional constituencies, in the Legislative Council, then the legitimacy and policy-making capability of the pro-Beijing HKSAR government are bound to be undermined. Furthermore, if the eighteen District Councils have most of the seats captured by the democrats, the authority of the HKSAR government to control the local administration would also be reduced and threatened. As a result, China's new united front work in Hong Kong has to stop the democrats from capturing half of the seats in the Legislative Council and prevent them from gaining control of the local advisory District Councils. Electoral competition with pro-democracy forces is necessary from the PRC viewpoint. Concomitantly, the PRC has to put all the necessary resources and manpower to back up pro-Beijing political forces in the HKSAR, empowering them to compete with and prevent the local pro-democracy forces from capturing political power at legislative and district levels.

"Democratic centralism" in Hong Kong's pluralistic setting is different from mainland China. The "democratic" aspects in Hong Kong embrace electoral competition and political opposition, while the mainland stifles such contest and contending forces. The "centralist" aspects in China entail personnel and political control imposed by the CCP on the mainland's polity, economy and society, but the "centralist" aspects in Hong Kong are played out in the personnel control of the top HKSAR leadership and the electoral mobilization at the legislative and district level. Comparatively, Hong Kong's political pluralism stands out to be a national security threat to the central government in Beijing.

Ideological Conflicts Between Authoritarian China and Pluralistic Hong Kong

Ideologically speaking, the PRC remains an authoritarian one-party state where its political culture is in conflicts with the relatively more pluralistic polity of the HKSAR. Authoritarian states are characterized by one-party

---

[96] Nelson, *Elite-Mass Relations in Communist Systems*, p. 32.

hegemony, the dominance of police power, the control over mass media and civil society, political and educational indoctrination and limited electoral competition.[97] Pluralism is traditionally associated with capitalist democracy where top political leaders are directly elected by citizens through universal suffrage, civil liberties are protected, interest groups thrive and compete among themselves, the rule of law exists and the state acts in the interest of "common good."[98] Limited pluralism in the HKSAR is characterized by the existence of civil liberties, some degree of electoral competition (the chief executive is elected by a small group of elites rather than directly elected by citizens through universal suffrage), the rule of law and the persistence of a relatively assertive civil society free from the penetration and control by the post-colonial state.[99] As the PRC's political culture is mingled with Hong Kong's counterpart, "patron-client pluralism" can be seen in the ways in which Hong Kong politics are conducted.[100] Yet, as President Xi Jinping came to power in the PRC in 2013, China's policy toward the HKSAR has been dominated by "conservative nationalists" whose value of upholding Beijing's national security clashes with the localist values of maintaining Hong Kong's social, economic and political uniqueness.[101] Under the circumstances of ideological conflicts between the PRC and the HKSAR, Beijing's united front work naturally faces resistance and opposition in the territory.

The ideological conflicts between China and Hong Kong can also be illuminated by a recent study of the PRC's "populist authoritarianism."[102] According to Tang Wenfang, China developed a political culture of "populist authoritarianism" in the early years of the CCP rule in which the concept of mass line was practiced in political mobilization, collectivization and the provision of social services.[103] Mass line became "the ideo-

[97] For a classic discussion of authoritarianism, see Juan J. Linz, *Totalitarian and Authoritarian Regimes* (Boulder, Colorado: Lynne Rienner, 2000), pp. 159–261.
[98] For a useful discussion of pluralism, see Martin Carnoy, *The State and Political Theory* (New Jersey: Princeton University Press, 1984), pp. 10–43.
[99] For an earlier argument that Hong Kong has a relatively pluralistic polity that is mixed with China's patron-clientelist politics, see Sonny Shiu-Hing Lo, *The Dynamics of Beijing-Hong Kong Relations: A Model for Taiwan?* (Hong Kong: Hong Kong University Press, 2008), Chapter 1, pp. 7–38.
[100] Ibid.
[101] Lo, "Ideology and Factionalism in Beijing-Hong Kong Relations," pp. 392–415.
[102] Tang Wenfang, *Populist Authoritarianism: Chinese Political Culture and Regime Sustainability* (New York: Oxford University Press, 2016), p. 152.
[103] Ibid.

logical foundation" of "populist authoritarianism."[104] Although the post-Mao leaders tried to avoid the personality cult of Mao Zedong, emphasized collective leadership and experimented with limited intra-party democracy, their "populist orientation" continues to dominate the CCP governance and to gain public support through political campaigns.[105] Another feature of populist authoritarianism in China is the utilization of "strong interpersonal trust and rich social capital."[106] Social capital is fully utilized for regime consolidation in the PRC where the Chinese concept of *guanxi* (personal networks) is important in human relations.[107] Tang notes that the model of populist authoritarianism embraces a high level of mass political participation and the encouragement of political contention, exposing members of the public to politics directly. Yet, political activism stems from mutual trust and strong personal bonds. The weaknesses of the PRC's populist authoritarianism include the relatively weak political institutions and the underdevelopment of the rule of law, intermediary social organizations and the electoral system.[108] This phenomenon reflects the CCP's attempt at creating a direct state-society connection in which "both sides can reach each other quickly without the filtering of the often protracted institutional processes."[109] To Tang, the "under-development of the intermediate institutions is both a cause and a result of the direct mass political participation."[110] The mass line ideology, mass participation in politics and the high level of political activism in China "require a highly responsive government for it to maintain political power and stability."[111] The populist authoritarian state "spends a lot of time and energy maintaining political power by responding to public demand."[112] As a result, citizens in the PRC tend to "believe that their government responds to their needs."[113] Strong political support for populist authoritarianism can be seen in the PRC where the regime can sustain itself with legitimacy, according to

[104] Ibid.
[105] Ibid.
[106] Ibid.
[107] Ibid., p. 155.
[108] Ibid.
[109] Ibid.
[110] Ibid.
[111] Ibid., p. 157.
[112] Ibid.
[113] Ibid.

Tang. However, the PRC is inherently politically unstable partly because "regime legitimacy and political trust based on the government's hyper-responsiveness cannot be easily sustained," and partly because "satisfying everyone's demands is simply too costly and too exhausting."[114] Without "institutional buffers such as elections and legal procedures, the public mood can swing violently and cause political earthquakes that can directly threaten the survival of the political system."[115] Tang concludes that "autocratic political trust, no matter how strong it may seem, is very costly to sustain."[116]

Tang's insightful analyses of the PRC can be applied to the Hong Kong case. First and foremost, PRC authorities who conduct new united front work in the HKSAR adopt the tenet of mass line to mobilize pro-Beijing forces in elections. They fully utilize interpersonal trust and social capital to stimulate mass participation in electoral politics. Yet, the Hong Kong setting is different from the PRC in that the former has the rule of law and relatively stronger political institutions. The HKSAR government has to learn how to respond to public demands assertively and effectively. Quite often, it has been criticized by the local democrats as being "weak" in both policy formulation and implementation. In January 2019, for example, the HKSAR government was heavily criticized by both pro-democracy and pro-Beijing politicians for failing to explain to citizens how HK$4000 of subsidy for each eligible citizen were distributed to the poor and the needy. The relatively "weak" capacity of the Hong Kong government in its policy formulation and implementation reflects that many principal officials are inexperienced, while the bureaucracy has lacked internal coordination and strong leadership. Unlike China where populist authoritarianism requires a responsive regime, Hong Kong is in lack of a responsive government equipped with strong performance legitimacy. The irony of China's united front work is that while it produces mass participation in support of the government, the administration remains relatively weak in its policy-making and policy-implementation capability. "Populist authoritarianism" can be partially implemented in the HKSAR because the CCP can only achieve mass participation and mobilization through the utilization of social capital and interpersonal trust in the pro-Beijing forces. Yet, the political institutions and policy-making as well as policy-implementation

[114] Ibid.
[115] Ibid.
[116] Ibid.

capacity are all outside CCP control, let alone penetration, of PRC agents responsible for united front work in Hong Kong.

RESISTANCE TO CHINA'S UNITED FRONT WORK AS NEW FORM OF HONG KONG CITIZENSHIP

Gerry Groot argues that China has been exerting its hegemony on the mainland society and groups through its united front work.[117] The same process can be seen in Hong Kong.[118] However, many Hong Kong's interest groups and individuals have been resisting China's united front work by having both passive and active resistance. Passively, some people tend to withdraw from receiving such united front inducements as monetary favors, socio-political status and appointments from the PRC and its agents. Actively, some Hong Kong people rely on political actions, like voting, protests and electoral competition, to prevent PRC authorities and their agents from encroaching into Hong Kong's political system.

In the study of citizenship, Jurgen Mackert and Bryan Turner have argued that most scholars have neglected the fact that the history of citizenship "is one of social struggle against pre-modern authorities, nobles and aristocracies, of class struggles and the demands of social movements, and no less of cultural, ethnic, indigenous protests against the long history of colonialism."[119] They also contend that citizenship can be interpreted as the "people's struggles for rights and their resistance to illegitimate and repressive authorities, unbearable economic living conditions, or discrimination with regard to religion, ethnic belonging and sexual orientation."[120] Moreover, violence has not been central to the studies of citizenship. In other words, if the new concept of citizenship embraces struggles, resistance and even violence, the case of Hong Kong deserves our scholarly attention. The 2014 Occupy Central Movement did represent a new mode of political participation involving various interest groups that were

---

[117] Gerry Groot, *Managing Transitions: The Chinese Communist Party, United Front Work, Corporatism and Hegemony* (London: Routledge, 2004).

[118] Lam Wai-man and Kay Lam Chi-yan, "China's United Front Work in Civil Society: The Case of Hong Kong," *International Journal of Chinese Studies*, vol. 4, no. 3 (December 2013), pp. 301–325.

[119] Jurgen Mackert and Bryan S. Turner, "Introduction: citizenship and political struggle," in Jurgen Mackert and Bryan S. Turner, eds., *The Transformation of Citizenship, Volume 3: Struggle, Resistance and Violence* (London: Routledge, 2017), p. 3.

[120] Ibid., p. 2.

mobilized by its leaders.[121] Robert Press has argued that in the process of "peaceful resistance," "repression triggers the initial resistance by individuals; the resulting activism, especially if it is able to gain some concessions, encourages organizational activism when it is safer to emerge into the open."[122] The case of Hong Kong shows that some people did resort to "peaceful resistance" because of the increasing intervention of PRC authorities in Hong Kong matters. While PRC officials and their supporters see Beijing's intervention as positive and rightful, those Hong Kong people who resist China's increasing encroachment also regard their resistance action as rightful. As a result, Beijing's united front work has been encountering various forms of resistance, ranging from apathy to denouncement, and from passive withdrawal to active participation in mass actions, including electoral mobilization, voting, protests and even violence. The Mongkok riot in February 2016 demonstrated how some localists and radicals resisted a government attempt at removing hawkers on the street, and how they used violence as a means to express not only their political discontent but also the reported abduction of several local publishers who published books critical of the PRC leaders, party-cadres and regime.[123]

Materialism Versus Post-Materialist Values

According to Ronald Inglehart, materialist values have the objectives of maintaining law and order, fighting rising prices, retaining a high rate of economic growth, ensuring that a country has strong defense forces, sustaining a stable economy and achieving effectiveness in crime control.[124] Post-materialist values include the need to "give people more say in the decisions of the government," to "protect the freedom of speech," to "give people more say in how things are decided at work and in their community," to "make their cities and countryside more beautiful," to "move toward a friendlier, less impersonal society" and to "move toward a society

---

[121] Sonny Shiu-Hing Lo, ed., *Interest Groups and the New Democracy Movement in Hong Kong* (London: Routledge, 2018).

[122] Robert M. Press, *Peaceful Resistance: Advancing Human Rights and Democratic Freedoms* (Aldershot, Hampshire: Ashgate, 2006), p. 28.

[123] Sonny Shiu-Hing Lo, *The Politics of Policing in Greater China* (London: Palgrave, 2016), Chapter 8, pp. 195–221.

[124] Ronald Inglehart, *Modernization and Postmordernization: Cultural, Economic, and Political Change in 43 Societies* (Princeton, New Jersey: Princeton University Press, 1990).

where ideas count more than money."[125] Citizens who hold post-materialist values support the values of mass participation in governmental decision-making, the protection of civil liberties, the maintenance of openness and transparency in their workplace and polity and the achievement of environmental protection and sustainable development.

Inglehart's insights can be combined with our study of China's united front work. United front emphasizes the use of materialistic incentives, such as financial support, socio-political status and economic influence, by PRC officials and agents to secure the support from the people of Hong Kong. Those pragmatic and materialistic Hong Kong people are vulnerable to the umbrella of China's united front work, especially business people who have the vested interest to increase their economic profits and maintain the socio-political status quo. Nevertheless, many young Hong Kong people tend to be more post-materialistic, possessing the strong values of human rights, civil liberties, the rule of law, sustainable development, the protection of cultural heritage of Hong Kong and the achievement of democracy defined in the Western sense of a political system where the chief executive is directly elected by citizens through universal suffrage. While the late Samuel Huntington defines democracy as having the hallmark of the rotation of political party in power, many people of Hong Kong do not envision this distant objective, because the current HKSAR polity does not really allow any political party to grasp political power and govern the city-state. Political parties are registered under the Company Ordinance in the HKSAR instead of any political party law. They operate like, to use Huntington's term, "legislative cliques" with struggles over government policies inside the Legislative Council.[126] At best, many post-materialistic and pro-democracy Hongkongers aspire to have the right to vote for their Chief Executive through universal suffrage. These post-materialistic Hongkongers tend to have a stronger sense of local Hong Kong identity, especially those who strive for the protection of the local cultural heritage and of environment in the territory.[127] Many localists have a strong sense of Hong Kong identity, seeing China's increas-

---

[125] Ibid., pp. 74–75.
[126] See Lo Shiu-Hing, "Legislative Cliques, Political Parties, Political Groupings and Electoral System," in Joseph Cheng and Sonny Lo, eds., From Colony to SAR: Hong Kong's Challenges Ahead (Hong Kong: The Chinese University Press, 1995), pp. 51–70.
[127] For concrete examples, like Eddie Chu Hoi-dick who was directly elected as a legislator in the 2016 Legislative Council direct election, see Sonny Shiu-Hing Lo and Jeff Hai-chi Loo, "An Anatomy of the Post-Materialistic Values of Hong Kong Youth: Opposition to

ing intervention in Hong Kong matters as politically unacceptable, intolerable and undesirable. The localists are post-materialistic because they uphold the values of environmentalism, good quality of life, personal esteem and individual self-expression.[128] Consequently, many of them have been determined to resist the PRC's united front work, which represents the penetration of mainland-style politics into the HKSAR.

Patron-Client Perspective

If those materialistic and pragmatic Hong Kong people are relatively susceptible to the PRC's united front work, they can be regarded as the potential and actual clients under the influence of material and non-material rewards from the patron, namely, Beijing and its agents. James Scott defines patron-client relations as "dyadic (two-person) ties involving a largely instrumental friendship in which an individual of higher socio-economic status (patron) uses his own influence and resources to provide protection or benefits, or both, for a person of lower status (client) who, for his part, reciprocates by offering general support and assistance, including personal services, to the patron."[129] A patron may have coercive powers and hold an official position of authority. Patron-client relations, to Scott, entail reciprocity in the sense that there are some exchanges between the patron and client, who both have disparity in their wealth, power and status.[130] A client is someone who enters an unequal exchange relationship in which he or she cannot reciprocate fully.[131] A second feature of the patron-client dyad is the face-to-face and personal quality of the mutually trustful and affectionate relationship.[132] The affection and obligation invested in the patron-client relations are critical to the process of political and electoral mobilization in China's united front work in Hong Kong, because the powerful patron can garner the support of his or her clients, who in turn return the patron's favor reciprocally by voting for him or her in elections.

China's Rising 'Sharp Power,'" in David Trotman and Stan Tucker, eds., *Youth: Global Challenges and Issues of the 21st Century* (New York: Nova Science), pp. 95–126.

[128] Ronald Inglehart, "Post-Materialism in an Environment of Insecurity," *American Political Science Review*, vol. 75, no. 4 (December 1981), pp. 881–882.

[129] James C. Scott, "Patron-Client Politics and Political Change in Southeast Asia," *American Political Science Review*, vol. 66, no. 1 (March 1972), p. 92.

[130] Ibid., p. 93.

[131] Ibid.

[132] Ibid., p. 94.

The study of patron-client politics has been largely neglected in Hong Kong politics.[133] The patrons in the context of China's united front work in the HKSAR include not only PRC officials, but also the Chief Executive, principal officials and pro-Beijing elites, especially the leaders of pro-Beijing political groups and unions. The entire hierarchy of patron-client politics in Hong Kong is complex, involving a variety of interest groups, as this book will show, such as women, labor unions, youth groups, religious groups, district-based federations and media organizations. United front represents the penetrative or infiltrative style of communist politics through the activities of mass organizations in a relatively pluralistic setting of Hong Kong.

Geopolitical Perspective

United front work is necessary for the political heartland, namely, the PRC, to exert control over its borderland, Hong Kong, which was ruled by the British from 1842 to 1997 and which remains a cosmopolitan and international city vulnerable to foreign influences. As China remains a political heartland apprehensive of foreign intervention, the traditional xenophobic sentiments of mainland Chinese leaders toward foreigners shape how Beijing has been dealing with Hong Kong. As such, united front work is indispensable for China to dilute foreign influences on Hong Kong politically and socially.

Geopolitically, Harold Mackinder argued in 1904 that the balance of power was tipped in favor of a political heartland.[134] As he wrote, "The actual balance of political power at any given time is, of course, the product, on the one hand, of geographical conditions, both economic and strategic, and, on the other hand, of the relative number, virility, equipment, and organization of the competing peoples."[135] From a geopolitical perspective, mainland China is huge in its physical size, population and resources compared with the miniscule Hong Kong, which lacks natural resources. However, geopolitically, Hong Kong has been historically located at China's borderland subject to the British colonialism and vul-

---

[133] The exception is Bruce Kwong, *Patron-Client Politics and Elections in Hong Kong* (London: Routledge, 2009). Also see Lo, *The Dynamics of Beijing-Hong Kong Relations: A Model for Taiwan?*.

[134] Harold J. Mackinder, "The geographical pivot of history," *The Geographical Journal*, vol. 23, no. 4 (April 1904), pp. 421–444.

[135] Ibid., p. 437.

nerable to Western influences. If mainland China as the political heartland sees the borderland Hong Kong as a possible chess board utilized by Western countries to influence, subvert and infiltrate the PRC, then there is arguably a genuine national security concern in the minds of Beijing. As a matter of fact, the PRC has seen Hong Kong's democratization as a Trojan Horse in which Western countries seek to not only change the HKSAR into a democratic polity under their influence but also shape the mainland's political system in the long run.[136] Under the circumstance in which Hong Kong has been perceived as a ploy utilized by Western states to subvert the PRC and undermine its sovereignty, China's united front work is destined to be the most important instrument by which Beijing has to reassert its political control and supremacy over the HKSAR.

INTEGRATED PERSPECTIVES AND UNDERSTANDING THE CONTEXT AND CONTENT OF NEW UNITED FRONT

Figure 1.1 integrates all the aforesaid perspectives and allows us to understand the context and content of China's new united front work in Hong Kong. The PRC regime under President Xi Jinping remains authoritarian, or "populist authoritarian" as Tang argues. It is the most powerful political patron influencing the HKSAR's political system. Three main factors shape Beijing's united front work in Hong Kong, namely (1) its determination to buttress the legitimacy of both the HKSAR leadership and the central government's policy toward Hong Kong, (2) its national security consideration (securitization) and (3) its geopolitical concerns about Hong Kong as a borderland vulnerable to Western influences. However, Beijing as the powerful political patron encounters the relatively pluralistic Hong Kong, meaning that its clients are mainly the HKSAR leaders and local ruling elites. Yet, the civil society and masses of Hong Kong remain politically heterogenous and divided into at least three parts: (1) a relatively materialistic and pragmatic segment vulnerable to Beijing's united front work; (2) a comparatively post-materialistic segment that resists and opposes it; and (3) an apathetic or indifferent segment that remains to be the target of lobbying from both Beijing and its agents on the one hand and pro-democracy local elites on the other. Hence, the civil society in the HKSAR, as argued in this book, is the arena of contention and struggle

[136] For this Trojan Horse view of Hong Kong, see Sonny Shiu-Hing Lo, *Hong Kong's Indigenous Democracy: Origins, Evolution and Contentions* (London: Palgrave, 2015).

1 A COMPREHENSIVE FRAMEWORK OF UNDERSTANDING THE CONTEXT... 41

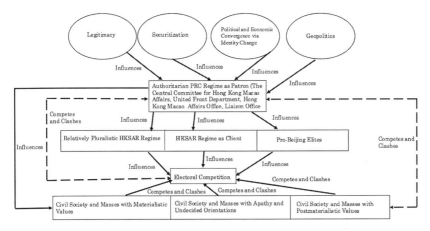

Fig. 1.1 A comprehensive framework of understanding China's new united front work on Hong Kong

between the relatively powerful patron Beijing and some pro-democracy Hongkongers. Their relations are conflict-ridden, especially as pro-democracy elites in the civil society are competing fiercely with pro-Beijing elites in elections at the legislative and district levels. Because the HKSAR remains a relatively limited pluralistic polity in which elections persist, civil liberties are protected and the rule of law exists, Beijing's united front work has to penetrate into all corners of the civil society and various mass organizations in order to stop the local pro-democracy elite from capturing most of the seats in the Legislative Council and most of the eighteen District Councils. As such, the battle for the hearts and minds of the people of Hong Kong is of utmost importance in the psyche of Beijing's policy-makers on Hong Kong, especially during the Xi Jinping era which shows that, to use David Shambaugh's term, the PRC is continuing with its "hard authoritarian repressive policies."[137] Shambaugh has recognized some "rising tensions in China's periphery," such as Beijing's relations with Japan, Taiwan and Southeast Asian states.[138] Yet, he has neglected the phenomenon that Hong Kong as an internal peripheral region of China has exhibited considerable "tensions" between the central authorities and local pro-democracy elites and masses.

[137] David Shambaugh, *China's Future* (Cambridge: Polity Press, 2016), p. 125.
[138] Ibid., pp. 138–145.

This book is organized into ten chapters. Chapter 2 will discuss the role of the Democratic Alliance for Betterment and Progress of Hong Kong (DAB) in China's new united front work, followed by Chap. 3 that will examine the activities of Fujianese interest groups. Chapter 4 will discuss the role of the pro-Beijing Federation of Trade Unions (FTU) and its competition with the independent and pro-democracy trade unions. Chapter 5 will focus on the role of women interest groups, while Chap. 6 will go through the six main religions in the HKSAR and examine the extent to which they are under the influence of united front operations. Chapter 7 will contend that the PRC's new united front work can be seen in the ways in which district-based federations and neighborhood (*kaifong*) associations are politically utilized and electorally mobilized. Chapter 8 will examine the role of pro-Beijing youth groups and those pro-democracy and radical youth groups that resist united front politics. Chapter 9 examines the PRC's influence on Hong Kong's civil society, absorbing the mainstream media but failing to capture the educational sector. As such, long-term migration, both inward to Hong Kong from the mainland and outward to Greater Bay Area from Hong Kong, is now encouraged. Chapter 10 will focus on the co-optation of business elites, democrats, former senior civil servants, educators and the Taiwanese, with external implications as foreign countries like Australia have seen united front work as politically dangerous and legally contentious. Finally, Chap. 11 wraps up our findings and cast lights on the operations of united front work, the features of penetrative politics, the integration of all academic perspectives and the implications for "one country, two systems."

CHAPTER 2

The Democratic Alliance for the Betterment and Progress of Hong Kong as Flagship of China's United Front Work

The PRC's united front work in the HKSAR since July 1, 1997, has been expanding to various strata of the society, including the businesspeople, workers, professionals, the youth, women and ethnic minorities, particularly after the revision of the United Front Work Regulations of the CCP in September 2015.[1] Chapter 8 of the revised Regulations has focused on the PRC united front work in Hong Kong, Macao and Taiwan. Article 29 states that the PRC united front work in Hong Kong and Macao aims at "comprehensively implementing the principles of 'one country, two systems,' 'Hong Kong people governing Hong Kong,' and 'Macao people governing Macao'"; "supporting the policies of the Chief Executives of the Special Administrative Regions and expanding the forces that love Hong Kong, Macao and China" and "strengthening the national identity and consciousness of the Chinese nation among the comrades of Hong Kong and Macao."[2] While Article 30 vows to oppose any "separatist activity of the Taiwan independence," Article 32 stresses that the CCP "supports democratic parties and individuals without party background to direct the related groups and associations that promote China's peaceful

---

[1] Wen Qiaoshi, *Tongzhan Gongzuo (United Front Work)* (Beijing: Chinese Communist Party History Publisher, 2008), pp. 178–179; see also "The United Front Work Regulations of the Chinese Communist Party," September 23, 2015, in *People's Daily*, September 23, 2015.

[2] "The United Front Work Regulations of the Chinese Communist Party," in *People's Daily*, September 23, 2015.

reunification to play their functions in united front work in Hong Kong, Macao, Taiwan and the overseas."[3] The implementation of Article 32, as this article will discuss, can be seen in the activities of the Democratic Alliance for the Betterment and Progress of Hong Kong (DAB), a pro-Beijing and "democratic" political party formed in Hong Kong in 1992. The DAB has been playing a crucial role in trying to win the hearts and minds of the people of Hong Kong through various activities, including its active participation in Legislative Council and District Council elections; its organization of training programs, forums and conferences and its coordination with other pro-Beijing interest groups in the support of Beijing's and the HKSAR government's policies. Most importantly, the DAB has been functioning as a major political force competing with the pro-democracy forces in the HKSAR. This chapter will examine the functions of the DAB and the extent to which it can fulfill the main objective of China's united front work in Hong Kong, namely, wining the hearts and minds of more Hong Kong "comrades" than ever before.

THE FUNCTIONS AND ORGANIZATION OF THE DAB

The DAB was founded in July 1992 by a group of 56 pro-Beijing political elites, declaring in its manifesto that "we love our country and we sincerely hope that China will be stable, prosperous, democratic and progressive," that "the relationship between Hong Kong and China should be one of cooperation and communication, as opposed to separation, alienation and antagonism," and that "we love Hong Kong and our guidelines are to work to protect Hong Kong's overall interests, to promote social stability, progress and development."[4] The DAB claims that it is a "big-tent party" and "not pigeonholed into serving the special interests of any social class."[5] In 2005, the DAB merged with a pro-business group named Hong Kong Progressive Alliance (HKPA), strengthening the business and professional background of the DAB members while simultaneously serving as a united front party that "crosses and transcends social and class boundaries in society."[6] In Table 2.1, the merger enhanced the profes-

[3] Ibid.
[4] Democratic Alliance for the Betterment and Progress of Hong Kong, *25th Anniversary Commemoration of the Democratic Alliance for the Betterment and Progress of Hong Kong: Choices and Promises* (Hong Kong: Democratic Alliance for the Betterment and Progress of Hong Kong, 2017), p. 6.
[5] Ibid., p. 12.
[6] Ibid.

Table 2.1 The background of founding members of DAB and HKPA

Background of founding members	DAB	HKPA
Entrepreneurs	7 (12.5%)	13 (40.6%)
Industrialists	0	5 (15.6%)
Professionals	33 (58.9%)	12 (37.5%)
Semi-professionals	10 (17.9%)	2 (6.3%)
Community organizers	8 (14.3%)	0
Total number	56	32

Sources: Yuen Kei-wang, *Hong Kong Road and the Democratic Alliance for the Betterment and Progress of Hong Kong* (Hong Kong: Chong Hwa Book Company, 2011), pp. 260–267; and Yuen Kei-wang, *Twenty Years of History of the Democratic Alliance for the Betterment and Progress of Hong Kong* (Hong Kong: Chong Hwa Book Company, 2012), pp. 20–28 and pp. 162–164.

Note: The two parties were merged in 2005 with a total of 4000 members. Entrepreneurs included businesspeople and company directors. Industrialists referred to manufacturers and industrialists. Professionals included doctors, lawyers, accountants, engineers, architect surveyors and professors. Semi-professionals embraced educators, nurses, social workers and office managers. Community organizers included trade unionist and leaders of the community organizations

sional, industrial and entrepreneurial profile of the DAB, which could then function as the united front umbrella reaching out to various strata of the society.

Organizationally speaking, the DAB was led by leaders who were not only politically loyal to Beijing but also projecting an image of being professional politicians fighting for the general interest of the Hong Kong people. Jasper Tsang, the DAB chairman from 1992 to 2003, was politically educated and groomed to be the leader of the pro-Beijing force. Born in Guangzhou city in 1947, Tsang migrated to Hong Kong at the age of two and his father had been a clerk in the pro-Beijing Chinese General Chamber of Commerce.[7] Tsang studied in the Saint Paul College and his brother Tsang Tak-sing was arrested in 1967 when he participated in the pro-CCP communist protests by distributing anti-government leaflets in Hong Kong. Jasper Tsang's political mentor was Ng Hong-man, a pro-Beijing veteran and a former Hong Kong member to the PRC National People's Congress. In 1993 and 1994, Tsang became an articulated politician arguing publicly with the last British Governor of Hong Kong, Christopher Patten, over the British Hong Kong administration's

[7] Jasper Tsang, *Straight Talk* (in Chinese) (Hong Kong: Cosmo Books, 1995).

Table 2.2 DAB chairpersons, 1992–2018

Name	Time	Educational background
Jasper Tsang Yok-sing	July 1992 to December 2003	Graduate of the University of Hong Kong, and a school headmaster of the pro-Beijing Pui Kiu Middle School
Ma Lik	December 2003 to August 2007	Graduate of the Chinese University of Hong Kong, and the vice president of the pro-Beijing *Hong Kong Commercial Daily*
Tam Yiu-chung	August 2007 to April 2015	Studied adult education at the Australian National University and later trade unionism at the London School of Economics and Political Science, and he was the former director of the pro-Beijing Hong Kong Federation of Trade Unions (FTU)
Starry Lee Wai-king	April 2015 to the present	Graduate of the Hong Kong University of Science and Technology and an accountant of KPMG

Sources: Yuen Kei-wang, *Hong Kong Road and the Democratic Alliance for the Betterment and Progress of Hong Kong* (Hong Kong: Chong Hwa Book Company, 2011), pp. 2–16, pp. 102–107 and pp. 211–217

political reform plan. In 1995, when Tsang ran in the legislative direct election, he was found by the mass media to have applied for immigration to Canada and eventually he was defeated in the electoral contest. After the defeat, Tsang was determined to stay in Hong Kong. He was directly elected to the Legislative Council (LegCo) in 1998 until 2016 and became its president from 2008 to 2016. As with Tsang, the late Ma Lik was born in Guangzhou and later migrated to Hong Kong. Ma became the secretary-general of the Basic Law Consultative Committee from 1985 to 1990 and then was appointed as the editor of the pro-Beijing *Hong Kong Commercial Daily* in 1991. Being a former student of Jasper Tsang, Ma was a famous writer for the pro-Beijing camp during the mid-1980s and severely criticized the British political reform plan by using a pseudonym, Sun Wai-sze, and he was gradually groomed to succeed Tsang as the DAB chair in 2003 (Table 2.2). After Ma passed away in 2007, a long-time pro-Beijing trade unionist Tam Yiu-chung became the DAB chair until 2015, when Starry Lee took over the leadership position. Lee was under the political tutelage of a pro-Beijing female district politician named Lee Lin in the 1990s, and she was groomed by Jasper Tsang to become a directly elected legislator in 2008.[8] All DAB leaders had one thing in common;

---

[8] Yuen Kei-wang, *Hong Kong Road and the Democratic Alliance for the Betterment and Progress of Hong Kong* (Hong Kong: Chong Hwa Book Company, 2011), pp. 211–216.

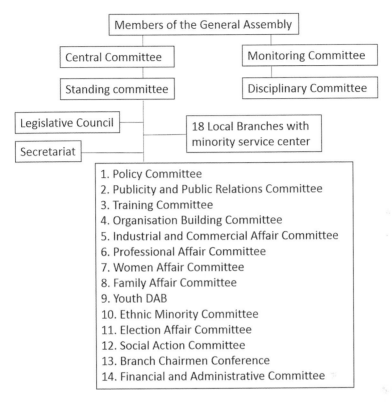

Fig. 2.1 The DAB organization chart. Source: "Organization Structure," in the website of the Democratic Alliance for the Betterment and Progress of Hong Kong, available in http://www.dab.org.hk/AboutUs.php?nid=234, access date: April 4, 2018

they had to be politically loyal to Beijing and to undergo a period of political training, tutelage and observation by PRC officials and agents responsible for Hong Kong matters.

Figure 2.1 shows that the DAB is tightly organized with a powerful nine-member standing committee led by the chairlady Starry Lee, five deputy chairpersons, five secretary-generals and one treasurer.[9] The standing committee is assisted by a 31-member central committee. There is no

---

[9] "25th Anniversary Commemoration of the Democratic Alliance for the Betterment and Progress of Hong Kong: Choices and Promises," p. 92.

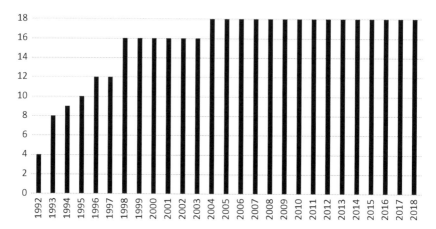

Fig. 2.2 Number of DAB district branches, 1992–2018. Sources: See the website of the Democratic Alliance for the Betterment and Progress of Hong Kong in http://www.dab.org.hk/branch.php, access date: April 4, 2018

overlapping membership between the central committee and the standing committee. Organizationally, the annual general assembly with the participation of ordinary members elects the members of both the standing committee and the central committee, thus demonstrating a "democratic" element in the CCP-style of "democratic centralism." In fact, the DAB is run in top-down manner, with the centralist element playing a dominant role in formulating party policies. There is a monitoring committee with party elders who oversee party affairs, together with a disciplinary committee. The internal checks and balances are instituted, but basically the DAB is led by a group of "oligarchical" leaders, because the top office-bearers and standing committee members are the most powerful elites within the party. The fourteen committees work side by side with the eighteen branches so that the party can conduct united front work that cuts across various strata of the society, including women, youth, ethnic minorities, professionals and industrial and commercial elites.[10] The DAB increased its district branches from four in 1992 to twelve in 1996, and then to eighteen in 2004 (Fig. 2.2). The objective of such expansion was to win the hearts and minds of more Hong Kong voters in local elections. The eighteen branches have offices with full-time directors being hired to con-

[10] Robert Michels, *Political Parties: A Study of the Oligarchical Tendencies of Modern Democracy* (Kitchener: Batoche Books, 2001).

duct daily operations of constituency work, thus broadening the umbrella of the united front work significantly.

The DAB Participation in Legislative and District Elections

Since the main objective of the DAB's united front work is to acquire voters' support in elections, the party has to demonstrate not only its performance in the local legislative and district elections, but also the political representation of its members at the levels of Hong Kong's top policy-making structures, such as the Principal Officials Accountability System (POAS) and the Executive Council, and of the PRC political system. The POAS was introduced by the HKSAR government under the leadership of Chief Executive Tung Chee-hwa (1997–2005) in July 2002 so that he could have his batch of appointed loyal officials. In Table 2.3, the DAB had more members who became principal officials and executive councilors in 2007, when the Chief Executive was C. Y. Leung (2012–2017), than the period from 2005 to 2012, when a former civil servant Donald Tsang was the Chief Executive. Leung was trying to empower the DAB at the top level of political leadership while Tsang only appointed one DAB member into the Executive Council. At present, the DAB is enjoying the political trust from Chief Executive Carrie Lam and has four members being appointed as principal officials. On the other hand, the DAB has traditionally demonstrated its influence in the memberships of both the PRC National People's Congress and the Chinese People's Political Consultative Conference (Table 2.3). The DAB representation at the level of the PRC's political system is significant; its heavyweight members can lobby the Chinese government for the interests of the Hong Kong people, thus projecting an influential image to win the hearts and minds of more Hong Kong residents.

Table 2.4 shows that the DAB as a united front machine could in general maintain its momentum in the direct elections held for the Legislative Council (LegCo) from 1998 to 2016, for its number of votes was maintained at 373,428 and 361,617 respectively. However, the DAB's share of seats in the LegCo actually declined from 25.1% in 1998 to 16.4% in 2016. The public support for the pro-Beijing and pro-government united front forces has shifted to other pro-establishment groups, whose votes increased significantly from 449,668 in 1998 to 918,278 in 2016, while their share of seats in the legislature also rose from 30.2% in 1998 to

Table 2.3 Major political representation of DAB members in Hong Kong and China

Year	Principal officials	Executive Council members	Hong Kong members to the National People's Congress	Hong Kong members to the Chinese People's Political Consultative Conference
1997	Elsie Leung Oi-sie	Tam Yiu-chung	Maria Tam Wai-chu, Ma Lik, Yeung Yiu-chung,	Jose Yu Sun-say, Kenneth Chow Chun-kay, Ann Chiang Lai-wan, Jasper Tsang Tak-sing
2002	Elsie Leung Oi-sie, Gary Chan Hak-kan	Jasper Tsang Yok-sing	Maria Tam Wai-chu, Ma Lik, Yeung Yiu-chung, Ip Kwok-him	Jose Yu Sun-say, Ambrose Lau Hon-chuen, Kenneth Chow Chun-kay, Cheung Hok-ming, Ann Chiang Lai-wan, Jasper Tsang Yok-sing, Tam Yiu-chung, Chan Kam-lam
2007	Gregory So Kam-leung, Raymond Cheung Man-to, Caspar Tsui Ying-wai	Lau Kwong-wah	Maria Tam Wai-chu, Yeung Yiu-chung, Ip Kwok-him, Choy So-yuk	Jose Yu Sun-say, Ambrose Lau Hon-chuen, Kenneth Chow Chun-kay, Cheung Hok-ming, Ann Chiang Lai-wan, Jasper Tsang Yok-sing, Tam Yiu-chung, Chan Kam-lam
2012	Lau Kong-wah, Gregory So Kam-leung, Bernard Chan Pak-li	Cheung Hok-ming, Starry Lee Wai-king, Ip Kwok-him,	Maria Tam Wai-chu, Yeung Yiu-chung, Ip Kwok-him, Choy So-yuk, Brave Chan Yung	Ambrose Lau Hon-chuen, Cheung Hok-ming, Tam Yiu-chung, Pang Chueng-wai, Chan Kam-lam
2017	Lau Kong-wah, Bernard Chan Pak-li, Caspar Tsui Ying-wai, Siu Ka-yi	Ip Kwok-him, Horace Cheung Kwok-kwan	Brave Chan Yung, Ip Kwok-him, Tam Yiu-chung, Choy So-yuk	Starry Lee Wai-king, Pang Cheung-wai, Leung Che-cheung

Sources: The data are collected from various official websites and government press releases, 1997–2017

41.7% in 2016. Hence, Beijing's strategy is to cultivate other pro-establishment forces, apart from the DAB, to win the hearts and minds of the voters with a view to blocking the advancement of pro-democracy forces. In fact, the pro-democracy votes increased from 979,199 in 1998

Table 2.4 The direct election results of the Legislative Council, 1998–2016

Total seats Party/force	1998 (20 seats)	2000 (24 seats)	2004 (30 seats)	2008 (30 seats)	2012 (35 seats)	2016 (35 seats)
DAB seats	5 (25.1%)	8 (29.4%)	8 (22.6%)	7 (22.8%)	9 (19.9%)	7 (16.4%)
DAB votes	373,428	391,718	402,420	347,373	366,140	361,617
Pro-establishment seats	5 (30.2%)	8 (34.6%)	12 (37.0%)	11 (39.5%)	17 (39.7%)	16 (41.7%)
Pro-establishment votes	449,668	461,048	660,052	602,468	730,363	918,278
Pro-democracy seats	15 (66.2%)	16 (60.0%)	18 (61.4%)	19 (59.2%)	18 (56.4%)	19 (54.8%)
Pro-democracy votes	979,199	799,240	1,096,272	901,707	1,036,998	1,206,420
Total votes that were cast by voters	1,489,705	1,331,080	1,784,131	1,524,249	1,838,722	2,202,283

Sources: *Report on the Legislative Council Election*, 1998, 2000, 2004, 2008, 2012 and 2016, downloaded from the website of Electoral Affairs Commission, in https://www.eac.gov.hk/, and *Election Information Compilation of Hong Kong* (published by the Hong Kong Institute of Asia-Pacific Studies, CUHK, 1996, 2001, 2005 and 2015)

Note: The Hong Kong Legislative Council election was partly directly elected, a proportion increased from 33% with 20 directly elected seats in 1998 to 50% with 30 directly elected seats in 2004, and to 50% with 35 directly elected seats in 2012. The pro-establishment camp includes the DAB, and other pro-Beijing and pro-government groups, such as the pro-business Liberal Party and pro-business Hong Kong Progressive Alliance in 1998, the pro-business New Forum in 2000, the pro-labor Federations of Trade Unions in 2008, the pro-civil service and pro-government New People's Party in 2012

to 1,206,420 in 2016, but the share of seats obtained by the pro-democracy forces declined from 66.2% in 1998 to 54.8%, mainly due to the proportional representation system adopted in the LegCo elections. This proportional representation system has been beneficial to the relatively smaller groups, including those from the pro-democracy and pro-Beijing camps. Although the democrats gained a considerable portion of votes in direct elections, this result could not be reflected proportionally in their capture of the seats in the LegCo, where half of the 70 seats are returned from geographical constituencies in which they have traditionally performed well and where half are returned from occupational groups in which pro-establishment and pro-Beijing forces are constantly dominant. In the 2016 LegCo direct elections and the March 2018 LegCo by-elections, the DAB candidates cooperated with other pro-Beijing united front groups, such as the New People's Party (NPP) led by the former Secretary for Security Regina Ip, and the Federation of Trade Unions (FTU). For instance, in the March 2018 by-election in the Kowloon West, the young DAB member Vincent Cheng defeated the pro-democracy candidate Edward Yiu by acquiring the strong support from the FTU and the NPP.

Figure 2.3 shows that the umbrella of China's united front work in Hong Kong has been expanded to other pro-Beijing forces apart from the DAB. In 1998, the other pro-Beijing forces managed to get 76,240 votes, but they gained 257,632 votes in the 2004 LegCo direct elections and then 556,661 votes in the 2016 legislative direct elections. Comparatively, the gains in DAB votes from 1998 to 2016 did not show drastic improvements, but the DAB's sustained momentum helped the overall pro-Beijing forces secure public support in LegCo direct elections, thus galvanizing the rapidly expanding pro-Beijing front to check and balance the pro-democracy forces electorally.

The DAB's dual functions of checking and balancing the pro-democracy forces while simultaneously providing a strong support base for the broader pro-Beijing united front can be seen in the Hong Kong District Council elections. Table 2.5 shows that the DAB performed strongly in

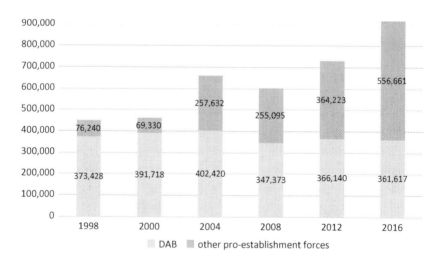

Fig. 2.3 Comparison of the votes gained by DAB and pro-Beijing forces in Legislative Council elections, 1998–2016. Sources: Votes gained were calculated from the official statistics in the website of the Electoral Affairs Commission

Table 2.5 The results of the District Council elections, 1999–2015

Year	1999	2003	2007	2011	2015
No. of candidates	798	837	907	915	935
No. of seats	390	400	405	412	431
No. of uncontested seats	76	76	74	76	66
Total votes	810,863	1,051,424	1,138,358	1,202,544	1,467,229
DAB					
No. of candidates[a]	188	200(3)	177(24)	182(24)	171(3)
Elected candidates	83	62	115	136	119
No. of votes	190,792	241,202	292,916	282,119	309,262
Percentages of the votes	23.5%	22.9%	25.7%	23.5%	21.1%
Pro-Beijing forces (including DAB):					
No. of candidates[b]	435	417	430	436	486
Elected candidates	233	201	298	299	298
No. of votes	442,286	491,067	614,621	652,840	788,389
Percentages of the votes	54.5%	46.7%	54.0%	54.3%	53.7%

Sources: *Reports on the District Councils Election* in 1999, 2003, 2007, 2011 and 2015; *Election Information Compilation of Hong Kong* (Hong Kong: Hong Kong Institute of Asia-Pacific Studies, the Chinese University of Hong Kong, 1996, 2001, 2005 and 2015)
[a]The double membership of FTU and DAB are indicated by the number inside the brackets
[b]The pro-establishment camp's candidates included those from the DAB, the FTU, Liberal Party (LP), Liberal Democratic Federation of Hong Kong (LDFHK, combined with HKPA in 1997), Hong Kong Progressive Alliance (HKPA, merged with the DAB in 2005) and other related districts' residential groups, such as Hong Kong Island Federation (HKIF, established in 1999 with 130,000 members), the Kowloon Federation of Association (KFA, established in 1997 with 200,000 members), and the New Territories Association of Societies (NTAS, established 1985 with 250,000 members)

District Council elections, increasing the number of votes from 190,792 in 1999 to 309,262 in 2015. It nominated between 170 and 200 candidates in the direct elections from 1999 to 2015, but the number of elected candidates increased from 83 in 1999 to 119 in 2015. This solid performance of the DAB provided a strong base of political support to the broader pro-Beijing united front forces, which overall captured 54.5% of the total votes in 1999 and 53.7% in 2015. The broader united front camp includes not only the DAB but also other pro-Beijing and pro-establishment groups, such as the FTU, the Hong Kong Island Federation (HKIF), the Kowloon Federation of Association (KFA) and the New Territories Association of Societies (NTAS). The overlapping memberships of DAB and FTU in running for District Council elections became the most prominent phenomenon in 2007 and 2012, when twenty-four candidates coming from both organizations. In the 2015 District Council elections, twenty-three pro-Beijing candidates participated in the name of the HKIF, eight candidates under the KFA and twenty-two affiliated with the NTAS, a phenomenon attributable to the increasing political mobilization of China's united front work in Hong Kong's electoral politics. Out of these fifty-three candidates, six from the HKIF, three from the KFA and seven from the NTAS were elected, showing a success rate of 30%. The HKIF, KFA and NTAS are united front organizations with which many residential and clan groups are affiliated. These united front groups could appeal to some voters who were either pro-government or pro-Beijing, but who did not see the DAB as the most politically active and attractive organization. In a sense, the DAB and these united front groups have a kind of political division of labor, offering more choices to the voters from the pro-Beijing and pro-establishment camps.

The political division of labor between the DAB and other pro-government forces has been designed so carefully that while the DAB has acquired the support of the traditionally pro-Beijing voters, other pro-establishment forces have succeeded in grasping the support from other voters, including many who are civil servants and those who are ideologically conservative. Usually, voters who are more satisfied with the government's performance and China, who have stronger emotional attachment to the PRC's national day and who have stronger Chinese national identity than the local Hong Kong identity tend to vote for the DAB and pro-Beijing forces rather than the pro-democracy camp.[11] Figure 2.4 proves that the DAB votes in District Council elections increased from 81,126 in 1994 to 309,262 in 2015, while other pro-government forces also rose from 292,944 votes in 1994 to 479,127 in 2015. Altogether, if the united front embraces both the DAB and other pro-government forces, it has been quite successful and expanding steadily since 1994.

The DAB itself has been undergoing tremendous consolidation since 1992, when it had only 235 members, one legislator and eight district councilors. From 1997 to 2006 (Table 2.6), the party did not have significant improvements in terms of the number of members and legislators, although it grasped 100 District Council seats and 105 such seats in 2000 and 2001, respectively. A turning point took place in 2008, when the DAB got 131 district councilors and had 12,300 members (Fig. 2.5). Since then the number of DAB district councilors has been maintained at

---

[11] Michael DeGolyer, "Local Elections, Long Term Effects? The Hong Kong District Council Elections of 2011," pp. 38–59, in http://hktp.org/list/district-council-elections.pdf, access date: April 8, 2018.

2 THE DEMOCRATIC ALLIANCE FOR THE BETTERMENT AND PROGRESS...   55

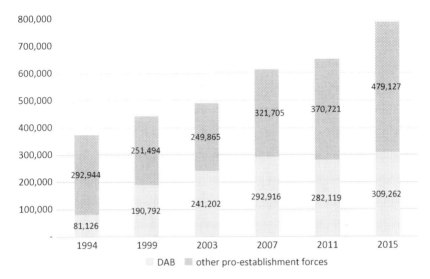

Fig. 2.4 Comparison of the voters gained by DAB and pro-Beijing forces in District Council elections, 1994–2015. Sources: Votes gained were calculated from the official statistics in the website of the Electoral Affairs Commission

a relatively high level, while the number of members jumped to 37,063 in 2018.

A deeper analysis of the DAB electoral performance in the eighteen districts (Table 2.7) shows that although the party candidates' success rate fluctuated from 1994 to 2015, some districts have already emerged as the power bases of the party. For instance, districts such as Wan Chai, Central and Western, Yau Tsim Mong, Kowloon City, Sai Kung, Kwun Tong, Wong Tai Sin and Islands became the DAB strongholds in 2015. Given the fact that the DAB, and its opponent pro-democracy forces, have traditionally seen the seats and votes captured at the district level as an indispensable bridge building up their electoral base and support for the higher-level legislative direct elections, the DAB's solid performance at the district and grassroots levels means that it does constitute a powerful political machinery to counter pro-democracy forces in local elections.

Most importantly, the DAB has been rejuvenating its memberships and it has nominated more young candidates in district elections from 1994 to 2015. Table 2.8 shows that the average age of candidates was maintained at 43 in 1994, 47 in 2007 and then 45 in 2015, and that the candidates

Table 2.6 Numbers of DAB legislators, district councilors and members, 1992–2018

Year	Legislative councilors	District councilors	DAB members
1992	1	8	235
1993	1	24	551
1994	1	37	714
1995	1	41	1086
1996	6	48	1205
1997	10	67	1406
1998	10	78	1366
1999	10	83	1800
2000	10	83	2021
2001	10	100	1956
2002	10	105	2012
2003	10	68	1877
2004	12	68	1800
2005	12	83	5486
2006	12	83	8270
2007	12	82	10,940
2008	13	131	12,300
2009	13	132	13,500
2010	13	132	15,300
2011	13	147	20,300
2012	13	136	22,489
2013	13	136	23,000
2014	13	136	25,000
2015	13	136	27,000
2016	13	119	33,000
2017	12	117	36,100
2018	13	117	37,063[a]

Sources: Democratic Alliance for the Betterment and Progress of Hong Kong, *Soar with Us to New Heights: Democratic Alliance for the Betterment and Progress of Hong Kong 15th Anniversary Commemorative Publication* (Hong Kong: Democratic Alliance for the Betterment and Progress of Hong Kong, 2007), p. 21, Yuen Kei-wang, *Twenty Years of History of the Democratic Alliance for the Betterment and Progress of Hong Kong* (Hong Kong: Chong Hwa Book Company, 2012), p. 165, Democratic Alliance for the Betterment and Progress of Hong Kong, *25th Anniversary Commemoration of the Democratic Alliance for the Betterment and Progress of Hong Kong: Choices and Promises* (Hong Kong: Democratic Alliance for the Betterment and Progress of Hong Kong, 2017), p. 13, and the website of the Democratic Alliance for the Betterment and Progress of Hong Kong in http://www.dab.org.hk/AboutUs.php?nid=1, access date: April 6, 2018

[a]Notes: DAB had 37,063 members in March 2018, http://www.dab.org.hk/AboutUs.php?nid=1, access date: April 6, 2018

2 THE DEMOCRATIC ALLIANCE FOR THE BETTERMENT AND PROGRESS... 57

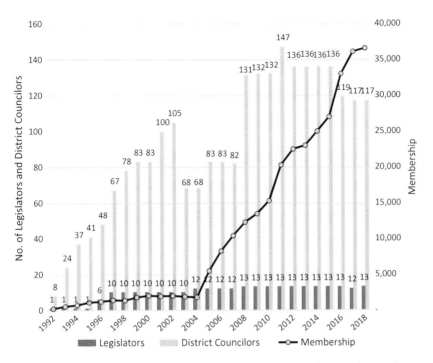

Fig. 2.5 Numbers of DAB legislators, district councilors and members, 1992–2018. Sources: Same as Table 2.6

under forty years old increased from 29 in 1994 to 76 in 2015. Those candidates who were at and under forty years old and who were elected increased from 12 in 1994 to 53 in 2015. Overall, the success rate of young candidates increased from 41.4% in 1994 to 69.7% in 2015, demonstrating a significant improvement in both membership rejuvenation and their chances of being directly elected. The electoral competitiveness of the DAB, has increased over time, fulfilling the ultimate objective of China's united front work in Hong Kong, namely, winning the hearts and minds of more young Hong Kong people, including those who join the party and those who vote for it. A good example of the DAB membership rejuvenation is lawyer Holden Chow, who was born in 1979 and who was the former chair of the Young DAB. In 2012 he was groomed to be the vice chairman of the DAB and was elected three years later as a district

Table 2.7 Success rate of the DAB candidates elected at various districts

Year	1994	1999	2003	2007	2011	2015
Eastern	33.3	59.1	54.1	70	94.1	76.9
Wan Chai	60	60	12.5	66.7	100	100
Central & Western	60	30	12.5	50	83.3	100
Southern	0	50	16.7	50	50	40
Kwun Tong	33.3	40	26.7	69.2	85.7	76.9
Wong Tai Sin	0	50	45.5	72.7	69.2	72.7
Kowloon City	25.0	37.5	22.2	60	70	88.9
Yau Tsim Mong	66.7	40	25	100	100	100
Sham Shui Po	57.1	23.1	7.1	42.9	50	62.5
Sha Tin	0	69.2	15.4	66.7	64.3	53.9
Sai Kung	0	62.5	40	69.2	70	72.7
Kwai Tsing	0	22.2	5.6	40	41.7	61.5
Tsuen Wan	50	20	16.7	60	66.7	66.7
Islands	66.7	100	100	80	100	75
Yuen Long	25	70	40	63.6	70	54.6
Tuen Mun	66.7	43.8	47.3	61.1	66.7	61.5
Tai Po	40	50	23.1	70	80	50
North	66.7	46.2	38.5	64.3	93.3	66.7
Total	44.6	47.2	30.1	65	74.7	69.6

Sources: Louie Kin-shuen and Shum Kwok-cheung, *Election Information Compilation of Hong Kong, 1982–1994* (Hong Kong: The Hong Kong Institute of Asia-Pacific Studies, The Chinese University of Hong Kong, 1996); Yip Tin-sang, *Election Information Compilation of Hong Kong, 1996–2000* (Hong Kong: The Hong Kong Institute of Asia-Pacific Studies, The Chinese University of Hong Kong, 2001); Yip Tin-sang, *Election Information Compilation of Hong Kong, 2001–2004* (Hong Kong: The Hong Kong Institute of Asia-Pacific Studies, The Chinese University of Hong Kong, 2005); Yip Tin-sang, *Election Information Compilation of Hong Kong, 2005–2012* (Hong Kong: The Hong Kong Institute of Asia-Pacific Studies, The Chinese University of Hong Kong, 2015); and Democratic Alliance for the Betterment and Progress of Hong Kong, *25th Anniversary Commemoration of the Democratic Alliance for the Betterment and Progress of Hong Kong: Choices and Promises* (Hong Kong: Democratic Alliance for the Betterment and Progress of Hong Kong, 2017), pp. 105–107, 109 and 111

councilor.[12] In 2016, Chow was directly elected to the LegCo and has become one of the most rapidly rising stars of the DAB. If the PRC united front work in the HKSAR targets at the youth, the rise of Holden Chow demonstrates how the DAB has been cultivating him as the young politician with bright political prospects.

[12] Yuen Kei-wang, *Twenty Years of History of the Democratic Alliance for the Betterment and Progress of Hong Kong* (Hong Kong: Chong Hwa Book Company, 2012), pp. 224–222.

Table 2.8 The success rate of DAB candidates in District Council elections, 1994–2015

Year	1994	1999	2003	2007	2011	2015
Number of nominated candidates	83	176	200	177	182	171
Numbers of elected candidates	37	83	62	115	136	119
Success rate of candidates	44.6%	47.2%	31%	65.0%	74.7%	69.6%
Average age of the elected candidates	43.0	46.1	47.9	46.9	45.2	44.7
Candidates at or under 40 years old	29	51	59	63	80	76
Elected candidates at or under 40 years old	12	14	11	35	53	53
Success rate of the young candidates	41.4%	27.5%	18.6%	55.6%	66.3%	69.7%

Sources: Louie Kin-shuen and Shum Kwok-cheung, *Election Information Compilation of Hong Kong, 1982–1994* (Hong Kong: The Hong Kong Institute of Asia-Pacific Studies, The Chinese University of Hong Kong, 1996); Yip, Tin-sang, *Election Information Compilation of Hong Kong, 1996–2000* (Hong Kong: The Hong Kong Institute of Asia-Pacific Studies, The Chinese University of Hong Kong, 2001); Yip Tin-sang, *Election Information Compilation of Hong Kong, 2001–2004* (Hong Kong: The Hong Kong Institute of Asia-Pacific Studies, The Chinese University of Hong Kong, 2005); Yip Tin-sang, *Election Information Compilation of Hong Kong, 2005–2012* (Hong Kong: The Hong Kong Institute of Asia-Pacific Studies, The Chinese University of Hong Kong, 2015); The website of the Election Affairs Commission, in https://www.elections.gov.hk/dc2015/eng/nominat2.html, access date: April 6, 2018; and Democratic Alliance for the Betterment and Progress of Hong Kong, *25th Anniversary Commemoration of the Democratic Alliance for the Betterment and Progress of Hong Kong: Choices and Promises* (Hong Kong: Democratic Alliance for the Betterment and Progress of Hong Kong, 2017), pp. 105–107, 109 and 111

ORGANIZATION OF TRAINING, FORUMS AND CONFERENCES

To broaden its base of political support, the DAB has been organizing various training sessions, forums and conferences. Table 2.9 shows that most training programs aim at educating the participants, including party members and assistants, to be young DAB leaders. These training activities that target at the young generation of DAB members have become far more prominent in Hong Kong after 2007, with diploma courses being institutionalized and regularized. Field visits to the PRC, United States and United Kingdom were arranged to broaden the horizon of DAB members. The socialization of DAB members embraced training in not only Hong Kong politics but also the mainland Chinese political system, socio-economic issues and their social communication skills.

While the quality of DAB members has been improved through various training activities, the party has made use of direction camps to hammer out its major policy directions (Table 2.10). From 1997 to 2017, the DAB held various camping activities in Southern China, notably Shenzhen, and

Table 2.9 The DAB training programs

Year	Topic	Cost	Content
2000	Political Professional Training	HK$ 2,400,000	To train participants to be the DAB leaders, including district councilors and assistants. Participants learnt politics, economics and media development of Hong Kong. They study US politics and presidential elections. Field visits to the United States were made.
2001	Social Leadership Training Program	HK$300,000	Trained DAB members as professional politicians, built up their district and community networks and improved their communication skills.
2007	Youth Political Professional Training Program	HK$1,800,000, for thirty participants who could visit the University of Cambridge. Many DAB policy spokespersons and district councilors were the participants.	Participants studied political and economic development, the implementation of the Basic Law and media politics. They also studied the mainland Chinese political system, western political system and democratization. Participants visited the Shanghai Pudong Cadre College and the University of Cambridge.
2010	New Generation Political Professional Training Diploma Course	The tuition fee for each participant was HK$2000	DAB members and outside participants were interviewed and attended a written test. Thirty-nine participants were admitted into the diploma program. The curriculum included international political conflicts, Hong Kong and Macau politics, Chinese and overseas national education and the Hong Kong people's national identity.
2012	New Generation Political Professional Training Diploma Course	Unknown	140 applicants but 43 were selected to study the course. The curriculum included Hong Kong values in historical perspectives, local identity, foreign values, Chinese values, Hong Kong politics and economy and the problem of social poverty.

(*continued*)

2 THE DEMOCRATIC ALLIANCE FOR THE BETTERMENT AND PROGRESS... 61

Table 2.9 (continued)

Year	Topic	Cost	Content
2014	New Generation Political Professional Training Diploma Course	Unknown	124 applicants and 52 were admitted. The curriculum included political reform, democracy, youth, civil society, civil disobedience, the rule of law, economic transformation, environmental protection and social poverty.

Sources: This table is compiled from news reports in *Wen Wei Po* and *Ta Kung Pao* from 2000 to 2014

invited guest speakers to enlighten its members on a variety of issues and topics, ranging from the question of universal suffrage to the quality of DAB's political participation, from party-building work to innovation and from the improvement of party image to its new positions in light of the changing political circumstances in the HKSAR.

Similarly, the DAB has held forums and conferences for the sake of maintaining a "high-quality" party image, especially among young members. In Table 2.11, the youth workshops embrace the study of localism, patriotism, moral education, career development, the local examination system, economic policy, social welfare, housing, technological innovation and Beijing's perception of the implementation of "one country, two systems." The objective was obvious: young DAB members are expected to be equipped with the necessary knowledge to tackle the current political, socio-economic and livelihood issues so that their good quality can reflect the DAB's strong professional image. If the DAB represents China's united front work in the HKSAR, its self-improvement, rejuvenation and expansion illustrate the united front's depth and breadth.

STRUCTURE OF UNITED FRONT WORK AND COORDINATION WITH PRO-BEIJING GROUPS AND LIAISON OFFICE IN SUPPORT OF GOVERNMENT POLICIES

Figure 2.6 depicts the structure of China's united front work in the HKSAR, where the Liaison Office's coordination department, social liaison department and social work department, together with the departments in the Hong Kong Island, Kowloon and the New Territories, have been

Table 2.10 DAB's direction camp

Time	Place	Theme	Keynote speakers
March, 1997	Shenzhen	The role of the DAB after the establishment of the HKSAR	Unknown
April, 1999	Panyu Hotel	The question of universal suffrage and the condition of DAB to be a shadow government	A former campaign manager of the US presidential election and the director of One Country, Two Systems Research, Shiu Sin-por, were invited.
March–April, 2001	Zhongshan Hot Spring Hotel	High-quality political participation and self-improvement	Senior civil servant Rafael Hui Si-yan, DAB leader Tsang Tak-sing, pro-Beijing elite Lau Nai-keung and academic Lau Siu-kai.
March, 2004	Shenzhen Seaview Hotel	Inspiring unity to embrace the future	Businesspeople like Gordon Wu and Eden Woon were invited.
December, 2004	Dongguan Silver City Hotel	Grasp the opportunity and dare to innovate in the future	Academic Ivan Choy and party leaders Jasper Tsang, Tam Yiu-chung and Ip Kwok-him.
April, 2006	Shenzhen Seaview Hotel	Building a political party with prospects	Academic Chan Kin-man and senior civil servants Rafael Hui and Stephen Lam
March, 2008	Shenzhen Kylin Villa	Continue to work diligently for Hong Kong	PRC official Qiao Xiaoyang and business elites Norman Chan and Jack So
May, 2009	Shenzhen Kylin Villa	Passing the torch and building the future	Academic Lawrence Kau and businessmen Henry Tang and Albert Cheng.
June, 2010	Shenzhen Kylin Villa	Develop and grow to meet the future challenges	PRC official Pang Qinghua and academic Wang Shaoguang
April, 2012	Shenzhen Kylin Villa	New situation and new development	Chief Executive C.Y. Leung and party leader Jasper Tsang.
October, 2014	Shenzhen Kylin Villa	Going with the difficulties	PRC official Zhang Xiaoming
April, 2016	Shenzhen Kylin Villa	Making progress on the basis of previous success and forging ahead into the future	Chief Executive Carrie Lam and PRC official Wang Zhenmin.

(*continued*)

Table 2.10 (continued)

Time	Place	Theme	Keynote speakers
April, 2017	Shenzhen Kylin Villa	How to activate the party's image and position and how to deal with political reform after the change of government and new Chief Executive	DAB heavyweights Jasper Tsang, Tam Yiu-chung, Ip Kwok-him and Chan Kam-lam.

Sources: Yuen Kei-wang, *Twenty Years of History of the Democratic Alliance for the Betterment and Progress of Hong Kong* (Hong Kong: Chong Hwa Book Company, 2012), p. 178 and this table is also compiled from news reports in *Wen Wei Po* and *Ta Kung Pao* from 1998 to 2017

Table 2.11 The DAB forums and conferences

Time	Forum topics
Youth workshops	
June, 2015	Political participation and localist sentiments
July, 2015	Education and training
August, 2015	Finding employment and career development
September, 2015	Patriotism, Chinese history and moral education
November, 2015	Workings of the territory-wide system assessment (TSA)
Roundtable discussions on economic development, the people's livelihood and the challenges and opportunities in Hong Kong	
October, 2015	Adjustment of Hong Kong's macroeconomic policy and the choices ahead
October, 2015	The way forward for Hong Kong's traditional industries
November, 2015	Coping with the welfare problems of Hong Kong residents
February, 2016	A roundtable discussion on the Mandatory Provident Fund
Roundtable discussions on new vision and new hope	
May, 2016	The implementation of "One Country, Two Systems"
May, 2016	The Gini coefficient and the income gap between the rich and poor
June, 2016	The housing problem and the distribution
July, 2016	New technological innovations

Source: Democratic Alliance for the Betterment and Progress of Hong Kong, *25th Anniversary Commemoration of the Democratic Alliance for the Betterment and Progress of Hong Kong: Choices and Promises* (Hong Kong: Democratic Alliance for the Betterment and Progress of Hong Kong, 2017), p. 37

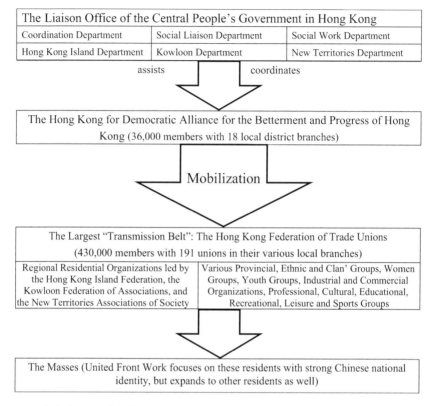

Fig. 2.6 The political structure of China's united front work in Hong Kong

working with the DAB intimately. During the non-election period, other pro-Beijing groups, especially the FTU, are playing the role of auxiliary organizations helping the DAB reach out to ordinary citizens and voters at the grassroots level, offering a whole range of constituency services, such as free legal aid, visits to mainland China and assistance provided to residents to deal with housing and social problems. During the electoral campaign period, all these constituency services have become an instrument through which the DAB, FTU as well as other united front groups, like the HKIF, KFA and NTFA, can garner and mobilize the support of voters solidly. The concept of "mass line" is implemented by the Liaison Office together with the DAB and FTU, which acts like one of the "transmission belts" together with various residents and clan groups, so that citizens at the district level develop a strong sense of belonging and identity to the pro-Beijing camp.

The strong DAB support at the grassroots level means that whenever by-elections are held for LegCo, it is well prepared and can mobilize popular support quickly. Table 2.12 shows that, except for the 2000 legislative by-elections in which the DAB performance was relatively weak, all other by-elections held for the LegCo in 2007, 2016 and 2018 demonstrated that the DAB obtained the voters' support that ranged from 52% in 2007 to 42% in 2018. The 2007 and 2018 performance was not so strong compared with the DAB's voting support in the 2016 LegCo direct elections in which the party acquired a range of 57 to 60% of the voters' support in the geographical constituencies of Hong Kong Island, Kowloon West and

Table 2.12 Number and percentage of votes for DAB in the 2016 legislative election and various by-elections

	Hong Kong Island	Kowloon West	New Territories East
2000 legislative by-election			
Registered voters	627,208	–	–
Votes cast	208,672	–	–
Voting rate (%)	33.27%	–	–
2007 legislative by-election			
Registered voters	618,398	–	–
Votes cast	321,938	–	–
Voting rate (%)	52.06%	–	–
2016 legislative by-election			
Registered voters	–	–	940,277
Votes cast	–	–	434,220
Voting rate (%)	–	–	46.18%
2016 legislative election			
Registered voters	627,807	488,129	97,5071
Votes cast	377,077	278,901	559,769
Voting rate (%)	60.06%	57.14%	57.10%
2018 legislative by-election			
Registered voters	623,273	489,451	988,986
Votes cast	270,597	215,333	412,325
Voting rate (%)	43.42%	43.99%	41.69%

Sources: The information is tabulated from the statistics of the Electoral Affairs Committee, in https://www.eac.gov.hk/en/legco/2000_report_2.htm, https://www.eac.gov.hk/en/legco/2007lcbe_hki_detailreport.htm, https://www.elections.gov.hk/legco2016by/eng/turnout.html?1522832011184, http://www.elections.gov.hk/legco2018by/chi/dps.html, and http://www.voterregistration.gov.hk/eng/statistic20161.html#1, access date: April 4, 2018

the New Territories West. The overall mobilization ability of the DAB in by-elections is quite strong, constantly constituting a serious threat to the pro-democracy camp.

During the Occupy Central Movement from September to December 2014, when some democrats used streets occupation to call for a faster pace and broader scope of democratic reform in the HKSAR, a surge of new united front groups took place to oppose the Occupy Movement. Figure 2.7 tabulates the rise of new united front groups, which cooperated with some existing ones, to oppose the occupiers. Many of these united front groups had close working relations with the DAB, such as the clan and ethnic groups and residential concern groups, which have traditionally helped the party to campaign in local and legislative elections. Provincial,

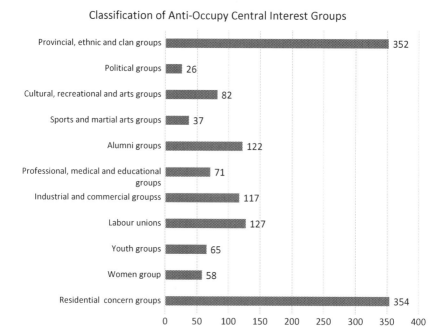

Fig. 2.7 Formation of united front groups against Occupy Central Movement. Sources: The data are collected and calculated from a website that showed a signature campaign mobilizing 1411 organizations to join the petition in 2014, available in: https://www.sign4peacedemocracy.hk/index.php?r=index/support, access date: April 4, 2018

ethnic, clan and residential groups stood out as the most important interest groups that rose up in opposition to the Occupy Central Movement in late 2014.

Although the DAB has been performing well in its united front work for China in the HKSAR, the party's political position often cannot be realized because of the China factor ironically. Table 2.13 shows that the DAB's political stance of advocating for universal suffrage is more a rhetoric than a reality, because it has to toe the official line of the central government in Beijing. Similarly, although the party claims to improve the judicial process in its manifesto, it supports the interpretations of the Basic Law by the Standing Committee of the National People's Congress in 1999 over the right of abode of mainland Chinese in Hong Kong, in 2004 over the procedures of directly electing the Chief Executive and in 2005 over the

Table 2.13 The DAB's political stance and political realities

Political stance	Political realities
Universal Suffrage—review the development of Hong Kong's constitutional structure before 2007, and strive to elect the subsequent Chief Executive by universal suffrage as well as to return all seats in the Legislative Council by universal suffrage.	In reality, the DAB adopts whatever position Beijing holds on the scope and pace of democratic reform in Hong Kong.
Improvement in the judicial process—Ameliorate Hong Kong's ordinances; raise the standard of quality of the judicial professionals and the administrative efficiency of the judicial organs; accelerate the implementation of bilingualism in the legal process; and promote communication between the judicial professionals of Hong Kong and that of mainland China.	The DAB supports all the interpretations of the Basic Law by the Standing Committee of the National People's Congress.
Memberships in international organizations—urge the Chinese Government to become a part of the "International Covenant on Civil and Political Rights," and the "International Covenant on Economic, Social and Cultural Rights" as early as possible.	The DAB is uncritical of any record of the PRC in violating human rights domestically. It also does not support the annual candlelight vigil held by the Hong Kong people on June 4 to commemorate the June 1989 Tiananmen tragedy in the PRC.

Sources: "Party Platform," in the website of the Democratic Alliance for the Betterment and Progress of Hong Kong, December 1997, in http://www.dab.org.hk/eng?t=1304, access date: April 4, 2018

length of office of the replacement Chief Executive.[13] The DAB is uncritical of the PRC's domestic violations of human rights. These pro-Beijing positions have imposed severe limitations on the DAB to acquire the support of all the voters, many of them are supportive of a faster pace and broader scope of democratic change in Hong Kong. These limitations explain why other pro-establishment and pro-Beijing groups have to be groomed and supported by PRC authorities so that the scope of united front work could become as broad as possible to counter the relatively strong pro-democracy forces.

Understanding its own limitations in reaching out to all voters and grasping their political support, the DAB has designed policy suggestions and initiatives to win the support of those Hong Kong people who live and work in mainland China, and those Hongkongers who attach more importance to livelihood issues than politically sensitive issues like democracy, human rights and Hong Kong's judicial independence vis-à-vis China. Table 2.14 shows that the DAB's new policy initiatives were carefully designed to acquire the support from Hongkongers who work and reside in the PRC, including the call for the provision of mainland identification documents, the need to grant them home mortgage loans, the exemption of mainland residence certification for them, the medical consultation for Hong Kong people who can enjoy national treatment, the recognition of associate degrees by mainland authorities and the ability of Hongkongers to apply for civil service positions in the mainland. If some or all these policy suggestions were accepted by the PRC government, these Hong Kong people who reside and work in the PRC would become a powerful source of voters in Hong Kong's elections, for the DAB would mobilize them to return to Hong Kong to vote for the party during the voting day. At the same time, the DAB attempts to strengthen its appeal to the Hong Kong people who live and work in the HKSAR through its policy advocacy work, including more support for children, young people and the elderly, less waiting time for housing applications and more distributive measures in the form of opening the fiscal reserves for the needy. The DAB has become a politically aggressive electoral machinery utilizing policy suggestions to lure the support of the Hong Kong people, including those who live and work in the mainland.

---

[13] Huang Zheping and Echo Huang, "A brief history: Beijing's interpretations of Hong Kong's Basic Law, from 1999 to the present day," in https://qz.com/828713/a-brief-history-beijings-interpretations-of-hong-kongs-basic-law-from-1999-to-the-present-day/, access date: April 8, 2018.

Table 2.14 The DAB's new policy suggestions and initiatives, 2017–2018

For the Hong Kong people working and residing in mainland China:
1. Provide mainland identity document to Hong Kong people working and living in China
2. Granting home mortgage loans
3. Exemption from mainland residence certification for Hongkongers living in Hong Kong
4. Medical consultation for Hong Kong people in the mainland to enjoy national treatment
5. Exemption for Hong Kong students to take mainland examinations if they want to study in the mainland
6. Expansion of associate-degree recognition by mainland education authorities
7. Introduction of compulsory moral education in primary and secondary schools
8. Improving the level of benefits for the elderly
9. Cancelation of restrictions to Hong Kong people who want to stay in the mainland's foreign-owned hotels
10. Opening up more non-service areas for Hongkongers in the mainland
11. Opening up the service industry in the mainland for Hong Kong people
12. Cancelation of individual business restrictions for Hongkongers who do business in China
13. Support the development of Hong Kong farmers in the mainland
14. Allow Hong Kong and Macao fishermen to hire mainland workers from various provinces in China
15. Exemption of applying for employment permits
16. Encourage the Hong Kong people to apply for civil service jobs

For Hong Kong people working and residing in Hong Kong:
1. Activate and stimulate the economy
2. Provide more space for the development of small and medium enterprises
3. Helping Hong Kong to nurture talents and attract global talents
4. Improve the people's livelihoods by utilizing fiscal reserves and share the benefits of economic growth
5. Create homes for all citizens: maintain the waiting time for public housing to three years
6. Bring happiness to families by preserving traditional family values and promoting local pregnancies
7. Establish an elderly care policy through the improvement of medical services for senior citizens
8. Bring joy to children through the introduction of the health care voucher scheme for children
9. Opening new roads for young people by developing their potential
10. Transform the community by improving environmental awareness and protection
11. Achieve social harmony by creating mutual trust in politics and improving the governmental efficiency of governance

Sources: Democratic Alliance for the Betterment and Progress of Hong Kong, *25th Anniversary Commemoration: Choices and Promises* (Hong Kong: Democratic Alliance for the Betterment and Progress of Hong Kong, 2017); and "A Proposal of Implementation of the Policy of Making Hong Kong People Enjoy National Citizens Privileges in the Mainland." Hong Kong: Democratic Alliance for the Betterment and Progress of Hong Kong, 2018, available in http://www.dab.org.hk/jm/images/news/1515118041.pdf, access date: April 4, 2018

There is evidence to show that PRC officials in the HKSAR, notably those from the Liaison Office, have been cultivating a very close working relationship with the DAB. Table 2.15 proves that the directors and deputy directors of the Liaison Office must attend to the important functions of the DAB, especially those activities held in the mainland and Beijing. Moreover, the Liaison Office tends to have a clear division of labor in dealing with DAB activities; when such activities are held at the local district level, the three departments in the Hong Kong Island, Kowloon and the New Territories must send officials to attend. During the fund-raising dinner in November 2016, the Liaison Office's director Zhang Xiaoming's calligraphy was sold with a price of HK$1,880,000 and a song by deputy director Lin Wu secured a donation of HK$7 million—a testimony of how the Liaison Office strongly and financially supports the DAB.

THE PRO-BEIJING CAMP'S COMPETITION WITH THE PRO-DEMOCRACY FORCE

The limitation of the pro-Beijing camp in general, including the DAB, can be seen in the overall election results of LegCo direct elections from 1998 to 2018. Figure 2.8 shows that the pro-democracy camp remains quite strong from 1998 to 2016, although the pro-Beijing camp narrowed the gap quite significantly from the 2012 legislative direct elections in the Hong Kong Island to the 2016 elections. The by-election in March 2018 showed a drop in the votes for the pro-democracy camp, implying that the PRC interpretation of the Basic Law over the oath-taking ceremony of localist legislators-elect in November 2016 did appear to have a dampening effect on the young voters, many of whom appeared not to vote in the 2018 by-elections.

Sources: Votes gained were calculated from the official statistics in the website of the Electoral Affairs Commission.

A similar pattern of the gradual rise in the pro-Beijing support can be seen in the direct elections held for the LegCo in the geographical constituencies of Kowloon West (Fig. 2.9). In Kowloon West, the gap between the pro-Beijing camp and the pro-democracy camp narrowed from 1998 to 2016. Most importantly, in the by-election held for the LegCo in 2018, the DAB candidate Vincent Cheng for the first time got 107,479 votes, a number slightly higher than the 105,060 votes acquired by pro-democracy candidate Edward Yiu. Cheng's victory was politically significant; the

Table 2.15 Activities showing the alliance between the Liaison Office and the DAB in 2017

Year	Activity	Department official from the Liaison Office who attended the event
May 2012	Celebrating the HKSAR anniversary	New Territories Department
November 2012	DAB fund-raising party	Director Li Gang and Deputy Director Lin Wu donated gifts, such as Chinese paintings and wine (*maotai*)
March 2013	A banquet in Beijing	Five directors attended, such as Zhou Nan, Jiang Enzhu, Gao Siren, Peng Qinghua and Zhang Xiaoming
March 2013	DAB visit to Qianhai and Nansha	Director Zhang Xiaoming
July 2013	DAB's 21st anniversary celebration in Hong Kong City Hall	Director Zhang Xiaoming
July 2013	DAB's 21st anniversary celebration in Sheung Wan district	Chen Fuzhong from the Social Work Department
November 2013	The marriage ceremony of the son of DAB's lawmaker Ip Kwok-him	Director Zhang Xiaoming
February 2014	DAB's Chinese New Year gathering	Wu Yangwei from the Hong Kong Island Work Department
February 2014	DAB's cocktail party for businesspeople	Yang Mao from the Social Work Department
March 2014	DAB's New Year Gala Dinner in Beijing	Director Zhang Xiaoming
April 2014	DAB fund-raising dinner	Director Zhang Xiaoming
September 2014	Funeral of DAB member Ip Kwok-chung	Yang Mao from the Social Work Department
January 2015	Opening ceremony of the youth summit chaired by DAB Youth Committee leader Holden Chow	Deputy Director Lin Wu
February 2015	Opening ceremony of DAB stall in Victoria Park during the New Year	Yang Mao from the Social Work Department
March 2015	DAB's Spring Lantern Festival Dinner	Director Zhang Xiaoming
July 2015	DAB's 23rd anniversary dinner	Director Zhang Xiaoming
July 2015	DAB visit to Beijing	Director Zhang Xiaoming
August 2015	DAB internship in Chongqing and Hangzhou	Li Yungfu from the Social Welfare Department

(*continued*)

Table 2.15 (continued)

Year	Activity	Department official from the Liaison Office who attended the event
February 2016	Dab cocktail party in Southern District	Fan Kesheng from the Hong Kong Island Work Department
February 2016	DAB cocktail party	Xie Lin from the New Territories Department
March 2016	DAB dinner during the meetings of the National People's Congress in Beijing	Director Zhang Xiaoming
April 2016	DAB directional camp in Shenzhen	Wang Zhenmin from the Law Department and Deputy Director Lin Wu
September 2016	DAB's Hong Kong students work scheme in the mainland	Deng Jianping from the Social Work Department
September 2016	Election of Legislative Council president	DAB chairlady Starry Lee openly admitted that the Liaison Office officials contacted DAB on this matter
September 2016	DAB's support of belt and road initiatives	Director Zhang Xiaoming
November 2016	DAB fund-raising dinner	Director Zhang Xiaoming's calligraphy was sold with a price of HK$1,880,000 and a song by deputy director Lin Wu got a donation of HK$7 million
February 2017	Opening ceremony of the office of DAB legislator Cheung Kwok-kwan	Yang Mao from the Social Work Department
February 2017	DAB's Spring Festival reception in Hong Kong Island	Wu Yangwei from the Hong Kong Island Work Department
February 2017	DAB Youth Committee's New Year Reception	Wu Yangwei from the Hong Kong Island Work Department
February 2017	DAB dinner in Beijing	Director Zhang Xiaoming
April 2017	Celebration of the HKSAR 20th anniversary in Yuen Long	Liu Lin from the New Territories Work Department
June 2017	HKSAR 20th anniversary in Shatin district where DAB's Elizabeth Quat attended	Liu Lin from the New Territories Work Department
July 2017	Celebration of DAB's 25th anniversary	Director Zhang Xiaoming and Deputy Director Lin Wu

(continued)

Table 2.15 (continued)

Year	Activity	Department official from the Liaison Office who attended the event
August 2017	Opening ceremony of the joint office of DAB legislators	Tang Weisheng from the New Territories Work Department
September 2017	Celebration show of DAB's 25th anniversary	Deputy Director Jing Jing
December 2017	Opening ceremony of DAB legislator in Tai Po district	Ye Hu from the New Territories Work Department
December 2017	DAB's study of the 19th Party Congress Work Report	Yang Mao for the Social Work Department

Sources: The data are compiled meticulously from the news reports in *Wen Wei Po* and *Ta Kung Pao* from May 2012 to December 2017

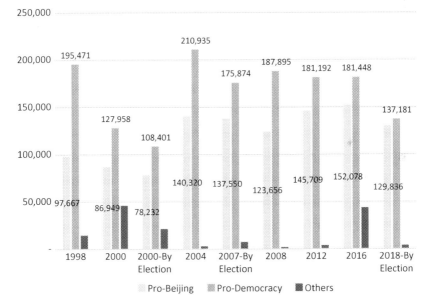

Fig. 2.8 Votes gained by the pro-Beijing and pro-democracy camps in Legislative Council elections in Hong Kong Islands, 1998–2018

DAB's united front with other pro-government forces achieved an unprecedented electoral success. However, a different pattern took place in the New Territories East (Fig. 2.10), where the pro-democracy force remained relatively strong from 1998 to 2016. Still, the gap between the pro-Beijing

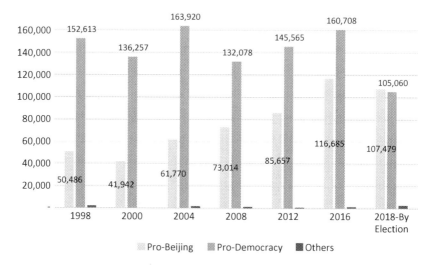

Fig. 2.9 Votes gained by the pro-Beijing and pro-democracy camp in Legislative Council elections in Kowloon West, 1998–2018. Sources: Votes gained were calculated from the official statistics in the website of the Electoral Affairs Commission

camp and the pro-democracy opponent narrowed in the by-election held for March 2018, showing that China's united front work did achieve some inroads from the perspective of electoral competition.

Conclusion

From the perspective of China's united front work in the HKSAR, the DAB has succeeded in expanding its membership and voters' support from 1992 to the present. It has been playing the dual roles of providing a solid base of political and electoral support for other pro-Beijing and pro-government forces, while simultaneously increasing its popular support to check and balance the influence of the pro-democracy camp. The DAB performs strongly at the local District Council elections and it has been working hand in hand with other pro-Beijing forces to narrow the gap of popular support with the pro-democracy camp in the recent years. Nevertheless, the pro-Beijing political positions of the DAB, including its rhetoric of supporting universal suffrage and its need to support all the policies of the central government in Beijing, have ironically become an electoral liability that constrains its popular support. Many pro-democracy

2 THE DEMOCRATIC ALLIANCE FOR THE BETTERMENT AND PROGRESS... 75

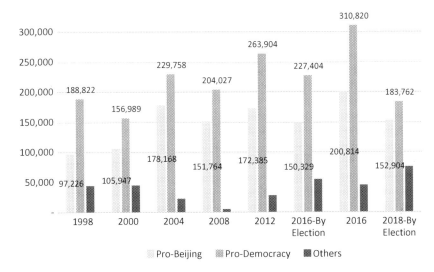

Fig. 2.10 Votes gained by the pro-Beijing and pro-Democracy camp in Legislative Council elections in New Territories East, 1998–2018. Sources: Votes gained were calculated from the official statistics in the website of the Electoral Affairs Commission

voters perceive the DAB as too pro-Beijing and lacking a clear platform in support of Hong Kong's democratization, human rights and judicial autonomy vis-à-vis Beijing. Despite its limitations, the DAB remains the most important united front agent for the PRC government to win the hearts and minds of more Hong Kong people.

CHAPTER 3

Political Participation of Fujianese Interest Groups

With at least 264,000 Hong Kong residents who spoke Fujianese as a dialect and language in 2016,[1] the political participation of the Fujianese in the HKSAR of PRC is a relatively neglected topic for research. This chapter attempts to fill in the gap in the existing academic literature.[2] The Fujianese political participation in the HKSAR is increasingly significant. On May 8, 1997, the Hong Kong Federation of Fujian Associations (HKFFA) was established, comprising 112 affiliated groups and representing a watershed in the Fujianese political participation.[3] As the PRC's

---

[1] "The 2016 Population By-Census," (Hong Kong: Census and Statistics Department, 2016), in https://www.bycensus2016.gov.hk/data/16bc-main-results.pdf, access date: April 22, 2018, p. 51. There were 3.4% of the Hong Kong population in 2006 who spoke Fujianese, compared with 3.5% in 2011 and 3.6% in 2016. In 2016, the population of Hong Kong reached 7,336,585 people (p. 25). It is unknown how many Hong Kong people who have Fujianese ancestry do not frequently speak Fujianese, although some Fujianese community leaders in Hong Kong claimed that there are 1.1 million Fujianese in the HKSAR in 2017. For the assertion of 1.1 million Fujianese who are residing in the HKSAR, see *Wen Wei Po*, August 3, 2017.

[2] There were a few anthropological and sociological studies on the Fujianese in Hong Kong from Gregory Elliot Guldin, "'Overseas' at Home: The Fujianese of Hong Kong," unpublished PhD thesis, University of Wisconsin, Madison, 1977. Also see Susanne Y. P. Choi, "Association Divided, Association United: The Social Organization of Chaozhou and Fujian Migrants in Hong Kong," in Khun Eng Kuah-Pearce and Evelyn Hu-Dehart, eds., *Voluntary Associations in the Chinese Diaspora* (Hong Kong: Hong Kong University Press, 2006), pp. 121–140.

[3] *Newsletter of the Hong Kong Federation of Fujian Associations*, January 1998, p. 1.

© The Author(s) 2019
S. S.-H. Lo et al., *China's New United Front Work in Hong Kong*,
https://doi.org/10.1007/978-981-13-8483-7_3

united front work in the HKSAR has been targeting at the expansion of pro-Beijing forces,[4] the Fujianese groups are, as will be discussed, increasingly prominent not only at the local legislative and district elections, but also at the high level of political representations in Hong Kong and mainland China, such as having members selected as Hong Kong representatives to the Chinese People's Political Consultative Conference (CPPCC) and the National People's Congress (NPC).

This chapter will first examine the HKFFA's organization, followed by an in-depth examination of its electoral participation. The relations between the HKFFA and the pro-Beijing political party, namely the DAB, will then be discussed. The representation of the Fujianese leaders in the high level of the political systems of Hong Kong and the PRC will be analyzed, including the membership of the Election Committee that selected the HKSAR Chief Executive. Finally, the chapter will explore the relations between officials of the Liaison Office—the PRC government's representative agency in the HKSAR—and the Fujianese activities, including how Fujianese groups have been mobilized to support the policies of the HKSAR government and Beijing toward Hong Kong.

The concept of interest groups is academically useful for our understanding of Fujianese political participation in Hong Kong. Interest groups refer to organizations in which members share their common interests and articulate their demands through various means, such as lobbying the government and legislators, participating in protests and rallies and utilizing the mass media.[5] They exist in the PRC's political system but are under much tighter control by the CCP than their counterparts in Hong Kong.[6] In Hong Kong, where China's united front work has been

---

[4] For China's united work in Hong Kong, see Cindy Yik-yi Chu, *Chinese Communist and Hong Kong Capitalists* (London: Palgrave Macmillan, 2010); Christine Loh, *Underground Front: The Chinese Communist Party in Hong Kong* (Hong Kong: Hong Kong University Press, 2010); and Ray Wang and Gerry Groot, "Who Represents? Xi Jinping's Grand United Front Work, Legitimation, Participation and Consultative Democracy," *Journal of Contemporary China* (2018), in https://doi.org/10.1080/10670564.2018.1433573, access date: April 22, 2018.

[5] Allan Cigler and Burdett A. Loomis, *Interest Group Politics* (Washington, D.C.: CQ Press, 1998).

[6] For China's interest groups, see Michael Waller, "Communist Politics and the Group Process: Some Comparative Conclusions," in David S. G. Goodman, ed., *Groups and Politics in the People's Republic of China* (New York: M. E. Sharpe, 1984), pp. 196–207, where Waller argues that interest groups in China exist "without pluralism." Also see Victor Falkenheim, ed., *Citizens and Groups in Contemporary China* (Ann Arbor: Center of Chinese

increasing since July 1, 1997, the role and political participation of Fujianese interest groups has been under-researched and neglected.

Traditionally, Fujianese interest groups have been active in the societies of Southeast Asia. In Malaysia's Kula Terengganu state, the Hokkien (Fujian) Association has propagated and maintained Chinese culture and retained an adaptive and a respectful attitude toward Islamic culture and festivals so that the Chinese and Muslims coexist comfortably.[7] The Fujianese have historically organized themselves as "voluntary groups" (*shetuan*) so as to articulate and protect their interests not only in the overseas Chinese societies, but also in their *qiaoxiang*—the ancestral hometowns of the Chinese diaspora.[8] The most famous Fujianese interest group leader in Southeast Asia was Tan Kah Kee, who was born in Fujian in 1874 and migrated to Singapore in 1890 and later established an anti-Japanese organization, the South Seas China Relief Fund Union (*Nanqiao Zhonghui*), in 1938.[9] In 1939, Tan sent nine batches of 3192 overseas Chinese drivers, engineers, repair workers and technicians to China for logistic work in support of the war against Japan.[10] In 1940, he visited Chongqing and was angry at the extent of political corruption of the Nationalist Party, triggering his political orientation of supporting the CCP.[11] Tan openly criticized the Fujian provincial administration during his visit in Fujian in November 1940, pointing out the "unfairness" in conscription, the abuse of power against the youth, the competition between the business sector and ordinary people and the unreasonable

Studies, University of Michigan, 1987). For interest groups in Hong Kong, see Sonny Shiu-hing Lo, ed., *Interest Groups and the New Democracy Movement in Hong Kong* (London: Routledge, 2017).

[7] Tan Yao Sua, Thock Ker Pong, Kamarudin Ngah and Goh Soo Khoon, "Maintenance and propagation of Chinese culture in a Malay state: the roles of the Chinese associations in Kuala Terengganu," *Asian Ethnicity*, vol. 13. No. 4 (2012), pp. 441–467.

[8] Hong Liu, "Old Linkages, New Networks: The Globalization of Overseas Chinese Voluntary Associations and its Implications," *The China Quarterly*, no. 155 (September 1998), pp. 582–583.

[9] Ibid., p. 589. For Tan's historical background and business development, see Yan Qinghuang, *Overseas Chinese Tradition and Modernization* (in Chinese) (Singapore: World Scientific, 2010), pp. 189–192. He expanded his rubber plantation business rapidly from 1914 to 1925 (pp. 196–197).

[10] Xia Yuqing, "Between the Family and State: *Nanqiao* engineers and the *Nanyang Huaqiao* society during the war years," *Southeast Asian Affairs* (in Chinese), vol. 2, no. 166 (2016), p. 66.

[11] Li Qirong and Xu Haoliang, "Tan Kah Kee's Spirit of Patriotism and the China Dream," *Overseas Chinese Journal of Bagui* (in Chinese), no. 2 (June 2016), p. 6.

high price of rice.[12] Tan appealed to the need to "utilize the power of the masses and of public opinion to fight and eliminate the corrupt officials."[13] In June 1947, when 13,632 overseas Fujianese joined the Fujian Overseas Chinese Association, the Nationalist Party attempted to infiltrate and control the returned overseas Fujianese interest groups.[14] With the PRC's establishment, the Fujianese interest groups leaders became the target of the CCP's united front work, including their flagship organization named Fujian Province Returned Overseas Chinese Association.[15] The CCP and the Fujian provincial government helped the overseas Fujianese in their remittance to their family members in Fujian. The CCP also assisted the residents in Xiamen, Quanzhou and Jinjiang on various matters, such as writing letters to their overseas Chinese relatives in Southeast Asia, setting up schools for the overseas Fujianese in Fujian and solving their employment problems in the local knitting and textile industry.[16] With the implementation of China's open-door policy, more overseas Fujianese Chinese were appointed to the National Returned Overseas Chinese Association, helping the PRC to develop economic modernization.[17] The Fuzhou city's united front department remarked in 2010 that it was necessary to deepen united front work, "using *xiangqing* (hometown affection) to cultivate friendship, and using friendship to seek *shangqing* (business affection), which in turn can consolidate *xiangqing*."[18] The Fujianese

---

[12] Tan Kah Kee, "Tan Kah Kee's speech criticizing the Fujian administration in the welcome ceremony of the Fujian *tongxianghui* (townspeople association)," November 24, 1940, in *Fujian Huaqiao Archival History* (In Chinese) (Fujian: Archive Publishing, 1990), pp. 1697–1703.

[13] Ibid., p. 1703.

[14] Shangguan Xiao-hong, "A Study of the Returned Fujian Overseas Chinese Associations in the Republic of China," *Journal of Overseas Chinese History Studies* (in Chinese), no. 3 (September 2017), pp. 87–90.

[15] *A Special Publication on the Establishment Meeting of the National Returned Overseas Chinese Association* (Zhonghua quan guo gui guo huaqiao lianhe hui) (Beijing: Gaihui, 1957) (no author), p. 54.

[16] Ibid., p. 55.

[17] In 1984, for example, Ye Fei was the honorary chairman of the National Returned Overseas Chinese Representative Conference. He was born in Fujian's Nanan and was an overseas Chinese in the Philippines. See *The Third National Returned Overseas Chinese Representative Conference* (in Chinese) (Beijing: National Returned Overseas Chinese Association, August 1984), pp. 77–83.

[18] Fuzhou city's United Front Department, "Consolidating the work on the representatives from Hong Kong, Macau, Taiwan and the overseas," *China's United Front Line* (Zhongguo Tongyi Zhanxin), August 2010, p. 40.

community has traditionally attached great importance to their *xiangqing*, and some of its overseas Chinese members from other countries, such as Italy, Hungary, Russia, Germany, South Africa and Israel, even returned to become village officials in Fujian's Mingxi county, including the positions of party-secretaries, deputy secretaries and directors.[19] If the Fujianese have shown a pattern of socio-political participation in Southeast Asia and Fujian, it is worthwhile to study their political participation in the HKSAR.

THE HISTORY AND ROLE OF FUJIANESE INTEREST GROUPS IN HONG KONG

While the Hong Kong Federation of Fujian Association (HKFFA) as an umbrella organization of the Fujianese interest groups was set up in May 1997, the earliest Fujianese interest group in Hong Kong was the Hong Kong Fukien Chamber of Commerce, which had been established in 1918 (Table 3.1). Other old Fujianese interest groups included the Fukienese Association, an organization composed of *tongxiang* (townsmen) associations, and the Fuzhou Association.[20] In 1997, under the leadership of Wong Kong-hon, the HKFFA was founded with the active participation of the Fukienese Association, the Fukien Athletic Club, the Hong Kong Fuzhou Association, the General Association of Xiamen and the Quanzhou Association. The number of affiliated groups of the HKFFA increased from 112 in 1997 to 234 in 2017.[21]

Several features of these interest groups stood out. First, they share the common political interest of supporting the PRC government and the HKSAR administration, especially the return of Hong Kong's sovereignty from Britain to the PRC on July 1, 1997 and Beijing's policies toward Hong Kong. During the outbreak of the Severe Acute Respiratory Syndrome (SARS) in the HKSAR from the end of 2002 to the summer of 2003, the HKFFA mobilized 7000 volunteers to support the residents and the community in resisting the spread of the infectious disease.[22] After

---

[19] Chen Feng-lan, "Transnational Mobilization of Overseas Chinese Village Officials and Qiaoxiang Social Governance: A Case Study of Mingxi Village in Fujian Province," *Journal of Overseas Chinese History Studies* (in Chinese), no. 1 (March 2017), pp. 19–28.

[20] The name Fukienese is used in this paper when it adopts the official name of the group concerned.

[21] See *Newsletter of the Fujian Members of the Chinese People's Political Consultative Conference* (*Zhengxue Tiandi*), vol. 7 (2017), p. 58.

[22] Ibid., p. 58.

Table 3.1 The main Fujianese interest groups in Hong Kong

Name	Year of formation	Platform and political ideas
Fukien Chamber of Commerce	1917	Promote patriotic business and Hong Kong's social affairs, and concern about the welfare of the Fujianese people in Hong Kong
The Fukienese Association	1939	Unite the *tongxiang* and fight against the Japanese during the Second World War
Jinjiang Clans Association	1985	Establish a stronghold in Hong Kong, being global in outlook, loving Hong Kong and loving the *jiaxiang* (homeland or home village), and friendly toward the neighbors
Jinjiang Clans Youth Federation	2007	Unite the young people from Jinjiang, strengthen the federation's vitality and consolidate the patriotic sentiment of loving Hong Kong and loving the homeland on the part of the young people
Fukien Athletic Club	1925	Being friendly toward the neighbors, serving the *tongxiang* and promoting the welfare of the society
Hong Kong Quanzhou Clans Association	1989	Unite the *tongxiang* from Quanzhou city, liaison with the *tongxiang*, consolidate their interactions and relations and strengthen the relations with the overseas *tongxiang* and groups
Hong Kong Foochow (Fuzhou) Association	1937	Unite the *tongxiang*, contact the townspeople, serving the society; maintain the principles of "loving the nation, Hong Kong and *jiaxiang*" and promote Hong Kong's economic prosperity
The General Association of Xiamen	1993	Enhance the friendship of *xiangqing*, promote *jiaxiang*'s infrastructure development, contribute to Xiamen city's reform and open-door policy, promote Hong Kong's stability and prosperity, helping the motherland to be wealthy and to make progress

Sources: Elite Group, *The Elites of Hong Kong's Fujianese Entrepreneurs* (in Chinese) (Hong Kong: Chinese Business Publisher, 2004); "The History of the Fukienese Association," in the website of the Fukienese Association, in http://fukienesehk.com/, access date: April 22, 2018, and "The History of the Fukien Athletic Club," in http://fkac.org/, access date, April 22, 2018. Also see "A Brief Introduction on the Hong Kong Fuzhou Associations of Societies," in http://www.hkcfalam.com/article-detail-aid-3.html, access date: April 22, 2018; and "A Brief History of the Fukienese Associations," in http://fukienesehk.com/side-navigation/, access date: April 22, 2018

the 19th Party Congress was held in the PRC, the Fujianese interest groups were mobilized to study and learn from the major policy pronouncements from the Congress. The Fukienese Association held a seminar to study the report of the 19th Party Congress in December 2017, inviting the HKFFA chair Chan Chung-chung to attend.[23] Chan appealed to the need for the Fukienese Association to "strengthen the patriotic forces" in Hong Kong and to reach out to more young people.[24]

Second, the Fujianese interest groups have become a bridge between the Fujianese in Hong Kong and their hometown in Fujian province, organizing various visits to the mainland and consolidating their social and business networks. In April 2018, the HKFFA's women committee sent a delegation to the Fujian province's Ningde city; the delegation was not only accompanied by officials of the Liaison Office in the HKSAR, but also received by Ningde's united front department.[25] Members of the delegation visited Ningde's scenic spots, strengthening their *guanxi* (personal) networks.[26] On the other hand, the Fukien Chamber of Commerce (FCC) has been playing a crucial role in uniting the Fujianese business people to invest and do business in the mainland.[27] The FCC has been active in receiving official and business delegations from the Fujian province to Hong Kong so that a mutually beneficial business relationship is entrenched.[28] The Fujianese have been regarded as a clan group attaching great importance to the development of business in a "pragmatic," "progressive" and yet "adventurous" manner, and as such, their *guanxi* networks in Hong Kong and the mainland are providing them with the necessary ingredients contributing to their successful business expansion to mainland China.[29]

Third, the Fujianese groups have become the united front organizations of the PRC government to publicize its policies. In April 2018, the HKFFA held a seminar and invited the Liaison Office deputy director

---

[23] *Wen Wei Po*, December 27, 2017, p. A14.
[24] Ibid.
[25] *Wen Wei Po*, April 13, 2018, p. A13.
[26] For the politics of *guanxi*, see Lucian W. Pye, *The Spirit of Chinese Politics* (Cambridge, Massachusetts: Harvard University Press, 1992), pp. 207–217.
[27] Remarks made by Lam Ming-sum, the FCC chairman, in *A Special Commemoration of the 95th Anniversary of the Fukien Chamber of Commerce and Hong Kong's 15th Anniversary of its Return to the Motherland* (in Chinese) (Hong Kong: The Fukien Chamber of Commerce, September 2012), p. 19.
[28] Ibid., pp. 54–63.
[29] Chong Kwok-to, "Discussing the Features of the Fujianese Humanitarian Spirit and their Mercantilism," in *A Special Commemoration of the 95th Anniversary of the Fukien Chamber of Commerce and Hong Kong's 15th Anniversary of its Return to the Motherland* (in Chinese) (Hong Kong: The Fukien Chamber of Commerce, September 2012), pp. 89–91.

Chen Dong to elaborate on the meetings of the NPC and CPPCC.[30] Chen emphasized the remarks made by the PRC President Xi Jinping in the NPC meeting, saying that Xi attached great importance to the "one country, two systems" and that the PRC constitutional revision was fully supported by the NPC members. The HKFFA chairman Ng Leung-ho commented that the HKSAR had to implement "the spirit" of the NPC and the CPPCC by "resolutely opposing all those activities that spilt the nation."[31] Similarly, the Quanzhou Federation of Associations (QFA) held a workshop in April 2018, inviting Liaison Office official Zheng Zhanliang to share his views on the NPC and CPPCC meetings.[32] The QFA chairman Yip Kin-ming added that Hong Kong should grasp the opportunity to be integrated into the Greater Bay Area and that Hong Kong should fully support the idea of co-location, which means that the high-speed railway from the mainland should arrive straight into the HKSAR where customs officers from both PRC and Hong Kong sides can deal with customs and immigration issues in the railway station located in Kowloon.[33]

Fourth, most of these Fujianese associations, such as the Quanzhou Association, have set up youth committees and volunteers' groups to groom young leaders for their organizations.[34] The Fukienese Association in April 2018 organized an award ceremony to express its appreciation of the work of volunteers, some of whom are recruited into its youth committee.[35] Finally, the HKFFA participates in politics actively, such as the mobilization of its young members to oppose the Occupy Central Movement in 2014, to help voters register in local elections and to nominate candidates to run in District Councils and Legislative Council direct elections.[36] In the 2016 Legislative Council direct elections, the HKFFA unprecedentedly nominated seven candidates, and all of them were elected to the lawmaking body.[37] Last but not least, the HKFFA reaches out to

---

[30] *Xianggang Shangpao*, April 10, 2018, p. A15.
[31] Ibid.
[32] *Xianggang Shangpao*, April 16, 2018, p. A12.
[33] Ibid. *Wen Wei Po*, April 16, 2018, p. A25.
[34] See the Facebook of the Quanzhou Association, in https://www.facebook.com/Hong-Kong-Quanzhou-Associations-Youth-Committee-893683283997735/?ref=py_c, access date: April 22, 2018.
[35] *Wen Wei Po*, April 3, 2018, p. A27.
[36] *Newsletter of the Fujian Members of the Chinese People's Political Consultative Conference* (*Zhengxue Tiandi*), vol. 7 (2017), p. 59.
[37] Ibid., p. 59.

ethnic minorities in the HKSAR, playing a crucial role in the implementation of China's united front work in the territory.[38]

THE HONG KONG FEDERATION OF FUJIAN ASSOCIATIONS (HKFFA) AND ITS ORGANIZATION

The HKFFA has eight types of affiliated groups (Fig. 3.1). The first type belongs to *tongxianghui* (townspeople) associations, examples of which include the Fukienese Association, Nanan Association, Quanzhou Federation of Associations and the Puxian Association (Table 3.2). This category occupies most affiliated interest groups. The Quanzhou Federation of Associations held a carnival in October 2017 to celebrate the PRC national day and to educate the members of the public by stressing how Japan exploited China from the Qing dynasty to the Nationalist era, and by emphasizing the need to oppose any talk on "Hong Kong independence."[39] Four officials from the Liaison Office attended, including deputy director He Jing. The Fujian province's united front department official Liu Changjiang came to Hong Kong to attend the event. Another example of how *tongxianghui* mobilized citizen participation in support of the HKSAR government and China's policy toward Hong Kong was the activities of the Puxian Association, which was formed in August 2017. The Puxian Association invited Liaison Office deputy director Chen Dong to preside over its inaugural ceremony, gathering 1500 new members, promoting cultural exchange between the Putian *tongxiang* in Hong Kong and the counterpart in Fuijian and providing *guanxi* networks for investment activities back in Fujian province.[40]

The second type of affiliated groups embraces the education and alumni associations, such as the Fukien Secondary School Alumni Association. These education groups are increasingly important as the HKSAR government has begun to encourage the implementation of national education in all primary and secondary schools. There are three Fuijianese secondary schools in Hong Kong, namely in Kwun Tong, Siu Sai Wan and North Point districts.[41] In January 2018, the Xiamen Double Ten Secondary

---

[38] Ibid., p. 59.
[39] *Xianggang Shangpao* (*Hong Kong Commercial Daily*), October 18, 2017, p. A21.
[40] *Wen Wei Po*, August 2, 2018, p. A19.
[41] See the websites of the school, in http://www.fms.edu.hk/, access date: April 26, 2018 and http://www.fssas.edu.hk/, access date: April 26, 2018.

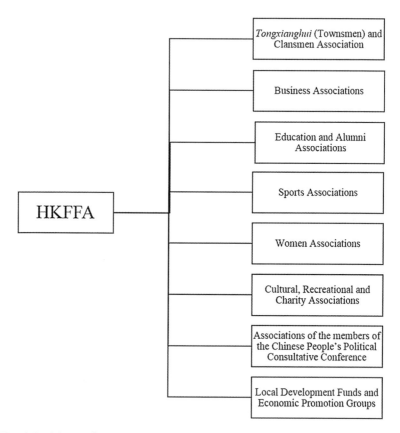

Fig. 3.1 Types of HKFFA affiliated groups. Source: Hong Kong Federation of Fujian Associations, *Special Issues*, vol. 10 (Hong Kong: Meijia Publishing Limited, October 2015)

School Alumni Association organized a tour to visit its sister school in Taiwan, participating in the 60th anniversary of the Taizhong Double Ten Secondary School, and enhancing friendships with the Taiwan educators who had Xiamen origin.[42]

The cultural, recreational and charity associations are the third common type of Fujianese interest groups in the HKSAR. They include welfare fund groups which organize cultural and sports activities, and which provide scholarships and subsidies to help families of the poor and the

[42] *Ta Kung Pao*, January 18, 2018, p. A20.

Table 3.2 Types of HKFFA affiliated groups

Types of affiliated groups	Examples	Total number
Tongxianghui (townspeople) and Clansmen Association	The Fukienese Association, Nanan Association, Quanzhou Federation of Associations and Puxian Clans Association	147
Business Associations	Hong Kong Pu Tian Commercial Association	2
Education and Alumni Associations	Fukien Secondary School Alumni Association, Xiamen Double Ten Secondary School Alumni Association	64
Sports Associations	Fukien Athletic Club	1
Women Associations	Hong Kong Fukienese Women Association	2
Cultural, Recreational and Charity Associations	The Fukien Calligraphy and Painting Association, and the Wing Chun Clansmen Welfare Fund Association	14
Associations of the members of the Chinese People's Political Consultative Committee	Hong Kong Fukienese (Provincial) CPPCC members Association	1
Local Development Funds and Economic Promotion Groups	The Fujian Charitable Education Fund, and the Min Kong Association	3
Total number		234

Sources: Calculations of different Fujianese interest groups from *Tai Kung Pao*, March 27, 2017, p. A21. Also see *Ta Kung Pao*, August 2, 2017, p. A19; October 18, 2017, p. A29; December 21, 2017, p. B1; January 18, 2018, p. A20; January 19, 2018, p. B11. *Wen Wei Po*, April 24, 2018, p. A15 and *Xianggang Shangpao* (*Hong Kong Commercial Daily*), October 18, 2017, p. A21

needy, especially the newly arrived immigrants from mainland China. The Fukien Calligraphy and Painting Association organized its 30th anniversary in January 2018 by inviting Liaison Office Deputy Director Yang Jian to attend. It appealed to members to "support the principle of 'loving the nation and Hong Kong' and promoting China's cultural enterprises."[43] The local development funds and economic promotion groups are supporting residents of lower-class families and the economic development of Hong Kong and the PRC. For instance, the Fujian Charitable Education Fund in December 2017 gathered a donation of HK$1 million to confer 200 scholarships on students from forty secondary schools, invited Liaison Office's educational deputy director Liu Jianfeng to attend and appealed

[43] *Ta Kung Pao*, January 19, 2018, p. B11.

to all award recipients to "love the nation, love the family and love themselves."[44] Between 1994 and 2017, the fund collected HK$350 million to support the construction of 607 primary schools in the PRC, including 249 schools located in the Fujian province.[45]

The HKFFA is composed of the socially and politically active Fujianese groups, cutting across occupational sectors, classes and gender. The Hong Kong Fukienese Women Association, which was set up in 2015 with 4000 members, held a celebration for International Women's Day on March 8, 2018. Its chairlady Choi Wong Ling-ling remarked that while Fujianese women had a good tradition of dealing with their families and working independently outside their families, the association strongly supported the policies of the CCP's 19th Party Congress, especially President Xi Jinping's comment on the role of women as "the creators of material and spiritual civilization."[46] The association visited the Fujian province in April 2018, and its delegation was received by not only the Fujian provincial party-secretary Yu Weiguo but also its united front department director Lei Chunmei.[47] Lei praised the Hong Kong women for being "an important force that promotes social development and progress and that comprehensively unites the female comrades in Hong Kong."[48] While Fujian officials updated the circumstances of Fujian to the Hong Kong delegates, they also appealed to the need of the association to participate in Fuzhou's development, to back up the policies of the HKSAR government, to support "one country, two systems," and to "continue promoting the excellent tradition of fostering patriotism" in Hong Kong.[49] All the affiliated groups under the HKFFA have become the target of united front work from the PRC.

ELECTORAL PARTICIPATION OF THE FUJIANESE

Traditionally, the Fujianese have been politically occupying their stronghold in North Point district, where many of them are residing. Table 3.3 shows that overall the Fujianese candidates performed well in their political stronghold in North Point; four local Fujianese politicians have

[44] *Ta Kung Pao*, December 21, 2017, p. B1.
[45] *Wen Wei Po*, April 2, 2018.
[46] *Xianggang Shangpao*, March 20, 2018, p. A20. *Wen Wei Po*, March 21, 2018, p. A15.
[47] *Wen Wei Po*, April 24, 2018, p. A15.
[48] Ibid.
[49] Ibid.

Table 3.3 Fujianese candidates and District Council election results in North Point District, 2007–2015

Constituency	1999	2003	2007	2011	2015
Mount Parker	Wong Kin-pan 1065 (49.0%)	Wong Kin-pan 1549 (55.9%)	Wong Kin-pan 2120 (81.7%)	Wong Kin-pan (uncontested)	Wong Kin-pan (uncontested)
Braemar Hill	Chan Ping-wun (uncontested)	Chan Ping-wun 1108 (55.6%)	Shiu Ka-fai 1385 (54.8%)	Shiu Ka-fai (uncontested)	Shiu Ka-fai (uncontested)
Fortress Hill	Lo Wing-kwan Frankie (uncontested)	Lo Wing-kwan Frankie 1385 (50.1%)	Lo Wing-kwan Frankie 1698 (58.6%)	Lo Wing-kwan Frankie (uncontested)	Lo Wing-kwan Frankie (uncontested)
City Garden	Hui Ching-on 995 (42.3%)	Hui Ching-on (uncontested)	Hui Ching-on 1698 (62.3%)	Hui Ching-on 2016 (63.2%)	Hui Ching-on (uncontested)
Kam Ping	Choy So-yuk (uncontested)	Choy So-yuk 1433 (44.5%)	Choy So-yuk 1804 (75.2%)	Choy So-yuk (uncontested)	Choy So-yuk (uncontested)
Provident	Wong Kwok-hing (uncontested)	Wong Kwok-hing 2665 (71.8%)	Kwok Wai-keung 2527 (89.8%)	Kwok Wai-keung (uncontested)	Kwok Wai-keung (uncontested)
Fort Street	Chu Hon-wah (uncontested)	Choy Sai-fu 944 (50.0%)	Hung Lin-cham (uncontested)	Hung Lin-cham (uncontested)	Hung Lin-cham (uncontested)

Sources: Reports of District Councils elections in 1999, 2003, 2007, 2011 and 2015, in https://www.eac.gov.hk/en/distco/report03.htm, https://www.eac.gov.hk/en/distco/1999_report.htm, https://www.eac.gov.hk/en/distco/2007dc_detailreport.htm, https://www.eac.gov.hk/en/distco/2011dc_detailreport.htm, and https://www.eac.gov.hk/en/distco/2015dc_detailreport.htm, access date: April 22, 2018

Note: The figures show their votes gained and also the percentage share of total votes

succeeded in becoming the elected District Council members from 1999 to the present. They are company executive Wong Kin-pan, studio trainer Lo Wing-kwan, accountant Hui Ching-on and businesswoman Choy So-yuk.[50] Wong Kin-pan was a member of the pro-Beijing DAB and he easily defeated Yan Wing-lok of the Democratic Party in 1999; the former got 1067 votes and the latter 488 votes. Wong's position remained secure in the 2003 District Council elections in which many DAB candidates were defeated, but he acquired 1549 votes to defeat Democratic Party's Wong Shing-fai, who was a Fujianese and who obtained 1222 votes. Wong Shing-fai as a pro-democracy Fujianese could not defeat Wong Kin-pan in 2003 when there was a strong public demand for democratic change. After Wong Kin-pan's landslide victory in the 2007 District Council elections, he has become an automatically elected incumbent easily.

Nevertheless, the Fujianese camp encountered opposition from other political forces from 2003 to 2010. In North Point's seven constituencies, the number of uncontested candidates remained at five in the 1999 District Council elections, but it was reduced to one in 2003, mainly due to the protest by half a million people against the performance of the HKSAR government on July 1, 1997. The massive public discontent with the Tung Chee-hwa administration in the summer of 2003 led to fierce competition in North Point. The competitive situation persisted in the 2007 District Council elections, but the Fujianese had a political comeback in the District Council elections in 2011, when six of the seven constituencies in North Point witnessed automatically elected candidates from the Fujianese community. The reassertion of the Fujianese political force could be seen in the 2015 District Council elections in which they captured all the seven constituencies without any opponent in North Point.

It is relatively difficult for a non-Fujianese candidate to get elected in the Fujianese stronghold of North Point. In Fort Street, DAB candidate Chu Hon-wah was automatically elected in the 1999 District Council elections, but he was later at loggerheads with the DAB and lost the support of the Fujianese camp in the 2003 elections.[51] The Fujianese camp claimed that Chu was not a Fujianese, and so it could not support him.

[50] Yip Tin-sang, *A Collection of Materials on Hong Kong's Elections, 1996–2000* (Hong Kong: Institute of Asia-Pacific Studies, the Chinese University of Hong Kong, 2001), pp. 67–68.
[51] *Pingguo Ribao* (*Apple Daily*), February 25, 2005, in https://hk.news.appledaily.com/local/daily/article/20050225/4691844, access date: April 23, 2018.

After his withdrawal from the DAB, Chu was defeated narrowly by a Fujianese candidate, Choy Sai-fu, by only one vote. Chu appealed to the court against the election result and he won the court case. However, prior to the 2005 by-election, Chu passed away and the DAB nominated Hung Lin-cham rather than Choy Sai-fu.[52] Hung, who works in the Fukien Secondary School, was elected and he has been re-elected without any opponent from 2007 to 2015. Hence, getting the support from the Fujianese political force could secure an upper hand in the electoral competition in the Fujianese stronghold of North Point.

At the level of Legislative Council elections, the Fujianese have become more politically active since 1997. Paul Cheng and Philip Wong were appointed by the PRC as members of the Provisional Legislative Council from December 1996 to June 1998 (Table 3.4). Choy So-yuk became a legislator selected by the Election Committee and she represented the pro-business and pro-Beijing Hong Kong Progressive Alliance. She later joined the DAB and was directly elected by citizens in the Hong Kong Island's geographical constituency. Ma Lik and Choy relied on the strong Fujianese votes in the geographical constituency of Hong Kong Island from 2000 to 2008. Another Fujianese, Wong Kwok-hing, participated in the pro-Beijing Federation of Trade Unions, while Gary Chan was a rising star affiliated with the DAB and succeeded in becoming a legislator in the 2008 Legislative Council (LegCo) elections in the New Territories East. Christopher Cheung Wah-fung became a legislator through the functional constituency representing the financial services and he joined the business group, the Progressive and Business Alliance.

The Fujianese political elites in the HKSAR have close relations with the DAB. Ideologically, the HKFAA and the DAB are pro-Beijing. They are mutually interdependent in local elections. While the HKFFA provides the Fujianese votes for DAB candidates, the DAB can deliver manpower and resources for the Fujianese to participate in local elections, including LegCo and District Council elections. Table 3.5 shows that most Fujianese political elites are also DAB members, including veteran politician Choy So-yuk and rising stars Brave Chan Yung and Gary Chan. Table 3.5 also illustrates the intimate relationships between the Fujianese and the high-ranking positions of the DAB. Table 3.6 demonstrates that the Fujianese advisors in the DAB are mostly businesspeople. The Fujianese business

---

[52] *Pingguo Ribao* (*Apple Daily*), February 26, 2005, in https://hk.news.appledaily.com/local/daily/article/20050226/4695264, access date: April 23, 2018.

Table 3.4 Fujianese legislators, 1997–2018

Legislative Council member	Constituency	Political party/group affiliation
Paul Cheng[a]	Nil	Nil
Philip Wong Yu-hong[a]	Commercial (second) 1998–2012	Nil
Choy So-yuk[a]	Election Committee (1998–2000)[b] Hong Kong Island (2000–2008)	Hong Kong Progressive Alliance Democratic Alliance for the Betterment and Progress of Hong Kong
Ma Lik	Hong Kong Island (2004–2007)	Democratic Alliance for the Betterment and Progress of Hong Kong
Wong Kwok-hing	Labor (2004–2008) New Territories West (2008–2012) Hong Kong Island (2012–2016)	Federation of Trade Unions
Gary Chan	New Territories East (2008–Now)	Democratic Alliance for the Betterment and Progress of Hong Kong
Christopher Cheung Wah-fung	Financial Services (2012–Now)	Business and Professionals Alliance for Hong Kong

Sources: Hong Kong Fujian Federation of Associations, *Special Issues* vol. 10 (Hong Kong: Meijia Publishing Limited, October 2015); See also Hong Kong Fujian Federation of Associations, *Newsletter of the Hong Kong Fujian Federation of Associations*, vol. 51 (Hong Kong: Meijia Publishing Limited, December 2016)

[a]Paul Cheng, Philip Wong and Choy So-yuk were members of the Provisional Legislative Council from December 1996 to June 1998

[b]In the 1998 LegCo election, ten legislators were elected from an Election Committee and Choy represented one of the ten elected legislators. This table is constructed from the biographies of LegCo members between 1998 and 2016

elites play a crucial role in the DAB leadership. For example, the HKFFA's honorary chairman Lo Man-tuen is also the chairman of the DAB Senate, which is a high-level body formulating the party's policy directions and which acts as a check and balance mechanism against any misconduct of DAB members. Lo was born in Quanzhou in 1948 and migrated to reside in Hong Kong in 1954. He became a successful businessman whose factories produced video cassettes in Hong Kong during the 1980s. In 2008, Lo was appointed as the CPPCC external affairs committee's deputy chairman.[53] In 2012, he became a deputy chairman of the PRC National

---

[53] See "Lo Man-tuen," in http://www.cppcc.gov.cn/CMS/wylibary/showJcwyxtInfoWylibary.action?tabJcwyxt.guid=11W001877, access date: April 24, 2018.

Table 3.5 Key Fujianese representatives in political parties as of 2018

Political party	Key Fujianese representative	Occupational background
Democratic Alliance for the Betterment and Progress of Hong Kong	1. Alan Chong Shaw-swee 2. Brave Chan Yung 3. Choy So-yuk 4. Gary Chan 5. Hung Lin-cham 6. Hung Kam-in 7. Lo Man-tuen 8. Iron Sze 9. Wong Ting-chung	1. Businessman 2. Social worker 3. District Council member 4. Legislative Council member 5. District Council member 6. District Council member 7. Businessman 8. Industrialist 9. Businessman
Federations of Trade Unions	1. Stanley Ng Chau-pei	1. Trade unionist
Business and Professionals Alliance for Hong Kong	1. Christopher Cheung Wah-fung	1. Businessman

Sources: Hong Kong Federation of Fujian Associations, *Newsletter of the Hong Kong Federation of Fujian Associations*, volume: 54 (Hong Kong: Meijia Publishing Limited, 2017). See also "People in the DAB," in http://www.dab.org.hk/AboutUs.php?st=1&nid=275&f1=235&f2=275, access date: April 10, 2018; "Organization Structure of Hong Kong Federation of Trade Union," in http://www.ftu.org.hk/zh-hant/about?id=13, access date: April 10, 2018; and "People in the Business and Professionals Alliance for Hong Kong," in http://en.bpahk.org/people/, access date: April 10, 2018

Chamber of Commerce.[54] Lo is now one of the members of the Board of Directors of the Hong Kong Association for Promotion of Peaceful Reunification of China, an organization set up by the PRC to conduct united front work to "unite the people of Hong Kong, to maintain the principle of 'one country, two systems,' to oppose Taiwan independence, and to deepen the relations between Taiwan and Hong Kong."[55] In the March 2017 Chief Executive election in the HKSAR, Lo openly asserted that the pro-democracy candidate John Tsang Chun-wah was not supported by the central government in Beijing, commenting like a spokesman who reflected the view of PRC officials responsible for Hong Kong

---

[54] For Lo's biography, see http://www.hsmrt.com/luwenduan/column/2259/, access date: April 25, 2018.

[55] See the mission of the Association in http://www.happrc.hk/tc/ourmission.php, access date: April 24, 2018.

Table 3.6 The Fujianese participation in the leadership of the Democratic Alliance for the Betterment of Hong Kong

Name	Positions in the DAB leadership
Alan Chong Shaw-swee	Member of the Senate, 2005–2013; Senate Vice-chairman, 2013–2019
Brave Chan Yung	Standing Committee member, 2011–2013; Vice-chairman, 2013–2019
Cheung Ming-man	Member of the Senate, 2005–2017; Senate Vice-chairman, 2017–2019
Choy So-yuk	Central Committee member, 2000–2019
Gary Chan Hak-kan	Central Committee member, 2009–2013; Standing Committee member, 2013–2015; Vice-chairman, 2017–2019
Hung Kam-in	Central Committee member, 2009–2013; Standing Committee member, 2013–2015; Deputy Secretary-General, 2015–2019
Hung Lin-cham	Central Committee member, 2009–2019
Jose Yu Sun-say	Senate Chairman, 2005–2015
Lo Man-tuen	Member of Standing Committee, 2005–2007; Senate Vice-chairman, 2007–2015; Senate Chairman, 2015–2019
Lo Wan-sing	Member of the Senate, 2005–2015; Senate Vice-chairman, 2015–2019
Ma Lik	Secretary-General, 1992–2003; Chairman, 2004–2007
Ting Kong-ho,	Member of Standing Committee, 2015–2019
Wong Kwok-hing	Central Committee member, 1992–2005

Sources: Democratic Alliance for the Betterment and Progress of Hong Kong (2017), *25th Anniversary Commemoration of the Democratic Alliance for the Betterment and Progress of Hong Kong: Choices and Promises*. Hong Kong: Democratic Alliance for the Betterment and Progress of Hong Kong, pp. 89–95

matters.[56] The rise of Lo in Hong Kong's political arena is a testimony of how a successful Fujianese businessman could become a politically influential elite linking Beijing and the HKSAR.

Table 3.7 shows that the Fujianese business elites have become the party and policy advisors to the DAB. While the DAB is an umbrella and a cross-class pro-Beijing party absorbing more businesspeople than before, many business elites who support and join the DAB come from the Fujianese. The Fujianese business people can provide not only policy advice but also financial support for the DAB, making the two political organizations work as partners in non-election time, when

---

[56] See Lo Man-tuen, "Why does the central government not support John Tsang to participate in the Chief Executive election?," *Sing Tao Daily*, March 24, 2017, p. A19.

Table 3.7 Fujianese advisors in the Democratic Alliance for the Betterment and Progress of Hong Kong

Types of advisor	Number (in total)	Fujianese leader	Occupation background
Party Affairs Advisor	1 (11)	Yu Sun-say, Jose	Businessman
Advisor for the DAB's policy directions and strategies (2017–2019 term)	8 (34)	Cai Yi	Businessman
		Hui Wing-mou	Businessman
		Hung Cho-hong	Businessman
		Lam Shu-chit	Businessman
		Ng Leung-ho	Businessman
		Sze Chi-ching	Industrialist
		Wong Ya-hong	Businessman
		Wong Yau-kar, David	Industrialist
Total	9 (44)		

Source: "Advisors," in http://www.eng.dab.org.hk/dab-people/advisors/, access date: February 11, 2018

constituency services are constantly offered, and in election period, as all their members and supporters are fully mobilized to compete with pro-democracy forces.

The Fujianese participation in the territorially based pro-Beijing groups is prominent. Table 3.8 shows that three pro-Beijing united front groups at the district level—the Hong Kong Island Federation of Associations (HKIFA), the Kowloon Federation of Associations (KFA) and the New Territories Federation of Societies (NTFS)—are composed of many Fujianese elites, who are mostly district councilors and businesspeople. A few Fujianese members of the three organizations are social workers and teachers. Traditionally, the HKIFA, KFA and NTFS have been campaigning for candidates of pro-Beijing forces, especially the DAB, in District Council and LegCo elections.[57] The participation of many Fujianese elites in the three united front organizations means that Fujianese candidates can easily acquire the manpower, logistical and electoral support from the entire pro-Beijing camp in a forceful manner.

[57] For District Council elections, see Shiu-hing Lo, Wing-yat Yu and Kwok-fai Wan, "The 1999 District Councils elections," in Ming Chan and Alvin So, eds., *Crisis and Transformation in China's Hong Kong* (London: M. E. Sharpe, 2002), pp. 139–165.

Table 3.8 Fujianese participation in pro-Beijing district-based groups, 2018

District Associations	Key Fujianese Representative	Occupational Background
Hong Kong Island Federation of Associations (HKIFA)	1. Cai Yi 2. Choy So-yuk 3. Hui Ching-on 4. Hung Chao-hong 5. Hung Lin-cham 6. Malcolm Lam 7. Stanley Ng Chau-pei 8. Ting Kong-ho 9. Wong Kin-pan 10. Wong Kwok-hing	1. Businessman 2. District Council member 3. District Council member 4. Businessman 5. District Council member 6. Former District Council member 7. Trade unionist 8. Secondary School Teacher 9. District Council member 10. District Council member
Kowloon Federation of Associations (KFA)	1. Chan Keng-chu 2. Hung Kam-in 3. Wong Ting-chung	1. Former District Council member and District Activist 2. District Council member 3. Businessman
New Territories Federation of Societies (NTFS)	1. Richard Chan Kam-lam 2. Chan Pok-chi 3. Chan Yung 4. Chong Yuen-tung 5. Gary Chan 6. Henry Tan 7. Lam Faat-kang 8. Nixie Lam Lam	1. Former District Council member 2. District Council member 3. Social worker 4. District Council member 5. Legislative Council member 6. Businessman 7. District Council member 8. District Council member

Sources: See "Hong Kong Island Federation of Associations: Organizational Structure," in http://www.hk-if.org/special.php?id=7, access date: February 11, 2018; "Kowloon Federation of Associations: Organizational Structure," in https://klnfas.hk/tc/DetailPage?vfljsifdio=dba132f6ab6a3e3d17a8d59e8 2105f4c, access date: February 11, 2018. "New Territories Federation of Societies: Organizational Structure," in http://www.ntas.org.hk/blog_post.jsp?rid=4&cate_id=3, access date: February 11, 2018

The Fujianese elites also participate actively in the selection of the HKSAR Chief Executive. Table 3.9 shows that sixty-six members of the 1194-member Chief Executive Election Committee in the 2017 Chief Executive election came from the Fujianese community, constituting 5.5% of the total membership.[58] The Fujianese occupied a large percentage of

[58] *Dongfang Ribao* (*Oriental Daily*), December 12, 2012.

Table 3.9 Participation of HKFFA members in the 2017 Chief Executive Election Committee

Sector	No of HKFAA members	Percentage of Fujianese in the Chief Executive Election Committee s	Key representatives	Occupational background
Industrial, commercial and financial sectors	24	36.36%	1. Jose Yu Sun-say 2. Margaret Ko 3. Iron Sze 4. Ng Chee-siong	1. Businessman 2. Banker 3. Industrialist 4. Property developer
The professional	3	4.54%	Chan Wing-kwong	Professional
Labor, social services, religious and other sectors	8	12.12%	1. Hung Cho-sing 2. Wong Ying-wai	1. Businessman 2. Solicitor
Members of the Legislative Council, members of the District Council, representatives of the rural advisory Heung Yee Kuk, Hong Kong deputies to the National People's Congress and Hong Kong members of the National Committee of the Chinese People's Political Consultative conference	27	40.91%	1. Cai Yi 2. Brave Chan Yung 3. Choy So-yuk 4. Hui Wing-mou 5. Lo Man-tuen 6. Ng Chau-pei	1. Businessman 2. Social worker 3. District Council member 4. Businessman 5. Businessman 6. Trade unionist
	Total: 66			

Source: Hong Kong Federation of Fujian Associations, *Newsletter of the Hong Kong Federation of Fujian Associations*, vol. 51 (Hong Kong: Meijia Publishing Limited, December 2016), p. 58

membership in several sectors, such as (1) the industrial, commercial and financial sector, and (2) local politicians sectors. Clearly, the Fujianese participation in local politics has a bearing on the election of the Chief Executive of the HKSAR. They have been providing a strong and solid support for pro-Beijing candidates in the Chief Executive elections.

Table 3.10 The elected Fujianese in the PRC National People's Congress Election, 2017

National People's Congress representative	Affiliated group(s) or institution(s)	Occupation background
Brave Chan Yung	New Territories Federation of Societies	Social worker
Cai Yi	Hong Kong Island Federation of Association	Businessman
Choy So-yuk	Democratic Alliance for the Betterment and Progress of Hong Kong	District Council member
Witman Hung	Internet Professional Association	Businessman
Lam Lung-on	The Hong Kong Chinese Importers' and Exporters' Association	Businessman
Stanley Ng Chau-pei,	Federations of Trade Unions	Trade unionist
Pauline Ngan Po-ling	The Chinese General Chamber of Commerce	Industrialist
Henry Tan	Fringe Backer	Industrialist
Wong Ting-chung	Hong Kong Industrial Commercial Associations	Businessman
David Wong Yao-kar	The Chinese Manufacturers' Association of Hong Kong	Businessman
Wong Yuk-shan	The Open University of Hong Kong	Professor and Vice Chancellor

Source: See *Wen Wei Po*, December 20, 2017, pp. A01–A03; See also HK01, "Supporting Candidates in NPC Elections in 2017," in https://www.hk01.com/, access date: December 4, 2017; and Hong Kong Fujian Federation of Associations, *Special Issues*, vol. 10 (Hong Kong: Meijia Publishing Limited, October 2015), pp. 12–17

Similarly, Table 3.10 shows that the Fujianese were influential in the selection of the Hong Kong members to the NPC in 2017. Eleven Fujianese were elected as Hong Kong members of the NPC. Out of thirty-six Hong Kong members of the NPC, almost one-third of them came from the Fujianese community in 2017—a testimony to the increasing political role of the Fujianese in Hong Kong's political relations with the PRC. Table 3.11 highlights the Fujianese who were appointed as members of the CPPCC in 2018. Three Fujianese leaders—Chau On Tat-yuan, Hui Wing-mou and Ng Leung-ho—are the CPPCC Executive Committee members, constituting one-sixth of the top-level membership and indicating the influence of the Fujianese political camp. Table 3.12 shows that, among the Basic Law Committee members, who decide on the issues relating to both Hong Kong and the PRC over Hong Kong Basic Law, two of them came from the Fujianese

Table 3.11 Fujianese community leaders appointed as members of the Chinese People's Political Consultative Conference in 2018

Key Appointed CPPCC members	Affiliated group(s) or institution(s)	Occupational background
Beau Kuok	Friends of Hong Kong Associations	Businessman
Chau On Tat-yuan[a]	Hong Kong Federation of Fujian Associations	Businessman
Choy Wong Ling Ling	All-China Women's Federation	Industrialist
Christopher Cheung Wah-fung	Business and Professionals Alliance for Hong Kong	Businessman
Chu Ming-chuan	All-China Federation of Industry and Commerce	Businessman
Hui Wing-mou[a]	New Home Associations	Businessman
Margaret Ko	Chong Hing Bank	Banker
Li Kuo-hsing	Hong Kong Jinjiang Clansman Association	Businessman
Ng Chee-siong	The Real Estate Developers Association of Hong Kong	Property developer
Iron Sze	The Chinese Manufacturers' Association of Hong Kong	Industrialist
Judith Yu	Kowloon East Associations	Businessman
Ng Leung-ho[a]	Hong Kong Federation of Fujian Associations	Businessman
Shi Qingliu	Hong Kong Fukienese (provincial) CPPCC members association	Businessman
Shi Weihung	Hong Kong Fukienese (provincial) CPPCC members association	Businessman
Tung Ng Ling-ling	Hong Kong Shine Tak Foundations	Businesswoman
Wong Ya Nam	Hong Kong Fukienese (provincial) CPPCC members association	Businessman

Source: *Wen Wei Po*, p. A05, January 26, 2018

[a]Note: Chau, Hui and Ng are three members of the eighteen-member CPPCC Executive Committee as of 2018. There were some 200 Hong Kong CPPCC members, because the number of "specially invited" Hong Kong members of the CPPCC is often unknown

community, namely, Wong Po-yan and Wong Yuk-shan. Both had a record of staunchly supporting China's policy toward the HKSAR, including the interpretation of the Basic Law by the NPC Standing Committee.[59]

[59] Wong Po-yan supported the NPC Standing Committee's interpretation of the Basic Law over the speed of political reform in March 2004. *Ming Pao*, March 29, 2004, p. A6. Wong Yuk-shan supported the NPC Standing Committee's interpretation of Article 104 of the Basic Law concerning the oath-taking behavior of two legislators-elect, Yau Wai-ching and Baggio Leung, in November 2016. *Xianggang Xinbao*, March 17, 2018.

Table 3.12 Fujianese as Basic Law Committee members as of 2018

Term	Fujianese representative	Occupation background
1997–2003	Wong Po-yan	Businessman
2003–2008	Wong Po-yan	Businessman
2008–2013	Wong Yuk-shan	University professor
2013–2018	Wong Yuk-shan	University professor

Sources: *The Basic Law and Hong Kong: The 15th Anniversary of Reunification with the Motherland*, 2012, in http://www.basiclaw.gov.hk/en/publications/15anniversary_reunification/index.html, access date: April 26, 2018; and "A List of the Basic Law Committee Members of the HKSAR under the Standing Committee of the National People's Congress," in http://www.npc.gov.cn, access date: April 26, 2018

Fujianese Alliance with PRC Officials and Participation in Political Activities

An alliance between PRC officials in the HKSAR and Fujianese interest groups can be seen in Table 3.13. By convention, PRC officials in the Liaison Office and from the mainland attend the functions organized by Fujianese groups. While mainland officials who visit Fujianese groups came from various departments, especially the united front department, the HKSAR-based officials must come from the Liaison Office, including the social liaison department and branch officials from the Hong Kong Island, Kowloon and the New Territories. Their attendance showed a high degree of endorsement from the PRC government for the Fujianese activities.

Table 3.14 shows that the HKFFA organized political activities in support of the HKSAR government, including the peaceful protest in support of the government's position on universal suffrage in August 2014, the anti-Occupy Central Movement's signature campaign from October to November 2014, the electoral mobilization during District Council elections and LegCo elections and a campaign in support of seven police officers who were charged of abusing their power over a protestor named Ken Tsang during the Occupy Central Movement. On August 17, 2014, the fifteen-member Committee for the Peaceful Protest in support of universal suffrage had seven Fujianese, including Iron Sze, Chau On Tat-yuan, Stanley Ng and Cai Yi.[60] A Fujianese community leader,

---

[60] "Fujianese give money and support in the anti-Occupy Central Movement," in http://www.post852.com/, access date: April 25, 2018.

Table 3.13 Chinese official attending the HKFFA's activities

Activities	Date	Key Chinese official present in the event
Shenzhen Fukiense Commercial Associations 2012 Chinese New Year Celebration. The HKFFA went to Shenzhen to celebrate the new year.	February, 2012	1. Li Zuke, Fujian CPPCC Deputy Director 2. Bai Tian, Shenzhen CPPCC director 3. Zhang Siping, Shenzhen party-secretary and united front department director
Celebration of the International Women's Day	March, 2012	1. Li Guo, deputy director of Liaison Office 2. Liao Xun, head of the coordination department of Liaison Office 3. Chen Xiurong, vice-chairman of the PRC All-China Women's Federation of Associations
The inaugural ceremony of the members of the ninth term of Board of Directors of the HKFFA	November, 2013	1. Wang Ginmin, vice chairman of the National Committee of the CPPCC 2. Zhang Changping, Fujian CPPCC director 3. Chen Zuoe'r, former deputy director of Hong Kong Macao Affairs Office 4. Lin Zhimin, deputy director of the PRC's United Front Department 5. Wang Zhiminm deputy director of the Liaison Office 6. Lin Wu, deputy director of the Liaison Office 7. Chen Weizhan, deputy commander of the People's Liberation Army in Hong Kong 8. Li Yuanming, deputy commissioner of the PRC Ministry of Foreign Affairs in the HKSAR
1. The inaugural ceremony of the members of the third term of the Board of Directors of the Hong Kong Dong Shi Town Fraternal Association. The HKFFA leaders attended the ceremony 2. The Chinese New Year Celebration of the Qiaosheng Middle Alumni Association, which is an affiliated group of the HKFFA	September, 2014	1. Huang Wai, head of the Liaison Office's Hong Kong Island social work department 2. Huang Jinzhan, party-secretary and the united front department of Jinjiang county in Fujian province
The HKFFA's Seminar on Hong Kong, China and Global Development	November, 2014	1. Song Ruan, deputy commissioner of the PRC Ministry of Foreign Affairs in the HKSAR

(continued)

Table 3.13 (continued)

Activities	Date	Key Chinese official present in the event
The Celebration of the establishment of HKFFA's New Territories West Branch	May, 2015	1. Liu Lin, head of the Liaison Office's New Territories work department
The inaugural ceremony of the members of the third term of the Board of Directors of HKFFA	September, 2015	1. Zhang Xiaoming, director of the Liaison Office
The Celebration of the 30th Anniversary of HKFFA's affiliated group, Hong Kong Jinjiang Clansman Association and the inaugural ceremony of the members of the 16th term of Directorate members of Hong Kong Jinjiang Clansman Association, which is affiliated with the HKFFA	2015	1. Lin Wu, deputy director of the Liaison Office 2. Lin Juan, chairman of the PRC All-China Federation of Returned Overseas Chinese 3. Zhang Changping, the chairman of Fujian CPPCC
The Celebration of the 90th Anniversary of Fukien Athletic Club and the inaugural ceremony of the members of the 19th term of Directorate members of the Fukien Athletic Club	2015	Wu Yangwei, head of the Liaison Office's Hong Kong Island work department
HKFFA's Celebration of the 67th Anniversary of the establishment of People's Republic of China	September, 2016	1. Lin Wu, deputy director of the Liaison Office 2. Hu Jianzhong, deputy commissioner of the PRC Ministry of Foreign Affairs in the HKSAR 3. Chen Fei, head of Fujian province's united front department 4. Li Wen, head of the Liaison Office's social liaison department 5. Wu Yangwei, head of the Liaison Office's Hong Kong Island work department 6. Liu Lin, head of the Liaison Office's New Territories work department 7. Li Baozhong, deputy head of the Liaison Office's social liaison department 8. Lu Ning, deputy head of the Liaison Office's Kowloon work department 9. He Ping, senior assistant of the Liaison Office's social liaison department

(*continued*)

Table 3.13 (continued)

Activities	Date	Key Chinese official present in the event
HKFFA's Kowloon West Branch Celebration of the 67th Anniversary of the establishment of People's Republic of China	October, 2016	1. Li Wen, head of the Liaison Office's Social Liaison Department 2. He Jing, head of the Liaison Office's Kowloon Work Department 3. Wang Xiaoling, deputy head of the Liaison Office's Kowloon work department
HKFFA's New Year Celebration	February, 2017	1. Lin Wu, deputy director of the Liaison Office 2. Chen Fei, head of Fujian province's united front department

Source: Hong Kong Fujian Federation of Associations, *Newsletter of Hong Kong Fujian Federation of Associations*, volumes 33–54 (Hong Kong: Meijia Publishing Limited, 2014–2017). See also *Wen Wei Po*, November 10, 2013, p. A13.; *Wen Wei Po*, October 1, 2016, p. A16; *Wen Wei Po*, October 24, 2016, p. A13

Hung Chao-hong, donated HK$3 million to the Committee.[61] Hung was responsible for coordinating all other Fujianese groups and subsidizing them to participate in the campaign.[62] Table 3.15 shows that Fujianese groups were heavily mobilized in the Alliance for Peace and Democracy, an organization opposing the Occupy Central Movement. Of the 1528 groups in the Alliance, 216 (14%) belonged to the Fujianese groups among which eleven came from Southeast Asia. These eleven groups under the HKFFA included the Myanmar Overseas Chinese Alumni Association, Bandung Alumni Association, Bali Alumni Association, Alumni Association of Pah Tsung High School (Jakarta, Indonesia), South Kalimantan Alumni Association, Machung Alumni Association, Surabaya Alumni Association, Macassar Alumni Association, Brunei Chinese Alumni Association and the Mianhua (Burma Chinese) High School Alumni Association.[63] Clans groups and alumni groups stood out as the most active interest groups in the process of political mobilization.

[61] *Pingguo Ribao (Apple Daily)*, August 17, 2014, in https://hk.news.appledaily.com/local/daily/article/20140817/18834891 access date: April 25, 2018.

[62] Ibid.; see also *Ta Kung Pao*, August 15, 2014, in http://news.takungpao.com/hkol/politics/2014-08/2674167.html, access date: April 25, 2018.

[63] See the Alliance website, in https://www.sign4peacedemocracy.hk/index.php?r=index/index, access date: April 23, 2018.

Table 3.14 Mobilization activities of HKFFA

Activities	Year	Objectives
8.17 Peaceful Protest in Support of Universal Suffrage	August, 2014	1. Anti-Occupy Central Movement 2. Support Political Reform Package 3. Mobilize some 250,000 citizens, including 36,500 Fujianese, to participate the protest in the signature campaign
Signature campaign to return the road to general public, restore the order and protect the judiciary	October to November 2014	1. Anti-Occupy Central Movement 2. Support the Hong Kong police 3. Mobilize 6000 Fujianese to be the volunteers in the signature campaign 4. Collect 180,000 signatures from citizens
Signature campaign in support of political reform plan initiated by the HKSAR government	May to June 2015	1. Support political reform in Hong Kong 2. Oppose the filibustering tactics used by democrats in the Legislative Council 3. Voter registration as to mobilize voters for the elections held for District Councils and Legislative Council
HKFAA's District Council election mobilization meeting	November 2015	1. Support pro-establishment candidates in District Councils elections to be held on November 22, 2015 2. Mobilize 4000 Fujianese to be the volunteers in the election campaign
HKFAA and its affiliated groups held a mobilization meeting for the Legislative Council direct elections	2016	1. Support and endorse pro-Beijing candidates in Legislative Councils elections 2. Opposed filibustering tactics used by democrats in the Legislative Council 3. Opposed candidates who advocate "Hong Kong independence" in Legislative Council elections
Cheng Le[a] Clansman protest against Hong Kong's "independence"	December 2016	1. Oppose any action in support of "Hong Kong independence" 2. Support the interpretation of the Basic Law by China's National People's Congress on Article 104 of the Basic Law with regard to the provocative and improper oath-taking behavior of two legislators-elect, Yau Wai-ching and Baggio Leung 3. Support Hong Kong police's action to handle the Occupy Central Movement and the Mongkok riot
Celebration of the newly elected chief executive Carrie Lam	March 2017	1. Support the victory of Carrie Lam in the chief executive election

(continued)

Table 3.14 (continued)

Activities	Year	Objectives
Fund-raising campaign to support seven police officers who beat up Ken Tsang in the Occupy Central Movement	August 2017	1. Support seven police officers who were accused of attacking Ken Tsang Kin-Chiu, an activist in the Occupy Central Movement 2. Support the Hong Kong police to maintain law and order
Voter registration campaign in the Kowloon West	August 2017	1. Voter registration campaign was launched to mobilize voters and supporters for the Legislative Council's by-election to be held in March 2018.

Sources: Hong Kong Fujian Federation of Associations, *Newsletter of the Hong Kong Fujian Federation of Associations*, volume 33–54 (Hong Kong: Meijia Publishing Limited, 2014–2017)

ᵃCheng Le is a village in Fujian Province and this protest was mobilized by the Cheng Le Clansman Association

Table 3.15 Fujianese participation and anti-occupy interest groups

Interest Groups	Total number	Fujianese group number
Provincial, ethnic and clan groups	355	131
Cultural, recreational and arts groups	82	0
Sports and martial arts groups	37	0
Alumni groups	161	62 from Fujian + 11 from Fujianese groups in Southeast Asia
Medical and educational groups	71	6
Industrial and commercial groups	155	4
Labor unions	167	0
Women groups	57	0
Youth groups	65	1
Residential concern groups	352	0
Political groups	13	1
Religious groups	13	0
Total	1528	216

Source: The website of the Alliance for Peace and Democracy, in https://www.sign4peacedemocracy.hk/index.php?r=index/index, access date: April 23, 2018

Note: This Alliance was led by Robert Chow Yung, who was a former radio host of the Radio Television Hong Kong and who is regarded as a pro-Beijing activist

Conclusion

Like all other interest groups, the Fujianese interest groups lobby the government, utilize the mass media and have members with shared interests. They have become increasingly active in the political arena of the HKSAR. Their uniqueness in Hong Kong lies in their intimate relations with China's united front work, supporting the PRC government's policies toward Hong Kong and the HKSAR administration. The political participation of the leaders of Fujianese interest groups, especially their business elites and local politicians, in the high level of politics in Hong Kong and Beijing-HKSAR relations is prominent, including the Legislative Council elections, the election of the chief executive, the election of Hong Kong members to the National People's Congress and the appointment of Hong Kong members to the CPPCC. At the grassroots level of the HKSAR politics, Fujianese interest groups have become an electoral machine for candidates from pro-Beijing political forces, notably the DAB, to mobilize the Fujian *tongxiang* to vote for them. The alliance between Fujianese groups and PRC officials in the HKSAR is noticeable in the activities held by the HKFFA and its affiliated groups. As such, the active political participation of Fujianese groups in Hong Kong is undoubtedly a hallmark of the territory's political development, demonstrating the depth and breadth of China's united front work in the HKSAR. In other words, Fujianese interest groups have been playing a crucial role in China's united front work in the HKSAR, trying to win the hearts and minds of more Hong Kong people, supporting the policies of the HKSAR and PRC governments and shaping public opinion in the territory in favor of pro-Beijing political forces. They have become an indispensable intermediary between the "patriotic" Hong Kong people and the PRC, providing strong manpower and logistical support for pro-Beijing forces in local elections, and constituting an agent or a "transmission belt" between China's united front work and the people of Hong Kong.

CHAPTER 4

Inter-Union Rivalry Between Pro-Beijing Federation of Trade Unions and Pro-Democracy Confederation of Trade Unions

While the studies on the fragmentation of Hong Kong's trade unions have been numerous, few attempts have been made to examine the political rivalries between the pro-Beijing Federation of Trade Unions (FTU) and the pro-democracy Confederation of Trade Unions (CTU) in the HKSAR under the sovereignty of the PRC.[1] This chapter attempts to fill in the gap in the existing literature, especially as inter-union rivalry and struggle have become a hallmark in the study of trade union politics in many countries in Europe, Africa and Asia.[2]

[1] For example, please refer to Linda Butenhoff, *Social Movements and Political Reform in Hong Kong* (Westport, Connecticut: Praeger, 1999); Stephen Chiu Wing Kai, *Strikes in Hong Kong: A sociological study* (Hong Kong: University of Hong Kong, 1987); Stephen Chiu Wing Kai and David A. Levin, "Contestatory Unionism: Trade Unions in the Private Sector," in Stephen Chiu Wing Kai and Lui Tai Lok, eds., The Dynamics of Social Movement in Hong Kong (Hong Kong: Hong Kong University Press, 2000), pp. 91–138; and Ng Sekhong and Olivia Ip, "Labour and Society," in Cheng, Joseph Y. S., ed., *The Hong Kong Special Administrative Region in Its First Decade* (Hong Kong: City University of Hong Kong Press, 2007), pp. 443–493.

[2] For example, please refer to Kristina, Ahlen, "Swedish Collective Bargaining Under Pressure: Inter-Union Rivalry and Incomes Policies," *British Journal of Industrial Relations*, vol. 127, no. 3 (November 1989), pp. 330–370; Matti Pohjola, "Union Rivalry and Economic Growth: A Differential Game Approach," *Scandinavian Journal of Economics*, vol. 86, no. 3 (1984), pp. 365–370; Valeria Pulignano, "Union struggle and the crisis of industrial relations in Italy," *Capital & Class*, vol. 79 (2003), pp. 1–8; Agnes Akkerman, "Union Competition and Strikes: The Need for Analysis at the Sector Level," *Industrial and Labor Relations Review*, vol. 61, no. 4 (July 2008), pp. 445–459; Anjan Chakrabarti and

© The Author(s) 2019
S. S.-H. Lo et al., *China's New United Front Work in Hong Kong*,
https://doi.org/10.1007/978-981-13-8483-7_4

The FTU was set up in April 1948, while the CTU was established in September 1990. The FTU has been described as "an agent of the Chinese Communist Party"[3] and "a 'transmission belt'" with the function of not only nominating candidates to run for local elections but also winning the hearts and minds of the working-class members of Hong Kong.[4] On the other hand, the CTU has formed a coalition with "its social movement allies and the pro-democracy political parties," like the Democratic Party, and competed with the FTU over the issues of political reform and the rights of the working class.[5] Hence, given the different political ideologies of the pro-CCP FTU and that of the pro-democracy CTU, it is academically and practically worthwhile to examine their political rivalries in Hong Kong since July 1, 1997.

INTER-UNION RIVALRY, SOCIAL MOVEMENT UNIONISM AND TRIPARTISM

The literature on inter-union rivalry has several characteristics. First and foremost, union rivalry is seen as a negative phenomenon. In Sweden, the common objective of trade unionists and employers was to "restrain interunion wage rivalry and to promote structural change by squeezing

---

Anup Kumar Dhar, "Labour, Class and Economy: rethinking Trade Union Struggle," *Economic and Political Weekly* (May 31, 2008), pp. 73–81; Miguel Martinez Lucio and Heather Connolly, "Transformation and Continuities in Urban Struggles: Urban Politics, Trade Unions and Migration in Spain," *Urban Studies*, vol. 49, no. 3 (February 2012), pp. 669–684; Nick Bernards, "The International Labour Organization and African trade unions: tripartite fantasies and enduring struggles," *Review of African Political Economy*, vol. 44, no. 153 (2017), pp. 399–441; Shafiqul Islam, "Gender Difference: How Does It Affect Trade Union Struggle? A Qualitative Study of Female Workers of Bangladeshi RMG Industries," *Socioeconomica: The Scientific Journal for Theory and Practice of Socio-economic Development*, vol. 6, no. 12 (2017), pp. 165–178; and Axel West Pedersen; Jon M. Hippe; Anne Skevik Grodem; and Ole Beier Sorensen, "Trade unions and the politics of occupational pensions in Denmark and Norway," *Transfer*, vol. 24, no. 1 (2018), pp. 109–122.

[3] Benjamin Leung and Steven Chiu, *A Social History of Industrial Strikes and the Labor Movement in Hong Kong, 1946–1989* (Hong Kong: Social Sciences Research Center, University of Hong Kong, 1991).

[4] Ng Sek-hong and Olivia Ip, "Labour and Society," in Cheng, Joseph Y. S., ed., *The Hong Kong Special Administrative Region in Its First Decade* (Hong Kong: City University of Hong Kong Press, 2007), pp. 443–493.

[5] Ming Chan, "Hong Kong Workers Towards 1997: Unionization, Labor Activism and Political Participation under the China Factor," *Australian Journal of Politics and History*, vol. 47, no. 1 (2001), pp. 61–84.

profits."[6] In Finland, union rivalry was seen as undermining "dynamic efficiency" of the economy.[7] Second, with the influx of migrants into some European states, union rivalry has taken the form of "community unionism," which refers to the phenomenon in which trade unions have to reach out to the immigrant constituencies, offer various services, recruit them and augment the public space after a certain period of authoritarianism. In Spain, trade unions developed a network of information offices and centers throughout the main Spanish cities during the early 2000s.[8] These centers provide a whole range of information services pertinent to employment, citizenship, social rights and housing. This service-driven direction of Spanish unions could be seen in the Global South, including countries like Brazil and the Philippines, where labor centers provide a crucial channel of interest articulation by trade unions.[9] The proliferation of labor centers in the process of union rivalry has implications for the HKSAR, because the FTU also expanded its membership and services in the 2000s by setting up various service centers to win the hearts and minds of new immigrants from the PRC.

Another feature of union rivalry is the debate over policy issues, ranging from occupational pensions to collective bargaining. In Norway and Denmark, trade unions in the 1990s actively promoted occupational pensions, although the scope of pensions, the degrees of risk sharing and the modes of governance differed from one place to another.[10] Furthermore, some scholars have found that strike incidence is higher where two or more trade unions bargain with an employer, but others have added that, under this multi-unionism, unions must make use of strikes to attract

---

[6] Kristina Ahlen, "Swedish Collective Bargaining Under Pressure: Inter-Union Rivalry and Incomes Policies," *British Journal of Industrial Relations*, vol. 127, no. 3 (November 1989), p. 330.

[7] Matti Pohjola, "Union Rivalry and Economic Growth: A Differential Game Approach," *Scandinavian Journal of Economics*, vol. 86, no. 3 (1984), p. 365.

[8] Ibid., p. 679.

[9] Kim Scipes, "Social Movement Unionism or Social Justice Unionism? Disentangling Theoretical Confusion within the Global Labor Movement," *Class, Race and Corporate Power*, vol. 2, no. 3 (2014), https://doi.org/10.25148/CRCP.2.3.16092119, in http://digitalcommons.fiu.edu/classracecorporatepower/vol2/iss3/9, access date: May 2, 2018.

[10] Axel West Pedersen; Jon M. Hippe; Anne Skevik Grodem; and Ole Beier Sorensen, "Trade unions and the politics of occupational pensions in Denmark and Norway," *Transfer*, vol. 24, no. 1 (2018), pp. 109–122.

more members and compete with each other by making more bargaining demands.[11]

The strategies of inter-union rivalry are diversified. In South Africa, for example, "social movement trade unionism" could be seen as trade unions forming alliances with community groups and political organizations in their workplace struggles.[12] If labor alone cannot push for the democratization of the workplace, then an alliance with other social movements is necessary.[13] Other scholars studying social movement unionism have found that trade union politics are intertwined with the activities of interest groups, political advocacy, students' organizations and residents' associations.[14] In Hong Kong, the CTU was regarded as utilizing the politics of social movement unionism during the dockworkers' strike from March 28 to May 6, 2013.[15]

Social movement unionism is described as an action in collaboration with community organizations to oppose union organizational functions, such as member representation.[16] The union alliance with community groups is strategic, protecting members' interests and enhancing the union capacity for mobilization. Unions with diverse and movement-oriented leaderships are more likely to campaign for social policies that affect workers beyond the represented workplace. Furthermore, by coping with the

---

[11] Agnes Akkerman, "Union Competition and Strikes: The Need for Analysis at the Sector Level," *Industrial and Labor Relations Review*, vol. 61, no. 4 (July 2008), p. 445.

[12] Tyanai Masiya, "Social Movement Trade Unionism: Case of the Congress of South African Trade Unions," Politikon, vol. 41, no. 3 (2014), p. 445.

[13] P. Waterman, "Social-movement Unionism: A New Model for a New World," no. 110 (The Hague Institute for Social Studies Working Paper Series, 1991).

[14] Frege Carola; Edmund Heery; and Lowell Turner, "The New Solidarity Trade Union Coalition-Building in Five Countries," in Frege Carola and John, Kelly, eds., *Varieties of Unionism: Strategies for Union Revitalization in a Globalizing Economy* (Oxford: Oxford University Press, 2004), pp. 137–158.

[15] Chris Chan King-chi; Sophia Chan Shuk-ying; and Lynn Tang, "Reflecting on Social Movement Unionism in Hong Kong: The Case of the Dockworkers' Strike in 2013," *Journal of Contemporary Asia*, vol. 49, issue 1 (2019), pp. 54–77, https://doi.org/10.1080/00472336.2018.1448429, in https://doi.org/10.1080/00472336.2018.1448429, access date: May 2, 2018.

[16] C. Engeman, "Social movement unionism in practice: organizational dimensions of union mobilization in the Los Angeles immigrant rights marches Social movement unionism in practice: organizational dimensions of union mobilization in the Los Angeles immigrant rights marches," *Work, employment and society*, vol. 29, no. 3 (2015), pp. 444–461.

rights of immigrants and other residents, unions can revitalize themselves and position well for future battles over workers' representation, contract negotiation and social policies.[17] The European approach to social movement unionism adopts a sociological standpoint in enhancing individual identity as group members are pursing post-industrial or post-materialist objectives. This approach argues that contemporary social movements are anti-hierarchical and non-ideological in the sense that they reject liberal, socialist or conservative visions of a good society for all.[18] Unions are now shifting their strategic orientation and promoting a new social movement unionism. Social movement unionism aims at organizing the unorganized, mobilizing the rank-and-file members, taking political action to consolidate union influence, reforming the labor laws to protect workers and changing the institutions of industrial relations.[19]

On the other hand, some unions opt for a more moderate strategy in their struggles. In Australia, the rapid downturn of the Australian steel industry in the early 1980s forced the unions to call for an integrated tripartite approach to deal with industrial actions and redundancy cases, leading to a gradual decline in strike levels and an improvement in industrial relations.[20] In Britain, the tripartism formula (government, business and trade unions) that involves inter-group cooperation in some policy areas may trigger conflicts between different classes.[21] In the United States, partnerships between the government, civic actors and worker centers can reach agreements on how to resolve difficult issues, accepting "dynamic tensions" in their relationships but injecting the elements of accountability and timely follow-up actions on all sides.[22] The International Labour

---

[17] Ibid.

[18] A. Vandenberg, "Social-movement Unionism in Theory and in Sweden," *Social Movement Studies*, vol. 5, no. 2 (2006), pp. 171–191.

[19] L. Turner and R. W. Hurd, "Building social movement unionism: The transformation of the American labor movement," in L. Turner, H. C. Katz and R. W. Hurd, eds., *Rekindling the movement: Labor's quest for relevance in the twenty-first century* (Ithaca, NY: Cornell University Press, 2001), pp. 9–16.

[20] D. Kelly, "Towards Tripartism: Industrial Relations in the Steel Industry 1978 to 1987," *Journal of Industrial Relations*, vol. 30, no. 4 (1988), pp. 511–532.

[21] D. Marsh and W. Grant, "Tripartism: Reality or Myth?," *Government and Opposition*, vol. 12, no. 2 (1977), pp. 194–211.

[22] Janice Fine, "Solving the Problem from Hell: Tripartism as a Strategy for Addressing Labour Standards Non-Compliance in the United States," *Osgoode Hall Law Journal*, vol.

Organization (ILO) has promoted "tripartism" in Africa, supporting the idea of "cooperation and compromise between workers, employers, and the state."[23] This idea originated from a "conservative response to revolutionary pressures stemming from the growth of trade unionism."[24] Tripartism is "ultimately rooted in a normative preference for reformism, compromise, and consensus building over radical change or agonistic politics."[25] Clearly, the ideology of tripartism has paid little attention to power relations, political conflicts and those structural constraints on industrial relations. As this chapter will argue, the FTU after July 1, 1997, has shifted from social movement unionism to a champion of tripartism, an approach that is contrary to the constantly pro-democracy and anti-governmental position of the CTU.

This chapter will argue that both the FTU and CTU adopted a strategy of social movement unionism in Hong Kong under the British rule; nevertheless, a turning point came in 1997 when the FTU changed its strategy to support tripartism. Rather than supporting the collective bargaining bill initiated by the CTU, the FTU rejected it on political grounds and voted against it just prior to the handover of Hong Kong on July 1, 1997. Immediately after the sovereignty transfer, the FTU supported a move by the Provisional Legislative Council to repeal the collective bargaining legislation. This strategic change on the part of the FTU was due to its need to support the policies of the HKSAR government and the PRC policy toward the maintenance of social and political stability in Hong Kong. As such, the FTU's positional change has made it far more politically moderate than before, while simultaneously cooperating with the pro-Beijing political groups and party, notably the DAB, to compete with the CTU and pro-democracy candidates in local elections, including LegCo and District Council elections. Due to the ideological differences between the FTU, which is bound to be pro-Beijing and pro-government, and CTU, which is pro-democracy and more radical in outlook and actions, this two-line struggle will likely persist in the HKSAR in the years to come.

50, no. 4 (2013), pp. 813–844.
[23] Nick Bernards, "The International Labour Organization and African trade unions: tripartite fantasies and enduring struggles," *Review of African Political Economy*, vol. 44, no. 153 (2017), p. 401.
[24] Ibid.
[25] Ibid.

Trade Union Politics in Hong Kong Under British Rule

The FTU, formed in 1948, was composed of various trade unions that had been founded in Hong Kong back to the 1870s (see Table 4.1). By 1989, the largest affiliated unions in the FTU included the Motor Transport Workers General Union, Hong Kong Union of Chinese Workers in Western Style Employment and the Hong Kong Seamen's Union. While the number of trade unions affiliated with the FTU was only 22 in 1948, the number increased to 135 in 1998 and then to 251 in 2016 (Table 4.2). With a total membership of 422,093 in 2016, the FTU is the largest trade union in the HKSAR, compared with the 138,856 members of the CTU in the same year (Table 4.3b).

Hong Kong's labor unions were traditionally split between the pro-Beijing FTU and the pro-Taiwan or pro-Nationalist Trade Union Council (TUC).[26] Union rivalry reflected the political struggle between the PRC and the Republic of China on Taiwan.[27] As such, political fragmentation and factionalism of trade unions in Hong Kong weakened the labor movement as a whole.[28] The FTU was founded in April 1948, five months earlier than the establishment of the TUC.[29] Due to the fact that the Hong Kong government under British sovereignty saw the leftwing FTU as a political and an ideological enemy, the FTU was bound to adopt a confrontational approach to dealing with the interests of the working class, including the use of strikes, lockouts and violent clashes, especially during the 1967 riots in which many leftists were imprisoned and suppressed by the colonial police.[30] In the early 1950s, the FTU participated in a series of strikes, including the electric car's driver strike and the milk company's

---

[26] Linda Butenhoff, *Social Movements and Political Reform in Hong Kong* (Westport, Connecticut: Praeger, 1999), p. 52. See also Joe England and John Rear, *Chinese Labour under British Rule: A critical study of labour relations and law in Hong Kong* (Hong Kong: Oxford University Press, 1975), p. 90.

[27] Butenhoff, *Social Movements and Political Reform in Hong Kong*, p. 53.

[28] Joe England, *Industrial Relations and Law in Hong Kong* (2nd ed.) (Hong Kong: Oxford University Press, 1989), p. 120. Also see Jeff Loo, "Workers as interest groups: Are they fragmented or powerless?," in Sonny Shiu-hing Lo, eds. *Interest Groups and the New Democracy Movement in Hong Kong* (London: Routledge, 2018), pp. 102–114.

[29] Chow Yick. *A History of the Struggles of Hong Kong Leftists* (in Chinese) (Hong Kong: Lee Man, 2002), p. 5.

[30] Ibid., p. 10 and pp. 223–260.

Table 4.1 Labor Unions affiliated with the Federation of Trade Unions

Year	Name of trade union (year of registration)	Members in 1989
1871	Hong Kong and Kowloon Sewing and Tailoring Trade Workers' Union (1949)	106
1874	Hong Kong and Kowloon Brick-laying Construction Trade workers' Union (1949)	2038
1896	Hong Kong and Kowloon Dockyards & Wharves Carpenters General Union (1949)	332
1917	Hong Kong and Kowloon European-Style Tailors Union	630
1919	Hong Kong and Kowloon Carpenters General Union	2821
	Hong Kong and Kowloon Painters General Union	2427
	Hong Kong and Kowloon Machine-Sewing Workers Union (1949)	834
1920	Logistics Cargo Supervisors Association	2261
	Motor Transport Workers General Union (1949)	26,801
	Hong Kong Tramway Workers Union	372
	Hong Kong and Kowloon Leather Trade Workers Union	2012
	Hong Kong and Kowloon Moulding and Glass Trade Workers' Union	503
	Hong Kong and Kowloon Ship Paint-Scrapers Painters Union	224
1921	Hong Kong Seamen's Union (1949)	13,028
	Small Craft Workers Union (1949)	2941
	Hong Kong Union of Chinese Workers in Western Style Employment	17,202
	Hong Kong and Kowloon Western-Styled Lady Dress Makers Guild	758
	Hong Kong and Kowloon Rattan Trade and Bamboo Wares Workers' General Union (1949)	941
1928	Hong Kong government Water-Works Chinese Employees Union	1331
1931	Hong Kong Electric Holdings Limited Workers Union	551
1937	Hong Kong Printing Industry Workers Union (1985)	6737
1939	Garment-Making Trade Workers Union	4830
1940	Government, Armed Forces and Hospitals Chinese Workers Union	4479
1946	Dairy Products, Beverage and Food Industries Employees Union	1435
	Bakery, Confectionery and Cake Trade workers Union (1949)	502
	Pacific Century Cyber Works Employees General Union (Hong Kong Telephone Co. Ltd. Chinese Workers Union)	1128
	Hong Kong and China Gas co. Ltd. Chinese employees Association	755
	Hong Kong and Kowloon Tobacco Trade Workers General Union	350
	Hong Kong and Kowloon Bamboo Scaffolding Workers Union	288
	Hong Kong and Kowloon Ship-building Trade Workers Union (1968)	630
	Hong Kong and Kowloon Coppersmiths General Union	147
	Hong Kong Department Stores and Commercial Staff General Union	5292

(continued)

Table 4.1 (continued)

Year	Name of trade union (year of registration)	Members in 1989
1947	Hong Kong Transportation, Decoration & Cleaning workers General Union (1949)	628
	Hong Kong Live Pig and Meat Trade Workers Union	325
	Hong Kong Plumbing General Union (1949)	647
	Hong Kong and Kowloon Spinning, weaving Dyeing Trade Workers General Union	10,043
	Hong Kong and Kowloon Rubber & Plastic workers General Union	3856
1948	Hong Kong and Kowloon Egg Workers Union	351
	Lighter and Cargo-Boat Transportation Workers Union	863
	Hong Kong Wooden Box Workers Union	239
	Hong Kong Postal Workers Union	1147
	China Light and Power Co. Ltd. Chinese Employees Union	1043
	Kowloon Live Pig Meat Trade employees Union	390
	Hong Kong and Kowloon Metal Industry Workers General Union (1949)	4409
	Hong Kong Chinese Clerks Association	991

Sources: Hong Kong Federation of Trade Unions, *Pass the Torch with Glorious Years: Collective Memories of Hong Kong Labourers, the Historical Photos of the Federation of Trade Unions, 1948–2008* (Hong Kong: Hong Kong Federation of Trade Unions, 2008), pp. 264–270, and Registry of Trade Unions, *Annual Statistical Report of Trade Unions in Hong Kong, 1989* (Hong Kong: Registry of Trade Unions, Labour Department, 1990)

Table 4.2 Summary of FTU's membership and number of labor unions, 1948–2016

Year	Number of members	Number of labor unions
1948	20,000	22
1958	127,000	57
1968	96,062	65
1978	210,650	63
1988	173,956	81
1998	280,039	135
2008	323,107	178
2016	422,903	251[a]

Sources: Hong Kong Federation of Trade Unions, *The Hong Kong Federation of Trade Unions Walk with You: 65th Anniversary History Collections* (Hong Kong: Chong Hwa Book Company, 2013), p. 280 and Registry of Trade Unions, *Annual Statistical Report of Trade Unions in Hong Kong, 2016* (Hong Kong: Registry of Trade Unions, The Labour Department of the HKSAR Government, 2017)

[a]Note: 251 unions included 190 affiliated unions and 61 associated unions. All the number of labor unions included affiliated and associated trade unions. The data of 2017 and 2018 are unknown as the FTU most recent publications have not stated the exact figures, in http://www.ftu.org.hk/m/zh-hant/magazine?id=39#magazine/ and http://www.ftu.org.hk/zh-hant/about?id=12, access date: April 10, 2018

Table 4.3 Unions and Membership of Hong Kong with the Hong Kong Federation of Trade Unions and the Hong Kong and Kowloon Trade Unions Council Affiliated Membership, 1967–1983

	Total unions		FTU		TUC	
Year	Members	Unions	Members	Unions	Members	Unions
1967	165,579	244	95,408	64	28,650	63
1968	169,676	254	96,062	65	32,604	68
1969	175,245	257	100,180	65	35,149	71
1970	196,299	272	114,387	66	36,280	93
1971	221,619	276	126,408	66	36,005	91
1972	251,729	280	145,521	66	37,817	87
1973	295,735	283	170,047	66	35,391	83
1974	317,041	293	184,440	67	32,099	85
1975	361,458	302	211,868	67	33,391	84
1976	388,077	311	224,544	67	33,462	84
1977	404,325	313	228,313	67	33,749	77
1978	399,995	327	214,848	67	33,471	76
1979	399,392	340	196,543	66	36,914	74
1980	384,282	357	182,601	66	36,723	71
1981	345,156	366	169,647	69	35,927	70
1982	351,525	378	171,073	71	35,521	70
1983	352,306	382	167,933	71	34,564	70

Sources: Ng Sek-hong, *Aspects of Labour Iusses* (Hong Kong: Wide Angle Press, 1984), p. 74

worker strike, forcing the employers to opt for arbitration.[31] At the same time, the Hong Kong government deported some leftwing unionists back to mainland China, keeping a tight lid on the assertiveness of leftwing trade unions.[32] The FTU from the 1950s to the 1970s allied with pro-Beijing activist groups in the educational, women and youth sectors to fight for the interests of the working class.[33] During the May 1967 riot in support of the mainland Maoists in Hong Kong, the FTU formed a 101-member "struggle committee against the persecution from the Hong Kong British," demanding that "patriotic comrades" should be released from prisons, that all repressive measures be stopped, that the government should apologize to victims who participated in the protests of a plastic factory and who were beaten up by the police and that no such repressive

[31] Ibid., pp. 52–58.
[32] Ibid., pp. 55–56.
[33] Ibid., p. 42.

event would reoccur.[34] The FTU's anti-colonial and anti-British positions could be clearly seen. From July to August 1967, the Hong Kong police arrested some 1500 leftists, including many trade unionists.[35] After the 1967 riot, the FTU gradually refocused on its union work and expanded its memberships; the number of unions slightly increased from 65 in 1969 to 71 in 1983, but the members rose from 100,180 to 167,933 during the same period (Table 4.3). On the contrary, the pro-Taiwan TUC was relatively stagnant, slightly decreasing the number of unions from 71 in 1969 to 70 in 1983, while seeing a drop of membership from 35,149 to 34,564 during the same period. Hence, the aftermath of the 1967 riot triggered the reorganization and growth of the FTU, while the TUC did not make any progress from the late 1960s to the early 1980s.

THE TRANSFORMATIONS OF FEDERATION OF TRADE UNIONS

After 1984, when Britain and China signed the joint declaration to prepare for Hong Kong's sovereignty transfer on July 1, 1997, the FTU position gradually changed from anti-colonial and anti-British to a partnership with the departing colonial administration. In 1981, the FTU participated actively in the Labour Advisory Board, a consultative body with representatives from the government, employers and employees.[36] It also promoted the revisions of existing labor ordinance to protect the interests of workers. Due to the FTU's gradual shift to support tripartism, it was no longer the target of political suppression by the Hong Kong British government. Most importantly, by 1997, the FTU position was drastically changed to one that would "support," "cooperate," "scrutinize" and "criticize" the HKSAR government, adopting the role of a loyal opposition.[37] This new position meant that the FTU abandoned its previous approach of adopting social movement unionism and that it would work with the HKSAR government under the principle of tripartism. The transfer of Hong Kong's sovereignty in 1997 was a watershed in the FTU's political position.

---

[34] Ibid., pp. 232–233.
[35] Ibid., p. 278.
[36] Federation of Trade Unions. *Federation of Trade Unions Walking with You: 65th Anniversary of Historical Essays* (in Chinese) (Hong Kong: Federation of Trade Unions, 2013), p. 79.
[37] Ibid.

Table 4.4 demonstrates that the FTU unions and membership continued to increase from 1984 to 2016, increasing its unions from 73 in 1984 to 190 in 2016, and expanding its members from 166,461 to 422,903 during the same period. The CTU, which was formally formed in 1990 but had some independent unions grouping together from 1984 to 1989, witnessed an increase of unions from 21 in 1990 to 80 in 2016, and an expansion of members from 74,038 to 138,856 during the same period. The pro-Taiwan TUC suffered from a gradual decline with a membership of 35,535 in 1984 to just 6724 in 2016. The independent Federation of Trade Unions (FTU), which was formed in 1984, envisaged a gradual increase of its unions and memberships from 11 and 11,889, respectively, in 1984 to 89 and 57,606 in 2016. The Federation of Hong Kong and Kowloon Labour Union (FLU) began to participate in electoral politics in 1994, when its representative Wong Kam-kuen was elected as a District Board member in Shumshuipo district, and then its leader Lee Kai-ming was elected as a legislator in 1995.[38] Politically, the FLU maintains friendly relations with the PRC government by sending its delegation to the mainland on May 1 annually.[39] As with the FTU, the FLU supports tripartism; from 1984 to now, each of the FLU, FTU and TUC got one representative in the Labour Advisory Board. The moderate position of FLU is its hallmark, being friendly to the PRC and supportive of tripartism. Hence, the FLU is regarded as pro-Beijing and pro-government, as with the FTU.

Table 4.5 sums up the largest four trade unions in Hong Kong, including their platform and ideology. The FTU emphasizes patriotism, solidarity and participation and is explicitly pro-Beijing. Although the FTU claims to support the labor movement, it is by no means supportive of strikes and radical action in the HKSAR after 1997 due to the pro-government stance. The FLU is pro-government and implicitly pro-Beijing, while the CTU is supportive of democracy and radical actions. The TUC remains pro-Taiwan but its influence has been declining rapidly.

The pattern of FTU activities from 1945 to 2008 demonstrated that it changed from social movement unionism to a moderate political position. Figure 4.1 shows that labor conflicts, lockouts and struggles were commonplace for the FTU from 1946 to 1979, but then a more moderate form of protests, demonstrations and petitions could be seen from the

---

[38] Federation of Labor Unions. *30th Anniversary of the Federation of Labor Unions* (in Chinese) (Hong Kong: Federation of Labor Unions, 2014).

[39] Ibid.

Table 4.4 Trade unions in Hong Kong, 1984–2016

Year	Members/unions	FTU	FLU	CTU	TUC	Others
1984	357,764(384)	166,461(73)	11,889(11)	45,380(14)[a]	35,535(71)	103,853(220)
1985	393,298(437)	167,832(70)	13,214(13)	48,084(18)[a]	35,116(70)	108,572(225)
1986	392,463(448)	169,822(72)	12,836(13)	49,265(19)[a]	31,477(68)	110,335(231)
1987	381,685(415)	168,550(/78)	14,329(17)	52,728(20)[a]	28,827(69)	123,799(236)
1988	416,136(430)	173,956(81)	13,958(17)	57,564(20)[a]	17,835(71)	158,937(245)
1989	437,939(439)	173,820(81)	26,630(18)	62,051(21)[a]	17,176(70)	163,594(253)
1990	468,746(446)	175,746(82)	24,152(18)	74,038(21)	30,693(70)	169,377(266)
1991	486,961(469)	181,498(84)	23,824(18)	70,524(24)	30,648(69)	185,492(279)
1992	525,538(481)	192,019(87)	21,008(18)	75,212(27)	30,769(69)	211,436(285)
1993	543,800(491)	199,862(89)	18,600(18)	78,498(28)	30,714(66)	221,158(295)
1994	562,285(506)	205,916(91)	16,680(19)	79,537(28)	31,143(65)	234,138(308)
1995	591,181(522)	222,448(97)	19,790(24)	81,686(29)	29,216(68)	243,209(309)
1996	624,327(535)	245,679(113)	21,746(31)	88,252(39)	28,212(66)	247,371(292)
1997	647,908(538)	260,118(118)	22,468(38)	91,245(40)	26,575(61)	254,505(288)
1998	657,019(558)	258,186(118)	23,902(41)	93,944(42)	25,438(64)	260,505(298)
1999	674,433(583)	278,063(130)	28,946(44)	983,79(47)	22,696(57)	251,465(310)
2000	673,375(594)	286,904(136)	28,530(45)	100,115(47)	19,520(55)	243,397(316)
2001	671,076(610)	287,233(143)	28,517(47)	10,6309(52)	17,983(52)	236,219(321)
2002	676,534(622)	296,516(147)	29,491(49)	113,331(56)	18,769(47)	223,635(328)
2003	668,532(644)	289,741(149)	29,818(51)	114,137(57)	18,385(40)	221,814(252)
2004	658,488(659)	285,403(154)	30,553(52)	113,324(61)	19,971(39)	214,711(358)
2005	655,159(686)	282,202(158)	31,209(55)	113,781(68)	19,260(36)	214,760(375)
2006	668,034(715)	292,671(174)	32,258(57)	117,137(73)	19,622(33)	212,651(384)
2007	686,371(731)	311,834(176)	34,125(62)	116,669(76)	19,264(30)	210,894(393)
2008	708,953(752)	335,945(178)	34,886(64)	117,650(77)	19,180(32)	207,981(407)
2009	730,519(768)	350,252(179)	36,038(68)	119,868(79)	18,233(34)	213,522(415)

(*continued*)

Table 4.4 (continued)

Year	Members/unions	FTU	FLU	CTU	TUC	Others
2010	770,890(780)	368,740(180)	41,587(70)	122,605(79)	24,519(33)	220,953(425)
2011	792,887(788)	380,009(183)	42,062(72)	126,265(80)	24,232(32)	228,081(428)
2012	813,891(800)	396,110(184)	44,052(74)	129,223(80)	24,082(28)	228,423(441)
2013	831,940(809)	405,516(184)	48,708(77)	133,038(81)	19,792(28)	233,129(446)
2014	826,729(819)	403,235(187)	51,662(85)	134,252(81)	7543(27)	238,479(446)
2015	869,528(821)	415,145(189)	53,333(87)	139,056(81)	7130(27)	263,401(444)
2016	888,466(828)	422,903(190)	57,606(89)	138,856(80)	6724(27)	270,533(449)

Sources: Ng Sek-hong *Aspects of Labour Issues* (Hong Kong; Wide Angle Press, 1984), p. 74 and Registry of Trade Unions, *Annual Statistical Report of Trade Unions in Hong Kong*, from 1984 to 2016 (Hong Kong: Registry of Trade Unions, Labour Department of the HKSAR Government, from 1984 to 2016)

Note: The number in brackets stands for the number of unions

[a]These numbers came from those unions affiliated with the Christian Industrial Committee, which was the predecessor of the CTU. The membership data of the FLU between 1984 and 1994 were not officially available and their memberships are found out by referring to the memberships of their affiliated groups and unions

Table 4.5 The largest four trade unions in Hong Kong: platform and ideology

Trade unions	Platform	Ideology
Hong Kong Federation of Trade Unions (FTU)	Patriotism, solidarity, rights, benefits, participation Promoting the labor movement, developing workers organizations, expanding and consolidating Hong Kong employees' solidarity	Explicitly pro-Beijing and pro-government
Federation of Hong Kong and Kowloon Labour Union (FLU)	Unite the working class, fight for reasonable rights, participate in democratic reforms and promote social prosperity	Pro-establishment and implicitly pro-Beijing
Hong Kong Confederation of Trade Unions (CTU)	Solidarity, dignity, justice, democracy	Pro-democracy Liberal and social democracy
Hong Kong and Kowloon Trades Union Council (TUC)	Strive for labor rights and liberal labor movement	Pro-Kuomintang (Taiwan)

Sources: From the websites of these four unions, in http://www.ftu.org.hk/en/about?id=12, http://www.hkflu.org.hk/fludata/fluintro.php, http://en.hkctu.org.hk/about-us/about-hkctu/, and https://www.facebook.com/pg/hktuc23845150/about/?ref=page_internal, and Regulations of Hong Kong Federation of Trade Unions, in http://www.ftu.org.hk/upload/page/12/photo/5a9621373ca64.pdf, access date: April 10, 2018

1980s onward. Furthermore, the FTU has paid more attention to political appointments made by the government to various consultative and advisory committees, and to electoral participation after the 1980s. Overall, the FTU changed from its action-oriented approach in the 1950s and 1960s to a drastically pro-establishment position since the 1980s. Organizationally, the FTU is like a quasi-political party with established committees dealing with membership, social affairs, women affairs, occupational safety, vocational training and rights and benefits (Fig. 4.2). Given the fact that many Hong Kong workers relocated to work in the mainland, the FTU set up a number of mainland consultation centers for them, including the service centers in Shenzhen, Guangzhou, Dongguan, Huizhou and Zhongshan.

Table 4.6 shows that the FTU is competing with the CTU for the support from the relatively large public-sector unions. The CTU succeeds in acquiring the support from the Professional Teachers' Union, while the FTU gets the support from the Government Employees Association. The FLU managed to obtain the support of Government Employees General

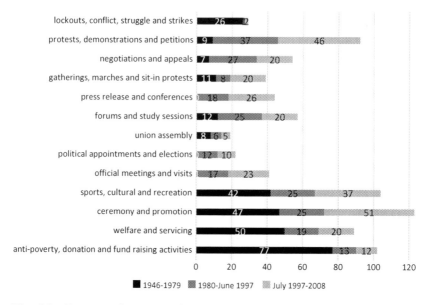

Fig. 4.1 Patterns of activities of the Federation of Trade Unions, 1945–2008. Source: Hong Kong Federation of Trade Unions (2008), *Passing the Torch with Glorious Years: Collective Memories of Hong Kong Labourers and the historical photos of the Federation of Trade Unions, 1948–2008*. Hong Kong: Xinhua Book Store

Union. Other civil servants' unions opt for neutrality and do not join either the pro-government/pro-Beijing FTU or the pro-democracy CTU, such as the Association of Hong Kong Nursing Staff, the Hong Kong Civil Servants General Union and the Government Disciplined Services General Union. Overall, Table 4.7 shows that 279 out of 379 civil servants' unions are not affiliated with FTU or CTU because many civil servants prefer to be at least apparently neutral.

Under the circumstances in which most civil servants wish to maintain their political neutrality, the FTU has been expanding its membership through the provision of services by its various centers at the grassroots level. Table 4.8 shows that the FTU centers have various functions, including the provision of medical services, the inculcation of patriotic attitude, the organization of cultural and sports activities, the provision of various skills-based training courses and the assistance of its members to

4 INTER-UNION RIVALRY BETWEEN PRO-BEIJING FEDERATION OF TRADE... 123

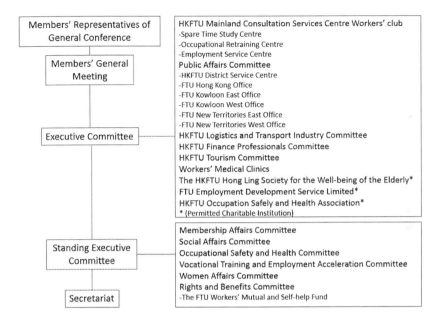

Fig. 4.2 The organization structure of the FTU. Sources: http://www.ftu.org.hk/en/about?id=13. *There are five mainland consultation services centers, location in Guangzhou, Shenzhen, Dongguan, Huizhou and Zhongshan, see the FTU website, in http://www.ftu.org.hk/en/participate?id=110, access date: April 28, 2018

find jobs and upgrade their knowledge. Through these centers, the personal data of the FTU members are easily obtained, thus providing the FTU with a powerful resource of political mobilization in election time. Since both the FTU and FLU are pro-Beijing, Fig. 4.3 shows that they both occupied about 12% of the memberships of unions in 2016, while the CTU merely got 3.6%. Overall, only 22.7% of the workforce participated in trade unions in 2016, reflecting the fact that many employees did and do not join trade unions. Hence, the FTU and CTU only compete against each other by focusing on the recruitment of existing and new unionized members. In spite of the relatively low degree of workforce participation in trade unions, the FTU stands out as the largest trade union in the HKSAR (Fig. 4.4).

Table 4.6 FTU, CTU and public-sector unions with more than 3000 members

Unions	Affiliated unions	Year of establishment	Membership
Hong Kong Professional Teachers' Union	CTU	1973	95,981
Hong Kong Chinese Civil Servants' Association	Independent	1949	68,284
Government Employees Association	FTU	1986	36,902
Association of Hong Kong Nursing Staff	Independent	1977	27,867
Hong Kong Civil Servants General Union	Independent	1978	14,512
Government Disciplined Services General Union	Independent	1998	10,506
HKSAR Government Employees General Union	FLU	2009	5959
Hong Kong Fire Services Department Staff General Association	Independent	1949	5737
Service Industry General Union	FTU	1985	5633
Hong Kong Public Medical Staff Association	FTU	2005	4057
Hospital Authority Staff Association	FTU	1992	3599
Hong Kong Public Doctors' Association	Independent	1990	3553
Hong Kong Fire Services Department Ambulancemen's Union	Independent	1970	3278

Sources: Registry of Trade Unions, *Annual Statistical Report of Trade Unions in Hong Kong, 2016* (Hong Kong: Registry of Trade Unions, Labour Department of the HKSAR Government, 2017)

Table 4.7 Civil servants' union membership

Unions	Number of unions	Membership
CTU	30	105,834
Joining both CTU and FLU	3	2411
FLU	25	17,631
FTU	38	70,011
TUC	2	80
Independent	279	212,535
Total	379	408,502

Sources: Registry of Trade Unions, *Annual Statistical Report of Trade Unions in Hong Kong, 2016.* Hong Kong: Registry of Trade Unions, Labour Department of the HKSAR Government, 2017)

Table 4.8 The Hong Kong-based service centers under the Federation of Trade Unions

Name	Year of formation	Functions
Workers' Children School	1946	Cultivating the sentiment of loving the country and loving Hong Kong, and producing the attitudes of activeness, sincerity, truth and innovation.
Workers' Medical Clinics	1950	Providing high quality and fair-priced medical services, including Chinese and Western medical clinics, dental clinics and X-ray and laboratory services.
Workers' Club	1964	Sponsoring various diversified activities in sports, culture and entertainment.
Spare Time Study Centre	1980	Assisting citizens to obtain professional qualifications by providing a diversity of programs including occupational, leisure and other training courses.
Employment Service Centre	1992	Providing job vacancy information to members and employees from various fields and referring suitable employees to employers, together with employment skills training and labor-related counseling services.
Occupational Retraining Centre	1993	Providing diversified occupational training to citizens, including those who are unemployed, housewives and the youths, thus helping them to re-integrate into the labor market.
Employment Development Service	2007	Endeavors in enhancing the competitiveness of local manpower and offering a practical training platform for those who have completed the training programs.

Source: The Federation of Trade Unions website, in http://www.ftu.org.hk/en/participate?id=98, access date: April 12, 2018

ELECTORAL PARTICIPATION AND COMPETITION

Since 1985, the FTU has been participating in politics through the LegCo functional constituency. The FTU had a representative, Tam Yiu-chung, being automatically elected to the LegCo from 1985 to 1991 (Table 4.9), while the TUC's Pang Chun-hoi had a similar experience during the same period. From 1995 to 2000, the FLU began to have a representative elected to the LegCo until the present. It is noteworthy that the pro-Taiwan TUC lost its influence in the LegCo starting from 2004 onward. From 2008 to the present, both the representatives from FTU and FLU have been automatically elected to the LegCo, reflecting the phenomenon of a political monopoly. The decline of the pro-Taiwan TUC and its replace-

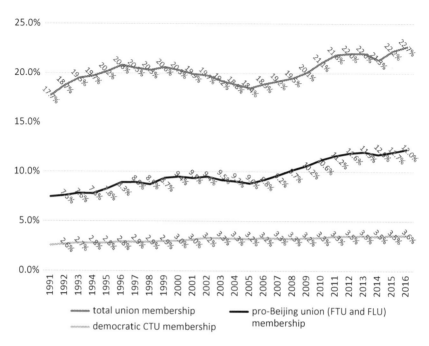

Fig. 4.3 Workforce participation in trade unions, 1990–2016. Sources: Registry of Trade Unions, *Annual Statistical Report of Trade Unions in Hong Kong*, from 1991 to 2016 (Hong Kong: Registry of Trade Unions, Labour Department), and Hong Kong Government, *Hong Kong Annual Report*, from 1990 to 2016, Hong Kong: Hong Kong Government

ment by the pro-Beijing FLU are politically significant, for union politics within the legislature is now dominated by the pro-Beijing faction.

Table 4.10 shows that the FTU has formed an alliance with the pro-Beijing DAB since the 1998 LegCo direct elections. In the 1998 and 2000 LegCo direct elections, the FTU and DAB formed a strategic alliance and got two and three candidates to be directly elected, respectively. The alliance continued until 2016, when the FTU itself nominated three candidates to run in the direct elections. Because the FTU remains the largest trade union in the HKSAR, the pro-Beijing and pro-establishment forces have been garnering its support to campaign for their like-minded candidates in LegCo's direct elections, constituting an effective check and balance against the pro-democracy camp. The pro-democracy camp's

4 INTER-UNION RIVALRY BETWEEN PRO-BEIJING FEDERATION OF TRADE... 127

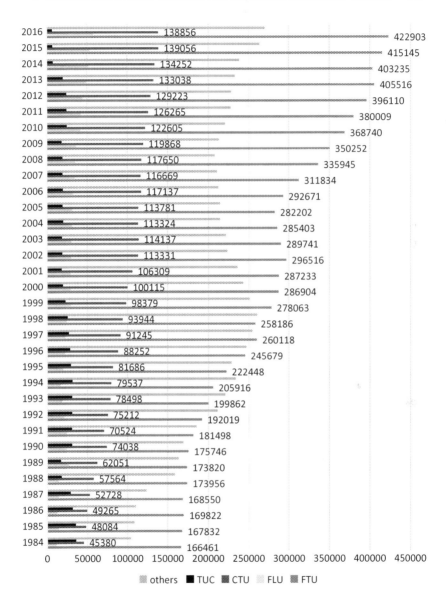

Fig. 4.4 Memberships of different trade unions, 1984–2016. Sources: Registry of Trade Unions, *Annual Statistical Report of Trade Unions in Hong Kong*, from 1984 to 2016 (Hong Kong: Registry of Trade Unions, Labour Department of the HKSAR Government, from 1984 to 2016)

Table 4.9 Election results of the Legislative Council's labor functional constituency, 1985–2016

Year	Hong Kong Federation of Trade Unions (FTU)		Federation of Hong Kong and Kowloon Labour Unions (FLU)		Hong Kong and Kowloon Trade Unions Council (TUC)		Independent workers' representatives[a]	
1985	Tam Yiu-chung	AE	No representative		Pang Chun-hoi	AE	No representative	
1988	Tam Yiu-chung	AE	No representative		Pang Chun-hoi	AE	No representative	
1991	Tam Yiu-chung	AE	No representative		Pang Chun-hoi	AE	No representative	
1995	Cheng Yiu-tong	684	Lee Kai-ming	533	Lee Kwok-keung	262	John Luk Woon-cheung	109
1998	Chan Wing-chan Chan Kwok-keung	212 204	Lee Kai-ming	212	Chan Yun-che	99	Ng Yat-wha	49
2000	Chan Kwok-keung Leung Fu-wah	226 259	Li Fung-ying	283	Leung Suet-fong	102	No representative	
2004	Kwong Chi-kin Wong Kwok-hing	288 278	Li Fung-ying	322	No representative		Chan Kwok-keung	105
2008	Ip Wai-ming Pan Pey-chyon	AE	Li Fung-ying	AE	No representative		No representative	
2012	Kwok Wai-keung Bill Tang Ka-bill	AE	Poon Siu-ping	AE	No representative		No representative	
2016	Ho Kai-ming Luk Chung-hung	AE	Poon Siu-ping	AE	No representative		No representative	

Sources: *The Reports of the Legislative Council Election* in 1998, 2000, 2004, 2008, 2012 and 2106, the Website of Electoral Affairs Commission, in https://www.eac.gov.hk/en/legco/lce.htm, access date: April 9, 2018; and *Election Information Compilation of Hong Kong* (Hong Kong: The Hong Kong Institute of Asia-Pacific Studies, The Chinese University of Hong Kong, 1995, 1996, 2001, 2005 and 2015)

Note: AE stands for Automatically elected

[a]Luk and Ng represented independent civil service unions, while Chan was a former FTU member being elected in 1998 and 2000, but he ran independently in 2004

Table 4.10 The FTU's participation results in Legislative Council Direct Elections, 1998–2016

Total seats Party/force	1998 (20 seats)	2000 (24 seats)	2004 (30 seats)	2008 (30 seats)	2012 (35 seats)	2016 (35 seats)
DAB seats	5 (25.1%)	8 (29.4%)	8 (22.6%)	7 (22.8%)	9 (19.9%)	7 (16.4%)
DAB votes	373,428	391,718	402,420	347,373	366,140	361,617
DAB alone	3(12.9%) 191,545	4(13.6%) 181,268	6(16.1%) 287,169	5(16.6%) 255,336	8(17.5%) 322,644	7(16.4%) 361,617
FTU & DAB alliance	2 (12.2%) 181,883	3(15.8%) 210,450	2(6.5%) 115,251	2(6.0%) 92,037	1(2.4%) 43,496	No alliance
FTU alone	No candidate	No candidate	1(3.0%) 52,565	2(5.7%) 86,311	3(7.0%) 127,857	3(7.8%) 169,854
Pro-establishment seats	5(30.2%)	8(34.6%)	12(37.0%)	11(39.5%)	17(39.7%)	16(41.7%)
Pro-establishment votes	449,668	461,048	660,052	602,468	730,363	918,278
CTU seats	3(10.7%)	3(9.4%)	2(5%)	1(3.5%)	3(6%)	1(4.6%)
CTU votes	159,785	125,742	89,185	52,919	112,140	101,863
Pro-democracy seats	15(66.2%)	16(60.0%)	18(61.4%)	19(59.2%)	18(56.4%)	19(54.8%)
Pro-democracy votes	979,199	799,240	1,096,272	901,707	1,036,998	1,206,420
Total votes that were cast by voters	1,489,705	1,331,080	1,784,131	1,524,249	1,838,722	2,202,283

Sources: *Report on the Legislative Council Election*, 1998, 2000, 2004, 2008, 2012 and 2016, downloaded from the website of Electoral Affairs Commission, in https://www.eac.gov.hk/, access date: April 10, 2018; and *Election Information Compilation of Hong Kong* (Hong Kong Institute of Asia-Pacific Studies, The Chinese University of Hong Kong, 1996, 2001, 2005 and 2015)

Note: The Legislative Council was partly directly elected from 33% with 20 directly elected seats in 1998, to 50% with 30 directly elected seats in 2004, and to 50% with 35 directly elected seats in 2012. The pro-establishment camp includes the DAB, and other pro-Beijing and pro-government groups, such as the Liberal Party and Hong Kong Progressive Alliance in 1998, the New Forum in 2000, the Federations of Trade Unions in 2008, the New People's Party in 2012

share of directly elected seats has declined since 1998, while the pro-Beijing and pro-government camp's share has increased, partly because of the mobilization ability of the FTU. The CTU had its representative Lau Chin-shek directly elected to the LegCo in 1991 and he joined the United Democrats of Hong Kong at that time. Lau defeated Chan Yuen-han of the FTU, signaling the first electoral rivalry between CTU and FTU. In

Table 4.11 Election Results of the pro-Beijing Candidates in District Council Functional Constituency under Legislative Council elections, 2012 and 2016

Name (Party)	Votes gained	Shares of popular votes (%)
Starry Lee Wai-king (DAB, elected)	277,143	17.41
Lau Kong-wah (DAB, defeated)	199,732	12.55
Chan Yuen-han (FTU, elected)	246,196	15.47
Total votes in 2012	723,071	45.42
Starry Lee Wai-king (DAB, elected)	304,222	15.93
Holden Chow Ho-ding (DAB, elected)	264,339	13.84
Wong Kwok-hing (FTU, defeated)	233,236	12.21
Total votes in 2016	803,797	41.98

Source: The votes were tabulated from the official website of the Electoral Affairs Commission, in https://www.eac.gov.hk/en/legco/2012lce_report.htm, and Report on the 2016 Legislative Council Election, in https://www.eac.gov.hk/en/legco/2016lce_report.htm, access date: April 9, 2018

1995, the CTU secretary general Lee Cheuk-yan was also directly elected to the LegCo. Lee held his LegCo seat until 2016 when he was defeated. While the CTU is now fighting for the interest of workers outside the existing political institutions, the FTU is lobbying for the government within the establishment. Overall, the CTU performance in LegCo direct election deteriorated from having three seats in 1998 to only one in 2016, but the FTU performance has improved over time. The electoral competition between the two unions remains prominent.

Table 4.11 shows that the FTU has been forming a solid alliance with the DAB to participate in the District Council constituency in LegCo elections in 2012 and 2016. Because of the popularity of Chan Yuen-han of the FTU, she was directly elected to the LegCo through the District Council constituency in 2012, while Lau Kong-wah of the DAB was defeated. In 2016, Wong Kwok-hing from the FTU was defeated. Nevertheless, the fact that FTU nominated candidates who had a strong showing in the LegCo direct election demonstrated the quasi-political party nature of the pro-Beijing union.

At the grassroots level, the FTU has been nominating candidates to participate in District Council elections. Table 4.12 shows that the number of FTU candidates increased significantly from one in 1999 to twenty-two in 2011, and then to forty-eight in 2015. In 2007 and 2011, the FTU formed an alliance with the DAB to compete in District Council elections. However, the number of FTU candidates directly elected as District Council members was twenty-four in 2007, thirty-five in 2011 and

Table 4.12 FTU District Councils members, 1999–2015

	1999	2003	2007	2011	2015
Candidates	8	9	30[a]	51	51
FTU alone	1	1	4	22	48
DAB alone	7	6	3	0	0
DAB/FTU alliance	0	2	22	29	3
Uncontested	2	0	0	6	7
Elected	8	6	24	35	29
Unelected	0	3	6	16	22
Successful rate	100%	66.7%	80%	68.6%	56.8%
Votes gained	10,860	15,248	49,153	82,290	95,583
Average votes obtained	1810	1694	1638	1829	2172

Sources: *Reports on the District Councils Election* in 1999, 2003, 2007, 2011 and 2015; *Election Information Compilation of Hong Kong* (Hong Kong: Hong Kong Institute of Asia-Pacific Studies, The Chinese University of Hong Kong, 2001, 2005 and 2015)

[a]One candidate Kwok Wai-keung declared himself as an independent candidate

twenty-nine in 2015, showing a decline in the success rate from 80% in 2007 to 69% in 2011 and to 57% in 2015. Although the average votes obtained by individual FTU candidates slightly increased from 1638 in 2007 to 2172 in 2015, the fierce competition in District Council elections meant that the FTU candidates as a collective group did not achieve any breakthrough in electoral competition. In the 2011 District Council elections, the FTU groomed a young female candidate Lau Kwai-yung to defeat Lee Cheuk-yan of the CTU, a political shockwave that demonstrated the success of the FTU in cultivating the rise of a local politician for nine years before she succeeded in election.[40] In the elections of the Labour Advisory Board, the FTU had a strong showing in 2016, when its representative Tang Ka-piu got 344 votes (Table 4.13). After the Occupy Central Movement from September to December 2014, when a group of students and democrats occupied several sites to push for democratic reform, some civil servants were concerned about the pro-democratic stance of Leung Chau-ting, who represented the Clerical Grades Civil Servants General Union. Eventually, Leung was defeated by Daniel Lau, a pro-government representative of the Government Disciplined Services General Union.

[40] *Wen Wei Po*, November 14, 2011, p. A03.

Table 4.13 Election results of the Labour Advisory Board in November 2016

Name	Votes	Union position	Affiliated union
Charles Chan Yiu-kwong[a]	300	Deputy Chairman, Hong Kong Civil Servants General Union	Independent
Wong Siu-han[a]	265	Secretary General, Hong Kong and Kowloon Trades Union Council	TUC
Chau Siu-chung[a]	294	General Secretary, Hong Kong Storehouses, Transportation & Logistics Staff Association	FLU
Tang Ka-piu[a]	344	Deputy General Secretary, Motor Transport Workers General Union	FTU
Daniel Lau Yuk-fai[a]	241	Chairman, Government Disciplined Services General Union	Pro-establishment
Leung Chau-ting	174	Chairman, Clerical Grades Civil Servants General Union	Social democratic
Lo Chak-man	27	President, Government Education Staff Union	Independent
Chan Che-bun Anderson	23	Chairman, Buildings Department Local Building Surveyors' Association	Independent

Sources: Labour Advisory Board Election of Employee Representatives, in http://www.labour.gov.hk/eng/news/LAB_Election2016.htm, and Five employee representatives elected to the Labour Advisory Board, in http://www.info.gov.hk/gia/general/201611/12/P2016111000567.htm?fontSize=1, access date: April 12, 2018

At the higher level of the political system in Hong Kong, the FTU is influential in its participation in the Chief Executive Election Committee's subsector election in 2016. It nominated 48 candidates and 26 of them won, ranging from 281 to 322 votes (Table 4.14). The pro-Beijing FLU nominated thirteen candidates, and twelve of them won. Other unions, namely, the pro-social democratic Hong Kong Federation of Civil Service Unions (FCSU) and pro-government Hong Kong Civil Servants General Union (CSGU), managed to get one candidate elected from each. With only one representative from a social democratic union elected to the Election Committee selecting the Chief Executive in 2016, the dominant labor voice was the pro-Beijing and pro-establishment FTU, whose representatives voted for the candidate, Carrie Lam Cheng Yuet-ngor, who was supported by the PRC government to be the Chief Executive of the HKSAR.

With regard to the political representation of FTU members in the higher level of the political systems of Hong Kong and mainland China, Table 4.15 shows that while the number of FTU members in Hong

Table 4.14 FTU Participation in the Chief Executive Election Committee's subsector elections, 2016

Union	Candidates	No. of elected members/votes		No. of defeated members/votes	
FTU	48	46	281–322[a]	2	209–211[a]
FLU	13	12	229–307[a]	1	70
FCSU	1	1	291	0	–
SGOA	1	0	–	1	82
CSGU	3	1	270	2	90–91[a]
GDSGU	2	0	–	2	37–78[a]
AHDSU	1	0	–	1	102
Total	69	60	229–322	9	37–211

Source: Elections Results of Election Committee Subsector Elections, in https://www.elections.gov.hk/ecss2016/eng/results_s3.html?1523254822767, access date: April 10, 2018

Note: By subsector, it means the labor sector that selected representatives to the Election Committee. The number of registered electors was 668 in 2017

FCSU pro-social democratic Hong Kong Federation of Civil Service Unions; *SGOA* pro-government Hong Kong Senior Government Officers Association; *CSGU* pro-government Hong Kong Civil Servants General Union; *GDSGU* pro-government Government Disciplined Services General Union; *AHDSU* pro-action and "radical" Alliance of Housing Department Staff Unions

[a]The figures with hyphens mean that the first number was the lowest number of votes obtained by the candidate and that the second number represented the highest vote obtained.

Kong's LegCo increased from one in 1985 to five in 2018, the union has a considerable number of representatives to the PRC National People's Congress (NPC) and the Chinese People's Political Consultative Conference (CPPCC). It means that the FTU has been politically well-positioned to support and lobby the PRC government's policies toward Hong Kong, playing the role of a united front intermediary to win the hearts and minds of more Hong Kong workers. Nevertheless, in terms of the ratio of FTU members to the overall number of Hong Kong members to the NPC, it has declined from almost 38% in the late 1970s and early 1980s to 8.5% in 2018–2022 (Table 4.16), reflecting a phenomenon that the PRC government conducted its united front work more on the business people and professionals in the HKSAR than on the working-class representatives.

Table 4.15 Higher-level political representations of the Federation Trade Unions members

Year	Legislative Councilors	The Chinese National People's Congress members	The Chinese People's Political Consultative Conferences members
1973		1.Yeung Kwong	
		2.Wong Yin-fong	
		3.So Yau	
		4.Kwok Tim-hoi	
1977		5.Lee Sung	
1978	No FTU legislator	1.Yeung Kwong	Chan Yiu-choi
		2.Wong Yin-fong	
		3.Chun Fai	
		4.Luk Tat-Kim	
		5.Woo Gau	
1982		6.Lee Sung	
1983		1.Yeung Kwong	Poon Kwok-wai
		2.Wong Yiu-fong	
1984		3.Chun Fai	
1985	Tam Yiu-chung	4.Luk Tat-kim	
		5.Chan Chik-Gwai	
1987		6.Tong Chi-on	
1988	Tam Yiu-chung	1.Cheng Yiu-tong	1.Yeung Kwong
		2.Luk Tat-kim	2.Poon Kwok-wai
1991		3.Tong Chi-on	
1992	Tam Yiu-chung		
1993		1.Cheng Yiu-tong	1.Yeung Kwong
1994		2.Lee Chak-tim	2.Poon Kwok-wai
1995	1.Cheng Yiu-tong	3.Luk Tat-kim	3.Lan Suk-yee
	2.Chan Yuen-han	4.Tong Chi-on	
1997	3.Chan Wing-Chan		
1998	1.Cheng Yiu-tong	1.Cheng Siu-tong	1.Yeung Kwong
1999	2.Tam Yiu-chung	2.Lee Chak-tim	2.Poon Kwok-wai
2000	3.Chan Yuen-han	3.Luk Tat-tim	3.Lan Suk-yee
	4.Chan Wing-Chan		
2001	1.Tam Yiu-chung		
2002	2.Chan Yuen-han		
2003	3.Leung Fu-wah	1.Cheng Siu-tong	1.Lam Suk-yee
2004	4.Chan Kwok-keung	2.Lee Chak-tim	2.Tam Yiu-chung
2005	1.Chan Yuen-han	3.Wong Kwok-kin	
2006	2.Tam Yiu-chung		
2007	3.Wong Kwok-hing		
2008	4.Kwong Chi-kin	1.Cheng Siu-tong	1.Lam Suk-yee
2009	1.Wong Kwok-kin	2.Wong Kwok-kin	2.Tam Yiu-chung

(continued)

Table 4.15 (continued)

Year	Legislative Councilors	The Chinese National People's Congress members	The Chinese People's Political Consultative Conferences members
2010	2.Wong Kwok-hing		3.Chan Yuen-han
2011	3.Ip Wai-ming		
2012	4.Poon Pui-mau		
2013	1.Wong Kwok-kin	1.Cheng Yiu-tong	1.Lam Suk-yee
	2.Chan Yuen-han	2. Stanley Ng Chau-pei	2.Chan Yuen-han
	3.Wong Kwok-hing		
	4.Mak Mei-yuen		
	5.Kwok Wai-keung		
2016	6.Tang Ka-biu		
2017	1.Kwok Wai-keung		
2018	2.Wong Kwok-kin	1.Tam Yiu-chung	1. Wong Kwok-kin
	3.Mak Mei-yuen	2.Cheng Yiu-tong	
	4.Ho Kai-ming	3.Stanley Ng Chau-pei	
	5.Luk Chung-hung		

Sources: Federation of Trade Unions, *Federation of Trade Unions Walking with You: 65th Anniversary of Historical Essays* (in Chinese) (Hong Kong: Federation of Trade Unions, 2013), p. 278 and Members List of 13th the National Committee of the Chinese People's Political Consultative Conference, in http://www.cppcc.gov.cn/zxww/2018/02/26/ARTI1519615396504299.shtml, access date: April 10, 2018

Table 4.16 FTU members in China's National People's Congress

Term of NPC	Year of the term	Total	FTU	Ratio (%)
1	1954–1958	2	1	50%
2	1959–1963	2	Nil	Nil
3	1964–1972	2	Nil	Nil
4	1973–1977	15	5	33.3%
5	1978–1982	16	6	37.5%
6	1983–1987	16	6	37.5%
7	1988–1992	19	3	15.8%
8	1993–1997	30	4	13.3%
9	1998–2002	36	3	8.3%
10	2003–2007	36	3	8.3%
11	2008–2012	36	2	5.6%
12	2013–2017	36	2	5.6%
13	2018–2022	36	3	8.3%

Source: The website of Hong Kong representatives of the National People's Congress, in http://www.npc.gov.cn/npc/gadbzl/xgdbzl_11/node_8514.htm, access date: April 19, 2018

Note: After 1997, the NPC Hong Kong members have been elected by the Electoral Committee, whose members increased from 400 increased to 1200 in 2016

Rivalries of FTU and CTU

Historically, the FTU and CTU have been locked in fierce rivalries over a number of policy issues in Hong Kong (Table 4.17). The pre-1997 LegCo approved a collective bargaining bill initiated by CTU's Lee Cheuk-yan, but it was then quickly repealed by the Provisional Legislative Council, which was established by the PRC to handle all the transitional issues relating to Hong Kong. The FTU Vice-Chairlady Chan Yuen-han claimed that the FTU supported collective bargaining, but due to the fact that the CTU had initiated a bill without sufficiently consulting public opinion, and also because such a bill "would not be beneficial to the solidarity of unions," the FTU did not support the collective bargaining bill proposed by Lee.[41] On the other hand, the Labour Advisory Board opposed Lee's bill, saying that it had not undergone thorough discussions.[42] Chan Yuen-han of the FTU reiterated that Lee Chek-yan had not consulted all the trade unions in Hong Kong. The pro-government and pro-Beijing *Wen Wei Po* even went so far as to argue that "radical unions made a surprise attack and evaded the mechanism of the Labour Advisory Board," and this would not be beneficial to the investment climate of Hong Kong because enterprises would suffer from a decline in productivity and profits.[43] As a result, in the LegCo, Chan of the FTU abstained from voting for the collective bargaining bill, saying that Lee's bill would split the local unions.[44] Similarly, Tam Yiu-chung, an Executive Council member from the FTU, insisted that time was not ripe for the collective bargaining legislation to be entrenched.[45] The political rivalries between the FTU and the CTU meant that Lee's collective bargaining bill was not only rejected by the FTU in the first place, but also bound to be repealed quickly later.

In 2007, a group of steel workers went on strike and demanded that their pay should be increased. The employer suggested a payment of HK$850 per day, but the steel benders counter-proposed HK$950 and eight-hour work per day.[46] The result was a settlement of HK$860 after thirty-six days of strike. In the incident, the CTU came out as the spokesman for the steel workers, while the FTU shied away from the strike until

---

[41] *Sing Tao Daily*, December 10, 1998, p. A9.
[42] *Tian Tian Daily*, December 10, 1998, p. A14.
[43] Wen Wei Po, December 4, 1998, p. A03.
[44] *Sing Tao Daily*, November 4, 1998, p. A16.
[45] *Hong Kong Commercial Daily*, October 5, 1998, p. B5.
[46] *Apple Daily*, August 12, 2007, p. A3.

Table 4.17 The political position of trade unions in controversial cases

Issues	Consequences	FTU's position	CTU's position
Collective bargaining bill was repealed by the Provisional Legislative Council, October 1997	The bill was passed by the Legislative Council before July 1, 1997, but then it was repealed by the Provisional Legislative Council after the handover.	FTU claimed that the bill did not have public consultation, that it would split the trade unions and that it should go through the consultative mechanism of the Labour Advisory Board.	CTU made a surprise attack by having the bill passed in the Legislative Council, but it did challenge the position of the FTU in the entire process from approving to repealing the bill.
Steel benders' dispute, August to September, 2007	The employer suggested HK$850 per day, but the steel benders counter-proposed HK$950 per day. The result was HK$860 after thirty-six days of strike.	It did not support the steel benders at the beginning, but later supported them after the twenty-six days of the strike.	It led the strike and acted as the benders' spokesman.
Bus drivers' dispute, August 2010	The bus companies suggested 1.8% salary increase but the union counter-proposed 2.2%. Their strike was unsuccessful.	It did not support them because the FTU itself reached a compromise with the bus companies.	The CTU led the strike and acted as a spokesman for the bus drivers.
Minimum Wage, November and December 2010	The government finally decided to set HK$28 as the minimum wage.	The FTU originally appeared to be demanding, but it eventually sided with the government.	The CTU was consistent in arguing for a higher level of the minimum wage.
Dock workers' dispute, March to May, 2013	The Hong Kong International Terminals Company Limited (HIT) suggested an 8.5% wage increase, but the CTU counter-proposed 23.5%. The result was a 9.8% increase after forty days of strike	It did not support the strike, but a FTU representative, namely Yau Mei-kwong, was a member of middle management of an outsourcing company, Global Stevedoring Service.	The CTU led the strike and acted as a spoken. They called public donations for helping the striking workers.

(*continued*)

Table 4.17 (continued)

Issues	Consequences	FTU's position	CTU's position
Aircrew officers' strikes, May 2015 and December 2017	The Aircrew Officers' Association and the Cathay Pacific Flight Attendants Union demanded an increase in the benefits of pilots and the salary of flight attendants respectively.	The FTU did not participate in any action because the two unions belonged to CTU.	CTU led the officers and flight attendants.
Kowloon Motor Bus dispute over a new salary package, February–March 2018.	A female bus driver, Yip Wai-lam, formed a coalition to fight for the interest of bus drivers. She was dismissed but after the protests from some drivers, together with the Labor Party, the League of Social Democrats, Yip was allowed to resume duty.	The FTU bus drivers' union was co-opted by the Kowloon Motor Bus and accepted the salary package initiated from the employer's side. It also openly rejected the use of strikes.	CTU had three bus drivers' unions and they all argued that the lack of collective bargaining power resulted in the dismissal of Yip Wai-lam.

after twenty-six days. The pro-Beijing *Wen Wei Po* labeled the CTU as "demagoguery" while praising the FTU as non-interventionist and rational.[47] The CTU supported the strikes of steel workers, and maintained law and order for them, while simultaneously exerting pressure on the construction sector to make concessions. Some students, intellectuals and educators went to sign their names in support of the strike, saying that the construction company should share the fruits of economic success with the workers.[48] At the beginning, the FTU claimed that it supported the workers, but it appealed to them to discuss with the government and the employer. Cheng Yiu-tong of FTU attempted to act as a middleman between the workers and the construction sector.[49] On the 21st day of the strike, FTU approached the strikers and got their consensus of making concessions if the construction company responded positively.[50] At the same time, some trade unionists from the American services and Australian

---

[47] *Wen Wei Po*, August 16, 2007, p. A12.
[48] *Hong Kong Economic Journal*, August 20, 2007, p. 9.
[49] Ibid., p. 10.
[50] *Apple Daily*, August 28, 2007, p. A12.

transport sectors supported the strikers by sending representatives to visit them.[51] Four hundred Catholics in Hong Kong followed suit.[52] While the CTU adopted social movement unionism to support the steel workers, the FTU harped on the same theme of using tripartism. On the 23rd day of the strike, 927 steel workers returned to work, expecting some concessions from both sides.[53] Interestingly, in early September, when the construction sector and the strikers' representatives began to negotiate a settlement, the FTU suddenly called for the strikers to continue with their strike, projecting a progressive image.[54] The FTU's changing strategy was to improve its image in the eyes of the steel workers, afraid of the likelihood that the CTU stole the entire limelight in the strike. A turning point came on September 5, when some strikers clashed with the police violently.[55] One construction contractor had privately began to pay HK$950 and eight hours per day to some steel workers, trying to end the strike.[56] But the unintended consequence of his action was to stimulate more steel workers to demand for the same treatment from other construction contractors.[57] The tug-of-war dragged on until the 36th day, when government succeeded in getting the Steel Benders Business Association to agree to pay HK$860 per day to the steel workers, while the workers insisted on the need for eight-hour work per day.[58] Due to the exhaustion on the part of many workers, who were eager to receive payment as soon as possible, the final settlement was HK$860 per day, but it was a Pyrrhic victory to the CTU, FTU and the steel workers. The rivalries between the CTU and FTU and the FTU's change of gesture did not really enhance the bargaining power of the steel workers. As a result of inter-union rivalries, the government easily became the victorious referee in the tripartism mechanism.

In August 2010, the fragmentation of trade unions into CTU and FTU could be easily discerned in the disputes between some bus drivers and their bus companies, including the City Bus, New World First Bus, Kowloon Motor Bus and Dragon Bus. Originally, the New World First

---

[51] Ibid.
[52] Ibid., August 29, 2007, p. A20.
[53] *Wen Wei Po*, August 30, 2007, p. A14.
[54] *Apple Daily*, September 3, 2007, p. A23.
[55] *Wen Wei Po*, September 6, 2007, p. A12.
[56] Ibid.
[57] *Apple Daily*, September 7, 2007, p. A14.
[58] Ibid., September 11, 2007, p. A4.

Bus drivers claimed to mobilize 1300 colleagues to go on strike to demand for better pay and benefits, but eventually, a minority of bus drivers launched the strike supported by the CTU.[59] The unionists demanded a pay increase of 2.2%, but the employers insisted on a slight increase of 1.8%. The FTU was silent and weak on the whole issue because its Vehicle and Transport General Union supported the employers, whereas the CTU remained the outspoken activist supportive of 90 bus drivers who went on strike on the first day. The 90 strikers occupied only 5.3% of all the drivers of the City Bus and New World First Bus, thus failing to constitute any threat to the bus companies. As a result of inter-union rivalry and the pressure of the bus companies on a large number of bus drivers on contractual terms, the strike did not even gain the support of many bus drivers on the second day. The CTU was seen as a "loser" in this battle, for the disunited unions in the first place rendered the strike attempt abortive.[60] The FTU was severely criticized by some commentators as supportive of the employers for the first time in its political history, abandoning any pro-labor position.[61]

The Minimum Wage Ordinance was enacted in the Hong Kong Legislative Council on July 17, 2010 and came into force on May 1, 2011. The turning point of the minimum wage issue in Hong Kong could be traced back to June 2009, when the Executive Council, a body that assists the HKSAR government in its policy-making processes, advised that the Minimum Wage Bill should be introduced to the LegCo. Eventually, the sixty-member LegCo passed the Minimum Wage Bill on June 16, 2010. The Secretary for Labour and Welfare of the HKSAR government, Matthew Cheung, said the passage of the bill marked a milestone in the protection of labor. The Provisional Minimum Wage Commission would review the minimum wage at least once every two years. For the HKSAR government, the objective of legislating on the minimum wage was to devise an optimal statutory minimum wage regime, which could forestall excessively low wages without unduly affecting labor-market flexibility, economic growth and competitiveness.[62] While local unions and labor groups asked for the minimum hourly wages of HK$33 to sustain the livelihood of the low-income citizens, leaders of the business community

---

[59] *Oriental Daily*, August 7, 2010, p. A03.
[60] *Hong Kong Economic Times*, August 11, 2010, p. A22.
[61] *Hong Kong Economic Journal*, August 11, 2010, p. 12.
[62] *BBC Monitoring Asia Pacific*, July 17, 2010.

argued that the rate was too high and it would lead to layoffs. The proposed minimum wage would protect low-income earners, such as toilet cleaners and security guards, some of whom earned only HK$20. Eventually, the bill was approved as legislation in the LegCo and the wages payable to an employee should not be less than the statutory minimum wage of HK$28.[63]

A tripartite committee composed of representatives from the government, employers and employees, namely, the Labour Advisory Board, discussed the possibility of exempting the elderly people from the minimum wage legislation, but there was no consensus.[64] The employee representatives argued that many elderly people worked in security and cleaning companies, and that they should not be exempted. All the three sides agreed that handicapped citizens should be protected by having 70 to 80% of the minimum wage protection. The security and cleaning workers organized protests and demanded that the minimum wage should be HK$30 to HK$35 per hour as some of them did not obtain HK$15 for an hour work.[65] About 70% of the security company staff received an hourly pay much lower than HK$24, according to the CTU.

The CTU was the most active trade union arguing for the urgent need of the minimum wage legislation for Hong Kong's workers. It called for the minimum wage of HK$30 per hour and a maximum eight working hours per day, apart from the call for the establishment of collective bargaining rights for workers.[66] One seventy-year old protestor said that he had joined a security company ten years ago, but there had been no pay adjustment for ten years. About 580,000 citizens who worked as security and cleaning staff had their monthly wage much lower than HK$6000, an income level that lagged behind the rising inflation and high living standard.[67] The Catering and Hotel Staff Union called for the need to set down the minimum wage of HK$33 per hour and it contrasted their staff members' situation with the hourly pay of the Chief Executive, Donald Tsang, who received HK$1600 per hour.[68] Workers in Hong Kong's restaurants received relatively low pay, ranging from HK$18 to HK$24 per hour. They argued that Hong Kong as a metropolitan city

[63] *China Economic Review*, May 3, 2011.
[64] *Sing Tao Daily*, February 15, 2008.
[65] *Ming Pao*, March 17, 2008.
[66] *Hong Kong Economic Journal*, May 2, 2008.
[67] Ibid.
[68] *Oriental Daily*, October 1, 2008.

was underdeveloped in terms of the protection offered to workers.[69] Critics of the government said that even Shenzhen, Hong Kong's neighbor, had implemented the minimum wage as early as 1994.[70] In May 2009, during a protest mobilized by the CTU and joined by 3000 citizens, the demonstrators called for the government to take care of the interests of all those workers affected by the 2008–2009 global financial crisis. The CTU argued for an hourly wage of no less than HK$33 and overtime pay for those working more than eight hours.[71] It mobilized citizens to boycott Café de Coral, which was found to exclude the lunch time of workers from their monthly wage.[72] The CTU also argued that foreign workers should be integrated into the minimum wage legislation.

A few Hong Kong businesspeople made remarks that angered working-class citizens, unintentionally exacerbating class contradictions and tensions. The remarks of Tommy Cheung Yu-yan, a legislator insisting that the minimum wage should be set at HK$20 in 2010, triggered public opposition. Two hundred low-income citizens protested outside the government headquarters and criticized Cheung as treating workers as "beggars."[73] One single parent criticized him in public, saying that HK$20 per hour would not enable her to feed her child.[74] A protest mobilized by the FTU attracted 2500 participants who called for the minimum wage legislation to protect working-class "dignity."[75] The CTU mobilized 3500 protests and criticized Cheung's comment as victimizing the working poor.[76] Cheung's provocative remark unexpectedly stimulated working-class protests. He eventually apologized to the public for his comment, while his pro-business Liberal Party colleague James Tien suggested an hourly minimum rate of HK$25 to appease the anger of some lower-class citizens.[77]

In July 2010, it was reported that the business sector would accept the minimum wage level of HK$28 an hour.[78] While the unionists insisted on

[69] *Ta Kung Pao*, October 13, 2008.
[70] *The Sun*, March 21, 2008.
[71] *The Standard*, March 15, 2010.
[72] *The Sun*, November 5, 2010.
[73] *Oriental Daily*, March 22, 2010.
[74] *Apple Daily*, March 22, 2010.
[75] *Wen Wei Po*, May 2, 2010.
[76] *Oriental Daily*, May 2, 2010.
[77] *The Sun*, March 27, 2010.
[78] *Hong Kong Daily News*, July 6, 2010.

HK$33 per hour, the Liberal Party announced that the small and medium enterprises would accept a HK$28 hourly minimum wage.[79] The conservative business sector, represented by Cheung, maintained that the business people would relocate their operations to China if the minimum wage would be fixed at HK$28 per hour.[80] The Provisional Minimum Wage Commission (PMWC), which was set up by the government to study the minimum wage level, concluded in November 2010 that, if the minimum wage were set at HK$33 per hour, employers would spend an additional amount of HK$84 billion and 81,000 citizens would be unemployed.[81] The PMWC claimed that 40,000 citizens would be unemployed if a minimum wage of HK$28 per hour were adopted. Although unionists insisted on a higher level of minimum wage than HK$28, the employers' representatives argued that the higher level of minimum wage would mean that a sudden economic downturn in Hong Kong would adversely affect many workers. Interestingly, the Employers Federation argued for a level of HK$24.3 per hour, while the restaurants and catering sector advocated a minimum wage level of HK$24 to HK$26, thus favoring the government to adopt a relatively lower level of minimum wage acceptable to all sides.[82] The government realized the need to implement the minimum wage legislation; utilized the PMWC to release findings relatively unfavorable to the maximum demands made by trade unionists; and used the Labour Advisory Board to reach compromises between the trade unionists and employers' representatives. The government decision of adopting the minimum wage of HK$28 per hour was a strategic move striking a balance between the interests of employees and that of employers, but the entire saga illustrated the relatively weak FTU and the more assertive CTU. A member of the top policy-making body, Executive Council (ExCo), Cheng Yiu-tong from the FTU, criticized Cheung Yu-yan's remark that the minimum wage should be set at HK$20 per hour and instead he proposed HK$34 in March 2010, ten months before his FTU changed its position to accept the government's proposed HK$28 per hour.[83] The FTU position appeared to be hardline, but in fact its pro-government stance meant that it made a gesture to disguise the flexible nature of its demands.

[79] *Apple Daily*, October 19, 2010.
[80] *The Sun*, September 4, 2010.
[81] *Oriental Daily*, November 11, 2010.
[82] *The Standard*, June 9, 2010.
[83] *Ta Kung Pao*, March 24, 2010.

When the bill was introduced to the LegCo for the first reading in June 2009, the government adopted multiple strategies. It allowed employers and employees to bargain among themselves in the Labour Advisory Board. It let the PMWC shape the focus of the debate in December 2010 to the public acceptability of HK$28 per hour. In November 2010, the ExCo approved the government's proposed HK$28 per hour. By January 2011, the FTU announced that 87.4% of its 181 affiliated unions accepted the level of HK$28 per hour. Another pro-Beijing FLU shifted its stance from insisting HK$33 per hour to accepting HK$28. At this juncture, the government succeeded in utilizing the PMWC, Labor Advisory Committee and pro-government FTU to legitimize the political acceptability of HK$28 per hour. The case of minimum wage debate showed that while the rivalries between the more action-oriented CTU and the pro-government FTU could be easily seen, the result was to allow the HKSAR government to make its final decision relatively easily.

From March to May 2013, the dock workers' strike erupted. The Hong Kong International Terminals (HIT) suggested a wage increase of 8.5%, but the CTU counter-proposed 23.5%. Both sides refused to give in, leading to forty days of strike. The CTU led the strikers from the beginning to the end, gathering donations from members of the public. But the FTU position was pro-harmony and pro-stability; its representative Yau Mei-kwong was found to be a member of the middle management of an outsourcing company named Global Stevedoring Service. The suspected conflict of role and interest of Yau was an embarrassment to the FTU, whose position remained far weaker than the CTU.

In May 2015 and December 2017, the aircrew officers launched strikes to demand for better pay and benefits for the pilots and better salaries of flight attendants respectively. In both cases, the Aircrew Officers Association and the Cathay Pacific Flight Attendants Union were affiliated with the CTU, adopting a more hard-line and action-oriented approach to fighting for their demands.[84] The FTU, however, did not participate in the actions because the two unions belonged to the CTU. In these two cases, the action-oriented approach of the CTU-affiliated unions was successful, for the inter-union rivalry between the CTU and FTU neither emerged nor gave a golden opportunity for the employer's side to play divide-and-rule tactics. Table 4.18 shows that the CTU-affiliated unions in the aviation industry remain strong, with the Cathay Pacific Airways

---

[84] *Sing Tao Daily*, May 31, 2015, p. A14.

Table 4.18 Trade unions in the aviation industry

Name of affiliated trade unions	Umbrella union	Year of registration	Membership in 2016
Cathay Pacific Airways Flights Attendants Union	CTU	1975	7222
Cathay Pacific Airways Local Staff Union	None	1979	874
Dragonair Pilots Association	CTU	1987	416
Hong Kong Dragon Airlines Flight Attendants Association	CTU	1989	1042
Airport Air Fright Employees' Association	FLU	1989	1268
Hong Kong Aviation Industry Employees General Union	FTU	1990	1377
Hong Kong Air Cargo Terminals Employees Union	FTU	2002	1083
British Airline Hong Kong International Cabin Crew Association	CTU	2003	64
Express and Airlines Pilots Association	None	2006	207
Hong Kong Airport Ramp Services Employees Union	FTU	2009	1844
JASL Employees Union	CTU	2010	200
Cathay Pacific Services Employees Union	FTU	2013	701
Cathay Pacific Services Limited Staff Association	None	2013	132
Virgin Atlantic Hong Kong Cabin Crew Union	CTU	2015	43

Source: Registry of Trade Unions, *Annual Statistical Report of Trade Unions in Hong Kong, 2016*. Hong Kong: Registry of Trade Unions, Labor Department of the HKSAR Government, 2017)

Flight Attendants Union as the largest union, thus enhancing their bargaining power vis-à-vis the employers, especially if inter-union rivalries do not erupt in any pay and benefits dispute.

In February 2018, a bus accident occurred in which nineteen passengers died and the bus driver was a part-timer working for the Kowloon Motor Bus (KMB) company. The KMB recognized only two of the five trade unions, one affiliated with the FTU and the other with TUC.[85] It came up with an improved salary package, which was however seen as undesirable by some drivers. One of the dissatisfied drivers, Yip Wai-lam, decided to form a coalition among the drivers, but she and her supporters were quickly fired by the KMB. The CTU, Labor Party, the League of Social Democrats and other drivers supported Yip and demanded that she

[85] Radio Television Hong Kong, May 2018.

should be reinstalled. After public outcry, the KMB decided to resume her duty. But the entire saga illustrated the lack of solidarity among trade unions; only two of the five unions were recognized by the KMB, which has been adopting a divide-and-rule tactic to negotiate with the two unions affiliated with FTU and TUC. The FTU-affiliated bus drivers' union openly said that it rejected the use of strikes, and that the negotiated salary package must be in conformity with the "acceptability" and "capability" of the KMB—a moderate position rejected by Yip and other drivers who argued that there should be collective bargaining to improve the interests and protect the rights of bus drivers.[86] Hence, while the FTU adopts a compliant attitude toward the KMB, the more action-oriented CTU has not shied away from using strikes to make their demands heard. Again, the KMB drivers' dispute showed that the fragmentation of trade unions has perpetuated the dominant power of the employer.

Conclusion

Both the FTU and CTU adopted a strategy of social movement unionism in Hong Kong under the British rule. Yet, a watershed took place in 1997 when the FTU changed its strategy to support tripartism and the HKSAR government wholeheartedly. Rather than supporting the collective bargaining bill initiated by the CTU, the FTU rejected it on political grounds and voted against it just prior to the handover of Hong Kong on July 1, 1997. Immediately after the sovereignty transfer, the FTU supported the move by the Provisional Legislative Council to repeal the collective bargaining legislation. The FTU's strategic change was due to its need to support the policies of the HKSAR government and the PRC policy toward the maintenance of social and political stability in the territory. However, the FTU's positional change has made it more politically moderate than before, while simultaneously cooperating with the pro-Beijing DAB to compete with the CTU and pro-democracy candidates in local elections, including both LegCo and District Council direct elections. Although FTU members have succeeded in becoming the Hong Kong NPC and CPPCC members, their numerical inferiority compared to the businesspeople and professionals means that it is far less politically influential at the higher levels of both the HKSAR and PRC political systems. Due to the ideological differences between the FTU, which is pro-Beijing

[86] Ibid.

and pro-government, and CTU, which is pro-democracy and action-oriented, this two-line struggle will likely persist in the HKSAR in the coming decades.

Moreover, inter-union rivalries between the FTU and CTU means that working-class interests have been undermined to some extent. When the FTU was virtually non-existent in some disputes, such as the Cathay Pacific pay dispute, the result was ironically in favor of the employees. When the FTU and CTU showed positional differences, such as the minimum wage legislation, the government and the employers' side could minimize the impacts of the workers' demands easily. Hence, inter-union rivalries continue to constrain the labor movement in the HKSAR, but the competition between the FTU and CTU will likely persist politically, and ideologically.

CHAPTER 5

United Front and Women Interest Groups from Pro-British to Pro-Beijing

China's united front work has also been focusing on women interest groups in the HKSAR since July 1, 1997, especially after the Occupy Central Movement in September–December 2014. Women interest groups have been relatively neglected in the study of Hong Kong politics, although some studies have explored the status and social participation of women.[1] Traditionally, women's status has been relatively low in Hong Kong, including their income level compared with men and their employment rate.[2] Most of the women interest groups are pro-government and

---

[1] For local studies on the status and social participation of women, see Wong Pik-wan and Eliza W. Y. Lee, "Gender and Political Participation in Hong Kong: Formal Participation and Community Participation," occasional paper series, Hong Kong Institute of Asia-Pacific Studies, The Chinese University of Hong Kong, 2006; Eliza Lee, "Gender and Political Participation in Hong Kong," *Asian Journal of Women Studies*, vol. 6, no. 3 (2000), pp. 93–114; Wai-man Lam and Irene L. K. Tong, "Political Change and the Women's Movement in Hong Kong and Macau," *Asian Journal of Women Studies*, vol. 12, no. 1 (2006), pp. 7–35; and Mok Hing-luen, "A Study of women's political participation in Hong Kong," Master of Social Sciences thesis, Department of Social Work, University of Hong Kong, 1991.

[2] In 2016, for example, women in the education sector were paid HK$9800 less than men each month, while women in the finance sector earned HK$8800 less than male counterparts. See Jeffie Lam, "We aim to close Hong Kong's gender pay gap and help half a million housewives, Women's Commission head says," in *South China Morning Post*, February 17, 2018, in http://www.scmp.com/news/hong-kong/community/article/2133651/we-aim-close-hong-kongs-gender-pay-gap-and-help-half, access date: June 16, 2018. In 2016, women also occupied 29% of the senior positions although they made up of 55% of the

© The Author(s) 2019
S. S.-H. Lo et al., *China's New United Front Work in Hong Kong*,
https://doi.org/10.1007/978-981-13-8483-7_5

pro-Beijing in the HKSAR, such as the flagship organizations, namely, the All-China Federation of Women Hong Kong Delegates Association, Hong Kong Federation of Women and the Hong Kong Women Development Association (HKWDA). Very few pro-democracy feminist interest groups exist, like the Association for the Advancement of Feminism (AAF), as this chapter will discuss in detail.

THE HONG KONG CHINESE WOMEN'S CLUB

In 1938, the Hong Kong Chinese Women's Club (HKCWC) was set up by the late Ellen Li Ts'o Sau-kuan (1909–2005), assisting China to fight against Japan during the Second World War.[3] From 1938 to 1941, when the Sino-Japanese war broke out, many refugees fled to Hong Kong from the mainland, while Chinese soldiers combating the Japanese invasion were wounded and retreated to Hong Kong. The club aimed at assisting the colonial British government to provide food, shelter, clothing, medical care, hospitalization, welfare services and rehabilitation work for these refugees, wounded soldiers and the people of Hong Kong.[4]

After the Second World War, the HKCWC increasingly became an influential pro-government interest group articulating the interest and welfare of women in Hong Kong. From 1946 to 1966, the club fought for the rights and status of women, striving for marriage reform, and the principle of equal pay for equal work for men. It also advocated the abolition of the concubine practices and opposed the legalization of soccer betting and illegal horseracing betting. In November 1985, a nursing and

---

overall workforce in Hong Kong. See Louise Moon, "Despite more women entering the Hong Kong workforce, few make it to senior management positions," in *South China Morning Post*, February 14, 2018, in http://www.scmp.com/business/article/2133286/despite-more-women-entering-hong-kong-workforce-few-make-it-senior, access date: June 16, 2018.

[3] See the life stories of the late Ellen Li, in http://www.elicf.com/eng/Dr%20Ellen%20Li.htm, access date: June 16, 2018. She was born in Fujian and got a business degree from the Hujiang University in Shanghai, a university established by the American Baptist Missionary Union in 1906. From 1964 to 1969, Li became an appointed member of the Urban Council and, later, she was the chairwoman of the Hong Kong Family Planning Association. She was the chairwoman of the Hong Kong Women Development Association. Li was the first female Legislative Council member from 1966 to 1974. She witnessed the implementation of marriage reform from tolerating concubines to monogamous marriage in 1971.

[4] For the activities of the Club, see http://www.hkcwc.org.hk/page.php?id=1, access date: June 16, 2018.

elderly home was established by the club to take care of the elderly, while promoting youth work and opening four night-time colleges for women. These colleges took care of the mature women who migrated from the mainland to Hong Kong and who wanted to study Chinese language, mathematics, bookkeeping and applied English language. In December 1965, the HKCWC Hioe Tjo Yoeng Primary School was set up, signaling the expansion of social and education work of the club.[5] In 1978, a secondary school was founded by the HKCWC in Shaukeiwan district, providing 1000 places for secondary school children. In September 1994, the HKCWC received government funding to establish a nursery center in Shaukeiwan district. Table 5.1 below summarizes all the social and educational activities of the HKCWC. It was crystal clear that the club

Table 5.1 The educational and social activities of the Hong Kong Chinese Women Club

Service centers	Location	Founding year	Service target
The HKCWC Hioe Tjo Yoeng Primary School	Shaukeiwan	1965	Primary school education
Hong Kong Chinese Women's Club College	Shaukeiwan	1978	Secondary school education
The HKCWC Fung Yiu King Memorial Secondary School	Shatin	1991	Secondary school education
The HKCWC Nursery	Shaukeiwan	1994	Children
The HKCWC Kindergarten	Shaukeiwan	2007	Children
The HKCWC Madam Wong Chan Sook Ying Memorial Care and Attention Home for the Aged	Yau Tong district	1985	The elderly people
The HKCWC Dr. Ellen Li Learning Centre	Yau Tong district	2006	Community organizations, adults and elderly people
Yau Tong Day Care Centre for the Elderly	Yau Tong district	2013	Elderly care services
Yau Lai Day Care Centre for the Elderly	Yau Lai	2013	Elderly care services

Sources: See the websites of all these organizations, including http://www.hkcwcc.edu.hk/, http://www.hkcwc-htyps.edu.hk/, http://www.fyk.edu.hk/, http://www.wcsyhome.org.hk/, http://www.hkcwckg.edu.hk/, http://www.ellcentre.org.hk/, http://www.hkcwcc.org.hk/, http://www.hkcwcc.org.hk/, access date: June 16, 2018

[5] See the School's website, in http://www.hkcwc-htyps.edu.hk/index/customIndex.aspx?nnnid=1, access date: June 16, 2018.

became an active and influential pro-government women interest group in Hong Kong under the British rule.

After the HKSAR was established on July 1, 1997, the HKCWC gradually became not only pro-administration but also pro-Beijing. As of 2018, its honorary chairwomen included former Secretary for Justice Elsie Leung, pro-Beijing legislators Priscilla Leung and Regina Ip and pro-government Miriam Lau Kin-yee.[6] Under the chairwomanship of Peggy Lam Pei Yu-dja from 1986 to 1991, the pro-government orientations of the HKCWC were firmly entrenched. After the 1997 transfer of sovereignty, the HKCWC became pro-Beijing. It organized a One Belt One Road talk for its members in early 2018, showing its natural drift toward a more pro-Beijing position than before. From March 2017 to March 2018, the HKCWC's budgeting income amounted to HK$526,664, but HK$305,166 or 58% of its income came from donations, including an undisclosed amount of government subsidies.[7] The rest of its income came from flag-day donations. Although the operating income was relatively moderate, the HKCWC can now be seen as both pro-government and pro-Beijing, demonstrating an inevitable evolution of the political orientations of many formerly pro-government interest groups in Hong Kong under the British rule to a pro-Beijing outlook after 1997.

The Women's Welfare Club

There are many pro-government district-based women interest groups in the HKSAR, such as the Women's Welfare Club (Eastern District), which was set up in 1955 and which provided a social platform for gathering among the relatively rich and affluent female elites in Hong Kong. It was supported by the Hong Kong government and was active in the provision of social welfare and services, such as the establishment of schools, nursery centers, family services and elderly services. The club's activities focus on the opening and operation of kindergarten and schools, such as the Women's Welfare Club (Eastern District) Hong Kong Kindergarten, the Women's Welfare Club (Eastern District) Hong Kong Nursery, the Women's Welfare Club (Eastern District) Hong Kong Lai Kwai Tim Day Nursery, the Ng Siu Mui Home Cum Care & Attention Unit for the

---

[6] For details, see its website http://www.hkcwc.org.hk/page.php?id=2, June 16, 2018.
[7] See the income and expenditure account, in http://www.hkcwc.org.hk/panel/editor/attached/file/20180328/20180328110843_95855.pdf, access date: June 16, 2018.

Elderly, the Wong Fung Ting Hostel for the Elderly, the Young Shu Cheung Neighborhood Elderly Centre, the Leung Lee Sau Yu Neighborhood Elderly Centre, the Leung Lee Sau Yu Neighborhood Elderly Center and the Kwan Kai Ming Memorial Chung Hok Elderly Centre. The transfer of sovereignty of Hong Kong from Britain to China has made the Women's Welfare Club (Eastern District) to adapt to the political circumstances. Its chairwoman was the pro-Beijing politician Ting Yok-chiu from 2000 to 2011. Since 1997, officials from the Liaison Office have become active in attending the activities of the Women Welfare Club (Eastern District). For example, in 2016, the Liaison Office deputy director Yin Xiaojing and an official from the social coordination department attended the club's Lunar Chinese New Year celebration.[8]

The Hong Kong Federation of Women

The main difference between the HKCWC and the Women's Welfare Club (Eastern District) is that, after the pro-government Hong Kong Federation of Women (HKFW) was set up in June 1993 by the pro-establishment elite Peggy Lam, the HKCWC became increasingly absorbed into the HKFW, but the Women's Welfare Club remains to be relatively independent. In other words, the HKFW has become one of the core united front organizations utilized by the PRC to infiltrate into the women sector in the HKSAR. Although the Women's Welfare Club has not joined the HKFW, it remains a political target of China's united front outreach, as Liaison Office officials have been attending some of the Club's activities.

The HKFW, which was set up in June 1993, currently has 76 organizations with 100,000 members. It is an umbrella organization with 1900 individual members.[9] The HKFW is explicitly pro-Beijing, holding the annual celebration for Hong Kong's return to China and making donations to mainland provinces and cities to build technical schools, service centers and clinics, especially during the occurrence of natural disasters in the PRC.[10] The mainland women organizations affiliated with the All-China Women Federation, such as the women group from Gansu province in December 2011, often visited the HKFW, illustrating the close

---

[8] *Wen Wei Po*, February 20, 2016.
[9] See the HKFW website, in http://www.hkfw.org/chi/intro.php, access date: June 16, 2018.
[10] See http://www.hkfw.org/chi/intro.php, access date: June 16, 2018.

relationships between the two umbrella united front organizations in the mainland and Hong Kong. The HKFW activities have become increasingly pro-Beijing after 1997, such as the holding of a seminar to publicize Beijing's White Paper on the implementation of the "one country, two systems" in June 2014, the support for the Hong Kong government's political reform proposal in February 2015 and the celebration of China's war victory over Japan in the Second World War in September 2015.[11] The HKFW was high-profile politically, supporting the Hong Kong police's action of dealing with the protestors during the 2014 Occupy Central Movement and donating money to families of police officers who were accused of abusing their power.[12] In March 2015, it also supported the Hong Kong government's political reform proposal with regard to the election method of the Chief Executive election in 2017.[13] On March 8, 2018, the HKFW celebrated Women's Day by attending a banquet at the central government offices together with 148 other women organizations.[14] The chief executive, Carrie Lam, delivered a speech and remarked that:

> Hong Kong has indeed made great strides in promoting women's development ... We are proud that Hong Kong has achieved gender equality in education. Despite having slightly more males than females in the 15-to-24 age group, females outnumber their male counterparts in higher education. In the last academic year, about 54 percent of students who enrolled in programmes funded by the University Grants Committee were female. In terms of professional degree programmes such as medicine, which have been dominated by male students in the past, these days females have an edge in terms of enrolment. For instance, in the last academic year, women accounted for about 51 percent of medical students in Hong Kong ... In 2016, 51 percent of women participated in our labor force, which is significantly lower than the 69 percent of men. Also in 2016, just one in three manager and administrator positions were filled by women. It is also noteworthy that the number of women in the workforce drops after the age of 30. This is understandable as this suggests that some women, including

---

[11] See the HKFW activities in http://www.hkfw.org/chi/event_archive.php, access date: June 16, 2018.
[12] See the *Annual Newsletter of the HKFW*, no. 74 (2017), in http://www.hkfw.org/chi/activities/publication/issue-74.pdf, access date: June 16, 2018.
[13] See its position in https://www.hkfw.org/chi/comment.php, access date: June 17, 2018.
[14] *Wen Wei Po*, March 28, 2018.

professionals, might not return to the job market after starting a family. My Government is committed to removing barriers for women to enter or remain in employment through various support measures. These include enhancing child care and elderly services, so as to create favorable conditions for women who wish to pursue their careers, and enable them to achieve a better work-life balance.[15]

Given the fact that the HKSAR encourages all women groups to create favorable working conditions for women, women interest groups have much room to enhance childcare and elderly services. As such, the HKFW and other pro-government and pro-Beijing like-minded groups can fill in the existing gaps in the delivery of services to women.

Organizationally speaking, the HKFW is composed of three large district-based organizations, namely, the Hong Kong Women Development Association (HKWDA), the Kowloon Women's Organization Federation (KWOF) and the Hong Kong Island Women Associations (HKIWA). As will be discussed below, the HKDWA was set up in 1996 and has become another flagship united front group. The KWOF was established in May 2000 and is a non-profit organization comprising twenty-four women groups at the grassroots level in such districts as Kowloon City, Shumshuipo, Yau Tsim Mong (Yaumatei, Tsimshatsui and Mongkok), Wong Tai Sin and Kwun Tong with altogether 24,600 members.[16] The HKIWA was established in 2005 and chaired by Carol Cheung Nga-lai Carol with 51 organizations, 30,000 members and 10 overlapping organizations with HKFW.[17] The HKIWA held celebrations on Hong Kong's 20th anniversary of its return to China in July 2017 and sent delegations to China to study the PRC's social, political and economic development.[18] The KWOF was established in 2000, chaired by So Lai Chun Ann and has 23 organizations with 25,000 members. It is explicitly pro-Beijing, vowing to "love Hong Kong and love China through social participation," opposing the

---

[15] "Speech by the Chief Executive at Women's Commission International Women's Day 2018 reception," in https://www.info.gov.hk/gia/general/201803/08/P2018030800787.htm, access date: June 17, 2018.

[16] For details, see the website of KWOF, in http://www.kwof.org.hk/web/index.php?option=com_content&view=article&id=53&Itemid=53, access date: June 17, 2018.

[17] For details, see the website of HKIWA, in http://www.hkiwa.org/web/, access date: June 17, 2018.

[18] For details, see the website of HKIWA, in http://www.hkiwa.org/web/album.php, access date: June 17, 2018.

Occupy Central Movement in 2014, denouncing the February 2016 Mongkok riot and supporting the government's political reform blueprint in 2015.[19] Its honorary patrons included not only a former Liaison Office deputy director, Yin Xiaojing, but also pro-Beijing women activists Peggy Lam, Ko Chi-wah and Chu Lian-fun.[20] Under all these district-based women organizations, there are many other smaller affiliated groups, thus infiltrating different strata and corners of the Hong Kong society.

As a united front flagship organization, the HKFW also reaches out to the female businesspeople and entrepreneurs. It sets up a committee focusing on the work of entrepreneurs in October 2001, vows to enhance interactions among women in the mainland, Hong Kong and Taiwan and aims at improving the political and socio-economic status of women in all three societies.[21] The united front activities of the HKFW are prominent, reaching out to not just the Hong Kong women but also linking mainland women with their counterparts in Taiwan. As of 2019, the HKFW had 9 "principal honorary presidents" (two passed away), 115 "honorary presidents" (four passed away) and 100 "honorary vice presidents" (nine passed away).[22] It is a cross-occupational elite group that co-opts women in different sectors, including industrial, commercial, monetary and financial, legal, educational, health, social welfare and science and technology sectors. The HKFW incorporates 430 members of the local executive committee members of many affiliated groups, including the Hong Kong Chinese Women's Club, which was formed in 1938 and which joined the Federation in 1993, and the Golden Bauhinia Female Entrepreneurs Association, which was formed in 2012 and which joined the Federation in 2018. Altogether the HKFW had eighty-four affiliated groups in 2018, including district-based women groups, the Hong Kong Girl Guides Association (formed in 1916 and joined the HKFW in 1993), the Eastern District Women Welfare Association (formed in 1955 and joined the HKFW in 1999) and the Hong Kong Aberdeen Female Fishermen Association (formed in 1996 and joined the HKFW in 2001). Although the Hong Kong Girl Guides Association is apparently more politically

---

[19] For details, see the website of KWOF, in http://www.kwof.org.hk/web/index.php?option=com_content&view=article&id=190&Itemid=56, access date: June 17, 2018.

[20] See the website http://www.kwof.org.hk/web/images/KWOF2017_17jun-361.jpg, access date: June 17, 2018.

[21] See the website https://www.hkfw.org/chi/event_hkfwwec.php, access date: June 17, 2018.

[22] See http://www.hkfw.org/chi/honorary.php, access date: January 8, 2019.

neutral rather than explicitly pro-Beijing, the fact that it has been co-opted can witness how united front work has been silently extending its arm to various women groups in the society of Hong Kong.

Politically, the HKFW is explicitly pro-government and pro-Beijing, saying that it aggregates the interests of women in different occupational sectors; implements the policy of "one country, two systems," supports the policies of the HKSAR government, actively promotes women participation in social matters; assertively advocates the equality for women and improves their quality in accordance with the ideals of the All-China Women Federation; cares about the interests of the minorities in the society and strengthens relationships with mainland women federation for the sake of bringing about "the prosperity of the motherland and Hong Kong."[23]

Since 2010, the HKFW has become more active in its local, regional and global activities, including the dispatch of a delegation to attend the 54th Session of United Nations Commission on the Status of Women in New York in March 2010, the donations and inspection to Tibet and Qinghai's schools construction in August 2011, the reception of mainland female cadres from the All-China Women Federation for exchange and study in Hong Kong in 2012, and the visit to the PRC State Council's Hong Kong and Macao Affairs Office (HKMAO) in October 2013. The visit to the HKMAO in October 2013 was politically significant; it involved not only a dialogue with the All-China Women Federation on how to enhance the status and welfare of women in the HKSAR and the PRC but also a lecture from mainland officials from the United Front Department on the (1) the need for Hong Kong to select a chief executive "who loves the nation and Hong Kong," (2) the necessity of adopting a gradual progress in Hong Kong's development of universal suffrage, and (3) the hope that Hong Kong women should explore a "democratic" model most suitable for the HKSAR.[24] In March 2018, the HKFW sent a 160-member delegation to Shenzhen to inspect the situation of the development of the Big Bay Area and to visit large mainland enterprises, such as Huawei, Tencent and Dajiang.[25] Most importantly, the delegation was led by an honorary leader, namely, the deputy director of the Liaison Office Tan

---

[23] For the platform, see http://www.wfda.hk/about.aspx?clid=151&lan=1, access date: January 9, 2019.
[24] Ibid.
[25] *Wen Wei Po*, April 7, 2018.

Table 5.2 The main leaders of the Hong Kong Federation of Women

Year	Name	Background and characteristics
2009–2010	Wong Siu-hwa	She graduated from the Xiamen University in 1974 with a degree in economics and then became the deputy director of a pro-Beijing business enterprise in Hong Kong. Wong was also the deputy chairwoman of the Hong Kong Fujianese Federation of Associations, the chairwoman of the Hong Kong Xiamen Clan Association, the deputy chairwoman of the Chinese Women Development Fund, an executive committee member of the All-China Women Federation and the standing committee member of the Xiamen city.
2011–2012	Tang Yeung Wing-man	She was the ex-officio member of the New Territories Heung Yee Kuk, the deputy chairwoman of the Hong Kong Overseas Chinese Federation of Associations, the deputy chairperson of the World Chinese Ningpo Chamber of Commerce, the deputy chairperson of the Shanghai-Hong Kong Business Development Association and the chairwoman of the Hong Kong Chau Shan Clans Association.
2013–2014	Wong Yeung Chi-hung	She was the member of the Guangdong People's Political Consultative Conference, the chairwoman of the Hong Kong Guangdong Federation of Associations and an executive member of a wine company.
2015–2016	Yip Shun-hing	She was the chairwoman of the Hong Kong Women Development Association and chairwoman of the Tuen Mun Women Development Association.
2017–2018	Wong Wai-ching	She was the director of the Kowloon Federation of Associations and the managing director of the Wong Sun Hing Enterprise Company.

Source: For details, see https://baike.baidu.com, https://www2.cgcc.org.hk, http://www.hkbu.edu.hk/tch/about/honlist/2015_HUF_ConnieWCWong.jsp, access date: January 9, 2019

Tieniu.[26] Clearly, the PRC has co-opted, lobbied, influenced and utilized the HKFW in its united front policy toward Hong Kong.

Table 5.2 outlines the main leaders of the HKFW. In 2018, the chairwoman was Wong Wai-ching, who is on the board of directors of the Wong Sun Hing Enterprise and the director of the famous united front group named the Kowloon Federation of Associations. The previous chairwomen were all politically active and pro-Beijing, ranging from Yip

[26] Ibid.

Shun-hing to Wong Yeung Chi-hung, and from Tang Yeung Wing-man to Wong Siu-hwa.

Overall, the HKWF is acting as an influential united front organization under the influence of the PRC to conduct extensive united front work on the successful professional women at the upper and middle levels of the society, to win the hearts and minds of the women at the grassroots level and to act as the bridge between mainland and Taiwan women interest groups. Therefore, the PRC's united front work in Hong Kong is operating through the HKWF in depth and breadth.

THE HONG KONG WOMEN DEVELOPMENT ASSOCIATION

Like the HKFW, which has become a pro-Beijing umbrella united front organization focusing on women, the Hong Kong Women Development Association (HKWDA) is another flagship organization established in 1996 and chaired by activist Yip Shun-hing. Yip is a Hong Kong member of the Chinese People's Political Consultative Conference (CPPCC) and she put forward a motion in March 2018 that it was necessary to enhance the Hong Kong youth's Chinese national identity and national consciousness.[27] The HKWDA has 30 affiliated organizations with 100,000 members, including 10 women organizations that have overlapping memberships with the HKFW. The organizational structure of HKWDA is composed of social services, social policy, women development and training, propaganda work and membership and volunteers' development. In June 2017, it sent a ten-member delegation to Fujian for a three-day forum between mainland Chinese and Taiwanese women, discussing a whole range of issues affecting women affairs, family construction and community governance.[28] The delegation was led by the deputy director of the Liaison Office, Song Wei, thus showing the close relationships between the HKDWA and PRC officials in the HKSAR. In early 2018, the HKWDA emphasized the development of its volunteers work while interacting with mainland delegates regularly, such as the delegations from Zhejiang and Guizhou provinces.[29] Locally, the HKDWA sets

---

[27] See her interview by the *Tai Kung Pao* internet, http://www.hkwda.org.hk/, access date: June 17, 2018.

[28] *Newsletter of the HKDWA*, no. 52 (November 2017), p. 17, in https://drive.google.com/file/d/1EP86s3d7v4t-9otbSQem9q5S1S3eiy0w/view, access date: June 17, 2018.

[29] *Newsletter of the HKDWA*, no. 53 (April 2018), in https://drive.google.com/file/d/17nUp8QFZAGXHqEVykC8AvuwrteYCRbgz/view, access date: June 17, 2018.

up six services centers for women, offering training courses for both the unemployed and employed and providing nursery services and leisure courses for the needs of women. Utilizing government support and PRC connections, the HKWDA constitutes another influential united front organization targeting women in Hong Kong.

While pro-Beijing women groups have remained very active in the HKSAR, little research has been conducted to explore whether women who participate in these groups are really aware of the fact that they are constantly under the target of united front work. It is safe to say that while the leaders of pro-Beijing women groups are perhaps aware of the united front function of their groups, many rank-and-file members may not be so politically sensitive. Yet, they appear to regard their participation in women interest group activities as more social than political. After all, many women in the HKSAR, especially those in pro-Beijing groups, tend to see politics negatively; the democrats are viewed as "demagogues" who stirred up such "radical" activities as the Occupy Central Movement in late 2014.

United front work in the HKSAR targets at women easily because many female citizens tend to cherish materialistic pursuits, including status, fame and concrete benefits like career guidance and professional networking for their personal advancement. Hence, once pro-Beijing women groups are linked up with the DAB and FTU, they constitute a powerful force to be reckoned with in elections at the legislative and district levels. The networking and personal *guanxi* (relationships) among women have become the political instrument through which pro-Beijing candidates could, can and will easily mobilize their solid supporters during elections. As such, united front work targeted at women does have an influential bearing on the power base of pro-Beijing candidates in election campaigns and on the voting day.

Figure 5.1 delineates the scope of women front groups in the HKSAR. The All-China Women Federation (ACWF) is a core group playing the leadership of the PRC's co-optation work targeted at local women. Spreading out from the core groups are three circles of other women groups, with the second layer including the Hong Kong Federation of Women (HKFW), the Hong Kong Women Development Association and the All-China Federation of Women Hong Kong Delegates Association (ACFWHKDA). The HKFW was set up in February 2009 and is another united front group, as mentioned in the section above. The ACFWHKDA is an organization under the umbrella organization, ACWF, and it mobilizes local delegates in the HKSAR to support the policies of Beijing and

5 UNITED FRONT AND WOMEN INTEREST GROUPS FROM PRO-BRITISH... 161

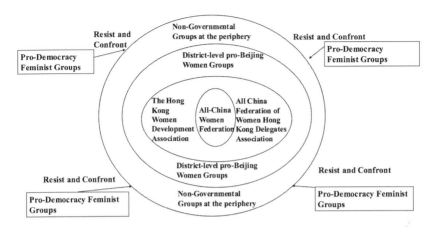

Fig. 5.1 Core and peripheral pro-Beijing women groups

the HKSAR government. The third outer circle embraces groups at the district level. These groups are indispensable for pro-Beijing forces to grasp the votes of women and mobilize their electoral support to check and balance against, and to defeat, the democrats in Hong Kong's legislative and district elections. The assumption of the pro-Beijing force is that, by expanding the electoral support base at the district level, this power base of voters in eighteen districts can be translated into the hardcore support for pro-Beijing candidates running for the direct elections held for the Legislative Council. The fourth circle of China's united front work on women in Hong Kong is built on the existing non-governmental organizations in the territory, but they are more peripheral, politically autonomous and not easily subject to the influence and mobilization of pro-Beijing core women groups.

Competing with all these pro-Beijing groups, the pro-democracy groups remain relatively weak, including the Trade Union Education Center under the Hong Kong Christian Industrial Committee (CIC) and the Association for the Advancement of Feminism, both of which were set up in 1984.[30] The pro-democracy Hong Kong Women Workers Association fought for the right of women to have maternity leave in 1982 and for the

---

[30] Sally Choi, "Feminist and Labor Movements in Hong Kong: Critical and Co-Constructive (Perspective)," a presentation in San Paulo, Brazil, July 30, 2013, in www.solidaritycenter.org, access date: January 7, 2019.

welfare of female cleaners and causal workers in 1989.[31] The voices of these small groups were critical in the fight for recognizing the rights of women workers. In 1995, they organized themselves into the Hong Kong Women's Coalition on Equal Opportunities, calling for an end to violence against women at the workplace. The pro-democracy women groups argued that although the Sex Discrimination Ordinance in 1995 prohibited sexual harassment, there was no stipulation that prohibited customers from sexually harassing female workers in the service and retail industries. They conducted a survey that pointed to 80% of female workers experiencing sexual harassment in the workplace of the catering industry. Eventually, the government revised the Ordinance in 2014, showing that pro-democracy women groups that came mainly from working-class background contributed to the fight for the interests and welfare of women in Hong Kong. Unlike the core pro-Beijing women groups that generally represent the upper-class women, the pro-democracy women groups tend to be working-class based.

Political Participation of Women in Hong Kong

From the perspective of political participation, both pro-Beijing and pro-democracy women groups have contributed much to the enhancement of women's interests, status and welfare. Table 5.3 shows that from 1966 to 1975, the top policy-making colonial body, the Executive Council, did not have any female unofficial (non-governmental) or official (governmental) members. The situation changed from 1976 onward.

In Table 5.4, women's participation in the Legislative Council began in 1966 when Ellen Li Ts'o Sau-kuan was appointed by the governor into the lawmaking body. She played a crucial role in lobbying the government's policy of abolishing polygamy through the amendment of the 1971 Marriage Bill. The number of women in the Legislative Council gradually increased from one in 1966 to six in 1984, including Hong Kong-born Lydia Dunn, who was appointed by Governor Murray MacLehose as a legislator in 1976, and who was later appointed by Governor Edward Youde as a member of the Executive Council in 1982. Politically, both Ellen Li and Lydia Dunn could be regarded as pro-British rather than pro-Beijing. Li was conferred upon as a Member of the Order of the British Empire in 1958 and later Commander of the Order of the

[31] Ibid.

Table 5.3 The gender distribution of Executive Councilors

Year	Unofficial members Female	Percentage	Unofficial members Male	Percentage	Official members Male	Percentage	Total
1966	0	0%	7	46.7%	8	53.3%	15
1967	0	0%	7	46.7%	8	53.3%	15
1968	0	0%	7	46.7%	8	53.3%	15
1969	0	0%	7	46.7%	8	53.3%	15
1970	0	0%	7	46.7%	8	53.3%	15
1971	0	0%	7	46.7%	8	53.3%	15
1972	0	0%	7	46.7%	8	53.3%	15
1973	0	0%	7	46.7%	8	53.3%	15
1974	0	0%	7	46.7%	8	53.3%	15
1975	0	0%	7	46.7%	8	53.3%	15
1976	1	6.7%	7	46.7%	7	46.7%	15
1977	1	6.7%	7	46.7%	7	46.7%	15
1978	0	0%	7	43.8%	9	56.3%	16
1979	0	0%	7	43.8%	9	56.3%	16
1980	0	0%	7	43.8%	9	56.3%	16
1981	0	0%	7	43.8%	9	56.3%	16
1982	1	6.3%	7	43.8%	8	50.0%	16
1983	2	12.5%	7	43.8%	7	43.8%	16
1984	2	11.8%	7	41.2%	8	47.0%	17

Source: The Association for the Advancement of Feminism, 1985, p. 111

British Empire in 1964. In 1995 Dunn retired from politics and returned to reside in Britain with her husband, the former Attorney General Michael Thomas.

The limited but gradual participation of women in Hong Kong's political institutions can also be seen in the evolution of the composition of the former Urban Council. Table 5.5 shows that the number of female unofficials who were appointed increased only from one in 1966 to three in 1983, but then dropped to two in 1984, while the number of female unofficial members who were elected only raised from two in 1966 to three in 1984.

The negotiation between Britain and China over Hong Kong's future from 1982 to 1984 provided a catalyst for more local women to participate in politics. Table 5.6 points to the gradual increase in the level of women participation in Hong Kong's Urban and Regional Councils from 1985 to 1997. While both bodies witnessed more female candidates contesting in the council elections, the success rate was relatively low for the

Table 5.4 The gender distribution of Legislative Councilors, 1966–1984

Year	Unofficial members Female	Percentage	Unofficial members Male	Percentage	Official members Male	Percentage	Total
1966	1	3.8%	13	50%	12	46.2%	26
1967	1	3.8%	13	50%	12	46.2%	26
1968	1	3.8%	13	50%	12	46.2%	26
1969	1	3.8%	13	50%	12	46.2%	26
1970	1	3.8%	13	50%	12	46.2%	26
1971	1	3.8%	13	50%	12	46.2%	26
1972	2	7.1%	13	46.4%	13	46.4%	28
1973	1	3.3%	15	50%	14	46.7%	30
1974	2	6.7%	15	50%	13	43.3%	30
1975	2	6.7%	15	50%	13	43.3%	30
1976	3	8.1%	15	40.5%	19	51.4%	37
1977	3	6.7%	21	46.7%	21	46.7%	45
1978	3	6.7%	21	46.7%	21	46.7%	45
1979	3	6.7%	21	46.7%	21	46.7%	45
1980	3	6.3%	22	45.8%	23	47.9%	48
1981	4	7.8%	24	47.1%	23	45.1%	51
1982	5	10%	23	46%	22	44.0%	50
1983	6	12.5%	19	39.6%	23	47.9%	48
1984	6	12.8%	17	36.2%	24	51%	47

Source: The Association for the Advancement of Feminism, 1985, p. 110

Regional Council, which covered the New Territories where male domination has become a tradition in rural politics. The Urban Council in 1986 witnessed 80% of female candidates being successfully elected—an unprecedented result in local electoral politics.

The overall improvement in women participation in local politics could be seen in the evolution of the Legislative Council elections. Table 5.7 illustrates that while women participation through functional constituencies and electoral college of the Legislative Council lagged behind male participation from 1985 to 2016, women did participate more actively in the legislative direct elections. The number of female candidates increased from six in 1991 to forty-five in 2016, an increase in sevenfold. Moreover, the success rate of female participation in legislative direct elections improved from 17% in 1991 to 24% in 2016, including an impressive success rate of 38% in both 1995 and 2004. Hence, the political transition from the early 1990s to the period of the HKSAR has witnessed a gradual increase in women participation in legislative direct elections.

Table 5.5 The gender distribution of Urban Councilors

	Female councilors			Male councilors		
	Unofficials		Officials	Unofficials		
Year	Appointed	Elected		Appointed	Elected	Total
1966	1(3.8%)	2(7.7%)	6(23.1%)	9(34.6%)	8(30.8%)	26
1967	1(3.8%)	2(7.7%)	6(23.1%)	9(34.6%)	8(30.8%)	26
1968	0(0%)	1(3.8%)	6(23.1%)	10(38.5%)	9(34.6%)	26
1969	1(3.8%)	1(3.8%)	6(23.1%)	9(34.6%)	9(34.6%)	26
1970	1(3.8%)	1(3.8%)	6(23.1%)	9(34.6%)	9(34.6%)	26
1971	1(3.8%)	2(7.7%)	6(23.1%)	9(34.6%)	8(30.8%)	26
1972	1(3.8%)	2(7.7%)	6(23.1%)	9(34.6%)	8(30.8%)	26
1973	1(4.2%)	2(8.3%)	0(0%)	11(45.8%)	10(41.7%)	24
1974	1(4.2%)	2(8.3%)	0(0%)	11(45.8%)	10(41.7%)	24
1975	1(4.2%)	2(8.3%)	0(0%)	11(45.8%)	10(41.7%)	24
1976	1(4.2%)	2(8.3%)	0(0%)	11(45.8%)	10(41.7%)	24
1977	1(4.2%)	2(8.3%)	0(0%)	11(45.8%)	10(41.7%)	24
1978	1(4.2%)	2(8.3%)	0(0%)	11(45.8%)	10(41.7%)	24
1979	1(4.2%)	3(12.5%)	0(0%)	11(45.8%)	10(41.7%)	24
1980	2(8.3%)	3(12.5%)	0(0%)	10(41.7%)	9(37.5%)	24
1981	2(8.3%)	3(12.5%)	0(0%)	10(41.7%)	9(37.5%)	24
1982	2(8.3%)	3(12.5%)	0(0%)	10(41.7%)	9(37.5%)	24
1983	3(10.0%)	3(10%)	0(0%)	12(40.0%)	12(40.0%)	30
1984	2(6.6%)	3(10%)	0(0%)	13(43.3%)	12(40.0%)	30

Source: The Association for the Advancement of Feminism, 1985, p. 110

At the level of District Council elections, women's participation has been constantly less active than men in the three main places, namely, Hong Kong Island, Kowloon Peninsula and the New Territories. Table 5.8 demonstrates this difference between women and men participation in district elections. Without the support from political parties, women candidates could not be easily elected. In fact, pro-Beijing forces have been realizing the weakness of women participation and recruiting a lot of women candidates, who are trained in their political marketing and campaign work. As a result, the gradual increase in the number of women candidates who were elected after July 1, 1997 could be attributable to their participation in political parties, ranging from pro-democracy to pro-Beijing ones. The pro-Beijing parties have given them a leverage over non-party affiliated candidates, because the former have better manpower and resources in not only the preparation of election campaigns but also the process of electoral mobilization.

Table 5.6 Women political participation in Urban Council and Regional Council

	Number of male members		Number of female members			
Year	Contested	Elected	Contested	Elected	Success rate	Overall percentage of female councilors
Urban Council						
1983	38	13	3	2	66.7%	13.3%
1986	34	11	5	4	80%	26.7%
1989	24	13	6	2	33.3%	13.3%
1991	31	13	6	2	33.3%	13.3%
1995	66	27	10	3	30%	10%
Regional Council						
1986	38	12	2	0	0%	0%
1989	21	12	2	0	0%	0%
1991	22	12	2	0	0%	0%
1995	50	24	11	3	27.3%	11.1%

Source: Louie, Kin-shuen and Shum, Kwok-cheung, *Election Information Compilation of Hong Kong, 1982–1994* (in Chinese) (Hong Kong: The Hong Kong Institute of Asia-Pacific Studies, The Chinese University of Hong Kong, 1996)

Table 5.9 shows that women participation had a much better performance, including success rate and the percentage of directly elected seats being occupied in the Hong Kong Island than both Kowloon Peninsula and the New Territories. Perhaps the voters in the Hong Kong Island tend to pay more attention to the role of women in local politics. In general, the Hong Kong Island remains a hotly contested place between pro-Beijing and pro-democracy forces. United front work conducted by pro-Beijing forces is constantly intense on the Hong Kong Island, where the PRC's official representative office, the Liaison Office, is located. The Liaison Office also conducts extensive united front work targeted at women, trying to minimize the chances of pro-democracy candidates to win district elections. As such, women participation in the Hong Kong Island is higher than that in Kowloon and the New Territories.

Political Mobilization of Women United Front Groups

The Hong Kong Federation of Women (HKFW) and other women groups played a crucial role in the mobilization of pro-Beijing forces against political enemies, such as Yau Wai-ching and Baggio Leung who in September

Table 5.7 Women participation in Legislative Council elections

Year	Direct elections – Male candidates number/Elected (%)	Direct elections – Female candidates no./Elected (%)	Electoral college – Male candidates no./Elected (%)	Electoral college – Female candidates no./Elected (%)	Functional constituency – Male candidates no./Elected (%)	Functional constituency – Female candidates no./Elected (%)
1985	Nil	Nil	36/12 (33%)	3/0 (0%)	24/10 (42%)	1/0 (0%)
1988	Nil	Nil	24/10 (42%)	2/2 (100%)	17/14 (82%)	3/0 (0%)
1991	42/17 (40%)	6/1 (17%)	–	–	39/20 (51%)	1/1 (100%)
1995	42/17 (40%)	8/3 (38%)	18/10 (56%)	0/0 (0%)	26/20 (77%)	3/1 (33%)
1998	66/16 (24%)	15/4 (27%)	21/8 (38%)	4/2 (50%)	54/26 (48%)	6/4 (67%)
2000	71/21 (30%)	17/3 (18%)	9/5 (56%)	1/1 (100%)	47/26 (55%)	10/4 (40%)
2004	75/25 (33%)	13/5 (38%)	–	–	58/25 (43%)	13/5 (38%)
2008	80/23 (29%)	31/7 (23%)	–	–	53/26 (49%)	6/4 (67%)
2012	164/26 (16%)	51/9 (18%)	15/3 (20%)	3/2 (67%)	52/30 (67%)	1/0 (0%)
2016	169/24 (14%)	45/11 (24%)	17/4 (24%)	4/1 (25%)	54/30 (65%)	1/0 (0%)

Male and female candidates: candidates who participate/candidates who are elected
Brackets represent the success rate
Sources: *Report on the Legislative Council Election*, 1998, 2000, 2004, 2008, 2012 and 2016, downloaded from the website of Electoral Affairs Commission, in https://www.eac.gov.hk/, and *Election Information Compilation of Hong Kong* (published by the Hong Kong Institute of Asia-Pacific Studies, The Chinese University of Hong Kong, 1996, 2001, 2005 and 2015)

Table 5.8 Differences in women and men participation in District Council elections

	Hong Kong Island				Kowloon				New territories			
	FP	FE	MP	ME	FP	FE	MP	ME	FP	FE	MP	ME
1982	8	3	72	23	7	1	140	49	4	1	170	55
1985	14	8	94	45	12	5	160	89	6	3	217	90
1988	19	10	85	47	17	10	150	86	15	6	186	103
1991	14	7	86	52	18	7	125	84	15	7	208	116
1994	25	11	139	62	23	10	217	101	47	14	303	146
1999	28	15	124	65	37	16	207	103	64	25	338	168
2003	30	16	127	64	40	22	224	99	75	30	343	173
2007	38	19	133	61	47	20	214	98	79	37	392	169
2011	34	20	133	61	37	20	220	100	91	39	375	174
2015	42	17	129	62	48	20	224	98	85	38	404	185

FP number of females participating in elections; *FE* number of females who are elected; *MP* number of males participating in elections; *ME* number of males who are elected

Table 5.9 The success rate and seats occupation rate of women candidates in District Council elections

	Hong Kong Island		Kowloon		New Territories	
Year	Success rate	Percentage of seats occupied	Success rate	% of seats occupied	Success rate	% of seats occupied
1982	37.5	4.5	14.3	2	25	1.8
1985	57.1	15.1	41.7	11.9	50	3.2
1988	52.6	17.5	58.9	10.4	40	5.5
1991	50	11.9	38.9	17.6	46.7	5.7
1994	44	15.1	43.5	18.5	29.8	8.8
1999	53.6	18.8	43.2	13.4	39.1	13
2003	53.3	20	55	18.2	40	14.9
2007	50	23.8	42.6	16.9	46.8	18
2011	58.8	24.7	54.1	16.7	42.9	18.3
2015	40.5	21.5	41.7	16.9	44.7	17

Sources: *Reports on the District Councils Election* in 1999, 2003, 2007, 2011 and 2015; *Election Information Compilation of Hong Kong* (Hong Kong: Hong Kong Institute of Asia-Pacific Studies, the Chinese University of Hong Kong, 1996, 2001, 2005 and 2015). Also see https://www.elections.gov.hk/dc2015/chi/intro_to_can.html, and https://www.elections.gov.hk/dc2015/chi/results_hk.html?1527837316296, access date: January 1, 2019

2016 showed disrespect to the PRC during the LegCo swearing-in ceremony. Days after the oath-taking stage, all the pro-Beijing women groups were mobilized to criticize the behavior of not only Yau and Leung but also legislator Edward Yiu, who later were all disqualified by the Hong Kong court from holding their positions in the Legislative Council. The HKFW took a leadership role and made a public announcement that Yau deliberately pronounced China as "Chee-na," a derogatory term used by Japan to refer to China during the Second World War, and that Yau and Leung humiliated the Chinese nation, violated the Basic Law, "blackened Hong Kong's civilization," "undermined the legislature's dignity," and "arrogantly challenged the spirit of the rule of law" in the HKSAR.[32] About 100 pro-Beijing women groups were mobilized to oppose and denounce the behavior of the radical pro-democracy legislators-elect. Table 5.10 below sums up all the main women organizations which were mobilized to advertise in the pro-Beijing media in opposition to the behavior of Yau and Leung. All the affiliated groups under the HKFW were listed in the public advertisement to join the campaign against the two legislators-elect.

THE CO-OPTATION OF WOMEN INTO POLITICAL INSTITUTIONS IN HONG KONG AND CHINA

While some formerly pro-British women groups in pre-1997 Hong Kong were co-opted by PRC authorities into the united front umbrella, and while pro-Beijing interest groups have been fully mobilized since the handover, more women have also been appointed into the political institutions of Hong Kong and the mainland. Table 5.11 shows that these institutions include the NPC, the CPPCC, the Hong Kong ExCo and the LegCo functional constituencies. As of 2018, the political representation of women in political institutions remained relatively low: 16.7% in the NPC, 8.9% of the Hong Kong members of the CPPCC, 25% in the ExCo and only 2.9% in LegCo's functional constituencies. Interestingly, although women representation in the direct elections at legislative and district levels cannot be matched with men, 31.4% of directly elected LegCo members in 2018 were women, a figure higher than that in District Councils in the Hong Kong Island, Kowloon and the New Territories. Hence, women participate more actively and voluntarily in legislative

[32] *Ta Kung Pao*, October 18, 2016.

Table 5.10 Political mobilization of pro-Beijing women interest groups in denouncing the oath-taking behavior of pro-democracy legislators-elect

Territory-wide women groups	Hong Kong Island's Women Groups	Kowloon's Women Groups	The Hong Kong Women Federation
The Women Committee of the Provincial People's Political Consultative Conference The Tianjin Industrial, Commercial and Professional Women Committee. Foshan Industrial and Commercial Association's Women Branch. The Women Committee of the Hong Kong Fujianese Federation of Associations. The Women Committee of the Hong Kong General Chamber of Commerce. The Women Committee of the Hong Kong Guangxi Federation of Associations. The Women Committee of the Hong Kong Chinese Manufacturing Association Hong Kong Women Alliance The Women Committee of the Hong Kong Guangdong Women Federation of Associations Hong Kong Overseas Chinese Women Association	The Hong Kong Island South Women Association Wah Fu Estate Women Federation The Stanley Women Club The Women Committee of the Chinese Reform Club The Aberdeen Female Fisherman Association The Women Association of the Central and Western Districts The Chai Wan Women Federation The Women Branch of the Hong Kong Southern District Federation of Associations The Women Branch of the Quarry Bay Residents Association The Women Branch of the Eastern District Progressive Association The Women Branch of the Shaukeiwan and Chaiwan Kaifong Welfare Association The Women Branch of the Hong Kong Fuchow Clans Association	Kowloon City District Women Progressive Association Yautsimmong Women Association Mei Foo Women Association Chui Ping Women Association Yau Tong Women Gathering Plaza Po Tat Women Association Kowloon Women Federation of Association Hiu Lai Women Association Kwun Tong Women Development Association Shamshuipo Women Association Chinese Women Affairs Association San Po Kong Women Association Laguna City Women Club Kwun Tong Women Federation East Kowloon Women Association	The Outlying Islands Women Federation Shatin Women Association Long Ping Women Club Kwai Chung Northwest District Women Club The Women Center of the New Territories Federation of Associations Cheung Chau Women Association Tuen Mun Female Fishermen Association Tsuen Wan and Kwai Tsing Women Association Tai Po Women Association The Northern District Women Association The Sai Kung and Cheung Kwan O Women Association Tuen Mun Federation of Women Tin Shui Wai Women Federation Yuen Long District Women Association Shatin Women Leadership Training Club

Source: For details, see the advertisement in *Ta Kung Pao*, in http://paper.takungpao.com/resfile/PDF/20161018/PDF/a11_screen.pdf, access date: January 9, 2019

Table 5.11 Political representation of Hong Kong Women in China's and Hong Kong's political institutions, 2018

Political bodies	Number of members	Number of women	Percentage of women (%)
China's National People's Congress	36	6	16.7%
Hong Kong members of the Chinese People's Political Consultative Conference	124	11	8.9%
Executive Council's official members (government officials and principal officials)	17	3	17.6%
Executive Council's unofficial members (non-government members)	16	4	25.0%
Legislative Council's functional constituencies	35	1	2.9%
Legislative Council's direct elections	35	11	31.4%
District Council members in Hong Kong Island	79	17	21.5%
District Council members in Kowloon	98	20	20.4%
District Council members in the New Territories	223	38	17.0%

Source: The authors' calculation from the existing data in the mass media

direct elections than local district elections, whereas they remain relatively underrepresented in China's two main representative bodies, the NPC and the CPPCC. To put it in another way, China's united front work on Hong Kong women has much room to be improved by not only encouraging more women to participate in Hong Kong's direct election at legislative and district levels, but also mobilizing more of them to join political institutions in the mainland.

Table 5.12 delineates the detailed political background of individual women who were co-opted in the CPPCC in 2018. The Hong Kong women who were appointed into the CCP have several features: successful professionals, loyal supporters who include the former pro-British elites and reputable activists who contribute to the social stability, charity work, economic prosperity and politico-legal development of both the HKSAR and the PRC.

DISTRICT-BASED WOMEN INTEREST GROUPS AS TRANSMISSION BELTS IN CHINA'S UNITED FRONT WORK

Many district-based women interest groups have emerged as the transmission belts in China's united front work in the HKSAR. For instance, the Hong Kong Outlying Islands Women Association (OIWA) was registered

Table 5.12 Political background of female Hong Kong members of the Chinese People's Political Consultative Conference, 2018

Name	Political and professional background
Rosanna Wong Yik-ming	Born in 1952, Wong became a politician and a social work activist. Since 1980, she has become the managing director of the Hong Kong Federation of Youth Groups. From 1985 to 1991, Wong was an appointed unofficial member of the Hong Kong Legislative Council. She became an appointed unofficial member of the Executive Council between 1988 and 1991. She withdrew from the political arena shortly after 1991, but then returned to the Executive Council in 1992. Governor Christopher Patten appointed her as the convener of the Executive Council in 1995, succeeding Lydia Dunn. In 1997, the British government appointed her as the Dame of the British Empire. After the sovereignty return of Hong Kong from Britain to China, Wong became one of the targets of China's united front work. In 2003, she was appointed as a member of the CPPCC National Committee.
Connie Wong Wai-ching	Born in 1960, Wong became a managing director of the Wong Sun Hing Company Limited. She is an executive committee member of the All-China Women Federation. Wong was also a member of the Kowloon City District Council, the deputy chairwomen of the Hong Kong Guangxi Federation of Associations and the deputy chairwoman of the Hong Kong Provincial CPPCC Members Association. In October 2010, she was appointed as the Hong Kong member of the CPPCC. She is now a deputy director of the Bills Committee of the CPPCC. Wong's involvement in the All-China Women Federation demonstrated her important role in united front work.
Pollyanna Chu Lee Yuet-wah	Born in Hong Kong, Chu is a famous entrepreneur and a philanthropist. In January 2018, she was ranked as the fourteenth richest person in Hong Kong, with assets worth US$4.8 billion. Her father was Lee Fok-shu, who was the owner of a golden VIP room in Macao's Lisboa casino. Chu was acquainted with many rich and famous people in Hong Kong and Macao, including Angela Leong On-kei, the fourth wife of casino tycoon Stanley Ho. In 2006, Chu was a member of the Election Committee of the Hong Kong Chief Executive. She was also the honorary president of the Hong Kong Federation of Women, the chairwoman of the Dongguan Clans Association and a member of CPPCC. As a successful entrepreneur, she became an easy target for China's united front work.
Starry Lee Wai-king	Born in 1974, Lee is now the chairwoman of the pro-Beijing Hong Kong Democratic Alliance for the betterment and progress of Hong Kong. She is a registered accountant and rose up the political ladder quickly in 2012, when she was appointed to the Executive Council as an unofficial member. She has become an obvious target of China's united front work, mainly due to her professional background and the lack of female leaders in the pro-Beijing political forces.

(*continued*)

Table 5.12 (continued)

Name	Political and professional background
Yeung Chi-hung	Born in the mainland, Yeung migrated to Hong Kong during the 1970s. In 1994, she was appointed a member of the Guangdong CPPCC. Later, Yeung became a member of the Standing Committee of the Guangdong CPPCC, and the deputy director and secretary-general of the Hong Kong Guangdong Federation of Associations. In 2005, she received the Bronze Bauhinia Medal from the HKSAR government. She was a donor and contributor to the poverty alleviation work and school construction in the provinces of Guangdong and Gansu. Her patriotic attitude toward China was a natural target of the mainland's united front work.
Yeung Lei-san	Yeung is the daughter of the famous Yeung Suen-sai, who was born in Fujian and became an overseas Chinese in the Philippines. Yeung Lei-san is a Hong Kong businesswoman and a member of the Standing Committee of the Beijing CPPCC. She has become very active socially and politically, participating in the Kowloon East Federation of Associations as the deputy chairwoman, and the Hong Kong Youth Development Enterprise Alliance as deputy chairwoman. In recent years, Yeung has written assertively to support the policies of Beijing and the HKSAR government, speaking against the democrats and criticizing the Taiwan leader Tsai Ying-wen after President Xi Jinping's speech that appealed for unity, dialogue and reunification with Taiwan in early January 2019. Yeung's political correctness and redness make her the staunch supporter and implementation actor in China's united front work in Hong Kong.
Margaret Chan Fung Fu-chun	Born in Hong Kong in 1947, Chan studied in Hong Kong for her secondary school years and then pursued undergraduate and graduate degrees in Canada, including her medical doctorate at the University of Western Ontario. She later came back to Hong Kong and joined the Hong Kong government in 1978. She was the director of the Health Department in 1994, later dealing with the outbreak of Severe Acute Respiratory Syndrome in late 2002 and early 2003. In 2007, with the support of China, she became the director-general of the World Health Organization until 2017. In March 2018, she was appointed as a member of the CPPCC. Clearly, this was Beijing's political reward to her service in the World Health Organization.
Eliza Chan Ching-ha	She is a senior consultant of a law firm and an attesting officer appointed by the PRC Ministry of Justice. Chan was appointed as a Justice of Peace in 2000, received the Bronze Bauhinia Star in 2000 and then the Silver Bauhinia Star in 2015. She is now a member of the CPPCC, member of the Tianjin CPPCC Standing Committee and chairwoman of the Hong Kong Provincial CPPCC Members Association.

(*continued*)

Table 5.12 (continued)

Name	Political and professional background
Meng Lai-hung	Meng is a successful entrepreneur and administrator in property investment, marketing, retail and health sectors. She is a member of the Guangdong CPPCC, member of the China Soong Ching-ling Fund, deputy chairwoman of the Guangzhou City Chamber of Commerce and the honorary principal of a secondary school in Guangxi. Her successful career and philanthropy work in China made her a natural appointment to the CPPCC.
Margaret Leung Ko May-yee	Born in 1952, Leung is now a deputy chairwoman and managing director of a bank in Hong Kong. She graduated from the University of Hong Kong in economics in 1978 and then later became a very successful manager and director in the banking industry. Leung was appointed by the former Chief Executive C. Y. Leung as a member of the Executive Council in 2012. Her successful career in the banking sector was the reason why she was appointed as a member of the CPPCC.
Tung Ng Ling-ling	Born in Fujian, Tung migrated to Hong Kong at the age of 17. She became a worker and later managed factories in mainland China during the 1980s. After she became a successful entrepreneur, she turned to charity and philanthropy work in both Hong Kong and China, emphasizing the need to nurture young people and stressing the importance of social harmony. Her successful career and hard-working spirit made her appointment to the CPPCC natural.

Sources: For details, see https://baike.baidu.com, http://paper.wenweipo.com/2010/04/12/zt1004120013.htm, http://news.takungpao.com.hk/hkol/politics/2016-03/3290561.html, http://www.zhonglun.com.hk/tc/people/eliza-chan.php, and http://ccgfie.com/zh-big/Chairman.aspx?id=644, access date: January 9, 2019

and established as a local group assisting women in various activities, such as helping them in taking care of their children, finding jobs, upgrading their skills in employment and establishing a local network of friends and supporters. As time passed, the OIWA evolved into a socially and politically active organization that emphasizes mutual aid among women, and that establishes more local branches in various districts, including Tai O in 1994 and Lamma Island, Ping Chau in 1996 and Tung Chung in 1998 and 2000. Under the support of the Hong Kong Jockey Club, the OIWA in 2002 set up a comprehensive service center for women. With the additional support from the HKSAR government in 2003, the association opened a nursery center in Tung Chung for local women, providing all kinds of services that ranged from childcare to health resources. All these centers and activities helped the OIWA to reach out to the community in a more extensive manner, winning the hearts and minds of more local women.[33]

Politically, the OIWA provides a crucial conduit for the pro-Beijing DAB to reach out to the potential voters before and during elections. The OIWA director, Chau Chuen-heung, is a DAB activist. The DAB utilizes the OIWA to penetrate deeper into the women sector. In 2002, the OIWA had only 2000 members, but the number jumped to 4000 in 2003, an increase due to the need to balance the rapid growth of pro-democracy forces after the July 1, 2003, anti-government protests. In 2008, the OIWA membership rose to 10,000, and in 2018 it had 16,000 members. The steady increase in the OIWA membership is a testimony to the perseverance in developing and expanding its activities. Financially, the OIWA relies on its income from three sources, the tuition fees for its training courses, street donations and government subsidies.

Electorally, the OIWA could nominate candidates, like Chau Chuen-heung, to participate in district elections and grasp seats, becoming a mini-political party at the local level. Chau worked hard in Tung Chung starting from the 1990s, articulating the interests of local residents, calling for the need for a local library and improved parking space, then becoming an elected District Council member. In 2003, she was made a Justice of Peace, and in 2010 she received a Bronze Bauhinia Star. Chau was also a member of the CPPCC in Hubei province. She has built up her political power base in the outlying islands, becoming the deputy chairwoman of the Outlying Islands Federation of Associations, a pro-Beijing united front group at the district level.[34] Table 5.13 shows that, in the outlying island District Council, the number of women candidates who won increased from one in 1991 to seven in 2015. While only one was directly elected in the 1991 District Council election, the figure increased to five in 2015, with a 50% women representation in the council. This result could be regarded as politically satisfactory.

Organizationally speaking, the OIWA has become like a mini-political party with functional and district-based committees. The district-based committees include six organizations: Tung Chung city center, Tung Chung's southwest area, Ping Chau Island, Tai O district and Mui Woo district. Because Tung Chung's population is much larger than other districts, the OIWA divided it into two sections for the ease of organizing

---

[33] See https://www.oiwa.org.hk/tc/, access date: January 9, 2019.
[34] For details, see https://baike.baidu.com, access date: January 9, 2019.

Table 5.13 Women participation in the District Council elections in outlying islands

Year	Number of candidates Participate	Win	Male Participate	Win	Female Participate	Win	% of success	% of women in the council
1982	17	5	17	5	0	0	0	0
1985	17	7	17	7	0	0	0	0
1988	17	7	14	7	0	0	0	0
1991	15	8	14	7	1	1	100%	12.5%
1994	14	6	12	5	2	1	50.0%	16.7%
1999	13	7	8	3	5	4	80.0%	57.1%
2003	17	8	13	4	4	4	100%	50.0%
2007	27	10	21	5	6	5	83.3%	50.0%
2011	24	10	18	6	6	4	66.7%	40.0%
2015	21	10	14	5	7	5	71.4%	50.0%

Sources: *Reports on the District Councils Election* in 1999, 2003, 2007, 2011 and 2015; *Election Information Compilation of Hong Kong* (Hong Kong: Hong Kong Institute of Asia-Pacific Studies, the Chinese University of Hong Kong, 1996, 2001, 2005 and 2015)

activities. Functionally speaking, there are six committees under the OIWA, dealing with elderly services, the development fund, policy and education, sustainable development, youth work and recreational and cultural work. Clearly, the OIWA is a mini-united front and district-based political party, fighting for the interests of local residents, and it is led by women activists supportive of the PRC and the HKSAR government.[35]

The OIWA's mission and vision are clear and it focuses on women interests and welfare. Its platform includes the objectives of promoting the solidarity and mutual aid among women in different districts, the protection of women interests, the promotion of women participation in social affairs and the organization of cultural, education, recreational, health and community services for residents. It is very active at the district level, arranging storytelling sessions for children, street donations, docent activities to appreciate cultural and historical heritage, talks on job search and skills enhancement and career guidance. The OIWA appears to be an

[35] For details, see http://www.oiwa.org.hk/tc, access date: January 9, 2019.

interest group caring for the livelihood of residents, but given Chau's close affiliation with the DAB, the group has actually become a vanguard of the DAB to maintain the support of voters at the district level and to organize constituency services to win the hearts and minds of the people.

There are many district-level women united front groups similar to the OIWA operation. Examples include the Tuen Mun Federation of Women (TMFW), which was set up in 1976 and which now has 40,000 members, and the Tin Shui Wai Women Association (TSWWA), which was established in 1996 and currently has 12,000 members.[36] The TMFW and TSWWA are district-based women groups that offer all kinds of services for women, including elderly care, youth development, on-the-job training, career counseling and childcare. Although their mission and vision are not explicitly pro-Beijing and pro-government, both organizations are led by DAB politicians, Yip Shun-hing in the case of TMFW and Kwong Yuet-sum from the New Territories Federation of Association in the case of the TSWWA. Yip is the chairwoman of the Hong Kong Women Development Association, and a CPPCC member from 2008 to the present. She was awarded the Bronze Bauhinia Star in 2014 and was a standing committee member of the pro-Beijing and pro-government Alliance Against the Occupy Central Movement in 2014. Yip has remained very active in fighting for the interests of women, including the concern about mainland women who came to give birth to their babies in Hong Kong and the call for lifelong learning for women.[37] Hence, infiltrating pro-Beijing and pro-government elites into the district-based women groups becomes a useful means by which the umbrella of united front work can be expanded. Kwong, the chairwoman of the TSWWA, comes from the pro-Beijing united front district organization, namely the New Territories Federation of Association, and she was an appointed District Council member in Yuen Long from 2008 to 2011. The TSWWA offers a variety of services for women in Tin Shui Wai, including the prevention of suicide problems of family members, the financial support for the poor and the needy and the provision of disaster relief for victims of various accidents. In December 2014, in celebration of its 18th anniversary, the TSWWA held an inaugural ceremony for its new office bearers and the representative from the Liaison

---

[36] For details, see http://www.tm-women.org.hk/attachment/public_pdf/2016May.pdf, and http://www.tswwa.org/our-company, access date: January 10, 2019.
[37] For her activities, see http://www.fhka.com.hk/zh-hant/node/372, access date: January 10, 2019.

Office's New Territories branch attended, together with DAB activists Yip Shun-hing and Leung Chi-cheung. Leung is not only a DAB member but was also the chairman of the Yuen Long District Council from 2008 to 2015. Obviously, the TSWWA became a peripheral organization of the DAB to grasp more votes through the delivery of constituency services. As such, both TMFW and TSWWA have a kind of division of labor, the former focusing on constituency work in Tuen Mun and the later in Yuen Long's Tin Shui Wai. The electoral power base of the DAB is therefore entrenched and expanded through the networking and constituency activities of the two district-based women groups.

Financial Support of Pro-Beijing United Front Groups and the Creation of District-Based Federations

Financially, pro-Beijing groups have been acquiring their support through various sources: donations from members of the public, honorary presidents and office bearers of the groups, pro-Beijing businesspeople and organizations and even governmental subsidies. A good example is the controversial financial support from the District Council to the Tsuen Wan Kwai Tsing District Women Association (TWKTDWA), which was formed in 1976 and which has gradually become a united front organization since 1997. The TWKTDWA held its 39th anniversary gathering in September 2015, when the attendees included not only a representative from the Liaison Office attended but also DAB legislator Chan Hang-bun, the leaders of the New Territories Federation of Associations and HKFW chairwoman Yip Shun-hing.[38] According to the chairwoman of the TWKTDWA, it had 6000 members in 2015 and obtained the support of many women through its activities, such as elderly care, job training and Chinese opera performance. In 2018, the association ran into a controversy over a subsidy from the Tsuen Wan District Council for HK$173,000.[39] One district councilor from the Democratic Party, Lee Hung-bo, criticized the District Council for having bias in favor of the association, which could easily gain HK$173,000, while thirteen social welfare groups had to compete for the amount of HK$280,000 and to

[38] *Ta Kung Pao*, September 12, 2015, in http://news.takungpao.com.hk/paper/q/2015/0912/3162732.html, access date: January 10, 2019.
[39] *Ming Pao*, May 20, 2018.

divide it up evenly. Lee charged that, from 2009 to 2016, the TWKTDWA could get the funding support from the Tsuen Wan District Council annually. He criticized the council's committee, which granted the subsidy to the TWKTDWA, for having bias in favor of the pro-government and pro-Beijing group. Yet, since the democrats were outnumbered in the working committee that approved the funding support, the subsidy to the association was easily supported by the pro-government and pro-Beijing councilors. Clearly, patron-client relations appeared in the Tsuen Wan District Council, where pro-Beijing members tended to support their like-minded district group, namely TWKTDWA.

In the PRC's united front work in the HKSAR, its supportive groups not only fully utilize the financial support from district councils but are also brought under the framework of district-based federations, such as the Kowloon Women's Organizations Federation (KWOF). The KWOF was founded in May 2000 and it has 24,600 members in 2019.[40] Its mission and vision are the same as other women groups, promoting the interests and welfare of women. But the KWOF activities are explicitly pro-government and pro-Beijing, such as its opposition to the Occupy Central Movement in 2014; its support of China's cooperation with the United Nations to hold the global women summit in New York in September 2015; its support of the development of the Greater Bay Area to integrate Hong Kong closer into the PRC in 2018; and its collaboration with the pro-Beijing Kowloon Federation of Associations to study and help relieve the pressure encountered by parents in August 2018.[41] While the KWOF president is Cheng Chun, its chairwoman So Lai-chun is a famous pro-Beijing activist at the district level. So is affiliated with the Kowloon Federation of Association (KFA), another famous district-based united front organization. In 2011, the KFA member, Wong Chun-ping, defeated a Democratic Party member in the Kwun Tong District Council elections, but Wong was discovered by the mass media as a suspected underground member of the Chinese Communist Party (CCP), who worked in the Liaison Office during the 1990s and who then left the office in 2002 to work in the KFA as a secretary-general.[42] When asked whether he was a CCP member, Wong told the media that "many residents knew"

[40] For details, see http://www.kwof.org.hk/web/index.php?option=com_content&view=article&id=53&Itemid=53, access date: January 10, 2019.
[41] Ibid.
[42] For details, see https://www.thestandnews.com/, access date: January 10, 2019.

Table 5.14 United front women groups in opposition to the 2014 Occupy Central Movement

Women Groups	Number of affiliated groups participating in the mass signature campaign in opposition to the Occupy Central Movement
Hong Kong Federation of Women's Center (set up in 1981)	Ten out of sixty-three affiliated groups
Hong Kong Federation of Women	Seven out of twenty-eight affiliated groups
Kowloon Women's Organizations Federation	Nineteen out of twenty-three affiliated groups
Other district-based women federations	Eleven out of sixty-one affiliated groups
Territory-wide women federations	9
(a) Hong Kong-based	4
(b) Kowloon-based	2
(c) New Territories-based	3

Note: Tabulated from websites and various media reports

his background.[43] As such, penetrating pro-Beijing loyalists into district-based federations is a means by which China's united front work in the HKSAR has been conducted.

Of the twenty-three affiliated groups under the KWOF, nineteen of them participated in an initiative of opening a hotline in September 2014 for parents, students and teachers to report on those students who decided to participate in the class boycott and the Occupy Central Movement.[44] Its move led to the immediate criticisms from pro-democracy groups, including the scholarism led by pro-democracy student leader Joshua Wong, which said that the KWOF might infringe on the privacy of individuals and the freedom of speech, and that it might create a "white terror" in the campus of secondary schools.[45] Table 5.14 shows that district-based federations were skillfully utilized by the pro-Beijing united front against

[43] Ibid.
[44] For details, see http://www.bbc.com/zhongwen/trad/hong_kong_review/2014/09/140916_hkreview_report_hot_line, https://www.voacantonese.com/a/beijing-loyalists-under-fire-for-reporting-hotline-20140910/2444843.html, and https://www.rfa.org/cantonese/news/HK-student-09082014094647.html, access date: November 23, 2018.
[45] For details, see https://www.voacantonese.com/a/beijing-loyalists-under-fire-for-reporting-hotline-20140910/2444843.html, access date: January 10, 2019.

the Occupy Central Movement in 2014. The KWOF cooperated with other like-minded groups in the process of political mobilization.

Table 5.15 shows that the KWOF leaders were co-opted into the mainland's political institutions in 2011, including CPPCC members in the mainland's southern cities and also special delegates representing Hong Kong in different women federations in the PRC. Such appointments to various mainland political institutions strengthened the subjective feelings of the co-opted elites on their recognition by PRC authorities and also

Table 5.15 Co-optation of leaders of the Kowloon Women's Organizations Federation into China's Political Institutions, 2011

Name	Office	Other positions	Appointed positions in China
Ngan Ng Yu-ying	Principal President	Nil	Shui Kwan City's CPPCC member
Ko Po-ling	Founding President	Kwun Tong District Council member	Hong Kong member of the NPC
Cheng Chun	Chairwoman	Nil	Special delegate of the All-China Women Federation
Lee Lin	Deputy chair	Kowloon City District Council member	Guangdong Federation of Women Executive Committee member
So Lai-chun	Chairwoman	Kwun Tong District Council deputy chair	Special delegate of Guangdong Federation of Women
Fung Mei-wan	Deputy chair	Kwun Tong District Council member	Anhui Federation of Women Executive Committee member
Wong Yuk-lan	Deputy chair	Nil	Special delegate to the Luwu District Federation of Women
Chiu Fung-yee	Deputy chair	Nil	Zhuhai Federation of Women Executive Committee member
Chan Yuen-yung	Deputy chair	Nil	Huizhou Federation of Women Executive Committee member
Wong Shu-ming	Secretary-general	YauTsimMong District Council member	Special delegate to Huixhou Federation of Women
Choi Pik-chi	Central Committee member	Nil	Special delegate to Luwu Federation of Women

Sources: See http://www.kwof.org.hk/web/images/%E5%89%B5%E5%88%8A%E6%9C%83%E8%A8%8A.pdf and www.kwof.org.hk/web/images/創刊會訊.pdf, access date: January 11, 2019

their sense of significance in the mainland political system at the national, provincial and local levels. In return, the co-opted women elites are determined to support Beijing's policy toward the HKSAR.

Like the KWOF, another women federation named the Hong Kong Island Women Association (HKIWA) was set up in April 2005 and was registered as a charity organization in August 2013. Its service centers spread out to the central and western district, Wan Chai, Eastern district and the Southern district on the Hong Kong Island. The political objective is clear: it aims at wining the hearts and minds of women voters in support of pro-Beijing forces in elections. Although its mission and vision dilute the political ingredient and focus on the promotion of the interests and welfare of women, it has 51 affiliated groups with 30,000 members.[46] Its chairlady Carol Cheung is explicitly pro-Beijing, saying that the association has to "love the nation and love Hong Kong."[47] The association's activities include the celebration of the HKSAR's 15th anniversary of its return to China, the mobilization of local women in the celebration, the organization of career guidance and jobs exhibition for members, the holding of cosmetics and English courses for women and the sending of delegations to Guangdong and Beijing to study the mainland's efforts at advancing the status and interests of women. The HKIWA supported the police in the 2014 Occupy Central Movement and it belonged to the so-called blue ribbon camp that opposed the democrats. During the annual inauguration ceremony of the HKIWA's new office bearers, officials of the Liaison Office attended its functions, showing a close partnership between the association and PRC authorities.[48] In the summer of 2015, the association visited the office of legislator Regina Ip, who welcomed its visit and introduced to them her work on women. On International Women's Day, on March 8, 2018, the HKIWA held a large-scale celebration ceremony, inviting three officials from the Liaison Office, two representatives from the Hong Kong Macao Affairs Office and the All-China Women Federation, the DAB deputy chairman Cheung Kwok-kwan and leaders from other local women federations to attend. Carol Cheung was reelected as the chairwoman in March 2018. Obviously, the HKIWA has emerged as one of the active united front women federations in the HKSAR, hav-

---

[46] See http://www.hiwa.org/, access date: January 11, 2019.
[47] Ibid.
[48] Those who supported the Occupy Movement wore yellow ribbons but those who opposed it wore the blue ribbons.

ing close connections with not only PRC officials but also the DAB and other united front groups.

It is noteworthy that the united front women federations sometimes share their affiliated groups but simultaneously reaching out to other different women groups in order to expand their power base. For example, the HKIWA and the Hong Kong Federation of Women (HKFW) share ten affiliated groups. These overlapping groups under two politically similar federations mean that they can share their manpower and resources in the event of socio-political mobilization. The ten common affiliated groups in the two federations are listed in Table 5.16.

The HKFW has more DAB members than the HKIWA. From 2015 to 2017, the HKFW had DAB members Starry Lee and Jasper Tsang Yok-sing as its honorary advisers. Other DAB members who were the advisers of the HKFW included Choi So-yuk and Sun Kai-cheong. In 2017, the honorary patron of the HKFW was the former Liaison Office deputy director Yin Xiaojing who retired in 2018. However, the leadership of the HKFW tended to dilute the role of DAB members; only Chau Chuen-heung from the DAB is the volunteer secretary-general of the association. The reshuffling of the leadership in the HKFW appeared to renew and recruit more pro-Beijing women into the organizational work. From 2017 to 2019, the new chairwoman of the HKFW is Pansy Ho, the daughter of Macao casino tycoon Stanley Ho. Interestingly, there are seven vice chairwomen, including Sophia Ko Ching-chi, who

Table 5.16 Ten affiliated groups shared by the Hong Kong Island Women's Association and the Hong Kong Federation of Women

Women group	Year of formation
Hong Kong Southern District Women's Association	1975
South Horizons Women's Association	1995
Kellett Bay Women's Association	1994
Shek O Women's Association	2000
Stanley Women Association	1997
Aberdeen Fisherwomen Association	1996
Wanchai District Women's Association	1982
Carnation Women's Association	2003
Lan Fong Woman Association	2004
Chaiwan Women's Association	1996
Shek Pai Wan Women Association	1985

Note: Tabulated from the websites of the two federations

was a former member of the government thinktank Central Policy Unit. Judging from the composition and reshuffling of the leaders of the two women federations, the idea was to refresh the leadership, groom new leaders, such as the younger Carol Cheung of the HKIWA, and to share manpower and resources with other affiliated groups. The combination of new and old leaders, and the inexperienced with the experienced, is a hallmark in the reshuffle of these pro-Beijing united front federations.

The overlapping leadership of the pro-Beijing federations can also be seen in the Hong Kong Eastern District Women's Association (HKEDWA), which was formed in 2015 as a united front group rallying district-based women groups in the Eastern district, and which currently has Carol Cheung, the chairwoman of HKIWA, as its honorary adviser. The HKEDWA chairwoman is Fung Chui-ping, and it joined the Hong Kong Federation of Women in 2016. The HKEDWA is explicitly pro-government and pro-Beijing; Fung remarked that it has to provide a platform for women to participate in the society and contribute to Hong Kong, and that the support of the central government in Beijing for Hong Kong is indispensable for the territory's economic prosperity and social harmony.[49] She expressed her gratitude to the financial support from the Eastern District Council, showing that the HKEDWA activities were funded by the directly elected local body.

In a nutshell, all the district-based federations are pro-Beijing united front organizations with overlapping affiliated groups and leadership. In non-election time, they all organize constituency services for women, utilizing the financial sponsorship from a variety of sources, including their honorary presidents, businesspeople, street donations and government subsidies. During elections, they have become a powerful alliance assisting pro-Beijing and pro-government candidates and political parties to grasp more votes. Moreover, these federations have become the auxiliary arm of not only Beijing but also the HKSAR government in supporting its policies. As such, the transmission belt functions of united front federations to win the hearts and minds of the ordinary people and to constitute a bridge between pro-Beijing elites and the masses have been fully achieved.

---

[49] See Fung's remarks as mentioned in http://www.hkedwa.com/word/, access date: January 11, 2019.

THE RELATIVELY WEAK PRO-DEMOCRACY FEMINIST GROUPS RESISTING UNITED FRONT WORK

Unlike the financially affluent and politically organized united front groups, the number of pro-democracy women groups in the HKSAR is very small, with the most active one being the Association for the Advancement of Feminism (AAF). The AAF was formed in March 1984 and aims at developing policy and research for the interests of women and raising their consciousness.[50] It has opened a hotline to receive women's complaints against sexual harassment, holds the annual pro-democracy rally and march on July 1, advocates the protection of human rights and the implementation of democratic political reforms, examines how to achieve sustainable development in the society, applies to district councils for funding support for its women activities and organizes arts appreciation and Buddhist courses to advance the spiritual development of women.[51] In July 2015, the AAF invited a pro-democracy activist, Lau Siu-lai, who was stripped of her position as a legislator by the court in 2017 over her "disrespectful" oath-taking behavior in October 2016, to talk about the role of women in the 2014 Occupy Central Movement.[52] It also advocates a peaceful approach to striving for women's equality and combatting violence against women. Although the AAF also acquires donations from members of the public and subsidies from district councils, its financial affluence is no match for the relatively larger and stronger pro-Beijing united front women groups. Table 5.17 sums up the financial situation of the AAF.

CONCLUSION

The PRC's united front work targeted at women groups and individual activists has become extensive and intensive since July 1, 1997. Some formerly pro-British and pro-colonial government women groups, such as the Hong Kong Chinese Women's Club and the Women's Welfare Club,

---

[50] See https://aaf.org.hk/, access date: January 13, 2019.

[51] For its activities, see https://aaf.org.hk/category/, access date: January 13, 2019.

[52] For Lau's role, see Shum Lok-kei, Jeffie Lam and Alvin Lum, "Ousted pro-democracy Hong Kong lawmaker Lau Siu-lai barred from Kowloon West Legislative Council by-election," *South China Morning Post*, October 12, 2018, in https://www.scmp.com/news/hong-kong/politics/article/2168359/ousted-pro-democracy-hong-kong-lawmaker-lau-siu-lai-barred, access date: January 13, 2019.

Table 5.17 Financial situation of the Pro-Democracy Association for the advancement of feminism

Year	Income (HK$)	Expenses (HK$)	Surplus (HK$)
1989	82,360	223,480	330,836
1990	287,644	233,467	383,544
1991	575,233	326,109	632,669
1992	371,598	404,229	600,036
1993	424,447	374,122	560,361
1994	460,168	444,857	525,306
1995	745,678	791,681	571,309
1996	547,879	566,835	552,353
1997	583,243	658,488	477,148
1998	657,672	716,824	417,996
1999	747,410	767,772	397,634
2000	1,244,808	770,937	871,505
2001	788,829	767,866	892,468
2002	1,051,635	966,058	978,045
2003	591,466	867,252	702,259
2004	764,147	835,708	630,698
2005	759,411	883,850	506,259
2006	710,323	855,299	361,283
2007	882,023	702,268	541,038
2008	682,484	792,955	430,567
2009	643,159	775,805	297,921
2010	964,303	923,328	338,896
2011	649,187	654,523	333,560
2012	554,418	416,744	471,234
2013	766,112	668,755	568,591
2014	708,569	706,966	570,194
2015	638,297	630,294	672,394
2016	576,732	607,967	641,159
2017	513,483	472,339	682,303

Sources: Tabulated from the annual reports of the Association for the Advancement of Feminism

have been co-opted and absorbed into the PRC's united front umbrella. Moreover, pro-Beijing women groups have grown by leaps and bounds, including the utilization of core groups such as the All-China Women Federation, the Hong Kong Federation of Women and the Hong Kong Development Association. Pro-Beijing women activists and groups have been politically encouraged and mobilized, and financially supported, to participate in legislative and local elections, thereby gradually increasing the quantity and quality of women participation in politics. At the same time, women activists have been politically appointed and co-opted into China's and Hong Kong's political institutions, strengthening their subjective feelings of being socially and politically recognized and of having their status elevated. Accompanying the enhancement of socio-political recognition is the continuing financial support of women groups by the rich, the famous women activists and other donors. In recent years, pro-Beijing women federations have envisaged their leadership rejuvenation and renewal, trying to sustain the momentum of development in the long run. On the contrary, pro-democracy women groups have remained relatively very weak, limiting to the most active Association for the Advancement of Women. The huge differences in the quantity of women groups between the pro-Beijing united front and the pro-democracy camp can be easily seen in the HKSAR, a testimony to the huge inroads of the PRC's new united front work that targets at women in the territory. Finally, the formation and mobilization of pro-Beijing women federations remain a hallmark of China's united front work in Hong Kong, for these federations can pool the manpower and resources, share leadership and affiliated groups and groom younger women leaders.

CHAPTER 6

United Front Work on Six Religions

The PRC authorities have been focusing on the co-optation of six main religions and their leaders in the HKSAR, including the Buddhist, Taoist, Confucian, Islamic, Christian and the Catholic. Comparatively speaking, the mainland Chinese co-optation of the Buddhist leaders in the HKSAR has been far more successful and much deeper than any other religions, including the Taoist, Confucian, Islamic, Christian and lastly the Catholic. This chapter examines how the mainland officials have been conducting united front work toward the six main religions, assessing the inroads and challenges ahead.

THE BUDDHISTS: FROM LOBBYING OF THE PO LIN MONASTERY TO UNITED FRONT TARGET

The religion of Buddhism in Hong Kong could be traced back to the Sung dynasty when mainland Buddhist monks went through Guangdong and Hong Kong to transfer their religious knowledge to Southeast Asia.[1] The Tuen Mun district was the place where mainland Buddhists first came to Hong Kong and where Buddhist statues and plaques were found. Hong Kong under the British rule tolerated religious practices, thereby allowing Buddhists to form their schools, build their temples, practice their religion and recruit their disciples. In August 1973, the six religions and their

[1] Tang Ka-jiao, *The 20th Century Hong Kong Buddhism* (in Chinese) (Hong Kong: Society of Hong Kong History, 2008), p. 1.

leaders in Hong Kong formed an alliance named Hong Kong Religious Alliance Camp, inviting several hundred participants to listen to historian Law Heung-lam's lectures on the evolution of religions in China and to let religious believers interact with each other harmoniously.[2] In June 1974, the Buddhist and Catholic leaders organized another larger-scale religious dinner and gathering so that the six religious believers could gather together and share their views on how to improve the society and bring about harmony. In 1976, the Buddhist leader Ven Sik (Sik Kwok-kwong) and Bishop Wu Cheng-chung formed an annual forum for the six religious leaders to share their insights in an annual setting and to deliver a joint New Year message. This convention of having six religious leaders to issue a joint New Year message has become a practice. The Buddhist leaders in Hong Kong opened many primary and secondary schools, set up the tertiary Nang Yan College in 1969, established a Buddhist hospital in 1971 and contributed to disaster relief efforts whenever there were victims from typhoon attacks and fire accidents.[3]

Politically speaking, the most significant lobbying activity of the Buddhists as an interest group in Hong Kong under British colonial rule was their interest articulation for the construction of a large Buddha statue starting from 1972, when the late Governor Murry MacLehose was the target of their lobbying efforts.[4] The colonial government supported the Buddhist leaders who set up a preparatory committee that involved the former Chief Secretary Sir David Akers-Jones as the principal patron. In 1974, the Hong Kong government bought a large piece of land in the Lantau Island to prepare for the construction of the Po Lin Temple, followed by the inception of its construction work in 1981. In the early 1980s, the Hong Kong Buddhist leaders visited Taiwan and collected almost half of the funding support for the construction of the Buddha status; nevertheless, the late director of the New China News Agency (the predecessor of the Liaison Office in the HKSAR), Xu Jiatun, heard about this. Xu sent some PRC officials from Beijing's United Front Department to lobby the Buddhist leaders against the Taiwan investment.[5] In 1986, the construction of the big Buddha was contracted out to a mainland

[2] Ibid., p. 151.
[3] Ibid., pp. 152–160.
[4] Ibid., p. 204.
[5] See "The Doubtful Representation of the Hong Kong Buddhist Association: Loving the Nation and Loving the Religion," October 31, 2015, in https://thestandnews.com/, access date: January 15, 2019.

technical consultancy company named China's Aviation Industry and Science, which eventually used three years to finish the design of the Buddhist statue in bronze.[6] The estimated cost of building the big bronze Buddha was HK$67 million. During the late 1980s, the funding for the completion of the Buddha status was insufficient and some Japanese monks visited the Po Lin monastery leaders, offering financial assistance. When Zhao Puchu, the chairman of the PRC Buddhist Association and the former chairman of the CPPCC, learnt about this visit from the Japanese, he called the Buddhist leaders of the Po Lin Monastery to stop them from accepting the Japanese offer.[7] Eventually, a mainland factory affiliated with the PRC Aviation Department was responsible for the completion of the Buddha statue in 1989. When the opening ceremony of the Buddha statue was held in 1993, Sik Chi-wai invited the last Governor, Christopher Patten, to attend the function. Yet, the NCNA director Zhou Nan regarded Patten as anti-PRC and refused to shake hands with the last governor—an event widely reported in the mass media. Hence, the politics of constructing the big Buddha statue on the Lantau Island's Po Lin Monastery were significant. Not only was the mainland united front work involved but the political wrangling between the PRC and Japan, and between Beijing and London, was apparent behind the scene.

On the other hand, the Buddhist leaders in January 1994 lobbied the colonial government to create a Buddha day, but since the British administration was departing and preparing for a transition to the Chinese rule, their lobbying effort had no concrete result.[8] The Buddhist leaders turned to lobby the Hong Kong Macao Affairs Office and the Preparatory Committee of the establishment of the first HKSAR government. Eventually, 54 Preparatory Committee members and 38 members of the Provisional Legislative Council supported the idea of having a Buddha day in the HKSAR after July 1, 1997. As a result, the HKSAR government designated the Chinese calendar of April 8 as the Buddha day every year. From the perspective of united front, the PRC government was delighted to witness the establishment of the Buddha day to incorporate Buddhism

[6] Also see Tang Ka-jiao, *20th Century Development of Hong Kong Buddhism* (Hong Kong: The History and Culture Society of Hong Kong Buddhism, 2007), p. 130.

[7] See "The Doubtful Representation of the Hong Kong Buddhist Association: Loving the Nation and Loving the Religion," October 31, 2015, in https://thestandnews.com/, access date: January 15, 2019.

[8] Tang Ka-jiao, *A History of Hong Kong Buddhism* (Hong Kong: Chung Hwa Bookstore, 2015), p. 279.

into one of its solid allies. After all, the Buddhist emphasis on social harmony fits into the ruling psyche of the PRC government, which has stressed the importance of maintaining economic prosperity and social stability in the HKSAR.

The management of some Buddhist monasteries was affected by scandals involving its Buddhist leaders. From 2005 to 2015, an abbot of the Po Lin Monastery, Sik Chi-wai, who was also a former Hong Kong member of the NPC in 1997 and a former chairman of the Hong Kong Federation of Buddhist Associations, was accused of not only financial mismanagement but also protecting two Buddhist monks, who got into "fake marriages" with a Buddhist nun named Sik Chi-ding, an abbess of Ting Wai Monastery.[9] In 2017, the Po Lin Monastery leader, Sik Kin-chiu, was found to have a mysterious relationship with a female Buddhist secretary named Sik Sum-wai, both going to Hawaii for holidays and spending a huge amount of money to buy life insurance.[10] Both of them were found to visit Hawaii for vacation. Sik Kin-chiu was originally named Lam Kwok-hing and a former chairman of the Macao Federation of Buddhist Associations as well as the deputy chairman of the World Federation of Buddhist Associations. He died of cancer in July 2018.[11] Sik Sum-wai was accused by the mass media of working for the PRC United Front Department's social work unit.[12] In 2016, the two Po Lin Monastery leaders—the late Sik Kin-chiu and Sik Sum-wai—attended the 67th anniversary celebration of the founding of the PRC in Beijing and participated in a dinner hosted by the mainland United Front Department. Leung Yiu-chung, a Hong Kong legislator, remarked that these leaders "were not real Buddhists and they have very close relationships with the mainland united front work."[13]

The Hong Kong Buddhist Association (HKBA), which was set up in 1945, has become politically pro-Beijing and pro-government since 1997.

---

[9] See *Apple Daily*, October 13, 2015. Also see Allen Au-yeung and Fanny W. Y. Fung, "Bad faith: director accuses chief nun of 'sham marriage, embezzlement' in Hong Kong monastery," *South China Morning Post*, October 13, 2015.

[10] See "Sik Kin-chiu dies and he was involved in scandals with life insurance and a nun," https://www.hk01.com, July 6, 2018, access date: January 15, 2019.

[11] See the report on his past and death in https://nextplus.nextmedia.com/article/2_603882_0, access date: January 15, 2019.

[12] See a report on the financial chaos within the Po Lin Monastery and its "close relationship" with the united front officials in the mainland, in http://www.epochtimes.com/b5/17/11/24/n9887395.htm, access date: January 15, 2019.

[13] Ibid.

In 2012, when student activists led by Joshua Wong's Scholarism opposed the government's national education policy, the HKBA supported the controversial policy. In October 2014, the HKBA issued a public statement, appealing urgently to all those Hong Kong people who participated in the Occupy Central Movement to "maintain calmness," to "leave the assembly places" and to "avoid bodily harm."[14] It also appealed to the leaders of the Occupy Central Movement to "abandon their prejudice" and to protect the safety of the participants. The HKBA urged that the government and the Occupy leaders should strive to achieve unity by having "mutual respect, sincere discussion and peaceful coexistence."[15] Ideologically, the Buddhist emphasis on social harmony fits into the pro-establishment mentality of the PRC regime. In September 2017, the HKBA, together with other Buddhist, Taoist, Islamic, Confucian and Christian leaders, celebrated the 68th anniversary of the founding of the PRC. The Liaison Office's deputy director Tan Tieniu attended the celebration. Leaders of the five religions came up with the following statement in support of the rise of China and its policy toward Hong Kong:

> Hong Kong is a fortunate place with success in the implementation of the two systems. We are glad to welcome the 68th anniversary of the PRC. We the religious leaders of Hong Kong congratulate our motherland for political smoothness, social harmony, public well-being, occupational flourishing and economic prosperity. Our motherland since the PRC establishment has grown from strength to strength, with the rapid development of science and technology which attracts the world, promotes world peace, and achieves mutual victories. Internally, our motherland severely penalizes bribery and corrupt acts and builds up the new style of clean governance, thus conforming to the wishes of the public. Hong Kong is relying on the motherland and should cherish the excellent opportunities provided by the "one country, two systems," and we should work hard and cooperate in unity to develop the economy, stop political disputes, and achieves the motherland's aspirations of Hong Kong. We should also safeguard Hong Kong's safety and prosperity, strive for the people's well-being, achieve a society with fairness and love, and contribute to the nation.[16]

---

[14] "An Urgent Appeal from the Hong Kong Buddhist Association," October 5, 2014, in http://www.hkbuddhist.org/zh/page.php?p=preview_detail&epid=26&cid=1, access date: January 15, 2019.

[15] Ibid.

[16] News Bulletin, "Hong Kong Religious Sector in Celebration of the 68th Anniversary of the PRC," in http://www.hkbuddhist.org/zh/page.php?p=preview_detail&epid=39&cid=1, access date: January 15, 2019.

It is noteworthy that the Catholic leaders, who tend to be more resistant to both the PRC regime and China's united front work, were excluded from the statement—a reflection of the difficulty of PRC officials in conducting united front work toward the Catholics in the HKSAR. In September 2018, the five religious leaders from the Buddhist, Taoist, Islamic, Confucian and Christian groups issued a statement in celebration of the 69th anniversary of the PRC, saying that they supported China's "One Belt One Road" initiative and its economic policy of developing the Greater Bay Area for the benefit of Hong Kong.[17] Again, the Catholic groups were not included in the joint statement in 2019.

The PRC authorities have long treated the Hong Kong Buddhists as the target of co-optation. On July 1, 1997, when Hong Kong's sovereignty was returned from Britain to China, a large-scale celebration of the handover was held in the Hong Kong Football Stadium with the active participation of the Hong Kong Buddhist Association and the PRC Buddhist Association. In May 1999, the PRC Buddhist Association arranged an exhibition of the Buddha's Tooth and Finger to Hong Kong, leading to the participation of 300,000 Hong Kong Buddhist believers and residents. In May 2004, the former minister of the PRC United Front Department, Liu Yandong, went to Hong Kong to celebrate the arrival of the Buddha's Finger in the HKSAR.[18] The Buddha's Finger exhibition was timed to enhance a sense of positive attitude among the people of Hong Kong, many of whom suffered psychologically, mentally and physically due to the outbreak of the Severe Acute Respiratory Syndrome (SARS) from late 2002 to mid-2003. Liu added that the exhibition of the Buddha's Finger in Hong Kong demonstrated Beijing's "care and love" for the people of Hong Kong.[19] Liu said that the religious sectors in both the mainland and Hong Kong belonged to "the same family" and that the PRC government insisted on the principles of "mutual respect, non-intervention, non-subordination" to interact with the religious leaders and believers of the HKSAR.[20] The PRC officials grasped the opportunity

[17] News Bulletin, "Hong Kong Religious Sector in Celebration of the 69th Anniversary of the PRC," in http://www.hkbuddhist.org/zh/page.php?p=preview_detail&epid=39&cid=1, access date: January 15, 2019.
[18] "Queues start earlier to see the Buddha's Finger blessed," *South China Morning Post*, May 27, 2004.
[19] Ibid.
[20] See the report in http://cppcc.people.com.cn/GB/34961/65233/65239/65802/4450761.html, July 27, 2004.

of the visit of the Buddha's Finger to Hong Kong to conduct united front work on all the religions in the territory. In 2012, during the 15th anniversary of the HKSAR return to China, another Buddha's Finger from Nanjing visited Hong Kong for five days, leading to the participation of 300,000 believers and residents. In 2015, the PRC Buddhist Association sent a delegation to visit its counterpart in Hong Kong, because the Hong Kong Buddhist Association celebrated its 70th anniversary. Through all these cultural exchanges and religious interactions, the foundation of the PRC united front work on the Hong Kong Buddhists has become very solid.

The Taoists Under United Front

The Hong Kong Taoist Federation of Associations (HKTFA) was formed in 1957 and has been co-opted by Beijing since 1997. It has five secondary schools, five primary schools and six kindergartens.[21] In 1984, the Hong Kong Taoists visited the PRC Taoist Association, opening a new chapter of mutual exchange and interactions. In May 1998, the HKTFA under the leadership of its chairman Tong Kwok-wah sent a 23-member delegation to Beijing, visiting the central authorities and their religious counterpart for the first time after 1997. During the visit, Tong said that the delegates were confident toward the "one country, two systems," and that Hong Kong would certainly continue as a prosperous and stable city. Most importantly, he remarked that, in the past, the Taoists in Hong Kong were "ignored" and "excluded" by the British, but after 1997, they adopted the principles of "loving China, Hong Kong and Taoism" to develop the traditional Chinese culture and to contribute to the prosperity of both Hong Kong and the mainland.[22] In July 2007, the PRC Taoist Association visited the HKSAR and celebrated its 10th anniversary together with the HKTFA.

In 2010, the Taoist association lobbied the government to designate an annual Taoist day. On the Sunday at the end of the second week of March 2013, the former Chief Executive C. Y. Leung attended the Taoist Festival Day as a formal gesture of respect to the Taoist religion in the HKSAR. The missions of the HKTFA, apart from its need to propagate the Taoist

---

[21] For details, see http://www.hktaoist.org.hk/index.php?id=112, access date: January 17, 2019.
[22] See *Zhongguo Zhongjiao* (*China Religion*), June 1998, p. 18.

religion, are to increase interactions with mainland religious authorities at the central and local level, to establish friendship with the mainland Taoist groups and to promote mutual exchanges.[23] These missions provide a golden opportunity for PRC authorities to conduct united front at the Hong Kong Taoists. In March 2015, the Taoist Festival Day in the HKSAR saw the participation of both the PRC Taoist Association and the Hong Kong Liaison Office's deputy director Lin Wu.[24] In June 2017, the PRC Ministry of National Religious Affairs received a delegation from the HKTFA led by chairman Leung Tak-wah, stressing that Beijing adopted the principles of "mutual respect, mutual non-intervention and mutual non-subordination" to deal with the Hong Kong religions.[25] In the same year, when the HKTFA visited Fujian province, the Fujian provincial united front chief Lei Chunmei met the delegation members and emphasized that Fujian recognized the important contributions of the HKTFA to the development of the Taoist faith, and that mutual operation between the mainland and Hong Kong Taoists would be able to contribute to the PRC's "One Belt, One Road" initiatives.[26] Lei also supported the HKTFA's action of helping the poor and the needy in Fujian's mountainous and ethnic minority areas, saying that the associational efforts would help the PRC realize its "dream of the Chinese renaissance."[27] In October 2017, the Shenzhen united front and religious officials visited the HKTFA in Hong Kong, saying that Taoism is a crucial element in the Chinese culture, and that Taoist exchanges between the mainland and Hong Kong would be in conformity with the PRC's objective of "globalizing the excellence of Chinese culture in the world."[28] In September 2018, the Guangzhou religious affairs department co-organized the first Guangzhou-Hong Kong-Macao Taoist cultural conference with the Hong Kong government's Home Affairs Department, inviting the Taoist groups in

---

[23] For details, see http://www.hktaoist.org.hk/index.php?id=112, access date: January 17, 2019.
[24] See http://www.taoist.org.cn, February 2015, access date: January 21, 2019.
[25] "Taoist Festivals in the Two Straits and Four Places," in http://zytzb.gov.cn/zjswxw/70116.jhtml, access date: February 3, 2019.
[26] "Lei Chunmei meets Hong Kong's religious leaders," in www.hktaoist.org.hk/index.php?id=317, access date: February 3, 2019.
[27] Ibid.
[28] See the report of the visit of the Shenzhen united front department to Hong Kong, in http://www.tzb.sz.gov.cn/xwzx/gzdt/tzsx/mzgz/zjgz/201710/t20171011_9336722.htm, access date: February 3, 2019.

Guangzhou, Hong Kong and Macao to attend. Academic experts in Taoism from the three places were invited to share their views, while religious leaders delivered speeches to support a joint declaration saying that "the three places will cooperate closely to spread the excellence of the Chinese cultural tradition and to realize the positive energies of the Chinese renaissance."[29]

In October 2018, the HKTFA cooperated with the Macao Taoist Federation to send a joint delegation to Beijing. The delegation was led by Zhang Qiang, deputy head of the Hong Kong Liaison Office's coordination department, and by Shing Gang, the deputy head of the Macao Liaison Office's coordination unit.[30] The HKTFA chairman Leung Tak-wah and the Macao counterpart Ng Ping-chi led 120 members to visit not only the central government's United Front Department but also the mainland's Taoist Federation of Associations. They shared views on how to develop and promote Taoism and to achieve world peace. Another common objective was to promote the excellence of the Chinese cultural tradition. Wang Zuoan, the deputy head of Beijing's United Front Department, stressed that all the Taoist leaders from Hong Kong, Macao and mainland "have to continue to propagate the excellent Chinese cultural tradition, to pay attention to the reorganization of Taoist scripts and literature, to consolidate international cooperation," and to invite foreign Taoists to attend the 2020 international Taoist forum to be held in the HKSAR.[31]

United front work targeted at religious groups is effective when PRC authorities utilize non-political activities as a means by which all these groups are participating collectively and cohesively. In 2003, the Taoists in the mainland collaborated with their counterparts in the HKSAR to set up an ecological forest in Gansu province for the sake of protecting the environment and dealing with deforestation. After the 2008 Sichuan earthquake in the PRC, the Hong Kong Taoists donated logistical supplies to the Sichuan and other affected provinces. In 2017, when the PRC Taoist Association celebrated its 60th anniversary, the Hong Kong Taoists donated 2 million yuan to the mainland work on the propagation of Taoism. Li Guangfu, the chairman of the PRC Taoist Association, said in

[29] *Wen Wei Po*, September 28, 2018.
[30] See the HKTFA Newsletter, in http://www.hktaoist.org.hk/usr/files/newsletter/2018/2018_11.pdf, November 11, 2018.
[31] Ibid.

2017 that these mutually beneficial activities could contribute to the "great process of the Chinese national renaissance and the realization of the Chinese dream."[32] The HKTFA chairman Leung Tak-wah added that the Taoist Festival Day could enhance the public understanding of the Chinese culture, and that Taoism and the Chinese culture are closely connected. Clearly, cultural activities provide a golden opportunity for the PRC side to conduct united front work on the local Taoists easily and effectively.

As with Confucianism, Taoism has been propagated and studied through the establishment of academic units, such as the Taoist Cultural Study Center (TCSC) under the Chinese University of Hong Kong. The TCSC was set up in 2005, organizing forums and study programs that attract the participation of not only Taoists from Hong Kong and the mainland but also the counterparts from Taiwan. In July 2015, the center held a study course that embraced the participation of 200 Taoists from the mainland, Taiwan, Singapore and Hong Kong.[33] The mainland participants, including the PRC Taoist Association's deputy chairman Meng Ziling and Wu Chenglin, delivered their talks on the Taoist beliefs, reforms and its development in the world. The center offered programs and certification for students specialized in the study of Taoism, thus becoming a platform for mutual educational exchanges and the PRC's united front outreach.

THE CONFUCIAN ACADEMY AND CONFUCIUS INSTITUTE

Confucius has been a traditional cultural and educational model for the Hong Kong society. The Confucian Academy is a non-governmental organization founded in 1930 by Chen Huanzhang to promote Confucianism, which emphasizes social harmony, moral conduct and proper rituals. Chen was born in Guangdong in 1881 and went to America to pursue his studies. In 1921, he established the Confucian Society with his teacher Kang Youwei, a conservative reformer, in Shanghai. After Chen died in 1933, the Confucian Academy was managed by Chu Yu-chun until 1942 when Lu Xiangfu succeeded him. Lu passed away in 1970 and Huang Yuntian assumed the leadership until 1992, when Tong Yun-kai took up the chairmanship. Tong was a Cantonese born in Sanshui in 1934

---

[32] *Zhongguo Zhongjiao*, June 2017, p. 26.
[33] *Zhongguo Zhongjiao*, April 2015, p. 34.

and obtained his doctorate in business management from the United States. He was politically co-opted by the PRC as the Guangdong CPPCC member and was also selected as a member of the Election Committee for the Chief Executive of the HKSAR from 1997 to 2016. In 2011, the PRC conferred a Confucian cultural award upon Tong, who in 2014 acquired a Silver Bauhinia Star from the HKSAR government.[34] Tong donated a lot of money to the establishment of Confucian temples, clinics, parks, schools and institutes in many cities in the mainland. In Hong Kong, the Confucian Academy set up a few secondary and primary schools, notably the Tai Shing Secondary and Primary School. As a quid pro quo, Tong has been politically rewarded by both Beijing and the HKSAR regime. In March 2018, Tong expressed his hope that the Confucian Academy would need the support of the government to reduce the land price so as to find a piece of land for the construction of a Confucius temple.[35] If the PRC is a patron supportive of its client Tong, and if the HKSAR government is also a client of Beijing, then the HKSAR regime is expected to facilitate the process of building a Confucius temple in the coming years.

Tong's remarks indicate that he is politically loyal to Beijing. He said that "the Confucian religion [in Hong Kong] has never confronted with the [Chinese] nation ... Our religion is wholeheartedly loving China and Hong Kong and this position has not changed ... We have never had any negative impact on the [ruling] party."[36] Tong's Confucian Academy has been actively promoting activities to care for the elderly and the needy, holding students' performance, public donations, Confucian festivals and free health care services. It also applied to the HKSAR government for support to build a Confucian temple in Hong Kong. Nevertheless, a critic of Tong accused him of "betraying" Confucius thoughts and of being too close to the CCP.[37] Lau Kwei-biu was worried that the advocacy of building the Confucian temple has a "hidden motive" of "maintaining political stability and social harmony in Hong Kong in the midst of an

---

[34] For details, see https://www.ourhkfoundation.org.hk/zh-hant/node/1026, access date: January 19, 2019. Also see *Ta Kung Pao*, September 2, 2013.
[35] *Oriental Daily News*, March 1, 2018.
[36] Tong's remarks are cited in Woo Chun-loong, "A traitor of Confucius and Mencius," in https://www.inmediahk.net/node/1006169, February 14, 2010, access date: January 21, 2019.
[37] Ibid.

authoritarian rule."[38] Lau adopted a critical democratic perspective and saw Tong as being a political client loyal to the patron, the CCP.

From a united front perspective, the Confucian Academy has been mobilized to participate in all kinds of pro-PRC activities. In June 2006, the PRC Minister of Religion Ip Xiaowen visited Hong Kong's Confucian Academy, saying that Confucianism emphasized "patriotism, solidary, development and self-strengthening efforts," and that the Hong Kong Confucian leaders could "contribute together to the good prospects" of the territory.[39] In June 2011, it participated in a large-scale exhibition of the life and historical events of the former PRC Premier Zhou Enlai, an exhibition that attracted the sponsorship and mobilization of other pro-Beijing interest groups, such as the Hong Kong Guangdong Federation of Associations, the Hong Kong Fujian Federation of Associations and the Hong Kong Chiu Chow Federation of Associations.[40] The exhibition ceremony was held at the Hong Kong Central Public Library and opened by the CPPCC vice-chairman Tung Chee-hwa and the Liaison Office's former deputy director Li Gang. In April 2012, the Confucian Academy participated in the celebration of not only Hong Kong's 15th anniversary of its return to China but also world peace, a large-scale social event that mobilized many other pro-Beijing interest groups, such as the Hong Kong Guangxi Federation of Associations, the Hong Kong Federation of Trade Unions, the Hong Kong Federation of Youth Associations and the Hong Kong Guangdong Federation of Associations. Clearly, the Confucian Academy was politically co-opted in the participation of celebration of all these apparently non-political and cultural activities.

The PRC united front work on Hong Kong's Confucius believers also extends to its support of the founding of the Confucius Institute of Hong Kong (CIHK) in 2006 through the collaboration of the PRC Office of Chinese Learning Council International (Hanban) and the Hong Kong Polytechnic University.[41] The CIHK aims at promoting the Chinese language and culture and facilitating cultural exchanges between the PRC

---

[38] Lau Kwei-biu, "Confucius Temple or Confucius Institute? A Tool of Maintaining Political Stability?," in https://www.inmediahk.net/node/1018023, access date: January 21, 2019.

[39] For his remarks, see "Minister Ip visits the Confucian Academy," in http://blog.sina.com.cn/s/blog_4b32f63a01000741.html, access date: January 21, 2019.

[40] See https://baike.baidu.com, access date: January 21, 2019.

[41] See CIHK background in https://cihk.org.hk/about-us/about-cihk/, access date: January 21, 2019.

and the world. It is the only Confucius Institute in the HKSAR holding various events like the Confucian Institute Day on October 27, 2018, the organization of workshops and seminars on Confucianism and other religions, such as Taoism, and the International Chinese Medicine Cultural Festival in July 2018.[42] It is noteworthy that, in 2013, Hanban and the Polytechnic University agreed to restructure the CIHK as a unit under the university so that the university community and students would benefit directly from the CIHK's activities and programs. Since 2014, the CIHK has been placed under the Polytechnic University's Faculty of Humanities. Therefore, the CIHK has enhanced its academic role and status and perhaps diluted the political sensitivity of being an organization affiliated with Hanban. The CIHK Council Chairman is Chu Hung-lam, an academic who was a Chang Jiang scholar appointed by the PRC Ministry of Education. The Chang Jiang scholars scheme was utilized by the PRC regime to co-opt overseas scholars, including Hong Kong academics, into the mainland academic circle quite effectively. The Council members have members of the Confucius Institute Headquarters (Hanban), thereby maintaining some degree of personnel connections with the PRC institutionally.

The PRC since 2004 has set up Confucius Institutes in many other parts of the world. As of 2017, there were 525 Confucius Institutes with 1113 programs in 146 countries in the world; they apparently teach Chinese language and cultures to peoples in the world, but since the Confucius Institutes are under the PRC's educational bureaucracy, many countries have become increasingly concerned about the mainland's possible influences and penetration into their campuses.[43] In particular, the institutes are led by academics and intellectuals who appear to be under the influence of PRC authorities. In the United States, a few universities terminated their collaborative relations with the Confucius Institutes, including the University of Chicago, Pennsylvania State University and the University of North Florida, where professors complained about the official PRC propaganda that penetrated into the content of the programs in Chinese culture and language education.[44] In Canada, McMaster

---

[42] See https://cihk.org.hk/past_event/, access date: January 21, 2019.

[43] *Apple Daily*, August 26, 2018.

[44] Sharon Bernstein, "Second U.S. University cuts ties with the Confucius Institute," October 2, 2014, in https://www.reuters.com/article/us-usa-china-confucius-institute-pennsyl/second-u-s-university-cuts-ties-with-chinas-confucius-institute-idUSKCN0 HQ4UZ20141001, access date: February 2, 2019. Also see "Confucius Institute closed at

University closed down the Confucius Institute in 2013 amid concerns about "human rights violation and discriminatory hiring practices."[45] In October 2014, the Toronto District School Board voted to cancel plans for a Confucius Institute because of its concern about China's human rights record and restrictions on human rights.[46] The ways in which some Confucius Institutes taught Chinese culture and education, and their linkage with the PRC educational apparatus aroused the great concern of some foreign universities. If Confucius Institutes represent the PRC's "soft power" in penetrating other parts of the world, this strategy has stimulated the political sensitivity of more foreign universities and institutes than ever before. Compounding the Western suspicions of the united front function of the Confucius Institute has been the assertive foreign policy adopted by the PRC under the Xi Jinping era. The American Congress expressed its concern about the possibility that the PRC government was utilizing not only the Confucius Institutes but also the overseas Chinese in its conduct and operation of united front work targeted at both foreigners and the overseas Chinese community.[47]

In the case of the Confucius Institute in Hong Kong, its only operation in the Hong Kong Polytechnic University was revamped by making it under the administration of the Faculty of Humanities, giving an image of some degree of autonomy from the PRC establishment. In the Hong Kong setting, the PRC's united front work focuses on other areas, especially interest groups in various occupational sectors, and therefore the Confucius Institute at the Polytechnic University is relatively insignificant as it focuses more on educational functions and cultural dissemination than on any political motivation.

US university amid concerns about Chinese influences on campuses," August 15, 2018, in https://www.scmp.com/news/world/united-states-canada/article/2159888/confucius-institute-closed-us-university-amid, access date: February 2, 2019.

[45] "McMaster University severs ties with Confucius Institute," March 2013, in https://bulletin-archives.caut.ca/bulletin/articles/2013/03/mcmaster-university-severs-ties-with-confucius-institute, access date: February 2, 2019.

[46] Austin Ramzy, "Toronto School District Cancels Plans for Confucius Institute," October 30, 2014, in https://sinosphere.blogs.nytimes.com/2014/10/30/toronto-school-district-cancels-plans-for-confucius-institute/, access date: February 2, 2019.

[47] *Apple Daily*, August 26, 2018.

THE HONG KONG MUSLIMS UNDER UNITED FRONT

In 2017, it was estimated that there were about 180,000 Muslims in the HKSAR.[48] At least one-third of them are Chinese, with the rest coming from locally born non-Chinese and foreign-born believers from Pakistan, India, Malaysia, Indonesia and Middle East and African countries.[49] The Muslim community in Hong Kong under the British rule became more prominent in the middle of the nineteenth century, especially as the British brought Muslim soldiers from India to other parts of Asia. Later, Muslim merchants arrived in Hong Kong. With the increase in the Muslim population, the British colonial government in Hong Kong granted them land to build mosques, schools and cemeteries.[50]

The Chinese Muslim Cultural and Fraternal Association (CMCFA) is the largest Islamic interest group in Hong Kong and was formed in 1917.[51] It was registered as a charity organization in 1963 and is now managed by a 15-member executive committee.[52] The CMCFA established a number of schools for Islamic children, including the Islamic Dharwood Pau Memorial Primary School, the Islamic Primary School, the Islamic Kasim Tuet Memorial College, the Islamic Pok Oi Kindergarten and the Islamic Abu Baker Chui Memorial Kindergarten. The group is constantly holding religious activities such as seminars, talks and lectures to study, propagate and publicize Islam. It also regularly pays visits to the Hong Kong prisons to guide the inmates to the direction of goodness and Islamic faith.

The CMCFA has been sending delegations to the PRC to enhance mutual understandings and relations. In July 1997, the PRC Islamic Association sent a seven-member delegation to visit Hong Kong after the invitation from the CMCFA, opening the door for mutual exchanges after the establishment of the HKSAR. In March and April 2006, the CMCFA and other local Muslim groups, such as the Hong Kong Islamic Federation, sent a 20-member delegation to visit Beijing and Yunnan province

---

[48] See Lau Chi-wai, "Muslims in Hong Kong," in https://www.bbc.com/zhongwen/trad/chinese-news-39124578, access date: January 22, 2019.

[49] Ibid. Also see "History of Muslims in Hong Kong," in http://www.islam.org.hk/en/?p=13&a=view&r=27, access date: January 22, 2019.

[50] Ibid.

[51] See http://www.cmcfa.com/e/action/ListInfo/?classid=1, access date: January 22, 2019.

[52] See http://www.islam.org.hk/en/?p=13&a=view&r=27, access date: January 22, 2019.

formally, marking the first visit of local Muslim leaders to Beijing after Hong Kong's handover.[53] Officials from the Hong Kong Macao Affairs Office, the United Front Department and the Religious Affairs Department met the delegates. In May 2013, Ningxia's CPPCC members visited the CMCFA through the introduction and support of the Hong Kong Liaison Office. In July 2015, the CMCFA sent a delegation to Qinghai and enhance mutual communication. In November 2017, the Liaison Office's deputy director Tan Tieniu visited the CMCFA, introducing the gist of the 19th Party Congress and appealing to the association and the Muslim community to maintain the "excellent tradition of loving China, loving Hong Kong and loving the religion," and to contribute to the PRC's developmental plan and strategies.[54] In December 2017, members of the PRC's CPPCC ethnic and religious committee visited the CMCFA, illustrating the importance of the local Islamic group to the PRC's united front work that targets at ethnic and religious minorities in the HKSAR. In April 2018, the Liaison Office organized a form to discuss the development of the Great Bay Area among the members of three interest groups, namely the CMCFA, the Guangzhou city's ethnic and religious affairs and the Guangzhou city's Islamic Religion Association. Clearly, the CMCFA has become the target of the PRC's official contacts and united front work.

A study of the historical development of the famous Hong Kong Islamic leader, Kasim Tuet (1919–1990), illustrated the harmonious relationships between the Muslims in the HKSAR and the PRC authorities. Tuet was a Muslim born in Hong Kong and had a Chinese name Chung Yin (Zhong Yin in Mandarin).[55] He was the former chairman of the Hong Kong International Islamic Association, chairman of the CMCFA and also the deputy chairman of the Hong Kong Religious Federation. As early as 1954, Tuet was the deputy chairman of an active local political interest group named the Civic Association. In 1978, he participated in London's Islamic study conference in the capacity of the representative from Hong Kong. He was appointed by the PRC government as the seventh CPPCC member. Tuet was described as an Islamic leader "loving China and loving the religion."[56] In March 1984, as a leader of the Islamic community in

---

[53] See the Liaison Office's announcement, in http://www.locpg.gov.cn/ldjl/zj/200701/t20070122_1153.asp, access date: January 22, 2019.
[54] *Wen Wei Po*, November 8, 2017.
[55] See https://baike.baidu.com/, access date: January 22, 2019.
[56] See http://www.cmcfa.com/e/action/ListInfo/?classid=1, access date: January 22, 2019.

Hong Kong, he wrote an open letter to the Hong Kong legislators, expressing his concern about the future of Hong Kong at a time when Britain and China negotiated the territory's political future. In 1985 he was appointed by the PRC government as a member of the Hong Kong Basic Law Consultative Committee, which was responsible for collecting public opinion on the drafting process of the HKSAR mini-constitution. Tuet was also an executive director of a cleaning company in Shenzhen and Shekou, showing that he was an active local Islamic business leader with business operations in the mainland. His ethnic minority origin, religious background and career development meant that Tuet was perhaps an ideal and a natural target of co-optation by PRC authorities.

In 2017, when the PRC government tightened its control over religions in the mainland, Hong Kong's Muslims were by no means affected and they could practice their religious beliefs relatively freely.[57] In March 2017, the mainland government integrated the Department of Religion into the United Front Department and ordered that the PRC national flag, constitution, socialist core values, and "the excellent Chinese cultural tradition" should be shown and demonstrated in all religious venues.[58] However, this directive was not really imposed onto the HKSAR. The PRC United Front Department has referred to the display of national flag, constitution, socialist core values and the Chinese cultural tradition in religious venues as an attempt at "Sinifying" Islam, protecting all religious groups and curbing religious extremism.[59] Yet, this process of Sinifying Islam has not been implemented in the HKSAR. On the other hand, many non-governmental organizations in the HKSAR, especially schools and interest groups, are encouraging citizens to understand more deeply about the Muslim cultural and religious practices, leading to a high degree of tolerance over Islam. Hence, while the Sinification of Islam has been carried out in the PRC, the Hong Kong Muslim community has been retaining its relatively high degree of cultural and religious autonomy.

---

[57] This was also the observation from journalist Lau Chi-wai in his "Islam in Hong Kong: Different Challenges in China and Hong Kong," March 1, 2017, in https://www.bbc.com/zhongwen/trad/chinese-news-39124578, access date: January 22, 2019.

[58] For the mainland practices, see *Sing Tao Daily*, July 4, 2018.

[59] See http://www.zjislam.org/show.aspx?id=1410&cid=24, January 5, 2019, access date: January 22, 2019.

The Christians Under United Front

The way in which the PRC treated the Christians during the 1950s has caused alarm to some Hong Kong Christians, who understand that they are constantly under Beijing's united front target and operation. After the CCP came to power in mainland China, it targeted at the Christian leader Wang Mingdao, who however refused to be co-opted and to accept the regime's principles of allowing the Chinese Christians to "be autonomous," to "cultivate" themselves, and to "propagate" their own religion.[60] In 1955, Wang was politically labeled as a "anti-revolutionary Christian clique." At the same time, the CCP sent agents to divide the mainland Christians internally, splitting them into two groups, one supportive of the CCP and the other opposing it.[61] The CCP strategy was to create political "enemies," isolate and attack them, and score victory by forcing those who tried to survive to change to a pro-regime stance. Wang's experiences of being politically persecuted remain vivid in the minds of a minority of Christians in the HKSAR. Ying Fuk-tsang, a religious expert, reminded the people of Hong Kong that Beijing's tight control over the Christians in the mainland displays six characteristics of official explanations: (1) such control is due to the local policy rather than the central government's directive; (2) the responsibility of any repression is shifted to local cadres; (3) the government's appeal to religious activists to stick to the law; (4) religious freedom in the mainland has made and will make progress; (5) religious leaders should adopt a moderate instead of a confrontational approach; and (6) religious activists should be aware of the danger of being utilized by the Westerners.[62] Ying's arguments attempt at alerting

---

[60] Ying Fuk-tsang, "Today we have to revisit a history of 'united front' work on Christians," January 28, 2019, in http://faith100.org/, access date: February 3, 2019. Ying is the director and professor at the Department of Religious and Cultural Studies at the Chinese University of Hong Kong. For an interesting contrast with the remarks made by Leung Yin-shing, an overseas Canadian Chinese Christian scholar who has been criticized as increasingly pro-Beijing, see "Pro-Beijing scholar Leung Yin-shing's remarks on the PRC protection of religious faith," in https://apostlesmedia.com/20180626/8195, access date: February 3, 2019. Also see "Comment on Leung's visit to China," in https://www.chinaaid.net/2018/06/blog-post_27.html, access date: February 9, 2019. Leung had taught at Hong Kong Baptist College and emigrated to Canada in 1990. He is seen by some Christian observers as being politically co-opted by the PRC.

[61] Ibid.

[62] Ying Fuk-tsang, "Using Facts to Convince Me: The Six Explanations in Defence of the Chinese Communist's Religious Policy," July 9, 2018, in http://faith100.org/, access date:

the religious leaders and activists in the HKSAR to the reality of the CCP's tight control over religious freedom in the mainland.

The PRC authorities started to conduct intensive united front work on the Hong Kong Christians in the early 1980s. The former deputy director of the NCNA, Li Chuwen, had been a Christian priest before he was sent to work in Hong Kong in 1983. After Li arrived in Hong Kong, one of his tasks was to conduct united front work on the Christian leader Kwok Nai-wang. Kwok was born in Hong Kong in 1938 and was the former secretary-general of the Hong Kong Christian Council from 1977 to 1988. He graduated from the University of Hong Kong in 1963 and then at the Yale Divinity School in 1966. Politically, Kwok is pro-democracy; he was one of the first ten supporters of the 2014 Occupy Central Movement and has consistently called for the direct election of the Chief Executive by universal suffrage.

When Li became the NCNA deputy director, he made friendship with Kwok, inviting the latter to visit mainland China frequently. In September 1984, a month prior to the 35th anniversary of the PRC, Beijing invited 200 famous Hong Kong elites to visit the capital, including the religious leaders from the six main religions. Kwok Nai-wang and Peter Kwong Kong-kit of the Anglican Church were among the seven religious leaders visiting Beijing.[63] In October 1985, on their way to visit Beijing, Kwong told Kwok "not to do anything that is not agreed by the Hong Kong religion."[64] However, during Hong Kong's democracy movement in support of the introduction of direct elections to elect both the Chief Executive and all the members of the Legislative Council in 1988, Kwok gave a pro-democracy speech in the Ko Shan theater with the participation of many other democrats. After his remarks and participation, Kwok was regarded as a member of the pro-democracy "faction" and became a target of political exclusion from Beijing's authorities. In 1985, when the Basic Law Consultative Committee was set up by the PRC government to consult the people of Hong Kong on the content of the Basic Law, Peter Kwong was co-opted as a member. Kwok remained politically defiant, maintaining that Hong Kong should be democratized. At this juncture,

February 3, 2019.

[63] "Li Chuwen and the united front work on the Hong Kong religions," in http://medium.com/civic-faither/c-e6aa60fe81bs, access date: February 3, 2019.

[64] "Interview with Kwok Nai-wang who appeal to the Hong Kong religious leaders and activists not to bow to those who are rich and powerful," October 10, 2018, in https://thestandnews.com/politics/, access date: February 3, 2019.

Beijing appeared to shift to co-opt Kwong and abandon Kwok in its united front work on the Christian leaders in Hong Kong. Peter Kwong became an easy target of political co-optation; he was co-opted into Beijing's political institutions, such as being a member of the Hong Kong Affairs Advisor, a member of the Hong Kong Preparatory Committee for the establishment of the HKSAR government and a member of the Election Committee of the first Chief Executive of the HKSAR. In 1998, Kwong was appointed by the PRC government as a Hong Kong member of the CPPCC. In 2007, the HKSAR government conferred upon Kwong a Golden Bauhinia Medal, recognizing his contribution to the religious community in Hong Kong.

While Kwong was groomed by the PRC and the Hong Kong authorities to be an authoritative spokesperson of the Hong Kong Christians, Beijing's officials began a campaign as early as the mid-1980s to oust Kwok from the Hong Kong Christian Council.[65] The Council was gradually controlled by pro-Beijing moderates, notably Ko Chiu-wah. Kwok eventually left the Council and founded the Hong Kong Christian Institute in 1988, cooperating with other democrats, such as Helena Wong Pik-wan, and calling for the need to promote democracy. Kwok reflected on the remarks made by So Shing-yat, the chairman of the Hong Kong Christian Council, who said during the religious sector's celebration of the national day of the PRC in October 2018 that the Christians "pray for the 'One Belt, One Road' scheme, the Greater Bay Area, the High Speed Rail, and the Hong Kong-Macao-Zhuhai bridge."[66] Kwok criticized the Hong Kong Christian leaders for "believing that being subservient to the [mainland] regime is a necessary path for the religion to protect itself and to survive."[67] According to Kwok, the six religions in the HKSAR are the "victims of their own success" because by building schools and getting the government's support, they have "eventually become part of the political establishment."[68] Most importantly, the religious leaders gradually cannot speak on issues to fight for social justice, and they are "afraid of antagonizing the PRC" because of their wish to propagate their religious faith in the mainland.[69] Kwok also warns that the PRC under President Xi Jinping is

[65] Ibid.
[66] Ibid.
[67] Ibid.
[68] Ibid.
[69] Ibid.

drifting slowly toward "totalitarianism," and that it does not loosen its political grip on Hong Kong's democratic development. Kwok's critique of the existing Hong Kong religious leaders and their willingness to be politically co-opted by PRC authorities is a testimony to his resistance to the CCP's united front work in Hong Kong.

Despite the fact that the leaders of the Hong Kong Christians appear to be politically co-opted, some other local Christians remain politically autonomous from Beijing's influence and they constantly provide insightful and independent analyses of the predicament of religious persecution in the PRC. For example, Choi Siu-kei provides an in-depth analysis of the PRC's religious policy and Xi Jinping's remarks on the need to "mainlandize" religions and to combine religions with socialism.[70] Other reports have been deeply concerned about the PRC's persecution of Christians in Henan province, where local authorities not only removed the church crosses but also changed the ten commandants and arrested those religious followers who leaked out the stories of official suppression to outsiders.[71]

Many other Christians in the HKSAR are under the united front work of the PRC. In October 2018, the Hong Kong Chinese Christian Churches Union sent a 45-member delegation to Beijing, studying various subjects such as China's aviation technology, defense modernization, foreign policy in light of the US-China trade war, Chinese cultural tradition, and the social contradictions in China under the new era.[72] Critics said that the Chinese Christian Churches Union, which claims to have a membership of 400,000, went to the PRC for a "brainwashing course" without any relationship with religious faith.[73] Indeed, the political philosophy of the leaders of the Union tends to be moderate, seeing their charity, donation and reconstruction work in Sichuan province after the 2008 earthquake as

---

[70] Choi Siu-kei, "How do Christians cope with the religious policy under Xi Jinping's era," June 6, 2015, in http://christiantimes.org.hk/, access date: February 3, 2019.

[71] "Henan officials ordered the deletion of command one from the ten commandants," January 3, 2019, in https://www.christiantimes.org.hk/Common/Reader/News/ShowNews.jsp?Nid=156717&Pid=102&Version=0&Cid=2141&Charset=big5_hkscs, access date: February 3, 2019. Also see Jiang Tao, "Authorities remove church crosses on flimsy pretexts," April 9, 2018, in https://bitterwinter.org/authorities-remove-church-crosses-on-flimsy-pretexts/, access date: February 3, 2019.

[72] See "Brainwashing the national situation," June 3, 2018, in http://apostlesmedia.com/20180603/7833, access date: February 3, 2019.

[73] Ibid.

meaningful.[74] It can be said that the Hong Kong Christians are politically divided into two groups, the mainstream one adopting not only a moderate attitude toward the PRC but also a more positive approach to engage with mainland authorities. However, a minority of local Christians tends to be critical of the CCP's persecution of the mainland Christians, aware and apprehensive of its united front work and resistant to any attempt at politically co-opting them.

THE CATHOLICS RESISTING UNITED FRONT

The Catholics are the most difficult religious followers whom the PRC united front has failed to gain significant inroads in Hong Kong. It is due to two main factors: the relatively strong Catholic leaders who tend to resist united front work and the CCP's record of persecuting mainland Catholics. In the PRC, there were 5.5 million Catholics, according to the official figures in 2014.[75] However, after the Vatican severed diplomatic relations with the PRC in 1951, the mainland Chinese Patriotic Catholic Association (CPCA) has remained pro-CCP while the underground Catholics have been politically suppressed. In 2018, for example, churches in Henan, Jiangxi, Zhejiang, Liaoning and Hebei provinces were ordered to fly the national PRC flag, abandon banners and images with religious messages, sing national anthem and display their loyalty to the CCP.[76]

As such, when an unprecedented "provisional agreement" between the Vatican and China was reached in September 2018 on the appointment of bishops, critics of the Vatican decision were deeply concerned about whether the deal would genuinely bring about an improved predicament to the Chinese Catholics. Pope Francis lifted the excommunications of seven bishops who had been ordained by the Chinese government but without the Vatican consent.[77] This important concession was made appar-

---

[74] See "Assist Sichuan after the 2008 Earthquake," no date indicated, in http://www.hkcccu.org.hk/news/Szechwan/index.htm, access date: February 3, 2019.
[75] "China's religious situation," in http://www.locpg.gov.cn/zggq/2014-01/04/c_125956454.htm, access date: February 4, 2019.
[76] Benedict Rogers, "China's war on Christianity," September 20, 2018, in https://catholicherald.co.uk/issues/sep-21st-2018/chinas-war-on-christianity/, access date: February 4, 2019.
[77] Cindy Wooden, "Vatican signs provisional agreement with China on naming bishops," September 22, 2018, in https://www.catholicnews.com/services/englishnews/2018/vatican-signs-provisional-agreement-with-china-on-naming-bishops.cfm, access date: February 4, 2019. In early 2018, two underground Catholic bishops were reportedly persuaded by a

ently in exchange for China's recognition of the final say of the Vatican over the bishop candidates to be nominated by the Chinese government. Cardinal Pietro Parolin, the Vatican Secretary of State, said in a statement that "the objective of the Holy See is a pastoral one," intending "just to create the condition, or to help to create the condition, of a greater freedom, autonomy and organization, in order that the Catholic Church can dedicate itself to the mission of announcing the Gospel and also to the contribution to the well-being and to the spiritual and material prosperity and harmony of the country, of every person and of the world as a whole."[78] Nevertheless, critics of the Vatican move have argued that Cardinal Parolin "betrays" the Catholic community by having an easy compromise with the PRC government without protecting the interests and predicament of many members of the underground Catholic Church in the mainland.[79]

The fiercest critic of the Vatican rapprochement with the PRC came from the Hong Kong Cardinal Joseph Zen Ze-kiun, who remarked that:

> In fact, the deal is a major step toward the annihilation of the real Church in China. I know the Church in China, I know the Communists and I know the Holy See. I'm a Chinese from Shanghai. I lived many years in the mainland and many years in Hong Kong. I taught in seminaries throughout China—in Shanghai, Xian, Beijing, Wuhan, Shenyang—between 1989 and 1996. Pope Francis, an Argentine, doesn't seem to understand the Communists. He is very pastoral, and he comes from South America, where historically military governments and the rich got together to oppress poor people. And who there would come out to defend the poor? The Communists. Maybe even some Jesuits, and the government would call those Jesuits Communists. Francis may have natural sympathy for the Communists because for him, they are the persecuted. He doesn't know them as the persecutors they become once in power, like the Communists in China.[80]

Vatican delegation to China to surrender their positions to two bishops nominated by the Chinese government.

[78] "Cardinal Parolin Comments on Holy See-People's Republic of China Agreement," September 22, 2018, in https://zenit.org/articles/cardinal-parolin-comments-on-holy-see-republic-of-china-agreement/, access date: February 4, 2019.

[79] Rod Dreher, "Rome Betrays Underground China Church," September 22. 2018, in https://www.theamericanconservative.com/dreher/vatican-betrays-underground-china-church/, access date: February 4, 2019.

[80] Cardinal Joseph Zen Ze-kiun, "The Pope Doesn't Understand China," October 24, 2018, in https://www.nytimes.com/2018/10/24/opinion/pope-china-vatican-church-catholics-bishops.html, access date: February 4, 2019.

Zen accurately points to the Pope's sympathy with the PRC and he has alerted the Catholic leaders of the need to observe how the mainland Catholics have been treated historically in the mainland.

> The Holy See and Beijing cut off relations in the 1950s. Catholics and other believers were arrested and sent to labor camps. I went back to China in 1974 during the Cultural Revolution; the situation was terrible beyond imagination. A whole nation [was] under slavery. We forget these things too easily. We also forget that you can never have a truly good agreement with a totalitarian regime. China has opened up, yes, since the 1980s, but even today everything is still under the CCP's control. The official church in China is controlled by the so-called patriotic association and the bishops' conference, both under the thumb of the party.[81]

It is Cardinal Zen who symbolizes not only arguably the Catholic conscience in Hong Kong and the PRC but also the Catholic resistance to the mainland's united front work. From a positive perspective, the Vatican has not yet abandoned its relations with Taiwan shortly after the 2018 deal with the PRC. If the Pope and his advisors were pressured to de-recognize Taiwan, the 2018 "secret agreement" could certainly be seen by critics as detrimental to the entire Catholic community. Critics of the provisional agreement also says that its content is secret, that Beijing aims to have the Vatican legitimize its selection of bishops, that Beijing conducts united front work on the members of the unofficial Catholic Church and that it would eventually exert pressure on the Vatican to de-recognize Taiwan. On the legitimacy of the bishops, the dual authority over their appointment from China and veto power by the Vatican will mean that both sides will need to negotiate further. Though the Vatican says that the provisional agreement is non-political, politics will be critical to its protection of the interests of the unofficial Catholic Church in China.

Cardinal Zen has been playing a critical role in the Catholic resistance to the PRC's united front work in both the PRC and the HKSAR. On July 1, 2003, Zen prayed and spoke for a pro-democracy rally, which attracted at least half a million citizens, against the HKSAR government. He openly criticized the HKSAR government's attempt at legislating on Article 23 of the Basic Law, a stipulation that banned subversion, sedition, secession

---

[81] Ibid.

and treason.⁸² In November 2005 Zen also spoke out against the government's political reform plan, which to him was piecemeal and conservative without a timetable and a territory-wide survey of democratization. In June 2010, Zen also participated in the mass action in opposition to the compromise political model between the Liaison Office and some moderate democrats. He appealed to all those mainland bishops to maintain their boldness in negotiating with Beijing without compromising their own principles.⁸³ Politically, Zen has been constantly pro-democracy and occasionally critical of the moderate democrats who choose to negotiate with PRC officials over the pace and scope of democratic reform in Hong Kong.

Joseph Zen was born in Shanghai in 1932 and made a Cardinal in 2006, making his name as a fierce critic of the PRC's religious policy. Although he retired in 2009, Zen has constantly spoken out on political issues that impinge on the well-being of Catholics in the mainland and Hong Kong. After his retirement, John Tong Hon was appointed by Pope Benedict to become the Bishop of the diocese from 2009 to 2017. Nevertheless, Tong was politically moderate and he, unlike Zen, tended to support and trust the Vatican and the PRC government to reach a consensus on how bishops should be appointed. Hence, shortly after Bishop Michael Yeung Ming-cheung, who succeeded Tong, died in January 2019, Tong was again appointed as an acting head of the local diocese until a new successor would be selected by the Vatican. Tong's surprise appointment was seen by some observers as a sign that the Vatican might hesitate in the appointment of Bishop Joseph Ha Chi-shing, who supported the Occupy Central Movement in 2014 and whose political views are far more liberal and pro-democracy than Tong.⁸⁴ On July 1, 2014, during the mass parade in support of Hong Kong's democracy movement, Joseph Ha remarked that the citizens should elect their political leaders, and that the Chief Executive of the HKSAR should ideally be elected by

---

⁸² "Reprimanding the PRC United Front Department, Joseph Zen appealed to the mainland Catholics not to abandon and betray the God," https://hkaboluowang.com/2009/0105/115369.html, access date: February 4, 2019.

⁸³ Ibid.

⁸⁴ Shirley Zhao and Ng Kang-chung, "Shock as Vatican brings Cardinal John Tong out of retirement to be acting head of the local diocese after death of bishop – blocking Occupy supporter Joseph Ha Chi-shing," *South China Morning Post*, January 7, 2019, in https://cdn4.i-scmp.com/news/hong-kong/politics/article/2181079/shock-vatican-brings-cardinal-john-tong-out-retirement-serve, access date: February 4, 2019.

the people of Hong Kong rather than a non-elected Election Committee.[85] Like Zen, Ha is politically liberal and pro-democracy in outlook. Unlike Zen, neither Tong nor Yeung was politically outspoken. Yeung was criticized for failing to speak out for the arrested and persecuted Catholics in the PRC.[86] It remains to be seen whether the local Bishops and Cardinals in the post-Joseph Zen era will be able to resist the PRC's united front work in the HKSAR.

While the Catholic leaders in the HKSAR play a critical role in resisting or accepting the PRC's united front work, the pro-democracy Justice and Peace Commission (JPC), which was set up in 1977, remains an interest group critical of the mainland's religious policy and practices. The JPC is composed of a group of Catholics who support human rights, social justice and the well-being of the Catholic Church.[87] The JPC calls for the release of those mainland Catholics who have been arrested and tortured by the mainland authorities, and it made a submission in July 2013 to the United Nations to request that the PRC government should respect the human rights, civil liberties and religious freedom of Catholics in the mainland.[88] Given the historical tradition of the JPC to speak out against religious persecution in the PRC, it will very likely remain the conscientious interest group critical of the mainland's united front work regardless of whether Zen's successors will maintain his politically defiant, critical and pro-democracy stance.

Beijing's Support of the HKSAR Governmental Co-optation of Six Religious Leaders

While the PRC government has made strenuous efforts at co-opting the six Hong Kong religious leaders, the same phenomenon can be said of the HKSAR administration. The HKSAR government asserts that Hong

---

[85] "Michael Yeung died and Joseph Ha is an temporary administrator dealing with religious affairs," January 4, 2019, in https://topock.kket.com/article/2243350, access date: February 4, 2019.

[86] "A Fading Vatican-China Agreement in the Midst of United Front," May 20, 2018, in http://kkp.org.hk/node/16793, access date: February 4, 2019.

[87] See its objectives in the JPC website http://www.hkjp.org/about_en.php?id=2, access date: February 4, 2019.

[88] See "Submission by the Justice and Peace Commission of the Hong Kong Catholic Diocese to the United Nations Human Rights Council for its Universal Periodic Review Regarding Religious Freedom in the People's Republic of China," July 18, 2013, in http://www.hkjp.org/focus_en.php?id=55, access date: February 4, 2019.

Kong has six main religions, namely the Buddhists with about 1 million believers, Catholics with 379,000 followers, Protestant Christians with 480,000 members, Muslims with 300,000 believers, and Taoists and Confucians whose supporters are unknown in numbers.[89] Apart from these six religions, there are about 100,000 members of the Hindi community from India, Nepal, Singapore, Thailand and other Asian countries.[90] In June 1978, the six major religious leaders from the Hong Kong Buddhist Association, Hong Kong Christian Council, Hong Kong Confucian Association, Hong Kong Chinese Muslim Cultural Fraternal Association, Roman Catholic Church of Hong Kong and the Hong Kong Taoist Association formed a conference gathering in which each religious leader would be rotated to be the chairperson.[91] From 1978 to 1986, they held several conference meetings every year. Starting from 1986, however, the conference has been held once per year. In recent years, due to the busy schedule of six religious leaders, the conference gatherings are held not necessarily annually but occasionally. In the 1980s the British colonial government attempted at creating a religious functional constituency for the Legislative Council's indirect elections, but because of the difficulties of selecting specific representatives from the six religions, the idea of having a religious functional constituency in the colonial legislature was shelved.[92] Nevertheless, in the selection of the HKSAR Chief Executive, it was decided that among the 1200-member Election Committee, 60 members came from the religious sector. Accordingly, each of the six main religions—Catholics, Christians, Muslims, Buddhists, Taoists and Confucians—got ten members in the selection of the Chief Executive of the HKSAR in March 2017, when Carrie Lam was elected as the Chief Executive with 777 votes. In December 2017, during the 40th anniversary of the conference gathering of the six local religious leaders, Chief Executive Carrie Lam attended and she made remarks illustrative of her government's united front work on the six religions. Lam said that the six religions had established a tradition of being enthusiastic in charity work,

[89] "Hong Kong: The Facts [on] Religion and Custom," May 2016, in https://www.gov.hk/en/about/abouthk/factsheets/docs/religion.pdf, access date: February, 2019.
[90] Ibid.
[91] Chow King-fun, "The Origins, Reflections, Unity and Friendship of Hong Kong's Six Religious Groups," in *Religious Reflections* (in Chinese), no. 27 (November 1995), pp. 73–81, in http://archive.hsscol.org.hk/Archive/periodical/spirit/S027k.htm, access date: February 2, 2019.
[92] Koo Sun-wing, "Who says Hong Kong has only six major religions?," October 17, 2016, in https://www.inmediahk.net/node/1045215, access date: February 2, 2019.

Table 6.1 Religious leaders who were politically co-opted before July 1, 1997

Position	Leaders of Hong Kong Religious Sector
Member of the Basic Law Drafting Committee	Peter Kwong Kong-kit (Christian)
	Sik Kok-kwong (Buddhist)
Member of the Basic Law Consultative Committee	Kasim Tuet (Muslim)
	Wong Wan-tin (Buddhist)
	Peter Kwong Kong-kit (Christian)
Hong Kong Affairs Advisors	Peter Kwong Kong-kit (Christian)
	Sik Kok-kwong (Buddhist)
Member of the Preparatory Committee of the first HKSAR Government	Peter Kwong Kong-kit (Christian)
	Sik Kok-kwong (Buddhist)

Source: Calculated by the authors from various news reports

Table 6.2 Hong Kong members of the Chinese People's Political Consultative Conference

CPPCC 7th term (1988–1992)	Kasim Tuet (Muslim)
CPPCC 8th term (1993–1997)	Wong Wan-tin (Buddhist)
CPPCC 9th term (1998–2002)	Peter Kwong Kong-kit (Christian)
CPPCC 10th term (2003–2007)	Peter Kwong Kong-kit (Christian)
11th term	No Hong Kong religious leader
CPPCC 12th term (2013–2017)	Paul Kwong (Anglican Church)
	Sik Koon-wun (Buddhist)
CPPCC 13th term (2018–2022)	Paul Kwong (Anglican Church)
	Sik Koon-wun (Buddhist)

Source: Calculated from various news reports

of encouraging the next generation to study religious wisdom and truth and of spreading out the message of love and peace. As such, she expected the six religions to continue to contribute to the Hong Kong society in the realms of social welfare, public health, education and the provision of services for the poor and the needy.[93]

Tables 6.1 and 6.2 show the political co-optation of Hong Kong's religious leaders by the PRC government before and after July 1, 1997. Christian and Buddhist leaders were the main target of political co-optation before the handover. After the HKSAR establishment, while

---

[93] "The 40th anniversary of the six religions' conference gathering," in http://www.hkcc.org.hk/acms/content.asp?site=hkccnew&op=showbyid&id=58427, access date: February 2, 2019.

Buddhist and Christian leaders have continued to be politically appointed into the CPPCC, Muslim leader Kasim Tuet and Paul Kwong of the Anglican Church have also become the target of appointments. Still, Catholic leaders have remained politically excluded. Confucian and Taoist leaders were not formally appointed to any political body under the PRC, perhaps pointing to their relatively insignificant influence on the local community. The pattern of political appointments to the PRC's political institutions has shown that Buddhist, Christian and Muslim leaders have been regarded as more politically "correct" than certainly the Catholic ones.

From the PRC's united front perspective, the HKSAR government's efforts at co-opting the local religious leaders into the existing political institutions are commendable. As Liu Yandong, the former minister of the United Front Department, remarked, the HKSAR is a society that accommodates various cultures and religions, which "have been playing a crucial role in the provision of services and charity for the society and which have been contributing immensely to the positive development of Hong Kong's social development and civilization."[94] She reiterated that Beijing adopts the principle of "mutual respect, mutual non-intervention, and mutual non-subordination" in coping with Hong Kong's religions, and that these tenets are the best in guiding Beijing's policy toward the religious leaders in the HKSAR.[95] Through regular gatherings to build up friendship, mutual trust and mutual respect, PRC authorities find it relatively easy to co-opt the leaders of the six religions in the HKSAR, apart from the efforts made by the Hong Kong government at cultivating harmonious relations, socio-culturally and politically, with the six major religious leaders.

In response to the friendly gestures and actions from both Beijing and the HKSAR administration, the six religious leaders have naturally no choice but to establish reciprocally friendly relations with them. In January 2017, the six religious leaders made a joint appeal in their new year message to the Hong Kong people, saying that the people of Hong Kong are "enjoying a privileged position under the 'one country, two systems' and that they should work hard, use wisdom to resolve disputes, elevate the educational quality for the youths, and to put the emphasis on the

---

[94] Liu's remarks are cited in "Buddhist Festival saw the participation of Liu Yandong in meeting the six Hong Kong religious leaders," CPPCC news bulletin, July 27, 2004, in http://cppcc.people.com.cn/GB/34961/65233/65239/65802/4450761.html, access date: February 2, 2019.

[95] Ibid.

principle of maintaining rites, justice, honesty and graceful actions."[96] Apart from the joint annual appeal and message to the people of Hong Kong, the six main religious leaders also conducted other activities to promote their religious faith and studies and to contribute to social harmony in the territory. For example, in April 2013, the six religious leaders held their annual conference at the Chinese University of Hong Kong, donating various historical religious documents to the university, and encouraging researchers to conduct research on the six religions and to preserve their historical documents digitally. In December 2018, during the conference gathering of the six religions, some religious leaders stressed that youths are the pillar of the PRC nation-state.[97] They appealed to the young people of Hong Kong to study and understand the Chinese history, to develop a stronger sense of serving the community and to nurture a sense of responsibility and mission in the new era. Such appeal to the youth in developing a stronger sense of nationalism and social responsibility was, strictly speaking, in conformity with the wishes of both Beijing and the HKSAR leaders, who have seen some radical youth since the emergence of the anti-national education campaign in the summer of 2012 and the eruption of the 2014 Occupy Central Movement as social "rebels." Hence, the religious leaders' appeal to the young people to contribute to the society of Hong Kong had a hidden political message supportive of the HKSAR regime. In February 2018, the six religious leaders issued a joint message hoping that the PRC would continue to be rich with ethnic harmony and appealing to the people of Hong Kong to support the local government, saying that the HKSAR government "can concretize its ruling philosophy, implement its policy platform, and maintain clean and virtuous governance."[98] They also appealed to the Hong Kong people to "strengthen the servicing spirit of the Executive and Legislative Councils," and "to remain united and respect each other mutually for the sake of constructing social harmony."[99] The six religious leaders said they were very confident with the future of Hong Kong, hoping that all the citizens could and would live happily, that elderly people would be respected, that moral education would be implemented, and that media

---

[96] "Six religious leaders issue a joint message in the Chinese New Year," January 27, 2017, in https://www.thestandnews.com/society/, access date: February 2, 2019.

[97] *Sing Pao*, December 16, 2018.

[98] "Six religious leaders issue a joint appeal in the new year, hoping the nation would be rich and Hong Kong having social harmony," February 15, 2018, in https://thestandnews.com/society/, access date: February 2, 2019.

[99] Ibid.

excellence could be achieved. Reading between the lines, the joint message was politically supportive of the government and socio-political harmony. A religious-governmental partnership between the six religions and the HKSAR government on the one hand, and that between the six religious leaders and Beijing on the other were firmly established.

Conclusion

The PRC's united front work in the HKSAR has gained considerable success in influencing and co-opting the leaders of the Buddhist, Taoist, Confucian, Islamic, Christian and the Catholic community. However, while the Buddhist leaders are the most vulnerable group under the united front co-optation, the Catholics remain the least vulnerable and the most resistant group vis-à-vis united front work. The Buddhist emphasis on social harmony and peace has much in common with the ideology of the CCP, thus making them an easy political ally. Similarly, the Taoist and Confucian values have laid much emphasis on social harmony and cultural values, leading to another relatively easy coalition with the CCP. The Muslims in Hong Kong have traditionally fallen under the PRC united front work. The Christian leaders have also been politically co-opted, but a minority of Christians have in the recent years been critical of the way in which these leaders embrace the PRC's united front work. The Catholics remain relatively the most politically defiant ones, perhaps mainly due to the work and legacy of Cardinal Zen.

On the other hand, the PRC's new united front work targeted at the six main religions in the HKSAR has displayed several characteristics: (1) the appeal to the use of religions to spread the Chinese cultural tradition in not only the Greater China region (mainland China, Hong Kong, Macao and Taiwan) but also countries in the world; (2) the mobilization of pro-Beijing Hong Kong religious leaders to participate in all kinds of religious and even political activities in support of China's renaissance; (3) the use of divide-and-rule tactics and the subtle political exclusion of those religious leaders and activists who are pro-democracy and critical of Beijing, such as religious priest Kwok Nai-wang and Cardinal Zen; and (4) the grooming of pro-Beijing religious leaders to take over the key positions of the leading religious groups in the HKSAR, gradually serving as the supporters and even spokespersons of the PRC government. The line between friends and enemies of the PRC regime can be easily seen in the evolution of its united front work on Hong Kong's religious sector.

CHAPTER 7

Penetrative Politics from Neighborhood Associations to District Federations: Electoral Mobilization and Competition

China's united front operation in the form of penetrative politics has been deepening in the society of Hong Kong at the district level, where neighborhood (*kaifong*) associations are the target of political capture and where pro-Beijing federations have been formed as umbrella organizations to rally all other like-minded interest groups. The ultimate objective is clear: during non-election time, all these pro-Beijing interest groups are organizing activities and providing constituency services to win the hearts and minds of the ordinary people, and then on the election day, groups and individuals are fully mobilized to support and vote for candidates of the pro-Beijing front. In this way, the pro-democracy forces and candidates could, can and will be defeated, thus stabilizing the HKSAR administration at the legislative and district levels. In mainland terminology, a huge amount of money has been spent for the PRC to "maintain stability (*weiwen*)" in the HKSAR, electorally and politically speaking. Perhaps, no researcher can really come up with an accurate estimate of how much money is annually used by PRC authorities and their agents as well as supporters to maintain Hong Kong's political stability, partly because the number of pro-Beijing interest groups is large and partly because their activities and constituency services are constantly tremendous. However, the challenge of China's united front work in the HKSAR is to sustain its momentum, especially as generational change means that some young people may not favor the materialistic benefits conferred upon them by the pro-Beijing elites. This chapter focuses on how united front work operates at the district level, discussing the role of *kaifong* associations and district federations and then examining how united front worked in two by-elections held for the Legislative Council in March and November 2018.

PENETRATING AND CAPTURING *KAIFONG* ASSOCIATIONS

Kaifong or neighborhood associations were first set up by the British colonial administration in 1949 when the Secretariat for Chinese Affairs encouraged residents to organize themselves voluntarily to help each other.[1] Even before World War II, the colonial authorities had long set up District Watch Committee in Hong Kong to co-opt 15 local Chinese leaders with the objective of maintaining law and order through the creation of a District Watch Force with 50–150 police officers.[2] However, the colonial rulers were apprehensive of strikes launched by workers, such as the 1922 seamen's strike and the workers' strike in Guangdong and Hong Kong from June 1925 to October 1926.[3] During the Japanese occupation of Hong Kong from December 1941 to August 1945, a ward system was established under the districts so that residents could look after their own street affairs. After the return of the British to govern Hong Kong, the colonial government encouraged the formation of *kaifong* associations to engender the development of a community spirit instead of allowing particularistic organizations, such as clans and district-based associations, to flourish and generate possible social conflicts.[4] Furthermore, the residential base of *kaifong* associations was similar to ancient China's *pao-chia* system in which several households were grouped together to maintain law and order and to fight local crime. In the 1940s, many Hong Kong residents were the migrants from mainland China and they had experienced the *pa-chia* system in China under the Nationalist rule. From the colonial government's viewpoint, the traditional conservatism of the *pao-chia* system was conducive to the social and political stability of Hong

---

[1] Aline K. Wong, *The Kaifong Associations and the Society of Hong Kong* (Taipei: The Orient Cultural Service, 1972), pp. 3–4. Also see Aline Lai-Chung Kan, *The Kaifong Associations in Hong Kong*, unpublished PhD dissertation, Department of Sociology, University of California at Berkeley, March 1970.

[2] Wong, *The Kaifong Associations and the Society of Hong Kong*, pp. 42–43.

[3] For details of these strikes, see Leung Po-lung, "The Workers' Movement in Hong Kong before the Japanese Occupation, 1937–1941," 2017, in https://wknews.org/node/1362, access date: February 9, 2019. Also see Hong Kong Seamen's Union website, in http://www.hksu1946.hk/main/pages.php?id=31, access date: February 9, 2019.

[4] Ibid., p. 4.

Kong. As such, *kaifong* associations began to develop gradually in Hong Kong under the British rule. However, the British colonizers were also concerned about the possibility that *kaifong* associations might be politicized and factionalized, generating chances for either the underground CCP or the Kuomintang (KMT) to penetrate into the society. Under these circumstances, the British colonial administration closely monitored the formation and development of *kaifong* associations, ensuring that they were pro-British rather than pro-CCP or pro-KMT. Interestingly, during and after the eruption of the Cultural Revolution in the PRC, the left-wing riots in Hong Kong from 1966 to 1967 led to the demands of many *kaifong* associations to support the maintenance of law and order, and to side with the colonial government in dealing with the rioters. During the 1966–67 riots in Hong Kong, some leftists went to plant bombs on the streets and assassinate an anti-CCP radio host named Lam Bun, losing the support of many Hong Kong people. Since the leftists were participating in terrorist activities, many *kaifong* associations supported the colonial police to suppress the leftist rioters. The creation of the Hong Kong week in late 1967 aimed at galvanizing the support of residents, including leaders of the *kaifong* associations, to support the colonial government and to create a new Hong Kong identity.[5] Overall, *kaifong* associations in Hong Kong under the British rule had various functions: acting as social welfare organizations to support charity work and disaster relief, to provide free education and free medical services, to help hawkers; performing as intermediary groups that narrowed the communication gap between the colonial authorities and the ordinary people; and serving as agents that provided social security, maintained law and order and assisted the process of community development.[6] If the British colonizers also conducted their own united front work in Hong Kong, *kaifong* associations were also their instruments of political penetration into the society.

The heyday of the development of *kaifong* associations was the period from the late 1960s to the 1970s, when the colonial government utilized them as intermediary organizations to engender a local Hong Kong identity, provide residents' feedback to government policies, submit annual financial reports for governmental scrutiny and subsidy support and assist the governmental delivery of such services as welfare relief, distribution of

---

[5] Clement Tze Ming Tong, *The Hong Kong Week of 1967 and the Emergence of the Modern Hong Kong Identity*, unpublished MA thesis, Department of History, University of British Columbia, August 2008, pp. 31–33.

[6] Wong, *The Kaifong Associations and the Society of Hong Kong*, pp. 50–104.

rice and clothes for the poor and the needy, and even the establishment of kindergartens for children.[7] In other words, *kaifong* associations acted like pro-government interest groups bridging the communication gap between the colonial rulers and ordinary citizens. Nonetheless, starting from the early 1980s, when District Board elections were introduced, *kaifong* associations displayed some leadership problems, partly because the aging community leaders who were usually local business elites not only had a communication gap with the local working class, and partly because they encountered political competition from the newly emerging political groups that participated in district elections. As a result, the *kaifong* leaders became either politically outdated or the targets of political co-optation from competing forces, including the nascent pro-democracy elites and most importantly the rapidly developing pro-Beijing elites. For the PRC authorities, they tried to secure the political support from more leaders of *kaifong* associations in preparation for the transfer of sovereignty from Britain to China in 1997.

The decline of *kaifong* associations in the 1980s was also attributable to the corresponding emergence of Mutual Aid Committees (MACs) and Owners Corporations (OC) which accompanied the rise of many public housing estates and new private buildings from the 1970s to the 1990s. MACs were set up in 1973 to help the government in its Fight Crime Campaign. They were composed of owners and tenants and responsible for building management; nevertheless, legally MACs were not statutory bodies and could not be sued.[8] The government then encouraged MACs to convert into OCs, which were independent statutory bodes under the Building Management Ordinance, and which could be legally liable. Since the 1990s, political parties, such as the pro-Beijing DAB, FTU and the pro-democracy Democratic Party, began to penetrate more MACs than ever before.[9] The actions of the DAB and FTU reflected the united front strategy of the PRC in the early years of the HKSAR. By infiltrating into

---

[7] Although the non-governmental voluntary groups appeared to decline in the 1970s, it can be argued that *kaifong* associations remained socially and politically significant for the colonial government to maintain its legitimacy. For the decline of voluntary groups in Hong Kong during the 1970s, see Lam Wai-Fung and James Perry, "The Role of Nonprofit Sector in Hong Kong's Development," *Voluntas: International Journal of Voluntary and Nonprofit Organizations*, vol. 11, no. 4 (2000), pp. 355–373.

[8] For details of the development and politicization of MACs and OCs, see Lo Shiu-Hing, "Party Penetration of Society in Hong Kong: The Role of Mutual Aid Committees and Political Parties," *Asian Journal of Political Science*, vol. 12, no. 1 (June 2004), pp. 31–64.

[9] Ibid.

MACs and OCs, pro-Beijing forces hope to garner the support of voters gradually at the grassroots level. For the *kaifong* associations, their leaders have also become the targets of political co-option by pro-Beijing political forces. On the contrary, most pro-democracy elites who emphasize the ideology of liberalism and democracy to appeal for public support naturally play down the significance of *kaifong* leaders in electoral competition. Under these circumstances, *kaifong* associations have provided a breeding ground for pro-Beijing forces to groom their community leaders and to recruit them into the umbrella of united front work.

The political orientation of *kaifong* associations has changed considerably in the HKSAR since July 1, 1997. Because the HKSAR government has to support Beijing's policies toward Hong Kong, *kaifong* associations are increasingly under the umbrella of governmental co-optation. The most important evidence pointing to the pro-HKSAR government and pro-Beijing proclivity of *kaifong* associations was their participation in a mass signature campaign launched by the pro-PRC Alliance for Peace and Democracy in opposition to the Occupy Central Movement from September to December 2014. The signature campaign involved some 1500 interest groups in which 27 *kaifong* associations in Kowloon and the Hong Kong Island and 31 rural committees in the New Territories participated (Table 7.1). Rural committees were established by the British colonial government to consult the opinions of the indigenous peoples in the New Territories. After 1997, rural committees have sided with the PRC government as their leaders are also the target of political co-optation by both the HKSAR administration and mainland authorities. Table 7.1 demonstrates the active participation of these *kaifong* associations and rural committees in opposition to the Occupy Central Movement in 2014.

CASE STUDIES OF THE TRANSFORMATION OF KWUN TONG AND MONGKOK *KAIFONG* ASSOCIATIONS

Since both the Kwun Tong *kaifong* association and the Mongkok counterpart were against the 2014 Occupy Central Movement, this section traces their evolution to show how they changed from pro-British intermediary groups to pro-Beijing organizations. Kwun Tong was one of the new towns in Hong Kong during the 1980s and it has a plenty of neighborhood associations. Table 7.2 shows the evolution of some *kaifong* associations in Kwun Tong. Those associations that have been politically captured by pro-Beijing forces include the Kwun Tong *Kaifong* Welfare Association,

Table 7.1 Participation of *kaifong* associations and rural committees in opposition to the 2014 Occupy Central Movement

Rural committees	Kaifong *associations (KA)*

Rural committees (RC) in the outlying islands
  1. Lantau South RC
  2. Lantau Four District RC
  3. Lantau South RC
  4. Tai O RC
  5. Mui Woo RC
  6. Lamma North RC
  7. Lamma South RC
  8. Lamma North RC
  9. Tsing Yi RC
  10. Cheung Chau RC
  11. Peng Chau RC
  12. Ma Wan RC
Rural Committees in Tuen Mun
  1. Tuen Mun RC
Rural Committees in Yuen Long
  1. Ha Village RC
  2. Ping Shan RC
  3. Pat Heung RC
  4. Shat Pat Heung RC
  5. Kam Tin RC
Rural Committees in North District
  1. Fanling District RC
  2. Fanling RC
  3. Sheung Shui RC
  4. Sheung Shui District RC
  5. Ta Ku Ling RC
  6. Shataukok RC
Rural Committee in Tai Po
  1. Tai Po RC
Rural Committee in Shatin
  1. Shatin RC
Rural Committee in Sai Kung
  1. Sai Kung RC
  2. Cheung Kwan O RC
  3. Hang Hau RC
  4. Sai Kung District RC
  5. Sai Kung North RC
	Central and Western District
	  1. Central KA
	  2. Mount Davies KA
	Wanchai District
	  1. Happy Valley Ngou Keng Bridge KA
	  2. Wanchai District KA
	  3. Causeway KA
	Eastern District
	  1. North Point District KA
	  2. Chai Wan KA
	  3. Shaukeiwan KA
	  4. Chai Wan KA
	Southern District
	  1. Nan Shan District KA
	Kwun Tong District
	  1. Sau Mau Ping KA
	  2. Yau Tong KA
	  3. Ngau Tau Kok KA
	  4. Lei Yue Mun KA
	Kowloon City Ditrict
	  1. Hung Hom KA
	  2. Tokwawan KA
	  3. Kowloon Wall City KA
	Yau Tsim Mong District
	  1. Yau Ma Tei KA
	  2. Mongkok KA
	  3. Yau Ma Tei *Kaifong* Promotion Association
	Shamshuipo and Mei Foo Districts
	  1. Mei Foo KA
	  2. Shek Kip Mei KA
	  3. Shumshipo KA
	  4. Shumshuipo *Kaifong* Promotion Association
	  5. Cheung Sha Wan KA
	  6. Shek Kip Mei KA
	  7. Lee Cheng Uk KA
	Cheung Kwan O District
	  1. Cheung Kwan O KA

Source: Calculated from the names of the associations and committees in https://www.sign4peacedemocracy.hk/index.php?r=index/support, access date: January 2, 2019

Table 7.2 The evolution of Kwun Tong *kaifong* associations

Kaifong *associations*	Evolution
Kwun Tong *Kaifong* Welfare Association	It was once an important neighborhood association. But its chairman Lam Hinfai, a restaurant owner, was appointed by the government as a chairman of the Kwung Tong District Board from 1982 to 1994. As a result, the association's affairs were neglected, and its activities stopped after the reconstruction of the Kwun Tong city center in the late 1990s.
Lei Yue Mun *Kaifong* Welfare Association	Its old members participated in the local guerillas who fought against the Japanese imperial army during World War II. After the war, the thriving seafood business in Kwun Tong helped the association's work. Later, its leaders became aging and the association also turned to support the PRC. This association is one of the very few which regularly holds the ceremony of hoisting the national flag of the PRC in its office.
Ngau Tau Kok *Kaifong* Welfare Association	It was set up when the Ngau Tau Kok upper and lower public housing estates were established. Its leaders migrated overseas and affected the association's work. Now it becomes close to the pro-Beijing DAB District Councilor Ngan Man-yu.
Tsui Ping Road *Kaifong* Welfare Association	It had an office and health clinic in Tsui Nam House. But the association became inactive due to the aging leaders. Now it survives by relying on the revenue from the clinic.
Lam Tin *Kaifong* Welfare Association	It still operates on the basis of the subsidies from the Social Welfare Department, providing services such as kindergarten, youth activities, family advice and elderly care. But it has fallen under the influence of a DAB politician named Or Chong-shing who is reportedly organizing the association's activities.
Yau Tong *Kaifong* Welfare Association	Its zenith involved four health clinics, a kindergarten and the organization of large-scale activities such as free vegetarian dinner for 1000 elderly people. Yau Tong's reconstruction affected the association's work, which was terminated at one time, but now it is under the influence of two pro-Beijing local politicians named Fan Wai-kwong and Lui Tung-hai. Fan is a member of the pro-Beijing interest group named Po Kin Hai Liu Association, which was set up in 1947, which has a platform vowing to love China, and whose website admits the strong support from the Liaison Office.
Jordan Valley *Kaifong* Welfare Association	It set up an elderly center with the subsidy from the Social Welfare Department. But when the Jordan Valley underwent demolition and reconstruction, the elderly center was relocated to a public housing estate. The association remains relatively politically neutral and is free from the penetration of any political force.
Sau Mau Ping *Kaifong* Welfare Association	It has traditionally been a pro-regime organization. Its office was relocated to a public housing estate after Sau Mau Ping's reconstruction and it remains operational.

(*continued*)

Table 7.2 (continued)

Kaifong associations	Evolution
Chau Kwo Ling Kaifong Association	It has traditionally raised the photo of the Chinese revolutionary leader Sun Yat-sen. The association is active in local Tin Hau Festival and it has no political affiliation.
Sin Cho Wan Kaifong Association	It originally took care of the residents in the Sin Cho Wan village. In 1981 the village was demolished and a number of Chiu Chow clansmen are responsible for managing a reconstructed temple in Sin Cho Wan.

Sources: The authors' interviews with local leaders in Kwun Tong district, 2017–2018. For the website of the pro-Beijing Po Kin Hai Liu Association, see http://www.pkhl.org/?xhjs&cid=19, access date: February 9, 2019. Also see Sonny Shiu-Hing Lo and Steven Hung Chung-fun, *A Research Project Report of the Development of Kwun Tong Non-Governmental Organizations: Roles, Development and Historical Changes* (in Chinese) (Hong Kong: Golden Horse Publisher, 2015)

the Lei Yu Mun *Kaifong* Association, the Ngau Tau Kok *Kaifong* Association, Lam Tin *Kaifong* Welfare Association and the Yau Tong *Kaifong* Welfare Association. Others remain relatively neutral or inactive. Hence, out of the ten neighborhood associations in Kwun Tong, half of them have already been captured by pro-Beijing political forces.

Another good example showing how a neighborhood association gradually changed from a pro-British organization to a pro-Beijing one is the Mongkok *Kaifong* Association (MKA). The MKA was set up in 1951 and got a large piece of land from the colonial government in 1974 to run its activities.[10] In 1980, a new center with five floors was opened, including a dental clinic, conference center, library and self-study rooms. As of 2011, the center hired hundred staff members, including thirty registered social workers, to deal with all kinds of services, including elderly care.[11] After 1997, its annual report must acquire the endorsement and support of a representative of the Liaison Office, for example the Kowloon work department chief Lin Wu in 2011.[12] Most importantly, after 1997, the MFA has obviously drifted toward the pro-Beijing stance, sending delegations to Guangzhou, Zhongshan, Shenzhen and Guangxi. In June 2010, the MFA participated in a pro-government political rally in support of the

---

[10] For details, see its website in https://mkkfa.org.hk/about/about.html, access date: February 9, 2019.

[11] See *Mongkok Kaifong Association, 1951–2011* (Hong Kong: Monkok *Kaifong* Association, 2011), p. 4.

[12] Ibid., p. 8.

government's political reform model.[13] After the DAB candidate Starry Lee Wai-king was directly elected to the Legislative Council in 2012, she visited the MFA which welcome her action, thus showing a loose alliance between the MFA and Lee, who later became the DAB chairwoman in 2015. Apart from the MFA participation in the anti-Occupy Central Movement's mass signature campaign in 2014, it joined a rally in the summer of 2015 which was organized by the Hong Kong and Kowloon Federation of *Kaifong* Associations in support of the HKSAR government's political reform blueprint on how the Chief Executive should be directly elected in 2017.[14] The explicitly political position of the MFA showed that many neighborhood associations have naturally become pro-HKSAR government and pro-Beijing organizations since the transfer of Hong Kong's sovereignty in 1997.

The Utilization, Organization and Mobilization of Three District-Based Federations

Three district-based federations are used by PRC authorities and their agents to conduct intensive and extensive united front work in the entire HKSAR. First, the New Territories Associations of Societies (NTAS) was established in 1985 with a membership of 250,000 residents. Its missions are "to love China and Hong Kong, to protect the Basic Law, to promote the linkages among groups in the New Territories, and to be concerned about the residents' welfare, interests, entertainment and friendship."[15] The explicit reference to "promote the linkages among groups in the New Territories" means that the NTAS is a united front organization rallying all other like-minded interest groups in the region. Second, the Kowloon Federation of Associations (KFA) was established in 1997 with 199 affiliated organizations and 220,000 members.[16] It openly emphasizes the concern about livelihood issues and the emotional attachment to the families in Hong Kong and to the motherland, China. Third, the Hong Kong Island Federation (HKIF) was set up in 1999 with 204 affiliated organizations and 130,000 members.[17] Its missions are to care about the

---
[13] *Mongkok Kaifong Association, 1951–2011*, p. 124.
[14] See https://mkkfa.org.hk/activity/activity_2_006.html, access date: February 9, 2019.
[15] Ibid.
[16] See https://klnfas.hk/tc/, access date: February 9, 2019.
[17] See http://www.hk-if.org/special.php?id=9, access date: February 9, 2019.

development of social welfare, to organize cultural and arts activities, to enhance cultural exchanges with the mainland, to help the poor and the needy and to provide a variety of services for the youth and women. When the KFA and HKIF were formed in 1997 and 1999 respectively, they appeared to reorganize all the formerly pro-Beijing groups and even the underground party cells in the territory, cooperating with the NTAS to become a new united front in the HKSAR. All the three federations tend to place much emphases on livelihood issues under which the real political objective is to win the hearts and minds of the residents in entire Hong Kong.

In terms of leadership, all the three district-based federations are led by political heavyweights with strong linkages to mainland political institutions (Table 7.3). The NTAS is led by president Leung Chi-cheung, a member of the CPPCC and also by managing director Chan Yung, a member of the NPC. The KFA is led by president Chan Chun-bun, a member of the NPC and by managing director Wong Wai-ching, a member of the CPPCC. The HKIF is led by Cai Yi, a member of the NPC. Since three top leaders of NTAS, KFA and HKIF are Hong Kong members of the NPC who are under the CCP's *nomenklatura* system, Beijing's officials responsible for Hong Kong matters can easily exert personnel and leadership control over the three district-based federations in the HKSAR. In a nutshell, the three federations constitute the influential united front mechanisms of the CCP.

Another hallmark of the three united front federations is the overlapping of core membership between the pro-Beijing political party, DAB and three regional organizations. Overlapping membership means that the DAB members can coordinate between the party's activities and the federation's, that they can pool the resources and manpower together easily to conduct constituency services during non-election time and that they can fully mobilize members of all affiliated groups to vote for DAB and like-minded candidates in the election period. The degree of overlapping membership between the DAB and the different regional federations varies. The DAB members have participated more extensively in the NTAS, followed by the KFA, but they participate relatively lightly in the HKIF (see Table 7.4). It reflects the significance that the DAB has placed on the electoral battles in the New Territories, where many migrants from the mainland tend to reside, while the electoral contests in Kowloon Peninsula is also critical to the party's performance. The Hong Kong Island is less important to the DAB, which can coordinate with other

Table 7.3 Leadership and organization of three main district-based federations, 2018

Region	Federation name	Formation	Groups	Members	Leaders	Background
New Territories	New Territories Association of Societies	1985	390	250,000	Leung Chi-cheung (President) Chan Yung (Managing Director)	Member of the Chinese People's Political Consultative Conference Member of the National People's Congress
Kowloon	Kowloon Federation of Associations	1997	199	220,000	Chan Chun-bun (President) Wong Wai-ching (Managing Director)	Member of the National People's Congress Member of the Chinese People's Political Consultative Conference
Hong Kong Island	Hong Kong Island Federation	1999	204	130,000	Cai Yi	Hong Kong member of the National People's Congress

Sources: Websites of the three federations, in http://www.ntas.org.hk/about.jsp, https://klnfas.hk/tc/, and http://www.hk-if.org/special.php?id=9, access date: February 9, 2019. Also see http://finance.takungpao.com.hk/special/2015cjlh_caiyi/, and http://hm.people.com.cn/GB/42280/357366/368975/, access date: February 9, 2019

like-minded groups and pro-Beijing independents rather than utilizing the HKIF as the mobilization machinery.

NEW TERRITORIES ASSOCIATION OF SOCIETIES

Before the NTAS was formed in 1985, a pro-Taiwan New Territories Associations Fraternization (NTAF) had been founded in 1979 with the inclusion of the flag of the Republic of China on Taiwan and the photo of Sun Yat-sen into its official association badge. The NTAF had sixty-eight affiliated interest groups, including clan associations, residents' welfare associations and sports organizations. It was clearly pro-Taiwan at the beginning. From the 1970s to the 1990s, the leaders of the New

Table 7.4 Key overlapping membership between the DAB and three district federations

New Territories Association Of Societies	Kowloon Federation of Associations	Hong Kong Island Federation
Leung Chi-cheung (DAB Yuen Long branch's chairman) Chan Yung (DAB vice chairman) Chow Chuen-heung (DAB member) Chan Hak-kan (DAB vice chairman) Wong Pik-kiu (DAB member) Chan Hang-bun (DAB Central Committee member) Ho Chun-yin (DAB Central Committee member) Lau Kwok-fun (DAB Central Committee member) Tam Wing-fun (DAB Central Committee member)	Chung Kong-mo (DAB member) Yeung Chi-hei (DAB Yau Tsim Mong branch's chairman) Lee Tak-hong (DAB Wong Tai Sin branch's chairman) Kan Chi-ho (DAB deputy secretary) Hung Kam-yin (DAB member)	Chu Lap-wai (DAB Central Committee member and Southern district branch's chairman) Lo Tin-sung (DAB member)

Source: Calculated from the websites of the three district federations. Also see http://finance.takungpao.com.hk/special/2015cjlh_caiyi/, http://hm.people.com.cn/GB/42280/357366/368975/, https://ntasnas.dsmynas.org:4433/, access date: February 9, 2019

Territories, such as Chan Yat-sun, Cheung Yan-lung and Lau Wong-fat, the former chairmen of the rural advisory body Heung Yee Kuk, were the targets of political co-optation by the British colonial government and later increasingly the foci of united front work from Beijing.

In 1985, when the NTAS was formally established, its chairman was the pro-Beijing elite, Lee Lin-sang, who was appointed as a Hong Kong member of the NPC in 1983.[18] During the World War II, Lee was a local guerilla fighting against the Japanese army. In the 1966–67 riot, Lee was one of the leftists who were imprisoned. When he died in 2015, the pro-Beijing *Ta Kung Pao* praised him as a person who loved China and Hong Kong.[19]

[18] *Hong Kong Commercial Daily*, April 7, 2015.
[19] See Chan Yung, "Lee Lin-sang engaged himself fully into the community," in http://news.takungpao.com.hk/hkol/politics/2015-04/2966923.html, access date: February 10, 2019.

The political background of Lee and his appointment as the founding chairman of the NTAS meant that the organization was politically patriotic.

Lee's position as the founding chairman of the NTAS had other political implications. First, Beijing's authorities were determined to absorb the pro-Taiwan NTAF into a pro-Beijing political machinery. Second, as Sino-British negotiation over the future of Hong Kong was completed in 1984, it was imperative for Beijing to reorganize all the pro-PRC interest groups in the New Territories. As such, the NTAS was formed with the leadership of Lee to achieve the objectives of reorganizing pro-Beijing groups and winning the hearts and minds of the rural residents from 1985 to July 1, 1997. Later, the three chairpersons of the rural Heung Yee Kuk—Chan Yat-sun, Cheung Yan-lung and Lau Wong-fat—were all appointed as the honorary chairmen of the NTAS, showing the PRC's strategy of co-opting rural leaders into the new pro-Beijing NTAS.[20] Third, the model of forming the NTAS as an organization rallying all the district-based interest groups was later replicated in both Kowloon and the Hong Kong Island, when the KFA and HKIS were established in 1997 and 1999, respectively. At the inception of its formation in 1985, the NTAS only had 26 affiliated groups with 40,000 members, but the figures expanded to 390 groups with 250,000 members by 2018—a drastic increase of 15 times for group affiliation and six-fold for individual membership. If united front entails the gradual expansion of pro-Beijing groups and individual membership, the NTAS model was a successful one.

A hallmark of NTAS expansion is its focus on trade unions, especially the Hong Kong Graziers Union led by Law Yuk-ching (HKGU) and the Hong Kong and Kowloon Flowers and Plants Workers General Union (HKKFPWGU) led by Leung Yuk-lam. The two traditionally agriculture-based trade unions occupied 25,000 members of the entire 40,000-member NTAS when it was formed. Although the two unions were pro-Beijing, they did not fall under the organization of the FTU. During the 1970s, agricultural trade unions gradually declined in Hong Kong under rapid industrialization, including their membership. Table 7.5 shows the gradual decline in the membership of both agriculture-based trade unions. They both had 25,000 members in 1985, decreasing to 15,000 members in 1992 and then 10,000 members in 2000, and 3500 in 2016.

---

[20] *The First Inauguration Ceremony and Office-Bearers of the New Territories Associations Fraternization* (Hong Kong: New Territories Associations Fraternization, 1979).

Table 7.5 Membership OF Agriculture-based Hong Kong Graziers Union and Hong Kong and Kowloon Flowers and Plants Workers General Union, 1973–2016

Year	Hong Kong Graziers Union	Hong Kong and Kowloon Flowers and Plants Workers General Union
1973	Not available	4556
1974	Not available	5133
1975	Not available	6235
1976	Not available	7186
1977	Not available	7864
1978	Not available	7610
1979	Not available	7380
1980	Not available	7011
1981	22,655[a]	6787
1982	22,019	6597
1983	21,317	6389
1984	18,801	6203
1985	17,983	5785
1986	17,321	5185
1987	16,126	4678
1988	14,481	4425
1989	13,551	4274
1990	12,625	4128
1991	11,766	4036
1992	11,155	3889
1993	10,780	3782
1994	10,380	3708
1995	10,126	3567
1996	9761	3464
1997	9474	2841
1998	9234	2634
1999	8817	2430
2000	7288	2376
2001	6267	2157
2002	5981	1996
2003	5640	1754
2004	5481	1680
2005	5205	1521
2006	4783	1501
2007	4549	1381
2008	4294	1311
2009	4162	1255
2010	4003	1157
2011	3968	1043

(*continued*)

Table 7.5 (continued)

Year	Hong Kong Graziers Union	Hong Kong and Kowloon Flowers and Plants Workers General Union
2012	3666	996
2013	3399	941
2014	3130	898
2015	2829	855
2016	2782	817

Sources: Tabulated from the annual reports of the Registry of Trade Unions, 1994–2016 and of the Annual Departmental Report of the Registrar of Trade Unions, 1973–1993 (Hong Kong: Hong Kong Government, 1973–1993)

ᵃThis was the first time that data appeared in the annual report published by the Registrar of Trade Unions, Hong Kong Government

When the NTAS was founded, it relied on some residents' associations, fishermen groups and women interest groups. In 1985, the NTAS's affiliated group, the New Territories West's Residents Association, had 2000 members and it has gradually expanded its membership in the 1990s.[21] On the other hand, the NTAS co-opted the fishermen associations, including the pro-Beijing Hong Kong Fishermen's Association. These associations became outdated and witnessed a decline in membership in Hong Kong during the 1980s and 1990s, when many fishermen and their children were relocated to work on the land, change their careers and reside in public housing estates. Despite the decline in the number of fishermen, the NTAS maintains its power base among women interest groups. In 1985, among the twenty-six affiliated groups of the NTAS, eight of them came from women groups, whose number has been increasing since Hong Kong's sovereignty transfer from Britain to China. By 1990, the NTAS's women groups encompassed many from various districts in the New Territories and some leaders later joined the DAB, such as Yip Shun-hing, Wong Mau-tai and Chow Chuen-heung (Table 7.6).

With the passage of time, the NTAS became an auxiliary organization for the election campaign activities of the DAB and other like-minded groups, especially the FTU. More members who were affiliated with the

[21] *Wen Wei Po*, December 27, 2011, http://paper.wenweipo.com/2011/12/27/AY1112270004.htm, and the facebook of the New Territories West's Residents Association, in https://www.facebook.com/, access date: February 10, 2019. Also see *Ta Kung Pao*, December 24, 2014 and January 15, 2016.

Table 7.6 Women interest groups absorbed by the NTAS in 1990

Women interest group	Chairwoman
Tuen Mun Women Association	Yip Shun-hing (later chair of the pro-Beijing Hong Kong Women Development Association)
Shatin Women Association	Wong Mau-tai (later DAB member)
Northern District Women Mutual Aid Association	Wun Kwun-dai
Sai Kung Women Association	Tong Yuen-hing
Tsuen Wan Women Association	Lee Kit-ming
Cheung Chau Women Association	Lee Kwei-chun (later DAB member)
Yuen Long District Women Association	Tang Mon-chu
Islands Women Association	Chow Chuen-heung (later DAB member)

Table 7.7 The district distribution of interest groups affiliated with the NTAS

District	1986	1987	1990	1996	1999	2005	2009
New Territories-based[a]	3	3	3	3	3	3	3
Northern	2	2	3	7	10	13	18
Tai Po	5	5	7	9	14	19	26
Shatin	2	2	3	6	12	20	26
Sai Kung	2	2	2	6	10	17	26
Yuen Long	9	10	15	13	21	33	44
Tuen Mun	3	4	3	5	5	28	35
Tsuen Wan	2	2	3	5	6	13	18
Kwai Tsing	1	1	1	2	4	7	9
Islands (Cheung Chau Island)	4(3)	8(6)	10(8)	15(11)	18(12)	23(15)	24(16)
Number of groups	33	39	50	72	104	176	219

[a]Note: The three New Territories-based groups are the Hong Kong Graziers Union, the Hong Kong and Kowloon Flowers and Plants Workers General Union and the Hong Kong Fishermen's Association

NTAS and DAB got directly elected as District Council members and Legislative Councilors. By 1990 the NTAS had 50 affiliated groups with 60,000 members. In terms of the distribution of the group membership, Table 7.7 showed that the affiliated groups mostly came from Tai Po, Shatin, Sai Kung, Yuen Long, Tuen Mun and Islands districts. Table 7.8 demonstrates the gradual increase in both the group and individual membership of the NTAS.

Table 7.8 Interest groups and individual membership of the NTAS

Year	Number of interest groups	Number of individual members
1985	26	40,000
1986	33	50,000
1987	39	Not available
1988	Not available	Not available
1989	Not available	Not available
1990	50	60,000
1991	Not available	Not available
1992	Not available	Not available
1993	Not available	Not available
1994	Not available	Not available
1995	Not available	Not available
1996	72	Not available
1997	97	Not available
1998	Not available	Not available
1999	104	60,000
2000	106	Not available
2001	127	70,000
2002	128	Not available
2003	154	83,000
2004	164	101,136
2005	176	109,129
2006	188	111,079
2007	199	133,100
2008	220	146,095
2009	Not available	Not available
2010	251	160,000
2011	Not available	Not available
2012	Not available	Not available
2013	Not available	Not available
2014	Not available	Not available
2015	Not available	Not available
2016	362	250,000
2017	372	250,000
2018	390	250,000

Sources: Tabulated from the various years of the NTAS annual reports

In 1999, Cheung Hok-ming became the NTAS chairman. He was directly elected as a District Council member in Tai Po in 1985 and then joined the DAB in 1992. When Cheung became the NTAS chair in 1999 he was also a member of the rural advisory body Heung Yee Kuk. Cheung's three positions—district councilor, DAB member and Heung Yee Kuk member—made him a natural leader of the NTAS, which was expected to conduct extensive united front work on the community leaders of the New Territories and to serve as the DAB's auxiliary electoral machinery. In 2018, Chan Yung was both a deputy chairman of the DAB and managing director of the NTAS, while Leung Chi-cheung was also a DAB member and the President of NTAS. Clearly, the alliance between the DAB and NTAS is more obvious and stronger than ever before.

After the mass protest against the Tung-chee hwa government on July 1, 2003, the NTAS was tasked and mobilized to participate in the District Council elections in November of the same year. It captured fifty-seven directly elected seats, but twenty of them were automatically elected. The NTAS played a crucial role to provide checks and balances against the ascending pro-democracy forces, which benefit from the mass protests and grasped almost 50% of the directly elected seats in all eighteen District Councils. On the other hand, some NTAS members were trusted by the HKSAR government; six of them were appointed as District Council members in 2011, while twenty-nine of them were directly elected. In 2015, the NTAS only had sixteen members directly elected, a decrease of thirteen members from 2011. It appeared that the NTAS members who were directly elected as District Council members gradually declined from 2003 to 2015. However, it can be argued that the division of labor between the NTAS on the one hand and the DAB and FTU on the other hand was increasingly clear. While the DAB performed as a political party nominating candidates to openly participate in District Council elections, and while the FTU focuses on the work and electoral participation of working-class representatives, the NTAS performed as an auxiliary electoral machinery mobilizing its affiliated interest groups and members to campaign and vote for the DAB and FTU candidates. In fact, most of the FTU candidates who participate in district elections have acquired the logistical and campaign support from the NTAS.

Financially, the NTAS does not publicize its annual expenditure, but there are regular reports on its activities of seeking public donations. For instance, the NTAS conducted donation activities by selling flags on November 11, 2017, acquiring almost HK$840,000.[22] In June 2010, the

---

[22] "Thanks for your support at our New Territories region flagday on 11 Nov 2017," Independent Assurance Report, in http://ntascs.hk/flagdayreport/Flagdayreport2017 1111chi.pdf, access date: February 1, 2018.

NTAS was registered as a charity and social organization that could conduct such social activities as the provision of social services, elderly care, dormitory and youth centers. As early as 2007, the NTAS received financial subsidies from the HKSAR government to set up social enterprises, including an ecological market in Tai Po waterfront, promoting the fishing culture and cruise services and providing job opportunities to the needy, the youth and women.[23]

In recent years, the NTAS has been reaching out to the youth in the New Territories, strengthening the PRC's united front work on the young people of Hong Kong. In 1997, the NTAS set up the Federation of New Territories Youth (FNTY), which has twenty-four affiliated groups in 2019.[24] As time passed, the FNTY operates more autonomously, while DAB members like Brave Chan Yung, Cheung Hok-ming and Leung Chi-cheung of the NTAS remain the FNTY's honorary chairpersons. The FNTY is explicitly pro-Beijing and claims that its "joint conference on elected politicians" has five legislators and twenty-eight District Council members.[25] The FNTY also provides mainland summer internship training for Hong Kong students; sends Hong Kong university students to visit, study and work in the mainland; and organizes fund-raising, cultural, music and other study activities.[26] In short, the FNTY originated from NTAS but it is now increasingly autonomous in operation and becoming a training ground for young people to be politically patriotic and active in the HKSAR.

The NTAS also functions as a stabilizing socio-political force in the HKSAR. It constantly supported government policies, denounced those localists who support "Hong Kong independence," opposed the 2014 Occupy Central Movement and supported the police who helped suppress the rioters of Mongkok in early 2016. In September 2017, when the son of an undersecretary for education Choi Yuk-lin committed suicide, some students from the Hong Kong University of Education posted a message to "congratulate his death"—an incident arousing the anger of many ordinary citizens. The NTAS mobilized its members to protest at the campus of the university, demanding that the university authorities should find out

[23] See http://ntascs.hk/Sea-LandMarket.php, and http://www.fnty.org.hk/slide.php?moduleID=121, access date: February 8, 2018.
[24] See http://www.fnty.org.hk/slide.php?moduleID=76, access date: February 10, 2019.
[25] Remarks made by the chairman Yip Kam-hung, in http://www.fnty.org.hk/slide.php?moduleID=-18, access date: February 10, 2019.
[26] See http://www.fnty.org.hk/news.php?moduleID=-1, access date: February 10, 2019.

the students concerned and that they should penalize the offenders.[27] Overall, the NTAS as a united front organization is like a pro-government and pro-Beijing interest group that can turn into an effective electoral machinery during the elections.

Kowloon Federation of Associations

The KFA was formed in 1997 and its current chairperson is Bunny Chan Chun-bun and managing director is Wong Wai-ching. It has 199 affiliated groups with a membership of 220,000.[28] Since Chan and Wong are a member of the NPC and a delegate to the CPPCC, respectively, the organization is politically influential and directly linked to the CCP's personnel control through the *nomenklatura* system. The KFA has the objectives of "deepening its services in various districts, performing the stabilizing and pillar functions in the society, and supporting the policies of the HKSAR government."[29] Many of its members are legislators, District Council members and also appointed members to serve the advisory bodies and committees of the HKSAR administration. Organizationally, Fig. 7.1 shows that it works like a semi-political party with special and district committees dealing with a whole range of issues from social policy to poverty and from specific districts in Kowloon to its affiliated interest groups. The district committees play a crucial role in constituency services during non-election time and political mobilization during the election campaign period. Table 7.9 illustrates the number of interest groups under the district committees, showing that the KFA adopts an interest group approach to unify the various pro-Beijing organizations in Kowloon. Many individual members are the active members of the Mutual Aid Committees and Owners Corporations of public housing estates and private buildings, thereby giving a comparative advantage to the KFA members who want to prepare and compete in district elections.

The KFA assists other pro-Beijing groups to prepare and participate in local elections. For example, in the November 2015 District Council elections, the KF contributed to the satisfactory performance of the

---

[27] "Severely condemning the remarks on the democracy wall of the Education University of Hong Kong, requesting the authorities that they should penalize the offenders," in http://www.ntas.org.hk/blog_post.jsp?rid=91&cate_id=2, access date: February 10, 2019.

[28] See https://klnfas.hk/tc/, access date: February 10, 2019.

[29] Ibid.

7 PENETRATIVE POLITICS FROM NEIGHBORHOOD ASSOCIATIONS... 241

Fig. 7.1 The organization chart of the Kowloon Federation of Associations. Source: See https://klnfas.hk/tc/, access date: February 8, 2018

Table 7.9 Interest groups under the district committees of the Kowloon Federation of Associations

District committee	Year of establishment	Number of interest groups
Kwun Tong	2006	43
Wong Tai Sin	January 2016	27
Kowloon City	April 2005	20
Yau Tsim Mong	July 2006	20
Shum Shui Po	March 2006	31
Affiliated Interest Groups	Various Years	50

Source: Tabulated from the website of the KFA

pro-Beijing Kowloon West New Dynamic (KWND) led by Priscilla Leung Mei-fun and the Positive Synergy (PS) led by Tse Wai-chun. The KWND and PS had twenty-one and twenty members, respectively, who were directly elected as District Councilors. Among the twenty-one elected KWND members, nineteen of them were simultaneously the members of the KFA. Of the twenty elected members of the PS and of another pro-Beijing group named East Kowloon District Residents' Committee, fourteen of them were affiliated with the KFA.[30] Hence, the role of KFA as an electoral machinery assisting pro-Beijing political groups could not be ignored. Table 7.10 sums up the findings on the linkages between the KFA and the two pro-Beijing political groups. In brief, the KFA functions as another auxiliary organization helping pro-Beijing groups and candidates in both non-election and election period.

The KFA is actually incorporating a lot of district-based pro-Beijing groups into its united front umbrella. Table 7.10 illustrates four major pro-Beijing district groups under the KFA. The East Kowloon District Residents' Committee (EKDRC) was set up in 1957 with 60,000 members and focused its work in the Wong Tai Sin area, while the Kwun Tong Residents Association (KTRA) was established in 1974 with 20,000 members (Table 7.11). The Kowloon City Residents Association (KCRA) was founded in 1988 with 30,000 members whereas the Shumshuipo Residents Association (SRA) was set up in 1976 with 6000 members. The SRA is now led by the experienced pro-Beijing activists, notably President Ng Yat-cheung and managing director Chan Keng-chou, who fought for the residents' interest by lobbying the government to increase the amount of subsidies to the elderly, and to reduce the rent for the poor and the needy who lived in public housing estates.[31] The SRA helped a lot of elderly people and mainland Chinese who migrated to Hong Kong. For example, its another managing director Rong Hai who migrated to Hong Kong from the mainland in 1989 helped many migrants and elderly people by acting as a bridge between the government and them, and by helping the lower-class women to equip with the necessary skills to find jobs.[32] Although these interest groups are small, they are very active in helping residents and can mobilize supporters to vote for pro-Beijing candidates effectively in District Council and Legislative Council direct elections.

The KTRA is an old district-based interest group whose activities are now comprehensive, ranging from youth leadership training to elderly service, from volunteering work to child care, from women study groups to arts and cultural events.[33] The SRA is also an active pro-Beijing interest

[30] Also see the report in http://news.takungpao.com.hk/hkol/topnews/2015-10/3206750_print.html, access date: February 10, 2019.
[31] *Wen Wei Po*, September 13, 2010.
[32] "The Forty-two years of linkage between the SRA and Shumshuipo," in https://kowloonpost.hk/2018/07/13/20180711p8/, access date: February 12, 2019.
[33] See the KTRA website, in https://ktra.klnfas.hk/tc/, access date: February 12, 2019.

Table 7.10 The linkages between Kowloon Federation of Associations, Kowloon West New Dynamic, East Kowloon District Residents' Committee and Positive Synergy

Constituency in the 2015 District Council elections	Name of the candidate	Group membership
Cherry	Chung Chak-fai	Kowloon West New Dynamic
Mong Kok North	Wong Shu-ming	Kowloon West New Dynamic
Mong Kok East	Wong Kin-san	Kowloon West New Dynamic
Mong Kok South	Chow Chun-fai	Kowloon West New Dynamic
East Tsimshatsui and King's Park	Tang Ming-sum	Kowloon West New Dynamic
Cheung Sha Wan	Lam Ka-fai	Kowloon West New Dynamic
Shek Kip Mei	Chan Kwok-wai	Kowloon West New Dynamic
Fu Cheong	Leung Man-kwong	Kowloon West New Dynamic
Lok Man	Yang Wing-kit	Kowloon West New Dynamic
Ho Man Tin	Cheng Lee-ming	Kowloon West New Dynamic
Prince Edward	Ting Kin-wa	Kowloon West New Dynamic
Kai Tak North	Leung Yuen-ting	Kowloon West New Dynamic
Kai Tak South	He Hua-han	Kowloon West New Dynamic
To Kwa Wan South	Lam Pok	Kowloon West New Dynamic
Hok Yuen Laguna Verde	Yue Chee-wing Edmond	Kowloon West New Dynamic
Whampoa East	Leung Mei-fun Priscilla	Kowloon West New Dynamic
Hunghom Bay	Cheung Yan-hong	Kowloon West New Dynamic
G22 Ka Wai	Lo Chiu-kit	Kowloon West New Dynamic
G24 Hoi Chun	Cho Wui-hung	Kowloon West New Dynamic
H01 Lung Tsui	Lee Tung-kong	East Kowloon District Residents' Committee
H07 Sun Po Kwong	Lui Kai-lin	East Kowloon District Residents' Committee, and Positive Synergy
H10 Lok Fu	Chan Wai-	East Kowloon District Residents' Committee, and Positive Synergy
H17 Ching	Chan Man-kai	East Kowloon District Residents' Committee
J01 Kwun Tong Town Center	Chan Wah-yu Nelson	Positive Synergy
J09 Shueng Shun	Fu Pik-chun	Positive Synergy
J12 Sau Mau Ping North	Wong Chun-ping	Positive Synergy
J13 Hiu Lai	So Lai-chun	Positive Synergy
J22 Yau Lai	Lai Shu-ho Patrick	Positive Synergy
J24 Yau Tong West	Lui Tung-hai	Positive Synergy
J26 King Tin	Chueng Shun-wah	Positive Synergy
J27 Tsui Ping	Cheng Keung-fung	Positive Synergy
J30 Hip Hong	Chan Chung-bun Bunny	Positive Synergy
J32 Ting On	Kam Kin	Positive Synergy

Note: Positive Synergy had four members in Wong Tai Sin and sixteen members in Kwun Tong who were elected as District Councilors. The Kowloon West New Dynamic had four members in Sham Shui Po, six members in Yau Tsim Mong and eleven members in Kowloon City who were elected as District Councilors

Table 7.11 District-based interest groups under the Kowloon Federation of Associations

Residents' interest groups	Year of formation	Number of members
Kwun Tong Residents Association	1974	20,000
East Kowloon District Residents' Committee	1957	60,000
Kowloon City Residents Association	1988	30,000
Shumshuipo Residents Association	1976	6000

Sources: See https://ktra.klnfas.hk/tc/, and https://www.facebook.com/pg/sspra.sspdc/photos/?ref=page_internal, access date: February 12, 2019

group which mobilized its members and supporters to vote for a pro-PRC independent candidate, Rebecca Chan Hoi-yan, in the by-election held for the Legislative Council in November 2018.[34] The KCRA is another active pro-Beijing group that often holds dinner, mainland visits and Chinese opera performance of the elderly people, trying to win their hearts and minds in non-election time.[35] During the 30th anniversary of the KCRA in January 2018, the Liaison Office's Kowloon branch deputy director Wang Xiaoning attended its celebration, together with DAB chair Starry Lee and deputy chair Vincent Cheng as well as pro-Beijing legislator Priscilla Leung Mei-fun.[36] Wang praised the KCRA as an organization loving China and Hong Kong through its support of the NPC interpretation of the Basic Law, the celebration of China's success in holding the 2008 Olympics Game, and its opposition to the Occupy Central Movement in 2014 and to Hong Kong independence from 2016 to 2018. Wang also remarked that 70% of the District Councilors in Kowloon City joined the KCRA in the past, and she hoped that the association would emphasize the importance of patriotic education and of Hong Kong's closer economic integration with the Greater Bay Area. The KCRA chairman Yeung Wing-kuen revealed that the KCRA had five members directly elected as District Councilors in November 2015, while its new president Poon Kwok-wah is a DAB member, saying that the group would continue to focus on livelihood issues.[37] The inauguration ceremony of its new office-bearers saw the attendance of the deputy District Officer of the

[34] See https://zh-hk.facebook.com/pg/sspra.sspdc/about/?ref=page_internal, access date: February 12, 2019.
[35] See its facebook, https://zh-hk.facebook.com/pg/, access date: February 12, 2019.
[36] *Hong Kong Commercial Daily*, January 11, 2018.
[37] Ibid.

HKSAR government in Kowloon City, the KFA managing director Lau Wai-wing and the police commander of the district. Clearly, the group had official endorsement from both the HKSAR regime and the Liaison Office.

THE HONG KONG ISLAND FEDERATION

The Hong Kong Island Federation (HKIF) was set up in 1999 with 204 affiliated interest groups and a membership of 130,000.[38] Its objectives are apparently non-political, focusing on the development of social welfare, the organization of cultural and arts activities, the consolidation of cultural exchange with the mainland, the assistance to the poor and the needy and the provision of services for the youth, women and the elderly. The federation's honorary advisers come from various pro-Beijing groups, including Regina Ip from the New People's Party, Starry Lee from the DAB, Cheng Yiu-tong and Ng Chau-pak from the Federation of Trade Unions and Chan Wing-kei from the Chinese Manufacturers' Association.[39] The united front function of the HKIF can be easily identified as it aims at uniting the elites from various groups and occupational sectors. The HKIF is composed of member groups which are politically pro-Beijing. For instance, the Wan Chai District Association holds annual celebration of the national day of the PRC, organizes study visits to the mainland, contributes donations to build schools and to support social welfare in the mainland and interacts with the PRC government on a regular basis.[40] Other groups affiliated and friendly with the HKIF include the Lan Fang Women Association, the Hong Kong Island Chaowen Association (a group composed of people of Chiu Chow ancestry), Hong Kong Island Women Federation, the pro-Beijing Po Kin Hai Liu Association, Hong Kong Volunteer Federation and Hong Kong Wanchai All-Sectors Association.[41] Regina Ip, a pro-Beijing legislator, often attended some of these gatherings, especially those organized by women groups.[42] The

---

[38] See the federation's website, in http://www.hk-if.org/special.php?id=9, access date: February 12, 2019.
[39] See the HKIF website, in http://www.hk-if.org/special.php?id=10, access date: February 12, 2019.
[40] See http://hkwanchai.lavendzpresspublishing.com/about.html, access date: February 12, 2019.
[41] See http://www.hk-if.org/msg.php?id=107, access date: February 12, 2019.
[42] See her attendance in an activity of the Lan Fang Women Association, in *Ta Kung Pao*, February 17, 2016.

intention was clear: she had to maintain regular contacts with some of these united front organizations to interact with voters frequently and thereby retaining her momentum to compete in the Legislative Council direct elections, while seeking the support of some of them for the electoral participation of members of her New People's Party.

Interestingly, there are three smaller federations under the HKIF, namely, the Wanchai District All-Sectors Association (WDAA), the Eastern District All-Sectors Association (EDAA) and the Southern District All-Sectors Association (SDAA). The WDAA held a celebration dinner and inauguration ceremony of its new office-bearers on June 20, 2017, with the participation of 1300 people and two directors from the Liaison Office's Hong Kong branch.[43] The association was the first local interest group which visited the Greater Bay Area after the announcement of its idea in the summer of 2018, showing that it was politically patriotic and eager to enhance cultural exchange and historical understandings between Hong Kong and the mainland. The WDAA also annually holds celebration dinner for the PRC national day, inviting dignitaries and local elites to express their hope that the "country would continue to be prosperous and stable."[44] Similarly, when the EDAA held the 10th anniversary of its establishment and also the 20th anniversary of the return of Hong Kong to China in August 2017, the Liaison Office and the Fujian province's United Front Department sent their officials to attend, showing that PRC officials attached great importance to such district-based federation activities in the Eastern district, where many Fujianese people are residing.[45] The SDAA, which was formed in 1992 by a group of pro-Beijing local elites, aims at expressing its concern about social affairs and promoting social harmony.[46] It supported the government's political reform initiative in 2014 and 2015, opposed the 2014 Occupy Central Movement and emphasized the need for Hong Kong to interact with the PRC intensively and deeply so that China's "One Belt, One Road" initiative could and would be realized. The SDAA also opposed those localists who called for "Hong Kong independence," becoming another district-based interest group supportive of the protection of the PRC's national security interest in the HKSAR.[47] The WDAA, EDAA and SDAA are like mini-federations within the larger

---

[43] *Ta Kung Pao*, June 21, 2017.
[44] *Hong Kong Commercial Daily*, September 18, 2017.
[45] *Wen Wei Po*, August 12, 2017.
[46] *Wen Wei Po*, September 16, 2015.
[47] *Wen Wei Po*, November 7, 2016.

HKIF to conduct extensive and intensive united front work in various districts on the Hong Kong Island.

In September 2017, the HKIF held its celebration of the 68th anniversary of the PRC. It planned a series of activities, including dinners, cultural festivals, movies appreciation, Chinese opera performance and other related carnivals from September to October, mobilizing the residents to understand their motherland in a deeper manner.[48] The HKIF chairman Choi Ngai stressed that Hong Kong must firmly grasp the consciousness of uploading the supremacy of "one country," and that they must strike a balance between the interests of "one country" and that of "two systems."[49]

A prominent 20th anniversary celebration and inauguration ceremony of its new office-bearers were held in January 2019, when the attendees included Chief Executive Carrie Lam, Liaison Office's deputy director He Jing, the deputy commissioner of the Ministry of Foreign Affairs Song Ru'an and the People's Liberation Army Garrison deputy commander Tian Rongjiang.[50] Lam appealed to the HKIF to assist and cooperate with the HKSAR government to maintain economic prosperity and social stability, and to integrate Hong Kong into China's developmental plan. She praised the HKIF for supporting government policies openly and assertively and displaying the function of a supportive network. Lam affirmed the stabilizing social function of the HKIF, showing that the HKSAR government welcomes the activities of the PRC's united front groups in Hong Kong. Echoing Lam, He Jing said that the HKIF under its leadership contributed to the growth of the forces that loved China and Hong Kong, and that it would and should continue to contribute to the "one country, two systems" and the "Chinese renaissance."[51] In response to Lam and He's remarks, the HKIF managing director So Cheung-wing admitted that the federation becomes one of the largest ones in the HKSAR and that he would continue the "excellent tradition" of supporting the government policies, serving the people and promoting Hong Kong's social and economic stability.[52] The ceremony witnessed the participation of the officials from the Liaison Office, the Guangdong province's United Front Department, Guangdong CPPCC, Foshan city's United Front Department, Foshan city's CPPCC, pro-Beijing legislators such as Regina

[48] *Ta Kung Pao*, September 6, 2017.
[49] Ibid.
[50] See the HKIF website, in http://www.hk-if.org/msg.php?id=411, access date: February 12, 2019.
[51] Ibid.
[52] Ibid.

Ip and Starry Lee and six Hong Kong members of the NPC and six local members of the CPPCC. Such high-profile and high-ranking participation of the Hong Kong elites and PRC officials were a testimony to the significant united front function of the Hong Kong Island Federation.

ELECTORAL MOBILIZATION: THE CASES OF THE VICTORY OF VINCENT CHENG AND REBECCA CHAN

The ways in which Vincent Cheng Wing-shun of the DAB and pro-Beijing independent Rebecca Chan Hoi-yan won the by-elections held for the Legislative Council in March and November, respectively, in 2018 demonstrated how the PRC's new united front work was conducted in the HKSAR. Table 7.12 shows the campaign expenditure claimed by the two

Table 7.12 A comparison of two by-elections held for Legislative Council in March and November 2018

Candidate	Political party affiliation	Upper limit of campaign expenditure	Actual campaign expenditure	Number of votes	Cost per vote ($)
By-election on March 11, 2018					
Vincent Cheng Wing-shun[a]	DAB	HK$1,821,000	HK $1,429,661	107,479 (49.9%)	HK $13.3
Edward Yiu Chung-yim Yiu	Independent	HK$1,821,000	HK $1,388,665	105,060 (48.8%)	HK $13.2
By-Election on November 25, 2018					
Candidate	Political Party Affiliation	Upper Limit of Campaign Expenditure	Actual Campaign Expenditure	Number of Votes	Cost per Vote ($)
Rebecca Chan Hoi-yan[a]	Independent	HK$1,821,000	HKD$1,462,000	106,457 (49.5%)	HK $13.7
Lee Chek-yan	Labor Party	HK$1,821,000	HKD$1,794,000	93,047 (43.28%)	HK $19
Frederick Fung	Independent	HK$1,821,000	HKD$1,020,000	106,457 (49.5%)	HK $82

Sources: *Hong Kong Economic Journal*, May 18, 2018, p. A18; *Hong Kong Economic Journal*, January 25, 2019, p. A12; *Apple Daily*, January 31, 2019, p. A09; *Wen Wei Po*, January 31, 2019, p. A14

[a]Directly elected candidate

Table 7.13 Some declared donors in Rebecca Chan's election campaign

Donor	Amount (HK$)	Political party or Clans group affiliation
Starry Lee Wai-king	20	DAB
Stanley Ng Chau-pei	20	FTU
Dominic Lee Tsz-king	20	Liberal Party
Vincent Cheng Wing-shun	20	DAB
Regina Ip Lau Suk-yee	20	New People's Party
Priscilla Leung Mei-fun	20	Business and Professional Alliance for Hong Kong
Elizabeth Quat	20	DAB
Cheung King-fun	1000	Liberal Party
Edmond Chung Kong-mo	1000	DAB
Ng Wai-kuen	1000	Hong Kong Hakka Association
Ho Chi-keung	1000	The General Association of Hong Kong Heiyuan Societies
Jimmy Tang Kui-ming	5000	Unknown
Chen Hongtian (a member of the CPPCC)	20,000	Federation of Hong Kong Community Organization

Sources: https://www.hkcnews.com/, access date: February 12, 2019

directly elected candidates as compared with other candidates in the two by-elections. Vincent Cheng of the DAB spent HK$13.3 per vote as compared with almost the same amount spent by pro-democracy independent candidate Edward Yiu Chung-yim. Moreover, Rebecca Chan appeared to spend even less than the two pro-democracy independents, Lee Cheuk-yan of the Labour Party and Frederick Fung Kin-kee. Nevertheless, the crux of the problem of the declared expenditure is that candidates are only required to report to the electoral affairs committee the amount of money they spent during the officially designated campaign period. Since united front work that assisted the campaign activities of Cheng and Chan took place well before the official campaign period, the seemingly lower amount of money spent on each vote hid the fact that most electoral engineering activities took place before the official campaign period.

Arguably, while the declared campaign expenditure for the officially designated campaign period hid the extent of united front activities during the non-election time, the same can be said of the declared donations from the candidates concerned. Table 7.13 demonstrates the donors and the relatively minimal amount they supported Rebecca Chan for her election campaign. While the amount was overall minimal, some united front

Table 7.14 Rental expenditure of Rebecca Chan's election campaign

Venue provider	Amount (HK$)
DAB	6900
Kowloon West New Dynamic	6600
Kowloon City Residents Association	1500
Shumshuipo Residents Association	1500
Yau Tsim Mong Federation of Associations	1500
Business and Professional Alliance for Hong Kong	1500
Federation of Trade Unions	800
King's Park Professional Union	800
Nam Cheong Residents Shoppers Association	800
Tai Kok Tsui District Residents Livelihood Concern Society	800
Hoi Wang Residents Association	800
Yau Ma Tei Concern for Residents Rights Association	800
Victoria Harbor Association	800
Neighborhood Power	800
Tai Nan Social Services Team	800
Ting Kin-wa and Cheng Lee-ming's District Councilors Joint Office	800
Total Amount	$31,800

Sources: See https://www.hkcnews.com/, access date: February 12, 2019

organizations, such as the Hong Kong Hakka Association, the General Association of Hong Kong Heiyuan Societies and the Federation of Hong Kong Community Organization, were involved in her electioneering activities. Other united front groups that were involved in Chan's election campaign provided venues and logistical support for her. Table 7.14 shows that many united front groups provided venues for her electioneering work, such as the Kowloon West New Dynamic, the Kowloon City Residents Association, the Shumshuipo Residents Association and the Yau Tsim Mong Federation of Associations.

Critics of these figures said that while Vincent Cheng's campaign expenditure of HK$1,380,000 was mostly supported by the DAB, Rebecca Chan got the financial support of pro-Beijing groups.[53] The reason was that Chan had become a so-called healthy ambassador weeks before the official campaign period, that she got the support of many united front groups and that *Tai Kung Pao* and *Wen Wei Po* staunchly supported her campaign and publicized her activities. Hence, some democrats estimated that Chan had used at least HK$10,000,000 in her real

[53] *Apple Daily*, November 20, 2018.

election campaign.⁵⁴ Her critics said that Chan's "healthy ambassador" image and activities were supported by the KFA. It was estimated that the public advertisement for her "healthy ambassador" cost at least HK$200,000 per month.⁵⁵ Similarly, Cheng's poster had long appeared in the constituency of Kowloon West in June 2017, showing that the DAB had prepared him for the election battle in March 2018. Due to the difficulties and impossibility of calculating the possible amount of expenditure before the officially designated campaign period, both Cheng and Chan might benefit from the loophole in Hong Kong's elections and they became the beneficiaries of continuous united front work in favor of their electoral preparation and early campaign.

The victory of Cheng was also attributable to his mobilization strategy at the end of the campaign period. He mobilized the former police commissioner Tang King-shing and also the former secretary for security Lau Tung-kwok to campaign for him, trying to grasp the votes of civil servants from the disciplinary forces in the constituency.⁵⁶ However, Edward Yiu's campaign assistants and workers were outnumbered, and his campaign strategy lacked a focus and failed to penetrate into the strongholds of the pro-Beijing forces. Compounding the lack of an effective campaign strategy of Yiu was the reluctance of many localists and middle-class citizens to vote for him. The Kowloon West constituency was vacated after the SCNPC interpretation of the Basic Law on Yau Wai-ching's disrespectful oath-taking behavior in October 2016. For the localists who supported Yau, they did not find Edward Yiu as politically appealing. In the eyes of some middle-class moderates who had voted for Yau, they were disappointed that Yau eventually misbehaved in the legislature, not to mention coming out to vote for Edward Yiu. Under these circumstances, Yiu's chance of being elected was substantially reduced, especially as he was one of the elected legislators who were also disqualified for the court in July 2017 for being improper in his oath-taking ceremony in the Legislative Council. Instead of allowing another pro-democracy candidate to participate in the by-election, Yiu remained politically defiant and attempted to get back his seat in the legislature. Furthermore, in September 2016 when Yiu was elected, he ran in the functional constituency for construction, surveying and urban planning. He did not have any experience in direct

⁵⁴ Ibid.
⁵⁵ See https://www.hk01.com/, access date: January 25, 2019.
⁵⁶ *Apple Daily*, March 12, 2018.

elections. Therefore, when Yiu decided to compete for the directly elected seat vacated by Yau Wai-ching in early 2018, his chance of being elected was undermined not only his inexperience in direct election but also the long preparation and strong mobilization of Vincent Cheng, as well as the unwillingness of many pro-democracy voters who formerly supported Yau to cast their ballots for Yiu.

Rebecca Chan's electoral victory represented the success of the PRC's new united front work in the HKSAR. She got the support of the new united front that was composed of not only the DAB but also pro-Beijing independents. Starry Lee, Ann Chiang and Vincent Cheng of the DAB all appeared on Chan's campaign leaflet, together with the pro-Beijing independent Priscilla Leung.[57] Other local elites who supported her election included Liberal Party members Cheung Yu-yan and James Tien, FTU leader Ng Chau-pak, New People's Party chairwoman Regina Ip, former Legislative Council President Jasper Tsang, member of the Executive Council Bernard Chan, and former Secretary for Food and Health Ko Wing-man.[58] Chan's campaign platform wisely focused on livelihood issues, such as "the call for alleviating the burden of the citizens at the grassroots level, the reduction of pressure on the middle class, the realization of dreams for the youth, and the need to regain the dignity for the elderly people."[59] On the contrary, Frederick Fung as a democrat came out to compete with Lee Cheuk-yan, thus diluting and dividing the votes from the pro-democracy supporters. Under these circumstances, Chan's victory was understandable and natural.

Conclusion

The creation, utilization and mobilization of district-based federations, together with the gradual political co-optation of *kaifong* associations, are the prominent united front strategies of the PRC authorities and their agents in the HKSAR. These *kaifong* associations and other local interest groups have been reorganized and regrouped under the new united front umbrella of district-based federations, constituting a powerful force in electoral preparation and mobilization of pro-Beijing voters and ensuring the victory of pro-Beijing candidates and parties in local direct elections.

---

[57] See Rebecca Chan's campaign leaflet in November 2018.
[58] Ibid.
[59] See Rebecca Chan's leaflet publicizing her campaign platform in November 2018.

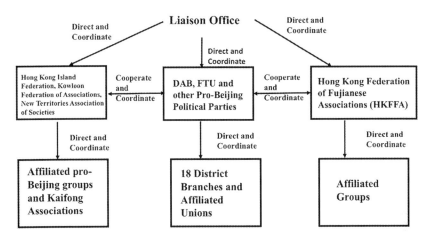

Fig. 7.2 Penetrative politics at the district level

At the territorial and district level, federations function as the united front machinery solidifying, coordinating and mobilizing all the affiliated interest groups and they provide constituency services regularly in non-election time. Furthermore, district-based federations are tasked to support the HKSAR government policies and expected to be a politically and socially stabilizing force in the society. Most importantly, they work side by side with the DAB, FTU and Fujianese interest groups to constitute powerful electoral machines in local politics, trying to win the hearts and minds of more Hong Kong people and mobilizing their supporters to vote for candidates of pro-Beijing forces in elections. Figure 7.2 sums up their relations and the coordinating and leadership role of the Liaison Office officials, who often attend, join and coordinate the activities of all these groups.

In a nutshell, district federations are like the "transmission belt" of the PRC's new united front work in the HKSAR, penetrating deeply and extensively to every corner of the society. Penetrative politics has one ultimate objective: to stop the democrats from grasping more directly elected seats at the legislative and district level and to increase the chance of success of the pro-Beijing candidates in the local elections.

CHAPTER 8

Youth Interest Groups from Pro-Beijing Front to Radical Resistance

The PRC's new united front work in the HKSAR is targeting at numerous youth interest groups, but it has also been adopting a hard-line policy toward those youth groups which are ideologically radical in resisting mainland Chinese influence on Hong Kong's political arena. This chapter firstly delineates the major youth interest groups that fall under the united front umbrella of Beijing and secondly discusses those young localist groups that resist the PRC's penetrative politics.

The Core Youth Groups Under United Front

Figure 8.1 shows the core youth groups that are under the varying degrees of influence of Beijing's united front work. At the core, the All-China Youth Federation plays a crucial role in co-opting some young Hong Kong people, who are appointed into this pro-Beijing youth organization. At the outer sphere, three Hong Kong-based interest groups stand out: (1) the Hong Kong United Youth Association, (2) the Hong Kong CPPCC Youth Association and (3) the Y Elites Association. At the outer boundary, other pro-Beijing local district groups persist, including the prominent uniformed cadet groups, such as the Hong Kong Army Cadet Association, which holds regular and annual summer activities for the young people to experience as army cadets. There are other non-governmental youth groups at the periphery; nevertheless, the localist interest groups appear to be uninterested in obtaining any monetary or

© The Author(s) 2019
S. S.-H. Lo et al., *China's New United Front Work in Hong Kong*,
https://doi.org/10.1007/978-981-13-8483-7_8

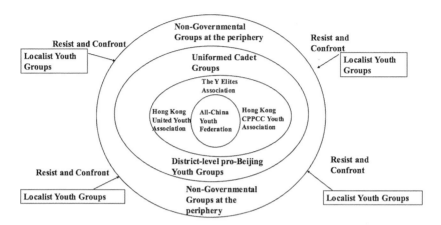

Fig. 8.1 Core and peripheral pro-Beijing youth groups

political support from the PRC and its agents in the HKSAR. The localist groups, as will be discussed, have all kinds of ideological inclinations, ranging from pro-democracy to pro-independence and from moderate to radical.

Basically, united front work is conducted more easily on those young people who have materialistic orientations, but it is more difficult to be achieved in the minds of those youths who are imbued with the ideas of democracy, human rights, social justice and sustainable development. Figure 8.2 highlights this major variation between the materialistic and post-materialistic young people of Hong Kong vis-à-vis Beijing's united front work. Naturally, those young people who are politically opportunistic, socially materialistic and culturally patriotic tend to be far more vulnerable to the PRC united front work than those who are politically pro-democracy, socially post-materialistic and culturally Chinese but not identified themselves with the CCP regime in the mainland.

Hong Kong United Youth Association

The Hong Kong United Youth Association (HKUYA) was established in August 1982 and some of its members are also the members of pro-Beijing All-China Youth Federation (ACYF). The ACYF was founded in 1949 that represents many youth groups in China, including notably the Communist Youth League. The former PRC Presidents, Jiang Zemin and

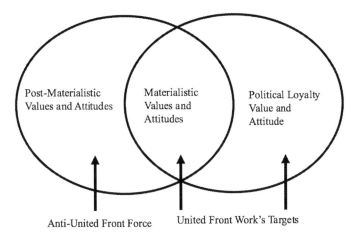

Fig. 8.2 The Values and Attitudes of Hong Kong Youths: Accepting or Resisting United Front Work

Hu Jintao, were both members of the ACYF. Through its 52-member organizations and some 77,000 individual members at all levels, the ACYF reaches over to an estimated 300 million young people across mainland China.[1] Its objectives are to "uphold the banner of patriotism and socialism"; "encourage young people to study Marxism-Leninism, Mao Zedong thought and Deng Xiaoping theory"; "represent and safeguard the legitimate rights and interests of young people of all ethnic groups and all walks of life"; "guide young people to actively participate in social activities and develop friendship with young people of Taiwan, Hong Kong, Macao and overseas Chinese" and to "consolidate the social stability and unity of China and to promote the reunification of the motherland."[2] Obviously, the federation conducts explicit united front work in the mainland.

The objectives of HKUYA are, like the ACYF, explicitly political, namely, "to support the Sino-British Joint Declaration, the Hong Kong Basic Law, and the HKSAR government policies; to promote mutual and deeper understanding between the young people who love China and Hong Kong and to unite local youths and train more local talents; and to promote the exchange between Hong Kong youth and mainland and

---

[1] See http://www.acyf.org.cn/, access date: February 17, 2019.
[2] Ibid.

overseas counterparts so as to achieve the motherland's peaceful reunification."[3] Most of the members in HKUYA are the elites in different social and occupational sectors, including university students.[4] There are seven committees under the HKUYA, including the (1) commercial and international affairs committee, (2) cultural and communication development committee, (3) social and women affairs committee, (4) innovation and start-up committee, (5) membership and training committee, (6) educational circles committee and the (7) sports development and leisure committee. The HKUYA has about 33,000 members, including 2000 individual members and 48 affiliated group members.

The chairmen of HKUYA have been actively participating in Hong Kong and Chinese politics through their appointments by the PRC government as members of the CPPCC and NPC. Table 8.1 illustrates that background of all the HKUYA leaders came from the business and professional sectors, showing that the PRC has been eager to co-opt mostly the business elites and members of the young generation since August 1992. In terms of class background, these co-opted Hong Kong elites came from middle and upper classes. Most importantly, the pattern of political appointment showed that most of them were appointed as NPC and CPPCC members at the national and local levels. Some of them were affiliated with All-China Youth Federation, such as Andrew Yao, Adrian Yip, Kenneth Fok, Johnny Ng and Andy Kwok. Their political affiliation reflects the significance of the All-China Youth Federation, which as mentioned before constitutes the core united front organization that grooms some Hong Kong elites to have overlapping leadership and membership of the HKUYA. Such overlapping leadership means that Beijing skillfully cultivates a group of young Hong Kong elites to strengthen the patriotic political forces in the HKSAR. It also demonstrates the role of the HKUYA as a "transmission belt" for the PRC to conduct its new united front work in Hong Kong.

Table 8.2 shows that the educational level of the HKUYA's General Committee members are relatively high with a range of 55–60% of them possessing Bachelor degrees and 36–43% acquiring Master degrees. On the other hand, many members of the HKUYA have been appointed to

---

[3] See the HKUYA mission and vision, in http://www.hkuya.org.hk/web15/web/subpage.php?mid=9, access date: February 17, 2019.

[4] "About HKUYA," in http://www.hkuya.org.hk/web15/web/subpage.php?mid=8, access date: February 17, 2019.

Table 8.1 Chairmen of Hong Kong United Youth Association, 1992–2018

Name	Institution affiliation	Occupational background	Key position in Chinese political institutions
Ian Fok Chun-wan	The Chinese General Chamber of Commerce	Businessman	1. NPC member, 2008 to the present 2. Member of Guangdong Province's CPPCC, 1997–2003
Peter Wong Man-kong	The Chinese General Chamber of Commerce	Businessman	1. NPC member, 1993 to the present
Dennis Sun Tai-lun	Does not have any institution affiliation	Businessman	Did not have any prominent position in Chinese political institution
Joseph Lee	The Federation of Hong Kong Industries	Industrialist	1. NPC member, 1997–2008
Eddy Li Sau-hung	The Chinese Manufacturers' Association of Hong Kong	Industrialist	1. CPPCC member, 2008 to the present
Kennedy Wong Ying-ho	New Century Forum	Lawyer	1. CPPCC Member, 2003 to the present
George Lung Chee-ming	Hong Kong Taiwan Youth Exchange Promotion Association	Businessman	1. CPPCC member, 2008 to the present
Wilson Wu Wai-tsuen	The Chinese General Chamber of Commerce	Businessman	1. Standing Committee member of the Liaoning Provincial Committee of the CPPCC, 2013–2018
Samuel Yung Wing-ki	Hong Kong Professional and Senior Executives Association	Businessman	1. CPPCC member, 2008 to the present
William Tsang Chi-hung	The Chinese General Chamber of Commerce	Businessman	1. Standing Committee member of the Hebei Provincial Committee of the CPPCC, 2013–2018
Andrew Yao	All-China Youth Federation	Industrialist	1. NPC member, 2013 to the present
Michael Hui Wah-kit	Hong Kong Chinese Importers' and Exporters' Association	Businessman	Did not have any prominent position in Chinese political institution

(*continued*)

Table 8.1 (continued)

Name	Institution affiliation	Occupational background	Key position in Chinese political institutions
Rock Chen Chung-nin	The Democratic Alliance for the Betterment Progress of Hong Kong	Businessman	1. CPPCC Member
Adrian Chun-to Yip	All-China Youth Federation	Businessman	1. Standing Committee Member of All-China Youth Federation
Kenneth Fok Kai-kong	All-China Youth Federation	Businessman	1. CPPCC member, 2018 to the present
Andrew Fan Chun-wah	Ningbo Overseas Association	Accountant	1. Member of the Zhejiang Provincial CPPCC
Johnny Ng	All-China Youth Federation	Businessman	1. CPPCC member, 2018 to the present
Andy Kwok Wing-leung	All-China Youth Federation	Businessman	1. Member of the CPPCC of the Zhanjiang Prefecture

Sources: Hong Kong United Youth Association, *We are Youth: The Celebration of the 23rd Anniversary of Hong Kong United Youth Association Limited* (Hong Kong: Hong Kong United Youth Association: 2015), pp. 36–37. See also "The Organization Structure of HKUYA," in http://www.hkuya.org.hk/web15/web/subpage.php?mid=10, access date: June 30, 2018

various governmental advisory and consultative committees. It is crystal clear that once the young professional and business elites join the HKUYA, they have a chance of being politically appointed to the Hong Kong and mainland's consultative bodies, thereby giving them better political status and more political influence. As such, the HKUYA remains attractive to those young professionals who have the aspirations and ambitions to climb up the political ladder in both Hong Kong and the mainland.

Table 8.3 illustrates that in 2015, the 12th ACYF leadership had a total of fifty-four members from the HKUYA, including one vice-chairperson, eleven members of the Standing Committee and forty-two committee members. The 12th ACYF meeting decided that "the most important theme is to realize the Chinese dream and renaissance during the new era of united front work on the patriotic youths."[5] The phenomenon that a large number of HKUYA were also the ACYF members demonstrated the "new era of united front work" through overlapping membership and

[5] See http://www.hua-jing.org/a/32427-cht, access date: February 19, 2019.

Table 8.2 Education background of General Committee members of the Hong Kong United Youth Association, 2012–2015

Education background of HKUYA's General Committee members, 2012–2015

Educational level	2012 (% of the total General Committee members)	2013 (% of the total General Committee members)	2014 (% of the total General Committee members)	2015 (% of the total General Committee members)
Bachelor	58%	55%	55%	60%
Master or Above	36%	38%	43%	36%
Others	6%	7%	2%	4%

Number of members of the Government's Advisory Committees in which HKUYA participates

Year	2012	2013	2014	2015
Number of Members in the Government's Advisory Committees	38	25	20	22

Sources: Hong Kong United Youth Association, *We are Youth: The Celebration of the 20th Anniversary of Hong Kong United Youth Association Limited* (Hong Kong: Hong Kong United Youth Association: 2012), p. 105; Hong Kong United Youth Association, *We are Youth: The Celebration of the 21st Anniversary of Hong Kong United Youth Association Limited* (Hong Kong: Hong Kong United Youth Association: 2013), p. 85; Hong Kong United Youth Association, *We are Youth: The Celebration of the 22nd Anniversary of Hong Kong United Youth Association Limited* (Hong Kong: Hong Kong United Youth Association: 2014), p. 69; Hong Kong United Youth Association, *We are Youth: The Celebration of the 23rd Anniversary of Hong Kong United Youth Association Limited* (Hong Kong: Hong Kong United Youth Association: 2015), p. 70

Table 8.3 Participation of HKUYA members in the 12th All-China Youth Federation

Position in the All-China Youth Federation	Number of HKUYA members
Vice-Chairperson	1
Standing Committee Members	11
Committee Members	42
Total	54

Hong Kong United Youth Association, *We are Youth: The Celebration of the 23rd Anniversary of Hong Kong United Youth Association Limited* (Hong Kong: Hong Kong United Youth Association: 2015), p. 118

leadership. Furthermore, a plenty of HKUYA members participated in various youth federations in the PRC at the city level. Table 8.4 shows that the youth federations in Guangdong, Yunnan, Hainan, Guangxi and Tianjin co-opted a lot of Hong Kong youth elites. In total, 442 members of the HKUYA were appointed into the mainland youth federations at

Table 8.4 Participation of HKUYA members in the 12th Chinese Youth Federations at the provincial and municipal levels

Province	Number of Vice-Chairperson	Number of Standing Committee members	Number of Committee members	Total
Beijing	2	3	9	14
Inner Mongolia	1	1	9	11
Tianjin	2	7	14	23
Liaoning	1	3	14	18
Hebei	2	4	10	16
Shanxi	1	3	5	9
Jilin	1	2	4	7
Heilongjiang	2	5	5	12
Shanghai	1	3	5	9
Jiangsu	1	2	14	17
Zhejiang	1	0	6	7
Henan	1	4	16	21
Shandong	0	2	8	10
Anhui	1	1	4	6
Fujian	1	4	6	11
Hubei	1	5	13	19
Hunan	1	4	6	11
Guizhou	0	0	3	3
Guangdong	1	7	48	56
Guangxi	1	5	18	24
Hainan	1	5	20	26
Chongqing	1	0	11	12
Sichuan	1	3	4	8
Qinghai	1	5	8	14
Yunnan	1	4	26	31
Ningxia	1	1	12	14
Shanxi	0	0	4	4
Total	28	82	312	442

Source: Hong Kong United Youth Association, *We are Youth: The Celebration of the 23rd Anniversary of Hong Kong United Youth Association Limited* (Hong Kong: Hong Kong United Youth Association: 2015), pp. 119–121

both provincial and municipal levels, including 312 committee members, 82 standing committee members and 28 vice-chairpersons. The extent of interlocking memberships between the HKUYA and the mainland youth federations is large, with the implications that they are politically interconnected at the horizontal level. Vertically, both the mainland youth federations at municipal level and the HKUYA are under the direct guidance and leadership of the ACYF.

In July 2015, it was reported that the ACYF made an unusual move by appointing two vice-chairpersons of the HKUYA, businessmen Adrian Cheng Chi-kong and Jaime Sze Wing-him as the ACYF deputy chairs.[6] By convention, the ACYF merely appointed the chairperson of the HKUYA as its deputy chairs. In 2015, the HKUYA chairman Kenneth Fok Kai-kong was in his mid-30s and was regarded as relatively young. Fok could wait for a few years to be appointed upward to the ACYF. Moreover, Sze was viewed as playing a crucial role in forming the pro-Beijing Y Elite Association, opposing the Occupy Central Movement in 2014 and leading the Hong Kong Federation of Fujianese Associations actively. Adrian Cheng works as the young leader of the New World Development Company and is regarded as the young generation of business people in the HKSAR. The co-optation of Cheng and Sze into the top leadership of the ACYF was politically significant, showing that the PRC's new united front work targets at the younger, prominent and successful business elites in the HKSAR.

Table 8.5 demonstrates the political participation of HKUYA members as legislators in Hong Kong. Two features stood out. First, most legislators of the HKUYA were affiliated with the pro-Beijing DAB, and the New Century Forum, meaning that the two political groups were the targets of political co-optation. Second, while the HKUYA has lots of members affiliated with the mainland youth federations at the central, provincial and municipal levels, those mainland young people who migrate to the HKSAR can practically join the HKUYA, constitute the new blood of the HKUYA and provide constant generational renewal, especially if there is a political will to staff the HKUYA with more young mainland migrants to Hong Kong. For instance, Gary Chan was born in Fujian and migrated to reside in Hong Kong, and he later graduated from the Chinese University of Hong Kong and Syracuse

[6] "The mystery of Jaime Sze becoming the ACYF vice-chairman," in https://hk.on.cc/hk/bkn/cnt/news/20150728/bkn-20150728222031319-0728_00822_001.html, access date: February 19, 2019.

Table 8.5 Participation of HKUYA members as Legislators, 1997–2018

Term	Name	Constituency and political party affiliation
1998–2000	Bernard Chan Charnwut	Insurance sector without political party affiliation
	Ma Fung-kwok	Election Committee and affiliated with the New Century Forum
2000–2004	Bernard Chan Charnwut	Insurance sector without political party affiliation
	Ma Fung-kwok	Election Committee and affiliated with the New Century Forum
	Henry Wu	Financial Services without political party affiliation
2004–2008	Bernard Chan Charnwut	Insurance without political party affiliation
	Wong Ting-kwong	Import and Export Industry, and affiliated with the Democratic Alliance for the Betterment and Progress of Hong Kong
2008–2012	Gary Chan Hak-kan	New Territories East, and affiliated with the Democratic Alliance for the Betterment and Progress of Hong Kong
	Wong Ting-kwong	Import and Export Industry, and affiliated with the Democratic Alliance for the Betterment and Progress of Hong Kong
	Samson Tam Wai-ho	Information Technology without political party affiliation
2012–2016	Gary Chan Hak-kan	New Territories East, and affiliated with the Democratic Alliance for the Betterment and Progress of Hong Kong
	Wong Ting-kwong	Import and Export Industry, and affiliated with the Democratic Alliance for the Betterment of Hong Kong
	Martin Liao Cheung-kong	Commercial constituency without political party affiliation
	Ma Fung-kwok	Sports, Performing Arts, Culture and Publication; and affiliated with the New Century Forum
	Chan Han-pan	New Territories West, and affiliated with the Democratic Alliance for the Betterment and Progress of Hong Kong
	Elizabeth Quat	New Territories East, and affiliated with the Democratic Alliance for the Betterment and Progress of Hong Kong
2016–Now	Gary Chan Hak-kan	New Territories East, and affiliated with the Democratic Alliance for the Betterment and Progress of Hong Kong
	Wong Ting-kwong	Import and Export Industry, and affiliated with the Democratic Alliance for the Betterment and Progress of Hong Kong
	Martin Liao Cheung-kong	Commercial constituency without political party affiliation
	Ma Fung-kwok	Sports, Performing Arts, Culture and Publication; and affiliated with the New Century Forum

(*continued*)

Table 8.5 (continued)

Term	Name	Constituency and political party affiliation
	Chan Han-pan	New Territories West, and affiliated with the Democratic Alliance for the Betterment and Progress of Hong Kong
	Elizabeth Quat	New Territories East, and affiliated with the Democratic Alliance for the Betterment and Progress of Hong Kong
	Holden Chow	District Council constituency, and affiliated with the Democratic Alliance for the Betterment of Hong Kong

Source: Hong Kong United Youth Association, *We are Youth: The Celebration of the 23rd Anniversary of Hong Kong United Youth Association Limited* (Hong Kong: Hong Kong United Youth Association: 2015), p. 71

University. He was elected to the Shatin District Council in 1999 and then directly elected to the Legislative Council in 2008. His gradual political rise was a testimony to how a young mainland-born Hong Kong resident could climb up the ladder in Hong Kong's political arena.

Politically, the HKSAR leaders and PRC officials attach great importance to the HKUYA. In August 2018, during the inaugural ceremony of the new leaders of the HKUYA, those who attended the event included Chief Executive Carrie Lam, deputy director of Liaison Office Chen Dong, and representatives from the PRC Ministry of Foreign Affairs and the People's Liberation Army (PLA).[7] Lam praised the expanding membership of the HKUYA to 33,000 young people, emphasized the importance for the youth to visit China and understand the motherland deeply in all aspects and appealed to the youth to nominate themselves to participate in the government's youth committee work.[8] Obviously, after the debacle of the anti-national education movement led by some pro-democracy young people, like Joshua Wong, and after the 2014 Occupy Central Movement and the early 2016 Mongkok riot, the HKSAR government was under tremendous pressure to conduct and consolidate its united front work on the youth. Chen Dong also appealed to the young people of Hong Kong to "follow the tradition of loving China and Hong Kong," to support the implementation of the "one country, two systems," to respect the Basic Law and the PRC constitution, and to oppose the call for "Hong Kong independence."[9] As the Hong Kong-based youth organization directly

---

[7] See "Chief Executive Carrie Lam attends the 26th anniversary of the HKUYA and its inaugural ceremony," in https://www.info.gov.hk/gia/general/201808/27/P2018082700848.htm, access date: February 19, 2019.

[8] Ibid.

[9] *Hong Kong Commercial Times*, August 28, 2018, in http://www.hkcd.com/content/2018-08/28/content_1100448.html, access date: February 19, 2019.

under the ACYF, the HKUYA leaders are likely under the PRC's *nomenklatura* system, and therefore the inaugural ceremony of its leaders are regarded as politically significant by the HKSAR government and PRC officials in Hong Kong.

THE Y ELITES ASSOCIATION

The Y Elites Association (YEA) was set up in May 2007 by a group of young Hong Kong people who attended the study and training sessions offered by the Chinese Academy of Governance, the Pudong Executive Leadership Academy, the China Youth University for Political Sciences and the Academy of Chinese Culture in the mainland.[10] The YEA has 900 young leaders coming from various occupational sectors, including commerce, art and culture, media and telecommunications, land and property, monetary and financial sector, information technology and sports. It set up fourteen committees to conduct research on areas like land development, Beijing-Taipei relations, technological innovation, membership affairs and student development. The YEA's objectives are to establish a platform for the "ignition of Hong Kong's younger generation to love China and Hong Kong, the organization of the young people to gain knowledge on China, to catch up with the generational tide and development, to strengthen the relations between its members and the society and mainland, to unite more Hong Kong young elites, and to become Hong Kong's societal pillar."[11] In 2018, the YEA had four Hong Kong members to the NPC, four local legislators, sixteen District Council members, thirty-three members of the Election Committee that selected the Chief Executive, ten members of the Hong Kong government's youth development committee, thirteen members of the youth commission and eight members of the civic education committee. Clearly, the YEA has the determination to participate actively in the political institutions of both China and Hong Kong.

According to the YEA chairman, Chong Kar-bun, who is also a businessman and land developer, the association supports the HKSAR government and PRC's efforts at achieving peaceful reunification and protecting national security.[12] He also said that the YEA opposes any call for "Hong Kong independence." The association organizes many youth activities, such as contributing news commentaries in pro-Beijing mass media to support the

---

[10] See http://www.yelites.org/web/subpage.php?mid=77, access date: February 19, 2019.
[11] Ibid.
[12] Ibid.

policies of the HKSAR administration, mobilizing the young students and undergraduates to visit China and work there as summer interns, encouraging them to participate in forums to understand the Greater Bay Area blueprint published by Beijing, and sending delegates to join the annual Boao youth forums in Hainan province. The YEA's delegation to the ACYF's 12th meeting in 2015 was led by seven Hong Kong members, including executive chairman Zhang Yi.[13] Other members include those representatives from the monetary, financial and legal sectors. Overall, the YEA is a pro-Beijing youth organization initiated by the local youth, playing the role of a pro-government interest group and actively participating in various activities supportive of the PRC and the HKSAR government.

Table 8.6 shows that high-ranking officials of the Liaison Office and the Hong Kong Macao Affairs Office attended the activities of the YEA. From 2008 to 2017, the YEA forums on such topics as the PRC's open-door policy, foreign policy, domestic development, Asia's transformations, the Belt and Road initiatives in China under Xi Jinping, and globalization were regarded as politically important and meaningful by the Chinese officials in both Hong Kong and Beijing. The Boao forums on Asia's development could be seen as the crucial YEA events that were in conformity with the PRC government's foreign policy. It was natural that the director and the deputy director of the Liaison Office, and representatives from the Hong Kong and Macao Affairs Office also attended many of the YEA activities, which mobilized the Hong Kong youth to participate in the events supported by the PRC government.

In terms of political participation in local politics, the YEA has recently since 2014 been actively encouraging its leaders to write commentaries and make remarks in support of both the HKSAR government and Beijing. In July 2014, the YEA organized youth activities to help mainland migrants to be integrated into the Hong Kong society, including the assistance provided to them to apply for public housing estates, so that the so-called contradictions between China and Hong Kong would be reversed.[14] The YEA also encouraged more Hong Kong youth to visit the mainland, including Shenzhen's Qianhai, Guangzhou's Nansha and Beijing, so as to understand rapid development in the PRC in a deeper way. In August 2014, the YEA chairman Leung Wang-jing mobilized its members to openly oppose the Occupy Central Movement, saying that it would be an action of "violating

---

[13] See http://www.hua-jing.org/a/32427-cht, access date: February 19, 2019.
[14] *Ta Kung Pao*, July 10, 2014, p. A17.

Table 8.6 Chinese officials who attended the activities of the Y Elites Association

Time	Activities	Objectives of the activities	Chinese officials who attended
July 30, 2008	A forum on the 30th anniversary of China's open-door policy	It aimed at reviewing China's thirty years of its open-door policy, achievements and challenges. The forum also discussed the role of the Hong Kong youth in China's developmental strategy, including their duties and responsibilities.	Gao Siren, the director of the Liaison Office
December 7, 2009	The 2009 Boao Youth Forum	The objective of this forum was to explore China's foreign policy and its economic and cultural development	Peng Qinghua, the director of the Liaison Office; Li Zhaoxing, the chairman of the PRC National People's Congress; and Zhao Heping, the vice-minister of the Ministry of Culture
November 26, 2010	The 2010 Boao Youth Forum in Hong Kong: Opportunities and Challenges in Asia after its economic recovery	Review the past, present and future of Asian development and reflect on the role and mission of youth, including their difficulties	Peng Qinghua, the director of the Liaison Office; Zhang Zhijun, the vice-minister of the PRC Ministry of Foreign Affairs; and Lu Xinhua, the Commissioner of the Ministry of PRC Foreign Affairs in the HKSAR
September 15, 2011	The 2011 Boao Youth Forum in Hong Kong: Asian Economy in Transition and Its Social Development with Implications for the Mission and Role of Youth	It aimed at investigating the role and the mission of the youth in Asia under economic and social transition.	Zhou Bo, the deputy director of the Hong Kong Macao Affairs Office; Wang Zhimin, the deputy director of the Liaison Office; Lu Xinhua, the Commissioner of the PRC Ministry of Foreign Affairs in the HKSAR; and Wu Hailong, the Assistant to the Minister of the PRC Ministry of Foreign Affairs

(continued)

Table 8.6 (continued)

Time	Activities	Objectives of the activities	Chinese officials who attended
November 2, 2012	The 2012 Youth Forum 2012: Consolidating and Creatively Cultivate the Soft Power of Youth	The objective was to strengthen the creativity of youth in their innovative thinking, and to unleash their soft power and potentiality in the development of the knowledge-based economy in Asia and the world	Wang Zhimin, the deputy director of the Liaison Office
September 9, 2013	The 2013 Boao Youth Forum in Hong Kong: Youth Innovation and the Innovative Asia	The objectives of this forum were to analyze Asia's development comprehensively from the perspectives of youth, education, culture and economy, and to examine how Asia's excellence and energies could be used to increase national innovation and competitiveness	Zhang Xiaoming, the director of the Liaison Office; Song Zhe, the Commissioner of the PRC Ministry of Foreign Affairs in the HKSAR; and Zhou Bo, the deputy director of the Hong Kong and Macao Affairs Office
May 20–21, 2015	The 2015 Boao Asia Youth Forum: Asia's Structural Reform and the Prospects and Role of Youth	The objective of the forum was to explore the role and opportunities of youth in promoting regional cooperation	Zhang Xiaoming, the director of the Liaison Office; Zhou Bo, the deputy director of the Hong Kong and Macao Affairs Office; Dong Xiaoling, the deputy commissioner of the PRC Ministry of Foreign Affairs in the HKSAR; Deng Zhonghan, the vice-chairman of the All-China Youth Federation
November 30, 2016	The 2016 Elite Forum: Promoting Social Innovation, "One Belt One Road" and Hong Kong's Future Development	This forum aimed at adopting the economic, youth, cultural and sports perspectives to explore how the Belt and Road initiatives could affect Hong Kong's future development	Qiu Hing, the deputy director of Liaison Office; and Dong Xiaoling, the deputy commissioner of the PRC Ministry of Foreign Affairs in the HKSAR

(*continued*)

Table 8.6 (continued)

Time	Activities	Objectives of the activities	Chinese officials who attended
November 2, 2017	The 2017 Elite Forum: Globalization and Free Trade and their implications for the Youth	The forum discussed how the youth could respond to the era of globalization and free trade, and how they should adapt to the changing economic and technological circumstances so that there would be new breakthrough for youth development	Wang Zhimin, the director of the Liaison Office; Xie Fong, the commissioner of the PRC Ministry of Foreign Affairs in the HKSAR; Chen Dong, the deputy director of the Liaison Office; Qian Yibing, director of the communication division of the Hong Kong and Macao Affairs Office; and Li Jiyi, the deputy director of youth working department of the Liaison Office

Sources: *Wen Wei Po*, July 31, 2008, p. A24; December 8, 2009, p. A18; November 27, 2010, p. A15; September 16, 2011, p. A14; November 3, 2012, p. A20; September 10, 2013, p. A4; May 6, 2015, p. B2; November 23, 2016, p. A23; October 20, 2017, p. A21; November 10, 2017, p. A15; and http://www.yelites.org/yelitesforum/YelitesForum_vip_2012.html, access date: February 20, 2019

the law and becoming violent."[15] He appealed to the youth to protect their families and believed that they would reject such radical action. Leung also contended that, in designing Hong Kong's democratic development, the young people should accept the model proposed by Beijing on August 31, 2014, and that the local democrats should abandon the call for having ordinary people to nominate the candidates for the Chief Executive election.[16] The YEA appealed to the young people to abandon the so-called international criteria of democratizing the political system of Hong Kong, and it reiterated that the HKSAR should develop its polity not only in accordance with the parameters set by Beijing but also in a "rational" manner.[17] The founding chairman of YEA, Jaime Sze Wing-him, argued that the local democrats who often referred to the Western models of democratization actually ignored the reality of the American president being elected by an electoral college.[18] The YEA also advocated the need for the Hong Kong

[15] *Ta Kung Pao*, August 18, 2014, p. 4.
[16] *Ta Kung Pao*, September 2, 2014, p. A15.
[17] *Ta Kung Pao*, July 24, 2014, p. A17.
[18] *Ta Kung Pao*, September 3, 2014, p. A4.

youth to study Chinese history and understand the motherland's arts and culture more comprehensively through curriculum reform.[19] It was believed that the curriculum of the Chinese history should be reformed in such a way that the patriotism of the Hong Kong youth could and would increase. In 2016, a YEA member Wang Peng, whose mother was a returned overseas Chinese from Indonesia to Hong Kong, contributed a commentary in *Ta Kung Pao*, appealing to the young people of Hong Kong to be more patriotic, to understand how China was politically and historically humiliated by foreign countries, to appreciate the PRC's impressive economic development and achievement and to support the motherland's developmental initiatives in accordance with the spirit of the May Fourth Movement.[20] The YEA stands out as one of the most pro-Beijing youth groups in the HKSAR.

Hong Kong CPPCC Youth Association

Another influential pro-Beijing youth association is the Hong Kong CPPCC Youth Association (CPPCCYA), which was set up in May 2014. The inaugural ceremony in May 2014 was attended by the Chief Executive C. Y. Leung, Chief Secretary Carrie Lam and Liaison Office director Zhang Xiaoming. Other representatives from the People's Liberation Army and the Ministry of Foreign Affairs in the HKSAR also attended. The founding president of the CPPCCYA, Karson Choi, the son of toy tycoon Francis Choi, donated his six luxurious watches which fetched up to HK$1 million for the association.[21]

The association is a provincial-level CPPCC organization that rallies not only the young people who are the members of CPPCC in various places in the mainland but also the local youth who are the targets of political co-optation. The objectives are to "serve the country, Hong Kong and members" of the CPPCC and to "comprehensively absorb the CPPCC's next generation, young entrepreneurs, professionals and community leaders."[22] Its current president Tam Chun-kwok said that the association is "one of the youth groups loving China and Hong Kong" and that it has the responsibility of "leading the youth to develop correct views toward their life, to reflect their opinions and to provide a platform

[19] *Ta Kung Pao*, October 30, 2014, p. 12.
[20] *Ta Kung Pao*, May 5, 2016, p. A22.
[21] See its website, http://hkcppccya.org/content.asp?pageid=3&newsid=3, access date: February 17, 2019.
[22] See its website, http://hkcppccya.org/default.asp, access date: February 24, 2019.

for them to contribute to the society."[23] Interestingly, the honorary donors of the CPPCCYA are business people and officials from the Liaison Office, including the current deputy director Tan Tieniu. Its structure includes committees on membership, external relations, professionals, social affairs, policy studies, sports development, charity work and information and technology. The external relations committee embraces mainland visits and delegations to study China's political, social and economic development. The application form for outsiders to apply to the association to join as a member asked the applicants whether they have relatives or whether they themselves are CPPCC members. The association has the right to reject any applicant without the need to give any reason, according to its website.[24] It appears that the membership process has to undergo internal screening so as to prevent anyone without direct or indirect CPPCC background from infiltrating the organization. However, the application form for the membership of the association's professional committee members is relatively loose; it does not ask for any direct or indirect membership of the CPPCC but it adopts a more liberal-minded attitude toward applicants from various professions, including law, accountancy, medicine, health, engineering, construction, information technology, education, social welfare, industry and commerce, monetary and finance, insurance, land and property, tourism, shipping and transport, export and import, textile, sports development, retail and wholesale, food and catering, fisheries and agriculture, district councils and the rural advisory body Heung Yee Kuk. All these sectors are those functional constituencies under the Legislative Council, showing that the CPPCCYA intends to co-opt young elites who can and will go into these sectors as political representatives. Hence, there is an elaborate plan for the CPPCCYA to co-opt the young people in the HKSAR in a politically strategic way, and to groom some of them as rising political stars in the future.

As with the YEA, the CPPCCYA supports the policies of the HKSAR government and Beijing. In September 2015, the association's founding president Karson Choi was invited to attend the military parade in Beijing, showing the importance of the CPPCCYA in the minds of Beijing's

---

[23] See http://hkcppccya.org/content.asp?pageid=2#president-message, access date: February 24, 2019.
[24] See http://hkcppccya.org/content.asp?pageid=2#committee, access date: February 24, 2019.

authorities.[25] Moreover, the CPPCCYA sent members to visit the mainland, including the Greater Bay Area, in 2018 so as to support the blueprint proposed by Beijing to strengthen the economic integration of Hong Kong and Macao into the mainland. Other associational activities included the opposition to the Occupy Central Movement in 2014, the support for a gradualist approach to political reform in April 2015, the mobilization of volunteers to help the poor and the needy in 2016, the sending of some members to study China's development in the Pudong Executive Leadership Academy in September 2016, the holding of a forum with government officials and association members on how to increase the competitiveness of Hong Kong students in 2017, and the mobilization of 800 members to participate in a forum on innovation and technology with school principals and teachers in December 2018.[26] All these events demonstrate that the CPPCCYA is increasingly active and assertive in the PRC's new united front work in Hong Kong, grooming a batch of young elites to support the policies of the HKSAR government and Beijing.

Uniformed Cadet Groups: The Hong Kong Army Cadets Association

The uniformed cadet groups include the Hong Kong Army Cadets Association (HKACA) and the Hong Kong Girl Guides Association. The Hong Kong Girl Guides Association was established in 1919 with the objective of training young girls to be the leaders and global citizens.[27] It remains relatively independent and does not easily fall into the PRC's united front work, although some Chinese officials have attended the activities of the Girl Guides Association (Table 8.7). Grasping the golden opportunity of more mainland visits from the Hong Kong Girl Guides Association, which had paid its first visit to China in 1988, PRC officials have established closer and harmonious relations with the leaders of the association since 1997. Furthermore, the All-China Youth Federation was one of the donors of the mainland visit of the delegation from the Hong

---

[25] See http://hkcppccya.org/content.asp?pageid=5&newsid=75, access date: February 24, 2019.

[26] See http://hkcppccya.org/content.asp?pageid=3&newsid=147, access date: February 24, 2019.

[27] See https://hkgga.org.hk/tc/content/vision-and-mission, access date: February 24, 2019.

Kong Girl Guides Association, reflecting an attempt by PRC authorities to enhance its united front work on the Hong Kong visitors.[28]

Compared with the Hong Kong Girl Guides Association, the HKACA has arguably become a relatively easier and more focused target of political co-optation. The HKACA was set up in 2015 to "train individual quality," to "nurture leadership quality" and to "promote the construction of Hong Kong and to assist and pay back the motherland loyally."[29] The six training objectives outlined in its website include self-confidence, self-discipline, self-strengthening, responsibility, leadership and service. The HKACA training activities are expected to be conducted in Putonghua. The cadets are organized into three types: mentors who are seventeen years old or above and whose applications are approved; elites who are between eleven and thirty-five years old and whose applications are approved to be cadet members; and district cadets who are recommended by school teachers and who are students from primary schools above level four and from secondary schools. The association was apparently formed in response to youth radicalism in the 2014 Occupy Central Movement, for the former Secretary for Education Ng Hak-kim said explicitly that many young people need to develop "correct values" and "self-discipline" and to "serve the community and the nation."[30] The HKACA arranges disciplinary and military-related training for the youth, including the invitation of PLA officers to talk about the basic knowledge of defense and the military in April 2018.[31] Through the summer camp in which the local cadets are trained, the pro-Beijing mass media highlight their training activities in order to instill a greater sense of patriotism among the young people of Hong Kong. In November 2015, the pro-Beijing Pui Kui Secondary School invited the HKACA to train thirty of its students, showing a partnership between the association and the local pro-Beijing school.[32]

When President Xi Jinping visited Hong Kong in June 2017 (Table 8.7), he paid a special visit to the Yuen Long's Junior Police Call Centre, saying that the young people need to nurture their consciousness of the rule of law, and that they should serve the society.[33] His high-profile visit to the

[28] *Ta Kung Pao*, August 2, 2016, p. B5.
[29] See its website, http://hongkongarmycadets.org/tc/, access date: February 24, 2019.
[30] *Ta Kung Pao*, January 25, 2015, p. A3.
[31] See http://hongkongarmycadets.org/ufiles/1522805224.pdf, access date: February 24, 2019.
[32] *Ta Kung Pao*, November 13, 2015, p. 3.
[33] *Oriental Daily*, June 30, 2017.

Table 8.7 Chinese officials attended the major events of the uniformed cadet groups

Time	Cadet groups	Activities	PRC officials who attended
July 24–31, 2016	Hong Kong Girl Guides Association	Hong Kong Girl Guides Centenary—Beijing: Inner Mongolia Exchange Tour in 2016	1. Li Yuanchao, the PRC Vice President met the delegation 2. Wang Yang, the Secretary of the All-China Youth Federation, Wang Yang
January 18, 2017	Hong Kong Army Cadets Association	The ceremony to celebrate the second anniversary of the establishment of the Hong Kong Army Cadets Association	1. Cai Yongzhong, the deputy political commissar of People's Liberation Army (Hong Kong Garrison) 2. Zhou Hong, the deputy director of the Liaison Office
June 30, 2017	Junior Police Call	Visit to the Pat Heung Junior Police Call Centre	1. PRC President Xi Jinping
January 14, 2018	Hong Kong Army Cadets Association	The Opening of HKACA Building and the ceremony of celebrating the third anniversary of the establishment Hong Kong Army Cadets Association	1. Wang Zhimin, the director of the Liasion Office
November 11, 2018	Hong Kong Girl Guides Association	Annual Dinner for the Hong Kong Girl Guides Association	1. Lu Ning, the deputy director of the Kowloon working department of the Liaison Office

Reference: *Oriental Daily*, in https://hk.on.cc/hk/bkn/cnt/news/20170630/bkn-20170630110900160-0630_00822_001.html, access date: February 21, 2019. Also see https://www.thestandnews.com/politics/, access date: February 24, 2019; *Ta Kung Pao*, August 2, 2016; *Hong Kong Commercial Daily*, November 22, 2018

Centre had united front implications: the young people of Hong Kong need to observe the law and order, and to serve the Hong Kong society dedicatedly. By implication, he criticized those localists who resorted to radical actions and remarks in opposition to the central government in Beijing. In February 2018, the mass media in Hong Kong highlighted a letter written by President Xi, who replied to a group of cadets sending him a Chinese New Year card. President Xi wrote back and expressed his gratitude to the card sent by the young cadets, and he appealed to the young people of Hong Kong to the necessity of demonstrating their "concrete action of loving China and Hong Kong."[34] He also added that the young people of Hong Kong should understand China more deeply. Obviously, Xi's replies could be seen as the new united front effort made by the PRC to win the hearts and minds of more young people of Hong Kong.

The HKACA was politically controversial. When it was set up in 2015, the HKSAR government said that the PLA did not participate in the process of forming and financially supporting its formation, even though the PLA commander Tan Benhong was the honorary sponsor of the HKACA.[35] However, critics of the HKACA said that the Home Affairs Department appeared to grant land and financial support to the association quickly, and they pointed to the former Chief Executive C. Y. Leung and principal official Lau Kong-wah as the honorary patrons of the association.[36] Pro-democracy legislator Kenneth Chan Ka-lok wrote to the HKSAR government and President Xi Jinping, asking whether the PLA intervened in the process of establishing the HKACA.[37] A localist group named Civic Passion set up a "passionate cadet group" to resist the formation of the HKACA. The Civic Passion leader Wong Yeung-tat criticized the HKACA for producing a batch of young people "loyal to the CCP" and he said the resistant group he formed aimed at training young people under eighteen years old to develop civic attitudes and be volunteers helping the poor and the needy.[38] Another media report revealed that the HKACA appeared to get preferential treatment from the government because two other larger Christian cadet groups with much longer history failed to acquire any land from the government quickly.[39]

In response to public suspicions, Lau Kong-wah said that there was no conflict of interest because the process of granting land and financial support was followed procedurally.[40] The HKACA chairman Chan Chun-bun asserted that the government did not have any bias in favor of his association. Yet, the media found that the HKACA got HK$2.6 million donation in a relatively short period of time, and that former police

---

[34] See https://www.hk01.com/, February 15, 2018, access date: February 24, 2019.
[35] *Ta Kung Pao*, February 5, 2015, p. A21. *Hong Kong Commercial Daily*, January 28, 2015, p. A2.
[36] Lo Chun's remarks, in *Sing Tao Daily*, December 4, 2016, p. A9.
[37] *Hong Kong Daily News*, January 21, 2015, p. 8.
[38] *United Daily News* (Taiwan), January 20, 2015, p. 12.
[39] *Ming Pao*, November 14, 2016, p. A3.
[40] *Sing Tao Daily*, November 25, 2016, p. A14.

commissioners such as Dick Lee and Tang King-shing became the members of the board of directors of the HKACA.[41] Dick Lee added that some young people of Hong Kong were negatively affected by the advocates and activists of the Occupy Central Movement in 2014, implying that the HKACA could direct the young people to the more "mature" path of their development and thinking.[42] Interestingly, the representatives of the unions of disciplinary forces, like immigration, custom and the fire services, in the HKSAR also echoed Lee's view, saying that the HKACA would not constitute any political "brainwashing" attempt at the young people, and that the youth should abide by law and order.[43] In 2017, the HKACA had 700 members, an increase in tenfold from its membership in 2015, while PRC officials continued to attend its annual summer activities.[44] The HKACA has become a pro-Beijing youth group increasingly playing the role of conducting united front work on the young students of Hong Kong.

In February 2018, the media reported that the fourteen youth cadet groups that have been participating in the annual ceremony of raising the PRC flag at the Golden Bauhinia Square in Wanchai on May 4 needed to follow the PLA-style of marching in military parade, even though thirteen of them traditionally adopted the British style of marching.[45] The HKACA chairman Chan Chun-bun came out to defend the decision, saying that Liaison Office officials who attended the preparatory meeting of the cadet groups for the annual flag-raising ceremony merely played the role of coordination without giving views toward the adoption of the PLA-style of march. Yet, representatives of three cadet groups told the media that Chen Lin, the director of the youth work department of the Liaison Office, did make a request to all cadet groups that the marching style could and should be changed to the PLA one.[46] Most representatives of the cadet groups had reservations over Chen's suggestion. Anyway, the revelation of the Liaison Office's request showed that the PRC authorities attempted to conduct united front work through the annual flag-raising and marching ceremony of the local uniformed cadet groups.

[41] *Ming Pao*, November 14, 2016, p. A3.
[42] *Ta Kung Pao*, July 21, 2015, p. 4.
[43] *Ming Pao*, October 26, 2015, p. A9.
[44] *Wen Wei Po*, January 25, 2017, p. A15.
[45] *Ming Pao*, February 9, 2018.
[46] Ibid.

New Public Outreach of the People's Liberation Army

The Liaison Office's request of the PLA-style of marching was in line with the gradual increase in public outreach of the Hong Kong Garrison in the HKSAR. In October 2018, a month after typhoon Mangkhut attacked Hong Kong, about 400 PLA soldiers in uniform were sent to clear the felled trees in MacLehose trail in the New Territories, an unprecedented move in the HKSAR.[47] Chief Secretary Matthew Cheung said that the HKSAR government did not request its help and that the action was voluntary community service from the PLA. Interestingly, before the PLA soldiers were dispatched to clean up the trees, they went to visit the Liaison Office and the event was highlighted by the pro-Beijing mass media. Since Article 14 of the Basic Law states that the PLA does not intervene in the affairs of the HKSAR, the PLA move could be seen as a united front action winning the hearts and minds of more Hong Kong people. Critics of the PLA, such as Tam Man-ho of the Civic Party, remarked that the PLA action of cleaning the trees and rubbish after the attack of typhoon Mangkhut was an act of "intervening in Hong Kong matters."[48] The reason was that, according to Tam, unlike the PLA action of cleaning the debris left by typhoon Hato in August 2017, which was requested by the Macao government, the PLA move of cleaning the fallen trees in the HKSAR was not precipitated by any formal request from the Hong Kong administration.[49] Despite the controversy over the PLA action of cleaning the trees in Hong Kong in 2018, many residents appeared to find the PLA move acceptable and some took photos with the soldiers who were removing the fallen trees on the MacLehose trail.

Since July 1997, and particularly since President Xi Jinping came to power in the PRC, the Hong Kong PLA has been conducting more activities to reach out to the members of the public in the HKSAR than before. It regularly pays visits to schools, the elderly centers and kindergartens, and it annually opens military camps so that ordinary people can visit them and watch the military exercises. Other activities of the PLA to reach out to the Hong Kong community included its action to mobilize soldiers to donate blood to the Red Cross twenty-one times from 1997 to 2018, to

---

[47] See https://www.hkcnews.com, access date: February 24, 2019.
[48] Ibid.
[49] Ibid.

plant trees eighteen times on the tree-planting day organized by the agricultural and fisheries department, to organize the Hong Kong military cadet summer camp fourteen times with the Department of Education during the same period, to visit elderly centers eleven times, to visit kindergarten ten times also from 1997 to 2018.[50] A total of 8450 PLA soldiers donated their blood to the Red Cross from 1998 to 2018. On August 16, 2018, there were 450 PLA soldiers donating their blood to the Red Cross, illustrating their active participation in the society of Hong Kong. On the other hand, a total of 15,900 PLA soldiers participated in the exercise of planting trees in the territory from 2000 to 2018. For the annual summer camp organized by the PLA and the education authorities, it began in July 2005 and the targets were the students from secondary school level three to level five, allowing local students to understand the life of the PLA and to have basic knowledge of military affairs and defense. The PLA also sent officers to train the participants of the training activities of the HKACA on the national affairs and to teach them on the methods of singing national anthem and increasing military morale. Finally, the PLA had visited elderly centers since 2006, including the centers under the management of various charity and non-governmental organizations, such as the Po Leung Kuk and the Tung Wah Hospital. In July 2017, when the aircraft carrier Liaoning and other Chinese frigates visited the HKSAR, twenty naval officers and forty soldiers from the Hong Kong Garrison visited the elderly centers and donated HK$60,000 for the welfare of the needy.[51] Similarly, since 2007, the PLA soldiers have been visiting various kindergartens and a school for the blind people. In January 2018, forty PLA soldiers visited a kindergarten and donated HK$60,000 for its development. Overall, the PLA could be seen as part of the new united front work conducted by the PRC government on the people of Hong Kong.

The Localist Resistance to United Front Work

In spite of the efforts made by the Liaison Office, the PLA and many pro-Beijing youth groups to win the hearts and minds of the local youth, the resistance to such co-optation work came mainly from the localists. If localism can be defined as a local ideology which attaches great

[50] Ibid.
[51] Ibid.

importance to local identity, history, values and cultural heritage while resistant to outsiders and external intervention, then it is quite strong among the psyche of many young people. Table 8.8 shows the critical Marxist youth groups and their political platform. These groups include the Socialist Action, Left Wing 21, the Proletariat Political Institute, the Civic Passion, the Hong Kong First, the Democracy Groundwork, the Community Citizen Charter and the Community March. In reality, Raymond Wong, Claudia Mo, Gary Fan and Wong Yeung-tat were the early localists with a very strong sense of local Hong Kong identity. Eddie Chu and others belong to the new and younger generation of the localists, but Chu's "self-determination" call has been regarded by Beijing as politically subversive. The reason is that when both Britain and China negotiated the future of Hong Kong from 1982 to 1984, they both regarded the "self-determination" of the Hong Kong people as impossible, for Hong Kong could not become politically and territorially independent. But the new generation of localists, like Chu, interpret the term "self-determination" broadly as the ability of the people of Hong Kong to voice out, decide and shape their political future, including the direction, scope and content of political reform. To Beijing, this broader interpretation of "self-determination" is politically and legally unacceptable.

Table 8.9 illustrates those interest groups that are composed of more radical localists who oppose China's united front work in the HKSAR. Most of these groups are regarded by the HKSAR government and Beijing as politically problematic and legally unacceptable. For instance, in September 2018 the Hong Kong government banned the Hong Kong National Party under the Societies Ordinance, for the government saw it as having activities, such as propaganda through the press, electoral participation, street booths, fund raising and distribution of leaflets to school children, which were detrimental to national security.[52] Even the relatively moderate group, the Demosisto, had its candidate like Agnes Chow, barred from participating in the Legislative Council by-election in early 2018 on the grounds that she advocated "self-determination or independence by any means."[53] Two Youngspiration members, Yau Wai-ching

[52] Kimmy Chung, "Ban of Hong Kong separatist party was on 'compelling' grounds and proportionate to risks: security minister John Lee," *South China Morning Post*, October 3, 2018, https://www.scmp.com/news/hong-kong/politics/article/2165592/ban-hong-kong-separatist-party-was-compelling-grounds-and, access date: February 24, 2019.

[53] Alan Wong, "Hong Kong Bars Democracy Advocate From Running for Legislature," *New York Times*, January 27, 2018, in https://www.nytimes.com/2018/01/27/world/asia/hong-kong-democracy-election.html, access date: February 24, 2019.

Table 8.8 Critical Marxist groups and their political platform

Name	Year of formation	Number of members	Key leaders (occupation and background)	Political platform
Socialist Action	2010	Unknown	1. Sally Tang Mei-ching Tang (trade unionist)	1. See the PRC and the HKSAR regimes as dictatorships 2. Fight for the realization of the immediate and full democratic rights, while rejecting a "gradualist" approach of the PRC liberals who fear revolutionary change while swallowing the "myth" that democracy and capitalist economy are inseparable
Left Wing 21	2010	Unknown	1. Steven Kwok Wing-kin (trade unionist) 2. Willis Ho (activist)	1. See the HKSAR government as serving the interests of the business elite through the state-business alliance and the protection of an "undemocratic" political system 2. The people of Hong Kong should create a truly democratic, free, equal and just society that respects individuals regardless of their gender, ethnicity and sexual orientations
Proletariat Political Institute	2010	Unknown	1. Raymond Wong Yuk-man (radio broadcaster)	1. See the HKSAR regime as Beijing's "puppet" 2. Believe that Hong Kong should "delegitimize" the PRC regime 3. Use "referendum" to amend the Basic Law so as to change the authoritarian rule imposed by Beijing on Hong Kong
Civic Passion	2012	Unknown	1. Cheng Chung-tai (university lecturer) 2. Wong Yeung-tat (media worker)	1. Fight against the "mainlandization" of Hong Kong 2. Fight against the "communist control" over Hong Kong affairs 3. Support the preservation of Hong Kong's local culture

(continued)

Table 8.8 (continued)

Name	Year of formation	Number of members	Key leaders (occupation and background)	Political platform
Hong Kong First	2013	Unknown	1. Claudia Mo (Legislative Council member) 2. Gary Fan (Legislative Council member)	1. Defend the "one country, two systems" 2. Support the idea of "Hong Kong people ruling Hong Kong" 3. Preserve Hong Kong's indigenous culture 4. Fight against the "mainlandization" of Hong Kong
Democracy Groundwork	2014	Unknown	1. Lau Siu-lai	1. Seek income redistribution and the improvement in the quality of life 2. Fight for the establishment of a comprehensive social welfare system 3. Fight for the construction of more democratic institutions in Hong Kong
The Community Citizen Charter	2015	Unknown	1. Eddie Chu Hoi-dick (Legislative Council member)	1. Use a bottom-up approach to incorporate democratic elements into the daily work and lives of citizens, because the social and political movements in the past were largely marked by an appeal to authority and an anticipation for governmental response. As a result, the spirits of "self-determination and self-organization" to strive for democratization have been sorely lacking

(*continued*)

and Baggio Leung, who were directly elected to the 2016 Legislative Council election, were disqualified from becoming legislators after their provocative remarks during the oath-taking ceremony in the legislative

Table 8.8 (continued)

Name	Year of formation	Number of members	Key leaders (occupation and background)	Political platform
Community March	2017	Unknown	1. Ben Lam (social worker) 2. Suzanne Wu (trade unionist)	1. It is crucial to initiate political reforms from the district level 2. Actively participate in district affairs as a way to solve social problems 3. The current institutional design has led to serious income gap and social inequality.

Sources: "About Community March," in https://www.facebook.com/pg/communitymarch/about/?ref=page_internal, access date: June 4, 2018; "About Us," http://left21.hk/wp/en/16-2/, access date: June 4, 2018; also see https://siulai.hk/, access date: June 4, 2018; "About us," in http://chinaworker.info/en/about-us-en/, access date: June 4, 2018; "Hong Kong First Establishment Manifesto," https://www.facebook.com/hongkongfirst/, access date: June 7, 2018; "About The Community Citizen Charter," in https://sites.google.com/site/hkcccharter/, access date: June 7, 2018; "The Manifesto of Proletariat Political Institute," http://www.hkppi.com/, access date: June 4, 2018; "The information about Civic Passion," in *The Stand News*, February 22, 2017, in https://thestandnews.com/politics/, access date: June 7, 2018

chamber. Yau and Leing pronounced China as "Jee-na,"[54] leading to the interpretation of the Basic Law's Article 104 on the oath-taking behavior by the Standing Committee of the National People's Congress (SCNPC). The SCNPC ruled that oath-taking must be conducted respectfully and appropriately, and then the Hong Kong court decided to deprive Yau and Leung of their elected seats because they failed to take the oath faithfully. Hence, the remarks and behavior of some radical localists were under the close scrutiny and swift responses of the authorities in both the HKSAR and Beijing.

---

[54] Tony Cheung, Joyce Ng and Stuart Lau, "Three rejections and multiple deviations mark Hong Kong Legislative Council swearing-in," *South China Morning Post*, July 20, 2018, in https://www.scmp.com/news/hong-kong/politics/article/2027413/three-rejections-and-four-deviations-mark-hong-kong, access date: February 24, 2019.

Table 8.9 Radical localist groups and their political platform

Name	Year of formation	Number of members	Key Leaders (occupation and background)	Political platform
Conservative Party	2015	Unknown	1. Alice Lai (activist)	1. See the 1984 Sino-British Joint Declaration as a failure and a document that cannot fully preserve Hong Kong's uniqueness and core values 2. Hong Kong should become Britain's overseas territory
Hong Kong Independence Party	2015	Unknown	No prominent leader	1. See Hongkongers as a "national" entity 2. Support the process of "nation-building" so as to allow Hong Kong to return to the British Commonwealth
Hong Kong Indigenous	2015	Around 60	1. Edward Leung (student)* 2. Li Tung-sing (activist) 3. Ray Wong (activist)	1. See Hong Kong as a "nation" 2. Intend to preserve the local culture of Hong Kong 3. See Beijing as a "threat" to Hong Kong's autonomy
Hong Kong National Party	2016	Around 50	1. Andy Chan Ho-tin (activist)	1. Believe that the people of Hong Kong should consolidate their "nationalistic sentiment" 2. The Basic Law of Hong Kong should be "abolished" as it cannot fully reflect and protect the rights of Hongkongers 3. Intend to establish the "Republic of Hong Kong"

(*continued*)

Table 8.9 (continued)

Name	Year of formation	Number of members	Key Leaders (occupation and background)	Political platform
Hong Kong Resurgence	2014	Unknown	1. Chin Wan (former university professor)	1. See Hong Kong as a "city-state" 2. Believe that Hong Kong can "annex" China 3. See Hong Kong's autonomy as a defense of the life of Hongkongers
Studentlocalism	2016	Unknown	1. Tony Chung Han-lin (secondary student)	1. See Beijing's intervention in Hong Kong as a phenomenon of "recolonization" 2. See Hong Kong as an "imagined community" 3. Hong Kong should become an "independent nation" 4. See Beijing as a "totalitarian" regime and the HKSAR as an "authoritarian" regime. 5. The youth in Hong Kong should prepare for the process of making Hong Kong "independent"
Valiant Frontier	2014	Around 30	No prominent leader	1. Hong Kong should be "separated" from the PRC 2. Support the "Hongkongers first" policy 3. Believe that Hong Kong can and should be an "independent country"

(*continued*)

Table 8.9 (continued)

Name	Year of formation	Number of members	Key Leaders (occupation and background)	Political platform
Youngspiration	2015	More than 100	1. Baggio Leung (activist) 2. Yau Wai-ching (activist)	1. Fight against the "mainlandization" of Hong Kong 2. Defend the local culture and local identity 3. Believe that Hong Kong should be "separated" from China 4. Believe that Hong Kong can manage its economic development independently from the mainland 5. Seek further reform of political institutions of Hong Kong
Demosisto	2016	Unknown	1. Joshua Wong 2. Agnes Chow 3. Nathan Law 4. Ivan Lam 5. Oscar Lai	1. Promote democratic "self-determination" 2. Use non-violence style of confrontation to build up Hongkongers' consciousness as to construct a just, free and equal society for all citizens

Sources: "Who is Ray Wong," available http://www.bbc.com/zhongwen/trad/china/2016/02/160211_hk_ray_wong, access date: June 4, 2018; "Interview with Valiant Frontier," available in http://polymerhk.com/, access date: June 4, 2018; "Background analysis on Studentlocalism," in *Wen Wei Po*, August 13, 2016; "The establishment of Youngspiration," in http://polymerhk.com, access date: June 4, 2018;"About Community March," in https://www.facebook.com/pg/communitymarch/about/?ref=page_internal, access date: June 4, 2018; "The Manifesto of Proletariat Political Institute," http://www.hkppi.com/, access date: June 4, 2018; "About Us," in http://www.hkip.org.uk/, access date: June 4, 2018; "An Introduction to Demosisto," in https://www.demosisto.hk/about, access date: June 4, 2018; "Hong Kong wants to rejoin UK, An Interview with Alice Lai," in https://www.facebook.com/peopleschartermbga/videos/1332278126820251/?hc_ref=ARTOi3avqOaUNgrbToKDzdFCy9e8LharrWLJEGgnUn9c_bDLsenT0rdm4sX8P464EXA, access date: June 4, 2018; *Tai Kung Pao*, April 21, 2015; "About Hong Kong National Party," in https://www.hknationalparty.com/, access date: June 4, 2018; *Wen Wei Po*, August 15, 2013; "About us," in http://chinaworker.info/en/about-us-en/, access date: June 4, 2018; "About The Community Citizen Charter," in https://sites.google.com/site/hkcccharter/, access date: June 7, 2018; "Hong Kong First Establishment Manifesto," in https://www.facebook.com/hongkongfirst/photos/a.139945929503000.31443.139741646190095/139946109502982/?type=3&theater, access date: June 7, 2018; "About Lab In HK," in http://www.labin.hk/about/#1498499367201-799e6c08-4e71, access date: June 7, 2018; "The information on Civic Passion," in *The Stand News*, February 22, 2017, in https://thestandnews.com/politics/, access date: June 7, 2018

CONCLUSION

The PRC's new united front work in the HKSAR is characterized by the creation of new youth groups, such as the HKUYA, CPPCCYA, YEA and HKACA, to win the hearts and minds of more Hong Kong people. The All-China Youth Federation remains the core pro-Beijing youth group which politically co-opts some young Hong Kong elites into the umbrella of united front work. Utilizing personnel appointment and an elaborate system of *nomenklatura*, PRC authorities skillfully maintain a close network of pro-Beijing youth groups which have further connections with young elites from political parties and other professional associations. In this way, the united front work of the PRC in the HKSAR can be expanded, renewed, rejuvenated, revived and sustained.

The creation of the HKACA was politically significant as it was established after the 2014 Occupy Central Movement. Clearly it aimed at winning the hearts and minds of more young Hong Kong people, hoping that they will gradually develop stronger sense of patriotism. The PLA was not directly involved in the HKACA creation, but its high-level honorary sponsorship and its officers' participation in the associational training activities demonstrated the new united front work of the Chinese military in Hong Kong. Other PLA activities that target at the young people include their opening camps, their visits to secondary schools and their volunteering efforts at cleaning up fallen trees after typhoon attack.

Finally, the localist groups that resist the PRC united front work appear to be weak. They are outnumbered and underdeveloped in terms of manpower and resources. The radical remarks and actions of some postmaterialistic localists were excessive and incautious, presenting golden opportunities for the authorities of Hong Kong and the PRC to initiate a crackdown. Under these circumstances, the PRC's united front work targeted at the young people can and will gradually gain inroads in the coming years, especially as many youths are imbued with materialistic values and the desire for more political influence and status in both the HKSAR and the mainland.

CHAPTER 9

Influencing Civil Society Through Mass Media, Education and Migration

Arguably, the two main pillars of the civil society in Hong Kong are the mass media and the education sector. The mass media have been traditionally seen as the fifth branch of the government, scrutinizing any regime and providing checks and balances against public maladministration. In communist states, the mass media have become the target of ideological propaganda and control, playing the role of an agent that can legitimize the ruling communist party. According to Georg Brunner, "mass agitation and mass media" in communist states "pursue the general aim of evoking a condition of consciousness in the population which induces all people to acknowledge party authority and through this state authority as legitimate and to comply with particular authoritative acts willingly and of their own accord."[1] Mass agitation aims at the adult population beyond the reach of training and educational institutions and it is conducted by social groups. Forms of mass agitation include lectures, organized leisure activities, adult education and oral as well as visual agitation, such as seminars and posters. In the context of Hong Kong, the pro-Beijing interest groups, such as women, youth, trade unions and clan associations, are instruments of mass agitation, as mentioned in the previous chapters. Another instrument of shaping social consciousness is the mass media, which can "propagate current party policies under the direct guidance of relevant sectors of the

[1] Georg Brunner, "Legitimacy Doctrines and Legitimation Procedures in East European Systems," in T. H. Rigby and Ferenc Feher, eds., *Political Legitimation in Communist States* (London: Macmillan, 1982), p. 35.

© The Author(s) 2019
S. S.-H. Lo et al., *China's New United Front Work in Hong Kong*,
https://doi.org/10.1007/978-981-13-8483-7_9

party machine."[2] Mass media have various types in the era of the globalization of technology: print media, electronic media, social media and the internet media.

Apart from mass media that can shape social consciousness, education is critical to any communist regime.[3] Education is a broad civil society sector that encompasses higher education, secondary and primary schools as well as kindergartens. At the higher education level, professors and researchers are the intellectuals whose research and ideas can shape how university students think. Similarly, at the level of secondary and primary schools, the role of principals and teachers is crucial in shaping the views and political culture of students. As Periklis Pavlidis has remarked, "those with a developed consciousness (cultivated in all here of its forms—moral, esthetic and philosophical) are in a position to understand in depth the human significance of their work and the social responsibility that it entails, and play a decisive role in developing students' consciousness, in identifying and exploring along with the students the meanings and purposes underlying the most active and creative attitudes towards reality, the strongest cognitive interest in it."[4] In communist states, education is indispensable in the processes of socialization and political legitimization. Brunner writes:

> In the teaching process relevant components of the ideology are conveyed partly directly and partly indirectly. The indirect method consists in the fact that all subjects are taught in the spirit of Soviet ideology [in former Eastern European states]. Under the direct method special ideological disciplines are included in the educational programme. In the general educational schools the direct method is applied only to a minor extent, the subject "social studies" or something similar being given in the higher classes.[5]

This chapter focuses on how PRC authorities target at and penetrate the two pillars of the Hong Kong civil society: mass media and education.

[2] Ibid.
[3] Kaarle Nordenstreng, "From Mass Media to Mass Consciousness," in George Gerbner, ed., *Mass Media Policies in Changing Cultures* (New York: John Wiley & Sons, 1977), pp. 269–283.
[4] Periklis Pavlidis, "Social consciousness, education and transformative activity," *Journal for Critical Education Policy Studies*, vol. 13, no. 2 (October 2015), pp. 1–37, especially p. 29.
[5] Brunner, "Legitimacy Doctrines and Legitimation Procedures in East European Systems," p. 35.

One recent study has found that surprisingly, in the PRC, higher education in a 2010 survey was associated with "an increasing level of skeptical attitude toward the government," even though it was traditionally assumed that education is designed to instill a sense of appreciation for the party-state and a love for the ruling party and the country.[6] This chapter does not adopt a quantitative approach to assess the impact of education on public trust toward either the Hong Kong government or the PRC. Rather, a historical approach is adopted to examine how PRC authorities have been attempting at penetrating both the media and education sectors in the civil society of Hong Kong, especially since July 1, 1997.

We will argue that despite the PRC's efforts at influencing the Hong Kong media and education, they have shown different patterns of penetrative politics. The PRC's political penetrative capability is stronger in the mass media than in the education sector, because the education sector remains politically more diverse, fragmented and pluralistic. Given the difficulties of shaping the educational sector easily in a short period of time, the PRC's new united front work adopts the policy of migration. Given the fact that 150 mainland Chinese have been allowed to have their one-way permits to enter and reside in the HKSAR since July 1, 1997, the number of mainland-born migrants coming to Hong Kong due to this migratory scheme is now almost one million. In early 2019, the PRC government announced the Greater Bay Area plan, stimulating the special administrative regions of both Hong Kong and Macao to integrate closer into the economy and society of nine cities in Guangdong province— Shenzhen, Zhuhai, Jiangmen, Zhongshan, Dongguan, Huizhou, Guangzhou, Foshan and Zhaoqing. The idea is to foster the development of science and technological development in the Greater Bay Area, generating a win-win situation and minimizing local competition in the Southern Chinese region. Preferential tax policies would be formulated by the PRC to facilitate the people of Hong Kong to move to the Greater Bay Area, to work and to reside there. If migration can be a "drive of political and social change," shaping the political attitudes and social norms of the citizens in the target places,[7] then inward migration from the mainland to the

---

[6] Ying Xie, Yunping Tong and Fenggang Yang, "Does Ideological Education in China Suppress Trust in Religion and Foster Trust in Government?," *Religions*, vol. 8, no. 94 (2017), pp. 1–11.

[7] Michele Tuccio, Jackline Wahba, and Bachir Hamdouch, "International Migration: Driver of Political and Social Change?," No. 9794 (Institute for the Study of Labor, Bonn, Germany, March 2016), in http://ftp.iza.org/dp9794.pdf, access date: March 8, 2019,

HKSAR, and outward migration from Hong Kong to the mainland, do have significant implications for united front work. With the influx of more mainlanders into Hong Kong, they can shape the social and political attitudes of some local people, while they themselves may ironically also be the target of social assimilations into the core values of the HKSAR. With more Hong Kong people going to work and reside in the mainland, they may also shape the socio-political attitudes of some mainlanders but simultaneously they are also the target of social assimilations into the mainland values. As such, through the economic integration plan of the Greater Bay Area, socio-economic integration between Hong Kong and the mainland would hopefully be achieved, thus paving the way for the possible success of the PRC's united front work, namely, winning the hearts and minds of the people of Hong Kong.

Indeed, inward and outward migration may not be able to achieve the PRC's united front work, if the mainlanders were assimilated into the Hong Kong core values and if the Hong Kong people moving to work and live in the mainland can and will influence the mainlanders' socio-political attitudes. In any case, the possible achievement of united front objectives through migration has not been studied seriously by Hong Kong-based scholars, but this chapter will cast light on some of the preliminary issues stemming from the politics of inward migration from the PRC into the HKSAR. Inward migration from the mainland to the HKSAR, from the perspective of localists, is a process of mainlandizing Hong Kong in such a way that the PRC's united front work can be smoothened and achieved more easily and rapidly. At the same time, if outward migration of some Hong Kong people to the mainland can and will be achieved, from the localist vantage point, a process of depriving Hong Kong of its local-born people can be accelerated, thereby quickening the mainlandization of Hong Kong. To put it bluntly, the PRC's "re-colonization" of Hong Kong can be and will be arguably achieved if both the inward and outward migration can bring about the politically nationalistic and patriotic attitudes of more Hong Kong people than ever before.[8]

pp. 1–42. Also see Douglas S. Massey, "The Political Economy of Migration in an Era of Globalization," in Samuel Martinez, ed., *International Migration and Human Rights: The Global Repercussions of U.S. Policy* (Oakland: University of California Press, 2009), pp. 25–43; and Sara Spencer, ed., *The Politics of Migration: Managing Opportunity, Conflict and Change* (Oxford: Blackwell, 2003).

[8] For the concepts of mainlandization and "re-colonization," see Sonny Lo, "The Mainlandization and Recolonization of Hong Kong," in Joseph Cheng Yu-shek, ed., *The*

This topic is beyond the scope of our book, but future researchers who are interested in the relations between migration and united front can conduct more studies on the political cultures of mainlanders and Hongkongers who participate in the processes of inward and outward migration respectively.

Mass Media Increasingly Under United Front Influence

It can be said that the mass media in the HKSAR have been increasingly under the influence of the PRC's new united front work since July 1, 1997. First and foremost, the media ownership and the political background of some media proprietors have been increasingly politically pro-Beijing. Table 9.1 demonstrates that most of the proprietors of the newspaper organizations are pro-Beijing, shaping to some extent the editorial stance of the newspapers concerned. With the entry of the Alibaba group, the editorials of the *South China Morning Post* have increasingly become pro-Beijing, ranging from their comments on the PRC's political development to its foreign policy.[9] Although its opinion page is composed of a variety of views, including letters and commentaries independent and occasionally critical of the PRC administration, the editorial stance tends to be consistently more pro-Beijing than ever before. While most newspapers' proprietors are pro-Beijing, a few of them are politically moderate, such as the *Hong Kong Economic Journal*, *Metro Daily* and *Ming Pao*. The only two pro-democracy newspaper organizations in the HKSAR are the *Apple Daily* and *Epoch Times*, which are also critical of the CCP regime in the mainland. In recent years, some local democrats have been shifting to Internet radios and programs as the platform to voice their views critical of both the HKSAR government and Beijing.[10] Nevertheless, there is no quantitative survey to show the percentage of population who are

---

First Decade of the Hong Kong Special Administrative Region (Hong Kong: The City University of Hong Kong Press, 2007), pp. 179–231.

[9] See, for example, Editorial, "Both Beijing and the Vatican gain from improved relationship," *South China Morning Post*, July 20, 2018, in https://www.scmp.com/comment/insight-opinion/article/2060265/both-beijing-and-vatican-gain-improved-relationship, access date: March 2, 2019.

[10] Kenneth Wai-Kin Ming, "Journalists as Interest Groups: Implications for Democracy Movement," in Sonny Shiu-Hing Lo, ed., *Interest Groups and the New Democracy Movement in Hong Kong* (London: Routledge, 2018).

Table 9.1 Newspapers ownership and the political background of media proprietors, 2019

Newspaper name	Owner/proprietor	Political position
AM730	Shih Wing-ching	Politically moderate and centralist
Apple Daily	Jimmy Lai Chee-ying	Pro-democracy
Epoch Times	Unspecified and unclear	Pro-Falun Gong, pro-democracy movement in Hong Kong and critical of the Chinese Communist Party
Headline Daily	Charles Ho Tsu-kwok	Pro-Beijing
HK01	Yu Pun-hoi	Pro-Beijing, but this newspaper shows views and comments critical of the HKSAR government and even Beijing's policy toward Hong Kong[a]
Hong Kong Commercial Daily	Sino United Publishing (Holdings) Limited	Pro-Beijing
Hong Kong Economic Journal	Richard Li Tzar-kai	Politically moderate and centralist
Hong Kong Economic Times	Lawrence Fung Siu-por	Pro-Beijing
Metro Daily	David Wee	Politically moderate and centralist
Ming Pao	Tiong Hiew King	Politically moderate and centralist
Oriental Daily News	Oriental Press Group	Pro-Beijing, critical of both the HKSAR government and local democrats
Sing Tao Daily	Charles Ho Tsu-kwok	Pro-Beijing
Sky Post	Lawrence Fung Siu-por	Pro-Beijing
South China Morning Post	Alibaba Group Holding Limited	Pro-Beijing
The Standard	Charles Ho Tsu-kwok	Pro-Beijing
Tai Kung Pao	Tangkung Wenwei Media Group	Pro-Beijing
Wen Wei Po	Tangkung Wenwei Media Group	Pro-Beijing

(*continued*)

Table 9.1 (continued)

Sources: This table is derived from the websites of different media organizations, see https://hk.appledaily.com/, access date: February 26, 2018; https://orientaldaily.on.cc/, access date: February 26, 2018; https://www.mingpao.com/, access date: February 26, 2018; http://std.stheadline.com/, access date: February 26, 2018; http://www.singpao.com.hk/index.php, access date: February 26, 2018; http://www.thestandard.com.hk/, access date: February 26, 2018; http://www.wenweipo.com, access date: February 26, 2018; http://www.takungpao.com.hk/, access date: February 26, 2018; http://www.hkcd.com/, access date: February 26, 2018; http://www.hketgroup.com/, access date: February 26, 2018; https://www2.hkej.com/landing/index, access date: February 26, 2018; http://www.hk01.com, access date: February 26, 2018; www.epochtimes.com, access date: February 26, 2018; http://www.scmp.com, access date: February 26, 2018; http://www.metrodaily.hk, access date: February 26, 2018; http://hd.stheadline.com, access date: February 26, 2018; https://www.am730.com.hk/, access date: February 26, 2018; https://skypost.ulifestyle.com.hk/, access date: February 26, 2018

ªNote: In February 2019, the HK01 laid off seventy employees, showing its financial difficulties in operation

interested in following the reports, discussions and comments of these Internet radios and programs.

Table 9.2 illustrates the editorial stance of some media organizations on the 2014 Occupy Central Movement. The *Apple Daily* obviously supported the Occupy Central Movement to push for democratization and to oppose the political parameters set by the central government of Beijing on Hong Kong's democratic reform on August 31, 2014. The pro-Beijing newspapers, such as *Oriental Daily News, Wen Wei Po* and *Ta Kung Pao*, saw the movement as a ploy made by foreign countries to foster a "color revolution" in the HKSAR and to challenge China's political authority. The other politically moderate newspapers, such as *Ming Pao, Hong Kong Economic Journal* and *Hong Kong Economic Times*, called for a trust-building process leading to dialogue between the pro-democracy activists and the Hong Kong government. The political divide between the pro-democracy media, the pro-Beijing ones and the moderate newspapers could be easily seen.

As the HKSAR has been increasingly politicized since the 2014 Occupy Central Movement, and especially the emergence of the Hong Kong National Party, the mass media's editorial position on the action of the HKSAR government to ban the National Party in September 2018 was also witnessing a clear political divide (Table 9.3). On February 26, the central government in Beijing issued a letter in support of the action of the HKSAR government to ban the Hong Kong National Party. In response, the media organizations editorialized and again the political divide between pro-Beijing and pro-democracy factions could be easily observed. The pro-democracy *Apple Daily* believed that Beijing's move would undermine the international confidence on the implementation of the

Table 9.2 The editorial position of media organizations on the 2014 Occupy Central Movement

Newspaper name	Editorial position on the Occupy Central Movement
Apple Daily	Supported the Occupy Central Movement as it was a means of opposing the "undemocratic universal suffrage model" initiated by Beijing. It believed that the direct election for the Chief Executive in 2017 should be really "democratic" and it should reflect the opinions of the masses rather than a "cosmetic" attempt at democratization. Its editorial also argued that the Occupy Central Movement was "creative and innovative," utilizing the mass to participate in political struggle against Beijing. It believed that the people of Hong Kong should not be politically "threatened" by the regime in power. Instead, the Hongkongers should use "propaganda and public opinion" to resist Beijing.
Hong Kong Commercial Daily	It saw the Occupy Central Movement as anti-government and socially and politically destabilizing.
Hong Kong Economic Journal	Its editorial believed the HKSAR government played a crucial role of tackling the problem of democratic reforms. It adopted a more moderate position by saying that the regime in power and the political opposition went to two extremes and confronted each other. Its editorial called for the Hong Kong government to take the initiative in defusing the political crisis during the early stage of the Occupy Central Movement because nobody on the democratic front appeared to call for a termination of the movement.
Hong Kong Economic Times	Its editorial called for mutual trust-building and concessions from both sides—the Hong Kong government and the protestors. They both should engage in dialogue and compromise rather than political confrontation and conflicts. Moreover, the central government should also cultivate political trust among the Hong Kong people, especially the youth.
Ming Pao	Its editorial remarked that the Hong Kong government and the democrats adopted the path of political conflicts and confrontations without the mind of compromise, leading to political and social chaos as well as uncertainties.
Oriental Daily News	Opposed the Occupy Central Movement as the foreign forces attempted at intervening in Hong Kong politically and fostering a "color revolution" as with the political development in the Middle East. In other words, foreign countries created social disorder, "paralyzed" Hong Kong's governance and "embarrassed" the central government in Beijing.
Sing Tao Daily	Opposed the Occupy Central Movement because it challenged the spirit of the rule of law in Hong Kong. Its editorial said that the Occupy Central movement undermined the social order and the masses who participated in it violated the law.

(*continued*)

Table 9.2 (continued)

Newspaper name	Editorial position on the Occupy Central Movement
Ta Kung Pao	Opposed the Occupy Central Movement because it has serious and tremendous harm on Hong Kong's governance, economy and social harmony. The movement led to unprecedented confrontation and social split in the HKSAR.
Wen Wei Po	Opposed the Occupy Central Movement as it captured the government's power. The movement is also shaped by foreign forces, notably the American and the British governments which expressed their support. The movement was comparable to the "orange revolution" in Ukraine and aimed at challenging the PRC government.

Sources: *Sing Tao Daily*, September 25, 2017, http://std.stheadline.com/daily/article/detail/1670418-%E7%A4%BE%E8%AB%96-%E5%8F%8D%E6%80%9D%E4%BD%94%E4%B8%AD%E3%80%80%E7%88%AD%E6%B0%91%E4%B8%BB%E8%AE%8A%E5%AE%B3%E6%B0%91%E4%B8%BB, access date: February 26, 2019; *Apple Daily*, May 13, 2013, https://hk.news.appledaily.com/local/daily/article/20130513/18258142?fb_comment_id=375484765901416_26677121, access date: February 26, 2019; *Wen Wei Po*, October 3, 2014, http://paper.wenweipo.com/2014/10/03/PL1410030006.htm, access date: February 26, 2019; *Tai Kung Pao*, March 31, 2017, http://news.takungpao.com.hk/hkol/politics/2017-03/3436848.html, access date: February 26, 2019; *Ming Pao*, September 29, 2014, p. A6; *Hong Kong Economic Journal*, September 29, 2014, p. A2.; Hong Kong Economic Times September 29, 2014, p. A12; and *Oriental Daily News*, September 29, 2014, p. A2

Table 9.3 The editorial position of the mass media on the PRC formal support of the Hong Kong Government's action of banning the Hong Kong National Party

Newspaper name	Editorial position on the PRC support of the Hong Kong Government's action of banning the Hong Kong National Party
Apple Daily	It believed that Beijing's action would undermine the international confidence on the implementation of the "one country, two systems," which was drifting toward "one country, one system." It also argued that Hong Kong's special status would be lost and that it would not be able to help China's "one belt, one road" initiative.
HK01	Beijing tried to emphasize its comprehensive jurisdiction over Hong Kong, but it also "exerted pressure on Chief Executive Carrie Lam" to deal with the Hong Kong National Party.
Sing Tao Daily	Beijing's authorities have zero tolerance of the "Hong Kong independence." The HKSAR government has to use its hardline policy to deal with this sensitive issue, especially as some organizations supportive of "Hong Kong independence" were still active.

(*continued*)

Table 9.3 (continued)

Newspaper name	Editorial position on the PRC support of the Hong Kong Government's action of banning the Hong Kong National Party
Tai Kung Pao	It believed that Beijing could show its support for the HKSAR administration. Under the "one country, two systems," Hong Kong's social institutions, legal systems and lifestyle enjoy the benefits of the "two systems." But the concept of the "two systems" is not applicable to China's national sovereignty right and national security issue. The Hong Kong people should and must support China's territorial integrity and fight against any separatist move. As such, they should accept the central government's letter supportive of the Hong Kong government action to ban the Hong Kong National Party.
Wen Wei Po	It supported the action of Beijing's authorities to illustrate the accurate understanding of Beijing-Hong Kong relations. This would protect Beijing's national security and developmental interest. The Hong Kong people should support the action of the HKSAR to ban the operation of Hong Kong National Party.

Sources: *Apple Daily*, February 27, 2019, p. A2; *Sing Tao Daily*, February 27, 2019, http://std.stheadline.com/daily/article/detail/1966717-%E7%A4%BE%E8%AB%96-%E5%85%AC%E5%87%BD%E7%99%BC%E8%A8%8A%E6%81%AF+%E8%A6%81%E6%B8%AF%E5%BA%9C%E7%9B%A1%E3%80%8C%E7%A6%81%E7%8D%A8%E3%80%8D%E8%B2%AC, access date: February 28, 2019; *Ta Kung Pao*, February 27, 2019, p. A2; *Wen Wei Po*, February 27, 2019, p. A14; HK01, available in: https://www.hk01.com/, access date: February 28, 2019

"one country, two systems," which was drifting toward "one country, one system." It also said that Beijing was determined to deal with the "Hong Kong independence" at the expense of the international society's perception of the "one country, two systems." Other pro-Beijing media, notably *Ta Kung Pao*, *Wen Wei Po* and *Sing Tao Daily* affirmed their strong support of the action of Beijing to back up the HKSAR government.

Although the HKSAR has a lot of media organizations, both local and foreign, they have been increasingly pro-Beijing in their political outlook. From the information provided by the Hong Kong Public Relations Professionals' Association, the classifications and the number of each classified media are listed in Table 9.4 below. Traditionally, the pro-Beijing media organizations had strong anchorage in Hong Kong under the British rule, including *Wen Wei Po*, *Ta Kung Pao*, *Hong Kong Commercial Daily* and the now-defunct *New Evening Post*. The pro-Beijing media were actually strong in the film industry, such as the Phoenix, Sun Luen and Cheung Shing (Great Wall).[11] The Sun Luen film company was set up

[11] See Ho Si-wing, "Hong Kong film commentary," October 30, 2010, in http://www.filmcritics.org.hk/film-review/node/2017/07/19/, access date: March 3, 2019.

Table 9.4 The classification and number of media in Hong Kong, 2018

Type of media organizations	Number of media organizations
Local Newspapers	17
Foreign Newspapers	9
Local TV and Radios	8
Foreign TV and Radios	8
Local Magazines	16
Foreign Magazines	6
Online Media and News Agencies	19
Non-local News Agencies	12

Source: "Media List," prepared by the Hong Kong Public Relations Professionals' Association, in https://prpa.com.hk/?p=164, access date: January 2, 2019

in 1952 and it was pro-CCP in political orientation while producing Cantonese films and movies. In 1982, a pro-Beijing film company named Sil-Metropole Organization Limited was founded, but it also cooperated with foreign companies to produce some films.

After the HKSAR was established, there has been a trend in which mainland companies have been cooperating with film producers, directors, actors and actresses from Hong Kong to produce a variety of films. In terms of profits maximization, such cooperation between the mainland and Hong Kong movie industries is natural and inevitable. From the perspective of united front work, the co-production of movies by aggregating movie directors, producers, actors and actresses from the two main places in Greater China has the tremendous political implication of attempting to unite the artists in the region. In September 2009, when the film named The Making of a Republic was shown in both the mainland and Hong Kong to celebrate the 60th anniversary of the PRC, especially its history from 1945 to 1949, its actors included not only famous mainland artists but also Hong Kong actors like Jacky Chan, Andy Lau Tak-wah, Donnie Yen, Chow Yun-fat and Leon Lai Ming (Table 9.5).[12] No Taiwan actor was involved in the making of this film in 2009. In 2011, the Beginning of the Great Revival was another film depicting the rise of the CCP and this film co-opted both Hong Kong and Taiwan actors, such as the Hong Kong-born Chow Yun-fat and Andy Lau and the Taiwan-born Chang

---

[12] The film was seen in Hong Kong as having the tone of political patriotism. See "Analyzing the Making of a Republic," September 9, 2009, in https://hk.appledaily.com/entertainment/art/20090909/13188390, access date: March 3, 2019.

Table 9.5 Participation of Hong Kong and Taiwan actors in the mainland's three political films. 2009–2017

Film	Hong Kong actors and director	Taiwanese actors
The Making of a Republic (2009)	1. Chan Ho-sun 2. Donnie Yen Chi-dan 3. Andy Lau Tak-wah 4. Leon Lai Ming 5. Jackie Chan Kong-sang 6. Tony Leung Ka-fai	No Taiwan actor participated in this film.
The Beginning of the Great Revival (2011)	1. Andy Lau Tak-wah 2. Michelle Xuan Ye 3. John Woo Yu-sen 4. Chow Yun-fat 5. Ray Lui 6. Tony Leung Ka-fai 7. Nick Cheung Ka-fai 8. Simon Yam Tat-wah 9. Alex Fong Chung-shun 10. Daniel Wu Yin-cho 11. Angela Yeung Wing 12. Miriam Yeung Chin-wah 13. Alex Fong Lik-sun 14. Eric Tsang Chi-wai 15. Wu Hang-yee	1. Chen Chang 2. Andrew Lien 3. Wang Po-Chieh 4. Wang Leehom
The Founding of an Army (2017)	1. Alex Fong Lik-sun Fong 2. William Chen Wai-ting 3. Andrew Lau Wai-keung	1. Wallace Huo 2. Tony Yang 3. Chen Chang

Sources: See http://www.chinadaily.com.cn/culture/2017-07/28/content_30278826.htm, access date: March 3, 2019; http://www.mediaasia.com/republic/, access date: March 3, 2019; http://ent.sina.com.cn/f/m/jdwy/, access date: March 3, 2019; and http://news.ifeng.com/a/20160801/49699817_0.shtml, access date: March 3, 2019

Chen. In 2017, the third film named The Making of an Army was shown in Hong Kong and the mainland. It embraced a Hong Kong director Andrew Lau Wai-keung, Taiwan-born actors Chang Chen and Wallace

Huo and its showing coincided with the visit of the PRC aircraft carrier Liaoning to the HKSAR.[13] While the Making of an Army was not well received by movie goers in 2017, the composition of the actors illustrated a gradual change from the participation of Hong Kong actors to the involvement of Hong Kong director, and from absence of Taiwan actors to their co-optation—a testimony to the PRC move of utilizing the production of films to conduct subtle united front work targeted at not only more Hong Kong actors but also the Taiwan counterparts in the film industry. Above all, the message of the three mainland-produced films was political, namely, the founding of the PRC, the CCP and the People's Liberation Army signaled the triple alliance between the state, the ruling party and the military in mainland China. If some Hong Kong and Taiwan actors participated in the production of this series of political films, it could symbolize some degree of legitimacy conferred by some Hongkongers and Taiwanese upon the state-party-military alliance in the mainland.

In the PRC's united front work, the boundary between friends and enemies is very clear. Friends are those who cooperate with the PRC government, but enemies are those who oppose it. As such, some Hong Kong actors, such as Anthony Wong and Chapman To, and actress like Denise Ho, who supported the 2014 Occupy Central Movement publicly and assertively are, according to news reports in 2016, "blacklisted" by mainland authorities (see Table 9.6).[14] Similarly, Taiwan's actresses, such as Bidai Syulan and Kulilay Amit, who are viewed by mainland authorities as supportive of "Taiwan independence," have not been welcome by the PRC. In the authoritarian politics of the PRC, political correctness determines whether a person is its friend or enemy. As some Hong Kong and Taiwan actors and actresses make remarks or take actions that exceed the bottom line of political tolerance by Beijing, they run the risk of being "blacklisted."

To influence the media industry in the HKSAR, the PRC needs to penetrate into the publishing houses. The Sino United Publishing (Holdings) Limited is Hong Kong's largest integrated publishing group and it was

[13] "From the Making of the Republic to the Making of an Army," July 16, 2017, in https://kknews.cc/zh-hk/entertainment/2mvjb8z.html, access date: March 3, 2019.

[14] Fifty-five actors and actresses in Hong Kong and Taiwan are "blacklisted" as the list was leaked out. See "Chinese cultural department leaks out a list of 55 actors and actresses," *Apple Daily*, December 30, 2016, in https://tw.appledaily.com/new/realtime/20161230/1024222/, access date: March 4, 2019.

Table 9.6 Prominent Hong Kong and Taiwan actors and actresses "blacklisted" by the PRC authorities

Actor/actress	Origin	Main reason block by Beijing's authorities
Kulilay Amit (Chang Hui-mei)	Taiwan	Mainland authorities reportedly see her as a Taiwanese supportive of "Taiwan independence" and she is in the "blacklist."
Bidai Syulan (Hsu Jo-Hsuan)	Taiwan	In 2010, she remarked that Japan was like her "adopted mother," leading to criticisms from some mainland Chinese, who labeled her as a Taiwanese supportive of "Taiwan independence."
Chapman To	Hong Kong	Supported the Occupy Central Movement in 2014
Anthony Yiu-ming Wong	Hong Kong	Supported the Occupy Central Movement in 2014
Denise Wan-see Ho	Hong Kong	Supported the Occupy Central Movement in 2014

Sources: See https://tw.appledaily.com/new/realtime/20161230/1024222/, access date: April 3, 2019. Also see https://theinitium.com/article/20170404-mainland-artists/?utm_medium=copy, access date: April 3, 2019

formed in 1988 by integrating some publishing agencies, such as the Commercial Press, the Chung Hwa Hong Kong, Hong Kong Joint Publishing and the Joint Printing Limited (Table 9.7). The publishing house is now engaging in not only publishing but also printing, wholesaling, retailing, new media and the dealer of calligraphy and art.[15] The company has thirty member companies in different places in the world, including the PRC, Hong Kong, Macao, Taiwan, Singapore, Malaysia, America, Canada, United Kingdom, France and Australia. Needless to say, all the bookstores under the Sino United Publishing Limited excluded all those books published by the Causeway Bay bookstore and Lee Bo, books which were critical of the PRC and which brought Lee and his associates into disappearance and troubles in late 2015 and early 2016.[16] Those

[15] See its website http://www.sinounitedpublishing.com/english/aboutus.html, access date: March 3, 2019.

[16] For details of the Lee Bo case, see Voice of America news, "Dissident Hong Kong Book Publisher Returns Home," March 24, 2016, in https://www.voanews.com/a/dissident-hong-kong-book-publisher-returns-home/3253265.html, access date: March 3, 2019. Also see "Missing Hong Kong book editor Lee Bo returns home," March 24, 2016, in https://www.theguardian.com/world/2016/mar/24/hong-kong-book-editor-lee-bo-returns-home-disappear-missing, access date: March 3, 2019.

Table 9.7 The evolution of the Sino United Publishing

Organization	Year of establishment	Features
Commercial Press Hong Kong	1914	The Commercial Press in Shanghai was founded in 1897 as the first modern publishing organization in China. In 1914, it established a branch in Hong Kong and launched the "Students' Magazine."
Chung Hwa Hong Kong	1927	The Zhonghua Book Company was founded in Shanghai in 1912. Later the Chung Hwa Hong Kong was set up in 1927.
Hong Kong Joint Publishing	1948	It was a bookstore chain and publisher founded in Hong Kong on October 18, 1948, as a result of a merger between three Shanghai publishers and bookstores, namely *Life*, *Reading* and *New Knowledge*.
Joint Printing (Hong Kong) Limited	1980	It resulted from a merger of two printers from China, namely the Hong Kong Commercial Press Printing Office (which was established in Hong Kong in 1924) the Chung Hwa Kowloon printing plant (which was established in 1933).
Sino United Publishing (Holdings) Limited	1988	In September 1988, the joint management office was reorganized under the Sino United Publishing as a holding company, which wholly owns the three main enterprises, namely the Joint Publishing, Chung Hwa, Commercial Press Hong Kong and also other publishing companies.

Source: Adapted from http://www.sup.com.hk/english/history.html, access date: March 3, 2019

books critical of corruption, political scandals and leaders in the PRC can only be found in some relatively smaller and independent bookstores and newspaper stalls in the HKSAR.

The Liaison Office is now controlling not only the three main enterprises—the Joint Publishing, Chung Hwa and the Commercial Press—but also a new publisher named Sinminchu (new democracy) publishing company. After the 19th CCP Congress in the PRC, the Sinminchu company has been publishing a series of books on the mainland, including the gist of the 19th Party Congress, the mainland's "deliberative democracy," the Chinese dream as espoused by President Xi Jinping, thereby playing a crucial role of disseminating the most updated and politically "correct" information about the CCP decisions and policies to the people of Hong

Kong. When asked by reporters on whether the Liaison Office's ownership of the local publishers might have "violated" the "two systems" in the concept of "one country, two systems," Chief Executive Carrie Lam replied diplomatically that so long as the Liaison Office possessed properties in accordance with the law, "we should not interfere with it."[17]

Overall, as many media proprietors are business people who have been maintaining friendly relations with the PRC, their newspapers organizations naturally adopt a certain degree of self-censorship, especially at the editorial desk where some editors have appeared to be more careful in writing about China and politically sensitive issues on Hong Kong than ever before. For a minority of liberal-minded media proprietors, they may allow a relatively high degree of autonomy and editorial freedom to their media organizations. Yet, the mainland ownership of media organizations is critical; once the mainland capital penetrates a media organization in the HKSAR, such organization is bound to be politically vulnerable to subtle self-censorship. The *South China Morning Post* is perhaps a typical example; since Jack Ma's Alibaba owned the media organization and its affiliates in December 2015, its editorials have become prominently pro-PRC although its opinion page and website contain a variety of views. In terms of the English newspapers, *The Standard* is also under the Sing Tao group and its political moderation is natural. Only the *Hong Kong Free Press* maintains a constantly critical stance on a whole of range of issues, ranging from Hong Kong politics to China's policy toward the HKSAR, and from human rights to the PRC's domestic development.[18] According to the Hong Kong Journalist Association, in 2017, nine of the twenty-six local mainstream media organizations were directly under the control and ownership of the mainland capital.[19] Moreover, 80% of the proprietors of the twenty-six mainstream media organizations were politically appointed to

---

[17] "Is the Liaison Office violating the two systems by possessing three publishers? Carrie Lam said we should not interfere as long as it was made in accordance with the law," May 29, 2018, in https://thestandnews.com/politics/, access date: March 3, 2019.

[18] See the website of the Hong Kong Free Press, in https://www.hongkongfp.com/, access date: March 3, 2019.

[19] "Hong Kong press freedom drops to 73 in the world and the red capital occupies 31 percent of the local media organizations," *Apple Daily*, June 6, 2017, in https://hk.news.appledaily.com/local/daily/article/20170606/20045536, March 3, 2019. Also see "Two Systems Under Siege," Release of the Hong Kong Journalist Association, July 2, 2017, in https://www.hkja.org.hk/en/press-release/two-systems-under-siege-hkja-releases-2017-annual-report/#more-1071, access date: March 3, 2019.

various positions of the HKSAR administration and the PRC government.[20] The CCP-style of penetrative politics in the Hong Kong media takes the forms of enhancing mainland ownership of media organizations, co-opting Hong Kong media proprietors and cultivating friendly relations with some influential editors so as to shape their political views toward both the HKSAR and the mainland.

At the level of the reporters, they have little choice but to report and write in a way acceptable to their higher-level editors. Surveys conducted by the Hong Kong Journalist Association have found that many reporters in the HKSAR are very concerned about press freedom in the HKSAR. Most importantly, while the press freedom index perceived by the journalists declined from 42 in 2013 to 40.3 in 2017, the index as seen by ordinary people also dropped from 49.4 in 2013 to 47.1 in 2017.[21] The average salaries of reporters are in general low, making it difficult to retain them in the media profession. Many reporters see their media profession as a stepping-stone to advance to other careers, like public relations managers and communication officers for corporate companies and politicians. Under these circumstances, the PRC's united front work in the mass media in the HKSAR can not only gain footholds easily but also penetrate deeply into the media organizations through ownership control and personnel appointments of media proprietors to the mainland political institutions, notably the CPPCC. The rapid economic rise of the PRC, accompanied by a large group of red capitalists who have become the instruments of the CCP to own Hong Kong's media organizations, has accelerated the process of the mainlandization of the media in the HKSAR.

Resisting the Mainlandization of Mass Media: The Rise of "Independent" Media in Hong Kong

Due to the increasingly compressed political space in the Hong Kong media, some media workers have formed their own "independent" media. The word "independent" does not mean that they advocate the independence of Hong Kong; it only means that their media organizations are politically autonomous from both the HKSAR government and Beijing, and that they voice views critical of the political authorities. These alterna-

---

[20] *Apple Daily*, June 6, 2017.
[21] "Hong Kong Press Freedom Index," July 11, 2018, in https://www.hkja.org.hk/en/survey-report/hong-kong-press-freedom-index/#more-3106, access date: March 3, 2019.

tive or "independent" media include the Stand News, which was founded in December 2014 by some Hong Kong people, including media professionals, who are keen "to maintain editorial independence and to protect democracy, human rights, freedom, the rule of law and social justice."[22] The Board of Directors of the Stand News include former legislator Margaret Ng, artist Denise Ho Wan-see, former editor Joseph Lian, social worker Fang Man-sang and media professionals like Choi Tung-ho, Chung Pui-kuen and Chow Tat-chi. The Stand News carries reports and commentaries critical of both the HKSAR government and the PRC regime.

Another alternative media is the Inmediahk, which is an Internet media established in 2004 to "promote the democracy movement" and "develop the civil society reporters."[23] It appeals to the members of the public to donate money to its work so that the role of an "independent media" can and will be maintained. Organizationally and ideologically, the Inmediahk has special sections on social movement and sustainable development in the HKSAR, maintaining a critical attitude toward the HKSAR government, covering stories on China's human rights and leadership struggle, emphasizing the need to improve the livelihood of citizens and the community and supporting the pro-democracy camp and youth groups.[24] As a matter of fact, the 2014 Occupy Central Movement stimulated the growth of the alternative media in the HKSAR (Table 9.8). Some alternative media participated in the movement, including the Passion Times Post 852, D100 and MyRadio, to name just a few examples. Post 852 has its website carrying commentaries and reports critical of both the Hong Kong government and Beijing, vowing to provide quality discussions and to protect press freedom.[25] Many young citizens like to use these alternative media as sources of their daily information and news, especially in the era in which the popular use of i-phones means that the younger generation develops a proclivity of reading news quickly through the alternative media in the HKSAR. Table 9.8 reflects the popularity of the new alternative media as compared to both the general media and the pro-government internet media in Hong Kong. In response to the rise of the pro-democracy Internet media, many pro-government groups establish their websites and

[22] See its website, https://thestandnews.com/about_us/, access date: March 3, 2019.
[23] See its website, http://www.inmediahk.net/donate, access date: March 5, 2019.
[24] See the stories in its website, https://www.inmediahk.net/, access date: March 5, 2019.
[25] See its website, https://www.post852.com/support-us/, access date: March 5, 2019.

Table 9.8 Internet media and popularity of their Facebook

Internet media	Year of formation	Owner and political orientation	Facebook favorites (likes) and followers
1. The General Media Websites			
HK01.com	2013	Yu Pun-hoi, the former owner of Ming Pao and it is politically moderate.	577,261/ 592,790
The Initium	2015	Zhang Jieping as editor and its investor is Cai Hua, a mainland Chinese who worked in the United States for some years. Its political stance is relatively moderate.	265,950/ 275,296
Bastille Post	2013	Lo Wing-hung and it is relatively politically moderate.	1,050,579/ 1,034,223
South China Morning Post	1903	Jack Ma of the Alibaba Group and it has been increasingly pro-Beijing.	1,427,362/ 1,716,574
The Standard	1949	The Standard Newspapers Publishing, part of the Sing Tao News Corporation, and it is politically pro-Beijing.	17,637/ 18,068
Apple Daily	1995	Jimmy Lai of the Next Digital and it is pro-democracy.	2,186,499/ 2,150,132
on.cc (Oriental Daily News)	1969	Ma Ching-kwan and it is pro-Beijing but critical of the HKSAR government and local democrats.	411,124/ 430,461
2. The Alternative Internet Media			
Post 852	2013	Yau Ching Yuen of the Freeman Develop Company Limited. It is politically autonomous and critical.	68,823/ 67,567
Inmediahk	2005	Ip Yam-chong and it is politically autonomous and critical.	483,479/ 461,829
The Stand News	2014	Choi Tony and it is politically autonomous and critical.	239,037/ 244,773

(*continued*)

Table 9.8 (continued)

Internet media	Year of formation	Owner and political orientation	Facebook favorites (likes) and followers
Passion times	2012	Wong Yeung-tat and it is politically autonomous and very critical of both the HKSAR government and Beijing.	403,737/ 381,097
Hong Kong Citizen News	2017	Lau Chun-to and it is politically pro-democracy, autonomous and critical.	56,081/ 60,738
Hong Kong Free Press	2015	Tom Grundy and Evan Fowler. It is pro-democracy, autonomous and critical.	85,032/ 87,355
3. Pro-government Facebook pages			
HongKongGoodNews	2014	Unknown	370,467/ 526,716
HKG Pao	2015	Chow Robert and pro-government.	128,279/ 136,941
Silent Majority	2013	Chow Robert and pro-government.	178,945/ 170,792
Speak Out Hong Kong	2013	Tang Yee-bong and pro-Beijing as well as pro-government. It is funded by the Hong Kong United Foundation.	324,050/ 312,399
Think Hong Kong	2018	Pro-Beijing and pro-government. It is funded by former Chief Executive Tung Chee-hwa.	107,190/ 110,245
Orange News	2014	Cloud Connect Technology Limited, Sino United Publishing (Holdings) Limited.	240,618/ 242,454
Wakeuphkpeople	2018	Unknown and pro-government.	16,295/ 16,559

Sources: See all the following Facebook pages: https://www.facebook.com/hk01wemedia/, https://www.facebook.com/theinitium/, https://www.facebook.com/Bastillepost/, https://www.facebook.com/standnewshk/, https://www.facebook.com/passiontimes/, https://www.facebook.com/hkgpaocom/, https://www.facebook.com/silentmajorityhk/, https://www.facebook.com/speakouthk/, https://www.facebook.com/thinkhongkong/, https://www.facebook.com/wakeuphkgpeople, https://www.facebook.com/hkorangenews, https://www.facebook.com/HongKongGoodNews/, access date: February 23, 2019

Note: The numbers of likes and follows were seen on their websites and Facebook pages on February 23, 2019

Facebook, bringing about a phenomenon of the politicization of the Internet media and a persistent struggle between the pro-democracy alternative media and the pro-government counterparts. Most of these pro-government Facebook, such as the Speak Out Hong Kong and Think Hong Kong, have been financially supported by pro-Beijing elites and foundation. As such, there are grounds for believing the PRC's united front work was in operation behind the scene, shaping the Hong Kong public opinion by helping the emergence of the pro-government voices in the cyberspace.

Penetrative Politics in the Education Sector

In the communist style of politics, education is the most important tool by which the ruling party can control how citizens think about the society and politics, thus shaping the regime legitimacy. Ideological indoctrination in communist-style political systems like the PRC and North Korea is commonplace. In the more pluralistic setting like the HKSAR, ideological indoctrination is not easy, like the public opposition to the 2012 national education policy formulated by the HKSAR government. However, there are other ways in which the PRC can penetrate its influence into the education system. First and foremost, the creation of pro-Beijing educational interest groups and schools is necessary for the PRC to enhance its political and social influences in the HKSAR. Second, a large scale of political appointments and co-optation of the local educational elites into the mainland's institutions is an effective means of achieving the objective of penetrative politics. Third, the idea of creating the Greater Bay Area in 2018 and the publication of its outline in early 2019 serve as a powerful instrument of luring the young children, school principals, university researchers and administrators and university students to participate in the process of socio-economic integration between Hong Kong and the Southern China.

The creation of pro-Beijing educational interest groups could be traced back to the Guangzhou-Hong Kong strike in May and June 1925, when some foreign police and military officers killed some mainland Chinese in Shanghai and Shamian, and when thousands of Hong Kong students and teachers went to Guangzhou to protest against foreign imperialism.[26] The

---

[26] Robert James Horrocks, "The Guangzhou-Hong Kong Strike, 1925–1926: Hongkong Workers in an Anti-Imperialist Movement," PhD thesis, Department of East Asian Studies,

Chinese Communist Youth League even penetrated some local Hong Kong schools, such as the Queen's College and St. Paul's College, to organize students to protest, to boycott classes and to join the protestors in Guangzhou.[27] In 1937, when Japan invaded China, a number of war relief associations were founded by the local Hong Kong students to assist the mainland Chinese in their fight against the Japanese imperial army. Many students from prestigious local schools, such as the King's College, participated in the operation of the war relief interest groups, which provided donation and medicine to the mainland Chinese refugees, and which however provided a fertile ground for some underground CCP members for secret penetration and recruitment.[28] The formation of the Hong Kong Students War Relief Association (HKSWRA) in September 1937 was a turning point, partly because it involved 24 local schools and the University of Hong Kong, and partly because it became a target of political infiltration by the communists. The CCP infiltration alarmed the Kuomintang (KMT), which later sent members to join the HKSWRA and engaged in a power struggle with the CCP members. In August 1938, the KMT mobilized the representatives of ten schools to participate in a meeting of the HKSWRA, accusing the communists of financial mismanagement. Due to the bitter power struggle between the CCP and KMT members, some school representatives left the HKSWRA, although there were other smaller war relief associations that remained active in Hong Kong under the British rule.

After World War II, some left-wing intellectuals from the mainland came to reside in Hong Kong and they tried to set up pro-communist schools in the colony. In the wake of the founding of the PRC in 1949, the British colonial government in Hong Kong disallowed the use of political propaganda in local schools and noticed that some schools were either dominated or infiltrated by the CCP. However, in July 1956, the PRC Premier Zhou Enlai met a group of Hong Kong intellectuals, including professor Chan Kwan-po and student Dorothy Liu from the University of Hong Kong.[29] Chan was a famous professor close to the CCP officials,

University of Leeds, October 1994, pp. 115–118.
[27] Ibid.
[28] Leung Po-lung, "Hong Kong's war relief associations and the Chinese Communist Party," February 10, 2017, in https://www.inmediahk.net/node/1047538, access date: March 5, 2019.
[29] "The meeting between Premier Zhou and the teachers and students from the University of Hong Kong," *China's United Front Magazine*, April 8, 2018, in http://www.locpg.hk/

while Liu was later regarded as a pro-Beijing Hong Kong lawyer participating in the drafting of the Basic Law of the HKSAR from 1985 to 1990. The PRC authorities saw Chan and Liu as the targets of its united front work in Hong Kong under the British rule. Dorothy Liu was shocked by the Tiananmen tragedy in the PRC on June 4, 1989. She later stood alone to express her condolence of the dead students in a meeting of the National People's Congress in 1990—an incident that shocked PRC authorities, who later tried to repeal her title as a member of the NPC, especially after her visit to observe Taiwan elections in 1994.[30] In March 1995, the former Liaison Office director Zhou Nan suggested that Liu's position as the NPC member should be canceled, but the NPC chairman Qiao Shi was tolerant and said that the NPC could tolerate different views to exist.[31] While Chan Kwan-po was the PRC's main target of united front in Hong Kong's higher education sector, Dorothy Liu's transformation from a politically patriotic student to a lawyer of conscience shortly after the 1989 Tiananmen tragedy in the PRC was illustrative of how co-opted patriot could change her political views over time.

In the 1970s, some students at the University of Hong Kong and the Chinese University of Hong Kong developed their Chinese national identity, forming associations that were concerned about the PRC's development, including its relations with Japan over the sovereignty of the Diaoyu Island. In 1973, the pro-Beijing faction led by the late Chan Yuk-cheung led the Student Union of the University of Hong Kong, signaling a shift toward pro-PRC attitudes among some university students.[32] Yet, in 1975, students at the University of Hong Kong were politically divided into the pro-Hong Kong and pro-Beijing factions, with the pro-Hong Kong one led by Mak Hoi-wah winning the election.[33] The identity split among the students was apparent; some believed that the student union should care more about the PRC while others argued that Hong Kong's society should be their focus of concern. The pro-Beijing sentiments of some Hong

jsdt/2018-04/08/c_129845662.htm, access date: March 5, 2019.

[30] "Remembering the fifteenth anniversary of the death of lawyer Liu Yiu-chu who loved Hong Kong," April 7, 2012, in https://www.bnn.co/news/gb/pubvp/2012/04/201204072307.shtml, access date: March 5, 2019. Liu died in March 1997 and was buried in the United States.

[31] Ibid.

[32] "The confrontation after 1967: the period from red fire to transition," November 12, 2010, in https://www.inmediahk.net/, access date: March 5, 2019.

[33] Ibid.

Kong students were dealt a severe blow in 1980, when a local student activist Lau Shan-ching, who supported the mainland's Democracy Wall Movement and its democrat like Wang Cizhe, was imprisoned in the PRC for ten years.[34] Those local students who were patriotic toward the PRC became more politically cautious and reflective, if not apprehensive, of the mainland's authoritarian politics.

The creation and expansion of pro-Beijing schools have become an effective instrument of the CCP's united front work in Hong Kong. During the 1980s, six pro-Beijing schools existed in the colony, including the Mongkok Workers' Children Secondary School, the Heung To Middle School, the Pui Kiu Middle School, the Hon Wah College, the Fukien Secondary School and the Chung Seng Middle School. These pro-Beijing schools found it difficult to operate and compete in an educational environment in which the government favored public schools and encouraged private schools to change into governmentally funded ones. Yet, toward the end of the British colonial rule, the government put forward a subsidy scheme for these pro-Beijing schools to transform themselves, and to allow them to establish branches. Under these circumstances, pro-Beijing schools had a new political life after the establishment of the HKSAR on July 1, 1997.

Table 9.9 illustrates the transformation of the pro-Beijing schools in the HKSAR. It shows that Heung To, Pui Kiu and Fukien schools expanded considerably, a testimony to the increase in the strengths of pro-Beijing schools in Hong Kong after 1997. Heung To increased its middle schools from one to three; Pui Kiu included not only middle school but also primary school and college; and Fukien secondary schools rose to three. It is noteworthy that Wong Cho-bau is a Hong Kong person but also a mainland Chinese land developer in Shenzhen. He was born in Guangdong's Chaoyang and migrated to Hong Kong at the age of three. In the 1960s, he lived in the squatter area, but he returned to build up the special economic zone of Shenzhen in the mid-1980s through his participation in the property and hotel businesses.[35] The historical development of Wong demonstrated how a mainland Chinese who migrated to Hong Kong could successfully transform himself into a famous entrepreneur assisting

---

[34] Lau Shan-ching, "My first encounter with uncle Kan," June 23, 2016, in https://www.inmediahk.net/node/1043023, access date: March 5, 2019.

[35] See the introduction to Wong Cho Bau in https://baike.baidu.com/, access date: March 7, 2019.

Table 9.9 The transformation of the pro-Beijing schools in Hong Kong after 1997

School	Establishment	Development
Workers' Children Secondary School	1946	Participated in the Direct Subsidy Scheme in 1991
Heung To Middle School	1946	Participated in the Direct Subsidy Scheme in 1991
Tin Shui Wai Heung To Middle School	2001	Under the Direct Subsidy Scheme
Tseng Kwan O Heung To Middle School	2003	Under the Direct Subsidy Scheme
Pui Kiu Middle School	1946	Participated in Direct Subsidy Scheme in 1991
Pui Kiu Primary School	2000	
Pui Kiu College	2005	
Hon Wah College (cum Primary Section)	1945	Participated in the Direct Subsidy Scheme in 1991 and it moved to Siu Sai Wan in 2000
Fukien Secondary School	1951	Participated in Direct Subsidy Scheme in 1991 and it moved to Kwun Tong in 2002
Siu Sai Wan Fukien Secondary School	1997	Government-aided school
Fukien Secondary School Affiliated School	2009	Took over the Pegasus Philip Wong Kin Hang Christian Primary School cum Junior Secondary School
Chung Sang Middle School	Unknown but it was founded before 1967	It was closed before 1997 because it did not have a formal school site beside the Silvery Theater although branch was located at the Wan Hon Street in Kwun Tong
Hong Kong Federation of Education Workers (HKFEW) Wong Cho Bau School	2001	Government-aided school
HKFEW Wong Cho Bau Secondary School	2001	Government-aided School

Sources: The authors constructed this table by using the information of the websites of all these schools
[a]Result announced for takeover of school sponsorship, http://www.info.gov.hk/gia/general/200907/10/P200907100130.htm; July 10, 2009

Hong Kong's educational development through his membership in the Board of the Directors of the Hong Kong Federation of Workers Wong Cho Bau School.

In general, pro-Beijing left-wing schools have acquired a lot of resources from the HKSAR government after 1997. One way of changing the image of the pro-Beijing schools is to alter the school name, such as the Scientia Secondary School which was originally named as the Workers' Children Secondary School in 1946.[36] However, the number of pro-Beijing schools in the HKSAR is relatively small. Most of the schools are dominated by English, Christian and Catholic ones.[37] As of 2017, one-fourth of Hong Kong's students studied in Catholic schools, which tend to be more autonomous from the government. Only thirty schools were pro-Beijing.[38] As such, even though Beijing was and is eager to see the introduction of national education in the HKSAR, the reality is that most of the schools, principals and teachers were and are not pro-Beijing and they lacked the determination and capability to support, let alone implement, the national education policy.

Due to the contextual difficulties of conducting united front work in Hong Kong's educational sector, the PRC authorities tend to focus on some pro-Beijing educational interest groups, notably the Hong Kong Federation of Education Workers (HKFEW). The HKFEW was established in April 1975 to rally teachers to adopt the position of "loving China and Hong Kong," to serve the educational professionals and to "promote the development of Hong Kong's educational enterprises."[39] It plays a crucial function of conducting united front work through coordination and lobbying efforts. The former presidents of the HKFEW, Jasper Tsang and Cheng Kai-nam, were DAB leaders who cultivated friendly relations with pro-Beijing teachers, who were then mobilized to vote for the DAB in legislative and district elections. In the Legislative Council elections, the HKFEW has been playing a crucial role in mobilizing

---

[36] See the website of the Scientia Secondary School in http://www.wss.edu.hk/about.aspx?clid=176&atid=98&lan=1, access date: March 7, 2019.

[37] See Wong Hoi, *An Analysis of Hong Kong's Social Strata* (in Chinese) (Hong Kong: Commercial Press, 2017), p. 147.

[38] Ibid.

[39] See its website in http://www.hkfew.org.hk/info.php?cid=28, access date: March 7, 2019.

pro-Beijing teachers to vote for like-minded candidates in the education functional constituency.

Table 9.10 shows that the performance of pro-Beijing forces in the education functional constituency elections was unsatisfactory. From 1985 to 2016, the pro-democracy candidates, the late Szeto Wah, Cheung Man-kwong and Ip Kin-yuen, won the seats returned from the educational functional constituency. Szeto won easily in 1985 and then became automatically elected in 1988. Although Cheung's votes fluctuated from 1991 to 2008, changing from a gradual increase in the number of votes to a steady decline, Ip picked up the votes easily and put up a relatively strong show in 2012 and 2016. On the contrary, the pro-Beijing candidates were all easily defeated from 1985 to 2016, showing that they are still no match with the pro-democracy counterparts in the education sector. It also means that the PRC's united front work in the education sector of the HKSAR has considerable gaps and it needs to catch up with the relatively powerful pro-democracy forces.

Table 9.10 Electoral results of the education functional constituency in Legislative Council elections, 1985–2016

Year Pro-democracy candidate	Votes gained	Opposing candidates	Votes gained
2016 Ip Kin-yuen	45,984	Choi York-lin	18,158
2012 Ip Kin-yuen	46,535	Ho Hon-kuen	15,170
2008 Cheung Man-kwong	37,876	Ho Hon-kuen	12,272
		Yu Yee-wah	2746
2004 Cheung Man-kwong	44,517	Yu Kai-chun	9155
2000 Cheung Man-kwong	35,793	Lee Kit-kong	5686
1998 Cheung Man-kwong	34,864	Li Sze-yuen[a]	5319
1995 Cheung Man-kwong	19,558	Leung Siu-tong	4495
1991 Cheung Man-kwong	15,193	Ho King-on	886
		Ng Chung-wang[a]	836
1988 Szeto Wah	Uncontested		
1985 Szeto Wah	12,706	Ip King-ping[a]	2655
		Ko Kay-yu[a]	2165
		Chan Yat-tong[a]	577
		Wu Siu-wai	409

Source: The news of the Professional Teachers' Union and the websites of elections and the Electoral Affair Commission

[a]Note: Li Sze-yuen was from the pro-democracy Professional Teachers' Union. Ng Chung-wang, Ip King-ping and Chan Yat-tong were independents. Ko was pro-Taiwan

Table 9.11 lists the political background of all those candidates who competed with the pro-democracy candidates nominated by the Professional Teachers' Union in running for the educational constituency

Table 9.11 Political background of candidates who competed with candidates from the Professional Teachers' Union

Opposing candidates	Political background
Choi York-lin	Vice-chairlady of the Hong Kong Federation of Education Workers, which is a pro-Beijing teachers' organization, and the school principal of a pro-Beijing secondary school.
Ho Hon-kuen	A graduate of National Taiwan University, the chairman of the Education Convergence, the school principal of a secondary school named Elegantia College.
Yu Yee-wah	Chairperson of the Hong Kong Federation of Education Workers, teacher of a primary school, member of the pro-Beijing Federation of Trade Union and chairwoman of the Education Employees General Union (which is a member of the Federation of Trade Unions).
Yu Kai-chun	A teacher of Tsuen Wan Chiu Chow Public School, the chairman of the Education Employees General Union and a member of the Hong Kong Federation of Trade Unions.
Lee Kit-kong	Headmaster of Sheng Kung Hui Kei Hin Primary School, and an executive committee member of the Education Convergence.
Li Sze-yuen	A member of the Professional Teachers' Union.
Leung Siu-tong	Chairman of the advisory management committee of the Hong Kong Teachers' Centre and an executive committee member of the Education Convergence.
Ho King-on	Chairman of the Hong Kong Federation of Education Workers.
Ng Chung-wang	Independent and he was the school principal of Yu Chun Keung Memorial College and a member of the Hong Kong Aid-school Teachers' Association.
Ip King-ping	Independent and he was the school principal of St. Stephan College, and a member of the Hong Kong Aid-school Teachers' Association.
Ko Kay-yu	Chairman of the pro-Taiwan and pro-Nationalist Hong Kong Teachers' Association.
Chan Yat-tong	Independent and he was the headmaster of the Yuen Long Catholic Primary School.
Wu Siu-wai	Vice-Chairman of Hok Yau Club, a group that was and is regarded as a pro-Beijing educational interest group.

Sources: See The Executive Committee of the Education Convergence, http://www.edconvergence.org.hk/committee_members(7th).htm, access date: March 8, 2019, and "Nationalist youth group under fire," *South China Morning Post*, July 18, 2012, in https://www.scmp.com/article/1007061/nationalist-youth-group-under-fire, access date: March 8, 2019

elections. Except for Li Sze-yuen and Ng Chung-yuen, all the opposing candidates came from the pro-Beijing forces. Clearly, patron-client politics were at work because pro-Beijing forces nominated these like-minded educators to compete with pro-democracy educators supported by the Professional Teachers' Union. The flagship of pro-Beijing educational interest groups remains the Hong Kong Federation of Workers, while the Education Convergence is also a pro-government committee absorbing pro-Beijing educators and the Education Employees General Union is affiliated with the pro-Beijing Federation of Trade Unions. Hence, a pattern of political participation of pro-Beijing educators could be seen from these interest groups, but their performance was consistently weak.

The PRC's penetration into the teachers' trade unions in the HKSAR remains relatively weak. Unlike the pro-democracy Professional Teachers' Union which exceeded 100,000 members in 2018, the Hong Kong Federation of Education Workers remains small and does not mention the number of members in its website.[40] Table 9.12 illustrates the major teachers' trade unions in the HKSAR and most of them are independent rather than pro-Beijing. The largest teachers' union remains the Professional Teachers' Union with a membership of 98,304 in 2017.

Some educational interest groups are not registered as teachers' unions. They include the Hong Kong Federation of Education Workers, the Hong Kong Subsidized Secondary Schools Council, the Hong Kong Association of the Heads of Secondary Schools, Education Convergence, the New Territories School Master Association, the Hong Kong Women Teachers' Organization and the Hong Kong Senior Education Workers' Association (Table 9.13). Most of them are politically neutral, but the Hong Kong Federation of Education Workers (HKFEW) and the Hong Kong Senior Education Workers' Association are pro-Beijing, relatively financially adequate and active in organizing activities. After the mass protest against the Tung Chee-hwa government on July 1, 2003, the PRC revived its united front work in Hong Kong by mobilizing the HKFEW to enhance its activities. The HKFEW has been holding annual dinners, which the Chief Executive and officials from the Liaison Office usually attend. It has also expanded liaison work with secondary schools so as to win the hearts and minds of more parents, students and teachers. In 2017, the number of liaison workers of the HKFEW increased to 1176 and they not only visited

[40] See its website, http://www.hkfew.org.hk/info.php?cid=28, access date: March 8, 2019.

Table 9.12 Major teachers' trade unions in Hong Kong, 2017

Name of the union	Year of registration	Declared membership	Political affiliates
Hong Kong Teachers' Association	1949	663	Independent
Education Bureau, Government, Grant-in-aid, Subsidized and Private Schools Junior Staff Union	1966	917	Federation of Hong Kong and Kowloon Labor Unions
Government Educational Staff Union	1973	401	Independent
Hong Kong Professional Teachers' Union	1973	98,304	Pro-democracy Confederation of Trade Unions
Association of Inspectors, Education Bureau	1975	193	Independent
Union of Government Primary School Headmasters and Headmistresses	1976	192	Independent
Union of Government School Teachers	1979	283	Independent
Association of Principal, Senior, Assistant and Certificated Masters and Mistresses of Education Bureau	1979	50	Independent
Association of Professional Teachers in English Foundation Schools	1980	342	Independent
Association of Principals of Government Secondary Schools	1982	31	Independent
Hong Kong Aided Primary School Heads Association	1983	370	Independent
Sheng Kung Hui Primary Schools Council School Principals Association	1986	50	Independent
Hong Kong Aided School Teachers' Association	1986	–	Stopped functioning
Association of Assistant Principals of Government Secondary Schools	1993	61	Independent

(*continued*)

Table 9.12 (continued)

Name of the union	Year of registration	Declared membership	Political affiliates
Association of Curriculum Officers, Education Bureau	1994	69	Independent
Social Welfare Department Teachers' Union	1996	11	Independent
Diocesan Boys' School Teachers' Association	2003	94	Independent
Education Employees General Union	2005	1045	Pro-Beijing Federation of Trade Unions
The Association of Deputy Heads of Government Primary Schools	2011	56	Independent

Sources: Registry of Trade Unions, *Annual Statistical Report of Trade Unions in Hong Kong* (Hong Kong: Registry of Trade Unions, Labour Department of the Hong Kong Government, 2017 and 2018)

Table 9.13 Educational interest groups that are not registered as Teachers' Unions

Educational groups	Year of establishment	Membership
Hong Kong Federation of Education Workers	1975	Unknown
Hong Kong Subsidized Secondary Schools Council	1971	345[a]
Hong Kong Association of the Heads of Secondary Schools	1964	356[b]
Education Convergence	1994	Unknown
New Territories School Master Association[c]	2006	932[d]
Hong Kong Women Teachers' Organization	2006	2000
Hong Kong Senior Education Workers' Association	1997	Unknown

[a]Member Schools, https://www.hksssc.edu.hk/schools.php

[b]The figure is the number of principals as their membership includes other than principals such as vice-principals and life and affiliated members. And there is overlapping of membership between the Hong Kong Subsidized Secondary Schools Council and the Hong Kong Association of the Heads of Secondary Schools

[c]致新界校長會朱景玄會長的公開信校長的腰板能挺直嗎?, Apple Daily, https://hk.news.appledaily.com/local/daily/article/20140613/18757025, 2014年06月13日

[d]新界校長會簡介, http://www.ntsha.org.hk/index.php?option=com_content&task=view&id=1&Itemid=2

209 schools but also invited 2257 people to join the association. Obviously, the HKFEW attempts to increase its strength gradually, although it is no match with the pro-democracy Professional Teachers' Union.[41]

Table 9.14 shows the historical dominance of the politically independent educational unions in Hong Kong. Most importantly, the pro-democracy Professional Teachers' Union (PTU) grew continuously from 1973 to 2017, while the pro-Beijing Education Employees General Union have remained weak from 2006 to 2017.[42] Hence, the PRC's united front work into the education sector has been hindered by the relatively strong pro-democracy forces.

The PRC's united front work in the teachers' unions of various tertiary institutions is also relatively weak. An overwhelming majority of these unions are politically neutral, except for four of them, namely the Vocational Training Council Non-Teaching Staff Union (which joins the CTU and FLU), the University of Hong Kong Employees Union (which also joins the CTU and FLU), the Chinese University of Hong Kong Employees General Union (which joins the CTU) and the Trade Union of Chu Hai College of Higher Education (which joins the CTU). All these unions are politically weak, failing to defend the interests of many academics, especially those who are on contractual and short-term contracts. Given that all these academic unions are fragmented without a united front, and that the university administration is usually stronger in the employer-employee relations, academics in the HKSAR are not really protected by their trade unions in tertiary institutions. For the PRC authorities, they cannot penetrate these trade unions easily. Table 9.15 shows the diversity of trade unions at the tertiary level and they are not easily captured by pro-Beijing forces. As such, PRC authorities tend to focus on the co-optation of the top individual leaders and office-bearers of various tertiary institutions, like some vice-chancellors, pro-vice-chancellors as well as some members and chairs of the higher-level councils, so that Beijing's policy against some localists' call for "independence," as will be discussed in the next chapter, could be easily adopted and implemented by the university presidents in 2018.

[41] See its website, https://www.hkfew.org.hk/info.php?cid=28, access date: March 9, 2019.
[42] For the strength of the PTU, see Steven Chung-fun Hung, "Professional Teachers' Union as interest group fighting for democracy," in Sonny Shiu-hing Lo, ed., *Interest Groups and the New Democracy Movement in Hong Kong*, pp. 87–110.

Table 9.14 Membership of Education Unions, 1955–2017

	HKTA	GESU	HKPTU	HKASTA	EEGU	EGSP
Establish	*1934*	*1973*	*1973*	*1986*	*2006*	*1966*
1955	2099					
1956	6003					
1957	5887					
1958	5812					
1959	5593					
1960	5007					
1961	4572					
1962	4454					
1963	3869					
1964	3854					
1965	3680					81
1966	5182					365
1967	2887					377
1968	3552					401
1969	3546					420
1970	3777					422
1971	2894					427
1972	2761					473
1973	2032	2092	8112			595
1974	2241	1951	9552			668
1975	1889	1968	12,697			851
1976	1676	2023	15,721			1126
1977	2027	1871	17,480			1374
1978	2113	1824	18,592			1966
1979	2203	1532	19,888			1698
1980	2150	1565	22,272			1837
1981	2083	1544	23,573			2016
1982	2136	1753	26,289			1996
1983	1790	1791	27,586			1972
1984	1686	1805	30,719			1864
1985	1561	1685	31,750			1972
1986	1604	1621	32,748	40		1929
1987	1528	1556	35,828	988		1846
1988	1346	1532	40,912	1051		1728
1989	1018	1469	44,089	1051		1613
1990	1019	1474	47,009	1127		1474
1991	939	1334	50,045	1131		1334
1992	948	1360	53,427	1313		1360
1993	904	1356	56,498	1314		1356

(*continued*)

Table 9.14 (continued)

	HKTA	GESU	HKPTU	HKASTA	EEGU	EGSP
Establish	*1934*	*1973*	*1973*	*1986*	*2006*	*1966*
1994	919	865	58,620	1312		1263
1995	911	761	61,416	1312		1249
1996	958	1225	64,196	1313		1193
1997	911	562	67,631	255		1194
1998	998	663	71,007	101		1223
1999	947	694	74,096	54		1186
2000	950	611	75,754	20		1112
2001	933	748	78,221	20		1128
2002	750	656	79,551	20		1020
2003	744	794	78,447	20		967
2004	733	801	76,887	20		907
2005	737	680	77,495	20	246	922
2006	737	637	78,423	20	2143	921
2007	717	595	78,974	20	3696	925
2008	722	542	79,988	20	4535	917
2009	742	563	82,206	20	4854	917
2010	736	575	84,616	20	5748	934
2011	734	594	88,261	20	4367	928
2012	717	610	90,551	–	3048	928
2013	652	443	93,170	–	2213	930
2014	659	443	93,996	–	1728	920
2015	653	412	95,685	–	1445	917
2016	659	384	95,981	–	1189	917
2017	663	401	98,304	–	1045	917

Sources: Annual Statistical Report of Trade Unions in Hong Kong, 1954–2017

Note: The shaded areas mean that there were no data for those years, for the unions did not exist at that time. HKTA: Hong Kong Teachers' Association; GESU: Government Educational Staff Union, formerly the Government School Non-Graduate Teachers' Union; HKPTU: Hong Kong Professional Teachers' Union; HKASTA: Hong Kong Aided School Teachers' Association; EEGU: Education Employees General Union; EGSP: Education Bureau, Government, Grant-in-Aid, Subsidized and Private Schools Junior Staff Union.

Similarly, the PRC has failed to control how the educators select their representatives to the Education Subsector of the Chief Executive Election Committee in 2006, 2011 and 2016 (see Table 9.16). The pro-Beijing HKFEW was no match with the pro-democracy Professional Teachers' Union in all these years, reflecting the limited inroads of the PRC into the educational sector, which possesses quite a lot of votes in the Election Committee selecting the Chief Executive.

Table 9.15 Different trade unions at Hong Kong's tertiary institutions in 2017

Institution	Year of establishment	Membership in 2017
The Academic Staff Association of the Education University of Hong Kong	1965	53
Vocational Training Council Teachers' Association	1971	583
The Hong Kong Polytechnic University Staff Association	1973	989
Technical Education Staff Association	1981	112
Hong Kong Polytechnic University General Staff Union	1981	55
Vocational Training Council Skills Centers Staff Association	1982	51
Staff Association of the Chinese University of Hong Kong	1982	1412
Education and Manpower Bureau Technical Education and Industrial Training Staff Association	1983	35
The Teachers' Association of the Chinese University of Hong Kong	1988	451
City University of Hong Kong Staff Association	1988	938
Vocational Training Council Non-Teaching Staff Union[a,b]	1989	711
Vocational Training Council Instructors & Training Centre Teaching Staff Association	1991	280
University of Hong Kong Employees Union[a,b]	1993	1456
Lingnan College Staff Association	1995	88
Vocational Training Council Academic Staff Association	1999	201
The Vocational Training Council Executive Officer Grade Association	2001	88
Vocational Training Council Technicians' Association	2002	152
Staff Association of The Education University of Hong Kong	2003	321
Hong Kong Baptist University Faculty and Staff Union[a]	2004	95
The Chinese University of Hong Kong Employees General Union[a]	2004	920
Vocational Training Council Learning Resources Centre Staff Association	2004	42

(*continued*)

Table 9.15 (continued)

Institution	Year of establishment	Membership in 2017
Staff Association of the Open University of Hong Kong	2005	66
City University of Hong Kong Teachers' Union	2006	10
Vocational Training Council Lecturers' Union	2007	388
The University of Hong Kong Staff Association	2008	1772
Hong Kong Design Institute Teachers' Association	2008	14
City University Substantiated Staff Union	2009	7
Academic Staff Association of the University of Hong Kong	2009	513
The Trade Union of Chu Hai College of Higher Education[a]	2016	7

Source: Registry of Trade Unions, *Annual Statistical Report of Trade Unions in Hong Kong 2017* (Hong Kong: Registry of Trade Unions, Labour Department of the HKSAR Government, 2017)
[a]Membership of the Hong Kong Confederation of Trade Union (CTU)
[b]Membership of the Hong Kong and Kowloon Federation of Labour Unions (FLU)

In view of the difficulties of penetrating the educational interest groups in the HKSAR, the PRC authorities have been shifting to the work of co-opting individual academics in Hong Kong. A number of measures were taken. First and foremost, the Chinese Association of Hong Kong and Macao Studies (CAHKMS) was established in Beijing in December 2013, trying to co-opt Hong Kong's academics and intellectuals into this think tank and legitimizing Beijing's policies toward the territory. The CAHKMS was registered in the Ministry of Civil Affairs and is under the supervision of the Hong Kong Macao Affairs Office (HKMAO) of the State Council.[43] As such, it is like a semi-governmental think tank on Hong Kong affairs. The association aims at "leading and coordinating the study and implementation of the theory of 'one country, two systems,' strengthening the exchange and cooperation between Hong Kong, Macao and the mainland, and promoting the function of a civilian think tank."[44] Because the think tank is directly under the HKMAO, its members are expected to conduct research and express their views along the line and policies of the

[43] See its website, http://www.cahkms.org/Page/AboutUs_1.html, access date: March 9, 2019.
[44] Ibid.

Table 9.16 The elected representatives from educational interest groups in the education subsector elections of Chief Executive Election Committee in 2006, 2011 and 2016

	No. of contesting	No. of elected	Highest votes (%share)	Lowest votes (%share)
In 2006: registered voters: 78,840, number of voters: 17,223, voting rate: 22.5%				
Professional Teachers' Union	12	12	12,843 (74.6%)	9752 (56.6%)
Education Convergence	5	4	6955 (40.4%)	3307 (19.2%)
Education Employees' Union	2	0	2511 (14.6%)	2113 (12.3%)
Federation of Educational Workers	3	0	3739 (21.7%)	3191 (18.5%)
Women Teachers' Organization	1	0	3034 (17.6%)	3034 (17.6%)
Others[a]	8	4	8992 (52.2%)	1509 (8.8%)
In 2011: registered voters: 88,618, number of voters: 20,084, voting rate: 22.7%				
Professional Teachers' Union	25	25	15,016 (74.8%)	11,831 (58.9%)
Education Convergence	6	3	6975 (34.7%)	2858 (14.2%)
Education Employees' Union	11	0	1885 (9.4%)	768 (3.8%)
Federation of Educational Workers	3	1	4159 (20.7%)	2628 (13.1%)
Women Teachers' Organization	2	1	4593 (22.9%)	3689 (18.4%)
Others	18	0	3544 (17.6%)	883 (4.4%)
In 2016: registered voters: 80,643, number of voters: 33,688, voting rate: 41.8%				
Professional Teachers' Union	30	30	26,684 (79.2%)	21,525 (63.9%)
Education Convergence	4	0	8492 (25.2%)	5247 (15.6%)
Education Employees' Union	3	0	4482 (13.3%)	2735 (8.1%)
Federation of Educational Workers	7	0	7827 (23.2%)	5300 (15.7%)
Women Teachers' Organization	1	0	5167 (15.3%)	5167 (15.3%)
Others	10	0	5088 (15.1%)	2221 (6.6%)

Sources: The 2006, 2011 and 2016 Election Committee Subsector Elections, Electoral Affairs Commission, in https://www.eac.gov.hk/, access date: March 9, 2019

Note: The minimum votes to be elected were 3801, 4105 and 21,525 for the year of 2006, 2011 and 2016 respectively

[a]In 2006, The PTU supported other three candidates, who were Ip Kin Yuen (8992 votes), Woo Hawk Yan (6852 votes) and Tang Yiu Nam (7156 votes), who were all elected. Also, Ada Mak Tse How-ling was elected with merely 3801 votes as she claimed to be an independent, although she was a member of the pro-Beijing DAB

Table 9.17 Hong Kong academics as the founding members of the Chinese Association of Hong Kong and Macao studies

University	Prominent Hong Kong Founding members
The University of Hong Kong	Richard Wong Yue-Chim (economist)
	Albert Chen Hung-yee (legal expert)
	Nelson Chow Wing-sun Chow (social work expert)
	Cheng Kai-ming (education expert)
The Chinese University of Hong Kong	Lau Siu-kai (sociologist)
	Yeung Yue-man (geographer)
	Sung Yun-wing (economist)
City University of Hong Kong	Chang Hsin-kang (engineering expert)
The Hong Kong University of Science and Technology	Francis T. Lui (economist)
The Hong Kong Polytechnic University	Lee Ming-kwan (sociologist)
Lingnan University	Li Pang-kwong (political scientist)
	Lau Chi-pang (historian)
The Education University of Hong Kong	John Lee Chi-kin (education expert)

Source: *Wen Wei Po,* January 3, 2014, in http://paper.wenweipo.com/2014/01/03/HK1401030015.htm, access date: March 3, 2019

central government in Beijing. The CAHKMS has three committees: law, economy and socio-administrative development. When it was formed in late 2013, there were 551 individual members in which 374 came from the mainland, 136 from Hong Kong and 41 from Macao. It publishes a magazine, *Gang Ao Yanjiu* (*Hong Kong and Macao Study*), four times per year for internal circulation and sharing of the research findings of members, although copies of the magazine are available in some bookstores and libraries in Macao and Hong Kong.[45] Table 9.17 shows the Hong Kong academics who were co-opted into the CAHKMS came from various local universities. Judging from their expertise, the PRC's new united front work targeted at individual academics coming from different disciplines and background. In 2019, the chairman of the CAHKMS is Xu Ze, a former deputy director of the HKMAO. The deputy chairpersons of the CAHKMS include sociologist Lau Siu-kai and politician Maria Tam, a former pro-British politician who has since July 1997 turned far more prominently pro-Beijing than ever before.[46] Lau denies that he is pro-

[45] See http://cahkms.org/hkmr/HKMR_10.html, access date: March 9, 2019.
[46] See http://www.cahkms.org/Page/AboutUs_3.html, access date: March 9, 2019.

Beijing, but his political role significantly changed from a former advisor of the British Hong Kong administration to the director of the Central Policy Unit of the HKSAR government from 2002 to 2007.[47] From 1993 to 1997, Lau was appointed by the PRC government as not only an advisor of Hong Kong affairs but also a member of the Preliminary Working Committee for the HKSAR. His political path reflected how Beijing targeted at him as a co-optee. In Macao, academic Wu Zhiliang, the chairman of the Macao Foundation, is one of the deputy chairpersons of the association, reflecting his political weight in the minds of the Beijing authorities. Overall, the PRC's appointment of Hong Kong and Macao academics into the CAHKMS demonstrates its political finesse in co-optation, widening the scope of academic friends in all disciplines and mobilizing their political support strategically.

In the process of co-opting individual educators, the PRC authorities have been adopting the principle of political redness to distinguish those friends from enemies. A good example is the rapid political ascendancy of Lee Ho-yin, who was appointed as a member of the CAHKMS in 2014 and who had studied law at Tsinghua University under the supervision of Basic Law expert Wang Zhenmin. He worked as an assistant in a mainland county for four years after his graduation from Tsinghua University, and returned to the HKSAR in 2012 as a rising star in Hong Kong politics.[48] When the former Chief Executive Tung Chee-hwa set up Our Hong Kong Foundation in September 2014 as a united front think tank to rally some Hong Kong elites, mainland experts and foreigners to give policy advice to Hong Kong for the sake of "promoting social harmony, economic prosperity, and sustainable development," Lee was invited to join the organization.[49] Rumors were rift that Tung even recommended Lee to Chief Executive Carrie Lam as a potential candidate for undersecretaries.[50] While Our Hong Kong Foundation is another Hong Kong-based think tank conducting united front work for the PRC, the CAHKMS is the most influential Beijing-based think tank that co-opts the elites of Hong Kong and Macao.

---

[47] *Apple Daily*, June 14, 2002, in https://hk.news.appledaily.com/local/daily/article/20020614/2658628, access date: March 9, 2019.
[48] See https://www.hk01.com/, July 9, 2017, access date: March 9, 2019.
[49] See https://ourhkfoundation.org.hk/zh-hant/node/36, access date: March 9, 2019.
[50] See https://www.hk01.com/, July 9, 2017, access date: March 9, 2019.

Enemies of the Post-Colonial State

As intellectuals are often conscientious in their political views, some Hong Kong academics have alienated the PRC authorities because their remarks and actions are deemed as endangering the security of the post-colonial HKSAR regime. The notable examples are legal expert Benny Tai Yiu-ting and political scientist Joseph Cheng Yu-shek, who have arguably contributed their ideas and efforts to the development of Hong Kong's democracy movement. The pro-Beijing mass media since the early 2010s have been targeting at both Tai and Cheng, attacking them as politicians upsetting the socio-political stability in the HKSAR. Objectively speaking, the political action and remarks of both Tai and Cheng appeared to upset the PRC authorities in several aspects. First, while Tai advocated and led the 2014 Occupy Central Movement, Cheng was accused of contacting foreigners, notably the Americans and the European Union, for funding support for the democracy movement in the HKSAR.[51]

Second, both played a crucial role in providing political insights and ideas to the pro-democracy camp in electoral contests of the Legislative Council and District Councils. While Benny Tai's "thunderbolt plan" in February 2016 attempted to assist the democrats to capture at least half of the seats in the Legislative Council in the September 2016 elections,[52] Cheng was a key coordinator in solving the internal disputes of various democratic factions in running for the directly elected seats in the eighteen District Council elections after July 1, 1997. Although critics of Tai questioned the effectiveness of his plan, Tai's usage of the smart phones to message and mobilize followers and supporters on how to vote in the September 2016 elections triggered the alarm of not only the pro-Beijing forces but also PRC authorities dealing with Hong Kong matters. The use

---

[51] For the accusation against Cheng, see Cheung Tat-ming, *What is the Evidence? Revealing the Black Hand Behind the Scene of Hong Kong's Chaotic Situation* (in Chinese) (Hong Kong: San See Cultural and Commercial Information, 2018). Cheung was one of Cheng's former research assistants. For the accusation on Cheng's links with the European Union, see *Ta Kung Pao*, November 14, 2018, in http://www.takungpao.com.hk/news/232109/2018/1114/204181.html, access date: March 9, 2019.

[52] Joyce Ng, "Thunderbolt plan: Benny Tai devises proposal for Hong Kong pan-democrats to win half of legislative seats in September poll," *South China Morning Post*, February 4, 2016, in https://www.scmp.com/news/hong-kong/politics/article/1909364/thunderbolt-plan-benny-tai-devises-proposal-hong-kong-pan, access date: March 9, 2019. For the concept of the "thunderbolt plan," also see http://www.interpreting.hku.hk/glossary/?p=59461, access date: March 9, 2019.

of smart phones as an instrument to mobilize pro-democracy voters to cast their ballots strategically, through the focus on the support of some candidates and an implicit abandonment of others, represented a Taiwan-style electioneering in the HKSAR. At the same time, Cheng's persistent efforts at coordinating the factions among the pro-democracy camp contributed to the success of the pan-democratic forces to compete with the traditionally powerful pro-Beijing camp at the district level. Both Tai and Cheng, in the eyes of PRC authorities dealing with Hong Kong elections, were the "unpleasant" thorns. As such, the pro-Beijing mass media kept on criticizing them as not only political "troublemakers" but also the "agents of foreign forces" that attempted to influence Hong Kong's political development.

Finally, both Tai and Cheng saw the PRC as an authoritarian empire obstructing Hong Kong's democratization and took action to promote the local democracy movement through their ideas and actions. If the PRC's united front also focuses on its attack at political foes, Tai and Cheng were the easy targets because both of them turned their political ideas into political action. In particular, Tai's public view toward the PRC was regarded as politically "incorrect" by the pro-Beijing media. He believes that the "one country, two systems" in Hong Kong has already been undermined by the PRC intervention, and that its rule of law, and freedom of speech, of press and of association have been "suppressed."[53] He also wrote optimistically:

> Some people feel that, in face of the strong CCP regime, the people of Hong Kong cannot do much and the prospects of democracy are bound to be difficult. But some people also believe that the phenomenon of the Umbrella Movement will surely reappear in Hong Kong. I believe that large-scale street protests and confrontations must accompany the development of democracy movement and they will reoccur one day. But like the experiences of democratization in other places, under the governance of the strong and authoritarian regime, we will have to wait for the transformations of the international political atmosphere, of the PRC's internal politics, and of the mainland Chinese society. At that juncture, the strong and authoritarian regime will not be so strong as we imagine. At that moment, it will be the time for the people of Hong Kong to fight back. But in the meantime,

[53] Benny Tai, "The hypocrisy of 'one country, two systems,'" *Apple Daily*, January 7, 2019, in https://hk.news.appledaily.com/local/daily/article/20190107/20585308, access date: March 9, 2019.

we are not passive and do nothing, but we should actively disseminate the ideas of non-violence, confrontation, social justice and democracy to the Hong Kong society. We have to utilize the existing space to manage the opportunities and contradictions that stem from Hong Kong's pluralistic civil society.[54]

Tai's ideas are, to the PRC authorities and the pro-Beijing elites, politically "subversive" because he is imbued with not only a very strong sense of Hong Kong identity but also a long-term vision of changing both the HKSAR and mainland China politically through the persistent democracy movement.

Due to the fact that both Tai and Cheng were pro-democracy educated intellectuals whose ideas and actions constitute a "threat" to the PRC's national security, which can be broadly defined as regime security including Hong Kong's regime legitimacy, they became the target of criticisms from the pro-Beijing mass media. Other academics who were singled out by the pro-Beijing media for criticisms were many, including political scientist Sing Ming and pollster Robert Chung. Sing was once critical of the role of the Liaison Office in Hong Kong's elections and he became a target of criticisms in the pro-Beijing press.[55] Robert Chung was accused of receiving foreign financial support in his surveys, but he publicly refuted such accusations.[56] Chung's surveys were sometimes questioned by the pro-Beijing media for their accuracy, because the findings of some surveys were unfavorable to the legitimacy of the HKSAR government. Compared with Tai and Cheng's experiences of being severely attacked and tarnished in reputation, Sing and Chung appeared to encounter relatively lighter criticisms. Overall, academics who are politically critical and autonomous, and who take action in the pro-democracy movement, are highly vulnerable to being labeled as the enemies of either the HKSAR regime or the PRC government. From the perspective of some pro-democracy critics,

---

[54] Benny Tai, "The First Umbrella," *Apple Daily*, December 31, 2018, in https://hk.news.appledaily.com/local/daily/article/20181231/20580418, access date: March 9, 2019.

[55] Lau Mong-hung, "Is Sing Ming an associate professor or an extreme professional politician," *Wen Wei Po*, December 5, 2011, in http://paper.wenweipo.com/2011/12/05/PL1112050001.htm, access date: March 9, 2019.

[56] See *Wen Wei Po*, August 7, 2012, in http://paper.wenweipo.com/2012/08/07/YO1208070016.htm, access date: March 9, 2019. For Chung's defence, see his press release, in August 9, 2012, in https://www.hkupop.hku.hk/chinese/release/release951.html, access date: March 9, 2019.

Tai and Cheng have become the "victims" of the authoritarianism of the PRC, whose tentacles have been creeping rapidly and extensively into the HKSAR since 2013.

CAN UNITED FRONT BE ACHIEVED THROUGH INWARD MIGRATION?

If the civil society in the HKSAR cannot be easily controlled by the PRC, especially in the educational sector, then migration is arguably the most efficient and effective instrument through which Beijing exerts its silent influence on the territory. Since the Greater Bay Area plan is relatively new, it takes time for us to observe whether the encouragement of some Hong Kong people to move to reside, work and retire in the mainland can and will work. Incentives, such as the provision of lower tax, the provision of preferential investment treatment and the issuance of Hong Kong and Macao residents' permits, can propel more residents from the two places to migrate inland, but the concerns about the provision of health care and social welfare remain the obstacles to outward migration. Inward migration from the mainland to the HKSAR, however, has been taking place since July 1, 1997.

Table 9.18 shows that a steady number of mainland-born Chinese arrived at the HKSAR annually from 1998 to 2017. If the quota of 150 mainlanders who can arrive Hong Kong every day on the basis of using one-way permit since July 1, 1997 is fully utilized, then the HKSAR can have 54,750 mainland migrants every year. But Table 9.17 illustrates that the quotas have not been fully utilized by the mainland government. From 1998 to 2017, there could be 1,095,750 mainland migrants if the quota of 150 persons per day was fully utilized. However, from Table 9.17, only 940,871 mainlanders came to reside in the HKSAR. The quotas appeared to be given to those sons and daughters of Hong Kong persons who got married with mainland spouses, who were mostly women. From 1998 to 2017, many mainland migrants were women and children, whose spouse and father, respectively, were Hong Kong men. Also, many of them were between 25 and 44. In the recent years, more elderly people from the mainland migrated to the HKSAR, but they were not a significant portion of the migrants.

There has been no research conducted on these mainland migrants, let alone their possible change in socio-political attitudes. From the perspec-

Table 9.18 Demographic and social characteristics of one-way permit holders, 1998–2017

Year/age	0–4	5–14	15–24	25–34	35–44	45–54	54–64	65+	Total
1998: Male	1182	14,304	2109	317	711	364	189	204	19,380
Female	1090	13,595	2419	3601	9036	3305	2351	1262	36,659
Total	2272	27,899	4528	3918	9747	3669	2540	1466	56,039
1999: M	4700	7193	1541	1684	1133	412	111	207	16,992
F	4422	7373	1604	11,360	9434	1867	805	757	37,633
Total	9122	14,566	3145	13,044	10,567	2279	916	964	54,625
2000: M	3699	6224	1698	3000	1501	623	330	348	17,423
F	3352	6349	1799	14,169	7527	2436	2326	2149	40,107
Total	7051	12,573	3797	17,169	9028	3059	2650	2497	47,530
2001: M	4859	4196	1191	3946	3219	511	346	244	18,512
F	4276	4245	1233	15,449	7030	1202	924	784	35,142
Total	9135	8441	2424	19,395	10,249	1713	1270	1028	53,654
2002: M	3994	3258	1472	1906	1764	462	271	236	13,363
F	3829	3208	1824	14,141	6000	1323	705	841	31,871
Total	7823	6466	3296	16,047	7764	1785	976	1077	45,234
2003: M	3437	4096	1551	1600	1682	604	253	190	13,413
F	3273	4061	1728	19,237	8425	1780	743	847	40,094
Total	6710	8157	3279	20,837	10,107	2384	996	1037	53,507
2004: M	2827	2914	1069	1132	1269	452	179	139	9981
F	2643	2936	1215	13,677	5508	1131	546	435	28,091
Total	5470	5850	2284	14,809	6777	1583	725	574	38,072
2005: M	2317	5176	2573	1783	2630	941	263	140	15,823
F	2315	4730	2591	19,109	7864	1744	599	331	39,283
Total	4632	9906	5164	20,892	10,494	2685	862	471	55,106
2006: M	1817	6779	3770	1519	4176	1371	282	157	19,871
F	1703	6092	3803	13,335	7114	1441	532	279	34,299
Total	3520	12,871	7573	14,854	11,290	2812	814	436	54,170
2007: M	1393	3332	2230	1069	2074	926	241	142	11,407
F	1289	3053	2284	9620	4298	1065	549	300	22,458
Total	2682	6385	4514	10,689	6372	1991	790	442	33,865
2008: M	1555	3754	3033	1098	2255	1082	283	158	13,218
F	1487	3379	3084	12,116	5933	1546	585	262	28,392
Total	3042	7133	6117	13,214	8188	2628	868	420	41,610
2009: M	1683	3424	2997	1621	2153	1031	292	159	13,360
F	1595	3031	3327	16,318	8018	2152	560	226	35,227
Total	3278	6455	6324	17,939	10,171	3183	852	385	48,587
2010: M	1690	2745	2659	1665	1955	895	296	151	12,056
F	1654	2464	3162	12,927	7256	2277	614	214	30,568
Total	3344	5209	5821	14,592	9211	3172	910	365	42,624

(*continued*)

Table 9.18 (continued)

Year/age	0–4	5–14	15–24	25–34	35–44	45–54	54–64	65+	Total
2011: M	1445	2427	2686	1742	3058	1344	404	138	13,244
F	1385	2206	3028	11,745	8156	2731	673	211	30,135
Total	2830	4633	5714	13,487	11,214	4075	1077	349	43,379
2012: M	1371	2198	2319	2697	6331	2885	1346	247	19,394
F	1378	1978	2484	11,273	11,446	4456	1898	339	35,252
Total	2749	4176	4803	13,970	17,777	7341	3244	586	54,646
2013: M	1693	2023	2027	2258	4172	1821	975	258	15,227
F	1582	1936	2325	10,543	8373	3069	1647	329	29,804
Total	3275	3959	4352	12,801	12,545	4890	2622	587	45,031
2014: M	2092	2004	2086	1716	3244	1291	665	244	13,342
F	1890	1883	2321	9649	7587	2420	1125	279	27,154
Total	3982	3887	4407	11,365	10,831	3711	1790	523	40,496
2015: M	1678	1928	2410	1808	2676	1650	709	262	13,121
F	1569	1740	2380	8644	6911	2686	1012	275	25,217
Total	3247	3668	4790	10,452	9587	4336	1721	537	38,338
2016: M	1838	3440	5660	2069	3725	4189	1492	586	22,999
F	1703	3048	5160	9370	8299	4700	1674	434	34,388
Total	3541	6488	10,820	11,439	12,024	8889	3166	1020	56,387
2017: M	1489	2814	4205	1860	3335	3204	1474	649	19.03
F	1446	2482	3777	7645	6722	3784	1596	489	27,941
Total	2935	5296	7982	9505	10,057	6988	3070	1138	46,971

Sources: See government statistics, available in https://www.had.gov.hk/file_manager/tc/documents/public_services/services_for_new_arrivals_from_the_mainland/report_2017q4.pdf, https://www.had.gov.hk/file_manager/tc/documents/public_services/services_for_new_arrivals_from_the_mainland/report_2012q4.pdf, https://www.had.gov.hk/file_manager/tc/documents/public_services/services_for_new_arrivals_from_the_mainland/report_2007q4.pdf, https://www.had.gov.hk/file_manager/tc/documents/public_services/services_for_new_arrivals_from_the_mainland/report_2002q4.pdf, access date: March 3, 2019

M Male, *F* Female

tive of united front work, since the mainland government controls who are the migrants coming to and residing in the HKSAR, it is difficult to analyze the background of the migrants, some of whom might be the siblings of high-ranking party officials. In March 2019, democrat Lee Wing-tat asserted that 21,000 mainland migrants after 1997 are CCP members, a speculation that promoted the immediate criticisms from the pro-Beijing media.[57] Regardless of the proportion of mainland migrants who might be CCP members, in recent years, the pro-Beijing DAB has

[57] *Apple Daily*, March 25, 2019.

been targeting at the relatively new migrants and providing constituency services to them, winning their hearts and minds. The pro-democracy groups are lagging behind the pro-Beijing forces in the systematic provision of services to the mainland migrants, who constitute a crucial source of voters in the HKSAR's direct elections at the legislative and district levels.

Despite the poverty of research focusing on the mainland migrants in the HKSAR, many clan groups have been set up by pro-Beijing forces so that the umbrella of the PRC's new united front can reach them extensively. For instance, the Hong Kong Zhuhai Women United Committee was established in 2018 to provide a platform to unite all female residents who came from and who were born in Zhuhai.[58] The chairlady is Cally Kwong Mei-yun, a Hong Kong member of the NPC and a singer who has become increasingly pro-Beijing in political outlook since July 1, 1997. The Committee aims at promoting women to participate in social affairs on the basis of the principle of "loving China and Hong Kong," to unite women through the formation of volunteer groups, to care for the interests of women and to provide training for them and to provide a platform for women in Hong Kong and Zhuhai to interact with each other.[59] The united front functions of the Committee were obvious. The influx of migrants from various parts of mainland China also provides a golden opportunity for many pro-Beijing groups to set up volunteer groups to assist the society in various capacity. For instance, the Hong Kong Guangxi Federation of Associations held a dinner celebrating the Chinese New Year in March 2019, inviting not only Chief Executive Carrie Lam but also officials from the Liaison Office and Beijing's United Front Department to attend.[60] The emergence of the Greater Bay Area provides another golden opportunity for many pro-Beijing groups, ranging from business to youth, to gather together and to forge partnerships with mainland groups and cities to implement the plan. For instance, fifteen interest groups from Guangdong, Hong Kong and Macao signed agreements in March 2019 to enhance training, technology transfer, resources sharing and the provision of services for young people in the three places.[61] Hence, the gradual influx of mainland migrants converge with the PRC's drive for

[58] *Ta Kung Pao*, March 7, 2019, pp. A12–A13.
[59] Ibid.
[60] *Wen Wei Po*, March 6, 2019, p. A15.
[61] *Wen Wei Po*, March 5, 2019, p. A9.

a new united front strategy, facilitating the formation of various clan associations and volunteer groups. On the other hand, the birth of the Greater Bay Area plan provides an additional and a legitimate platform for all pro-Beijing groups to reorganize themselves, to forge closer partnerships with the mainland and Macao counterparts and to mobilize the youth to participate in the blueprint of socio-economic integration.

Conclusion

This chapter proves that while the PRC's new united front work is successful in the media sector of the Hong Kong civil society, its penetrative politics are less forceful in the educational sector. As such, the long-term plan of accelerating socio-economic integration between the HKSAR and mainland China is conducted through the Greater Bay Area blueprint. It remains to be seen whether the Greater Bay Area plan will be successful in achieving the PRC's new united front policy of speeding up the socio-economic integration between Hong Kong and the mainland. But judging from the relatively limited inroads of the pro-Beijing forces in the educational sector of Hong Kong, it will take some years and perhaps decades for the PRC's new united front work to be really successful.

CHAPTER 10

Co-opting Individuals with External Implications: Business Elites, Democrats, Civil Servants, Educators and Taiwanese

Introduction

The PRC's new united front in the HKSAR has been expanding its outreach to four key social groups, namely, the business elites, democrats, civil servants and educators, with implications for the Taiwan people and even some overseas Chinese in other parts of the world. This chapter focuses on how the PRC authorities have been co-opting the business elites, some democrats, civil servants and educators in Hong Kong, and how they have been reaching out to the Taiwan people, ranging from the members and leaders of the Kuomintang (KMT) to that of the New Party. The external implications of mainland China's new united front work are significant, because they are now reaching out to overseas Chinese and some foreigners, raising the deep concerns of foreign countries, especially as the rapid economic rise and the increase in military strength of the PRC are seen as the "existential threats" in many parts of the world.

Pro-Business Political Parties as Targets

The two most important pro-business political parties that are under the prime targets of political co-optation by the PRC authorities are the Liberal Party (LP) and the Business and Professionals Alliance (BPA). The LP was founded by the former Legislative Council member Allen Lee Peng-fei in 1993 and was originated from the Cooperative Resources Center (CRC). The CRC was a loose grouping of business elites formed in 1991 and led by Lee to gather twenty-one politically conservative legislators to counter the rapid rise of the democrats after the introduction of direct elections to the legislature in 1991. In fact, the CRC could be seen as a "legislative clique," to borrow from the late Samuel Huntington, to protect the business interests and to resist the pro-welfare demands and agendas of the directly elected democrats.[1] Originally, the PRC authorities attached great importance to the role of the LP in its united front work against the pro-democracy forces; nevertheless, a turning point came in July 2003 when the former LP chairman James Tien publicly opposed an attempt by the Tung Chee-hwa administration to legislate on Article 23 of the Basic Law—a stipulation that requires the HKSAR government to enact its own legislation against subversion, treason, secession and sedition. Tien's prominent role in resigning from the Executive Council and the lack of support from LP members in the legislature forced the HKSAR government to postpone the legislation on Article 23 indefinitely until March 2019, when the Carrie Lam administration was reportedly expected by Beijing to study how the legislation would be revised and re-introduced to the legislature as soon as possible. Tien's act of political defiance was widely seen as politically disloyal to Beijing, but he and LP member Selina Chow became so politically popular in the September 2004 legislative elections that they were both directly elected to the legislature.

The relatively politically autonomous line of the LP members continued to be a hallmark that irritated PRC authorities. In the March 2012 Chief Executive election in the HKSAR, the LP supported a pro-business candidate Henry Tang Ying-ren and opposed C. Y. Leung, who was backed up by Beijing. The electoral competition between Tang and Leung was marred by fierce accusations and scandals, with supporters of both sides pointing to the other candidate's deficiencies. On February 27, 2012, it was reported that C. Y. Leung got the support of Xi Jinping, the chairman of Beijing's Central Coordination Committee on Hong Kong, and that he would very likely be endorsed by the Beijing leaders and then elected as the next Chief Executive.[2] Due to Beijing's view that Tang was plagued with personal scandals, it tended to favor Leung, but the central

---

[1] Sonny Lo, "Legislative Cliques, Political Parties, Political Groupings and Electoral System," in Joseph Cheng and Sonny Lo, eds., *From Colony to SAR: Hong Kong's Challenges Ahead* (Hong Kong: The Chinese University Press, 1995), pp. 51–70.

[2] "Predicting Xi Jinping's support and C. Y. Leung would be elected," *Apple Daily*, February 27, 2012, in https://hk.news.appledaily.com/local/daily/article/20120227/16105897, access date: March 16, 2019.

government officials would politically support both of them in public. Interestingly, this report turned out to be accurate, because the pro-Beijing *Ta Kung Pao* editorialized two days before the election day in a way that demonstrated the proclivity of Beijing leaders' support of Leung. The editorial put Leung in front of Tang although it praised both candidates:

> In personal aspects, Leung is a talent rising from the grassroots level and his patriotic attitude toward the country is unquestionable. He was trusted by the central government when he was the secretary general of the Hong Kong Basic Law Drafting Committee [from 1985 to 1990]. After the return of Hong Kong's sovereignty, he has become an indispensable pro-establishment representative in the Executive Council. Henry Tang has joined the government since the sovereignty return, becoming the Financial Secretary and later the Chief Secretary, serving the members of the public and sitting in the Legislative Council to face the scolding and criticisms from such legislators as "Long Hair" [Leung Kwok-hung] and Raymond Wong. He has the heart of serving Hong Kong and the "one country, two systems." From the personal angle, both Leung and Tang are talents and they have ideals, vision and capability. The only difference is their lifestyle.[3]

The last sentence of the pro-Beijing newspaper appeared to point to the relatively luxurious lifestyle of Tang, implying that Leung was implicitly more acceptable. After Leung's victory, some LP members including Tien continued to be critical of his administration, making PRC authorities feel that the LP is by no means a reliable political ally.

As a result, PRC authorities have turned to groom and support another pro-business group, the BPA. The BPA was founded in October 2012 by some former LP members, such as Andrew Leung Kwan-yuen, Jeffrey Lam Kin-fung, the late Lau Wong-fat, Abraham Shek Lai-him, and some other pro-Beijing legislators like Priscilla Leung Mei-fun. Leung and Lam were the former core members of the LP and could be seen as political opportunists as they withdrew from the LP after its poor performance in the 2008 legislative elections without any party candidate directly elected to the legislature. The decline of the LP continued after the electoral debacle in 2008, because James Tien criticized Chief Executive C. Y. Leung in October 2014 and asked him to resign from the HKSAR

---

[3] "Leung and Tang are acceptable, but casting blank votes is unacceptable," *Ta Kung Pao*, March 22, 2012, p. A2.

leadership position.[4] Tien's position as a Hong Kong member of the CPPCC was immediately revoked by Beijing because his remark critical of Leung was regarded as not only anti-Leung but also anti-PRC.[5] According to businessman and Hong Kong CPPCC member Chan Wing-kei, the central government staunchly supported C. Y. Leung in dealing with the Occupy Central Movement that began from September 2014, and therefore Tien's open remark calling for Leung's resignation was deemed as exceeding Beijing's political bottom line.[6] Tien argued that the LP was "politically neutral" and that it was by no means a "super pro-emperor party," and he refused to retract his remarks on Leung.[7] After Tien's membership in the CPPCC was revoked, he resigned from his chairmanship from the LP. Although the LP member Selina Chow said that Zhang Xiaoming, the director of the Liaison Office, still saw the LP as a political party that "loves the country and Hong Kong," the central authorities gradually shifted their political support to the BPA.[8] The case of Tien shows that once his remarks exceeded the red line of political tolerance from Beijing, he was politically "penalized." The political boundary between the PRC's friends and enemies was clear; one has to back up the Chief Executive and his or her policies and such personal support is equivalent to the support of the central government in Beijing.

After the resignation of Tien from the LP, his successor Felix Chung Kwok-bun has strengthened his harmonious relations with both the Chief Executive and Beijing, thus trying to change the image of the LP in the eyes of the central authorities. Occasionally, the LP opposes the government policy, such as its concern about the proposed extradition arrangement between the HKSAR and mainland China in March 2019, because some business people were concerned that those Hong Kong people involved in commercial crime, apart from serious criminal offences such as

---

[4] "James Tien's position in the CPPCC is revoked and he refuses the retract his remarks," *Oriental Daily News*, October 29, 2014, in https://hk.on.cc/hk/bkn/cnt/news/20141029/bkn-20141029195749995-1029_00822_001.html, access date: March 16, 2014.

[5] "James Tien opposes Leung, central government punishes him," *Apple Daily*, October 29, 2014, in https://hk.news.appledaily.com/local/daily/article/20141029/18916544, access date: march 16, 2019.

[6] Ibid.
[7] Ibid.
[8] "James Tien resigned from the LP chairmanship and refuses to withdraw his remark," October 30, 2014, *Hong Kong Economic Times*, in https://paper.hket.com/article/460635/, access date: March 16, 2019.

Table 10.1 Comparison between the Liberal Party and the Business and Professionals Alliance for Hong Kong, 2019

Membership in the political institutions of the PRC and Hong Kong	Liberal Party	Business and Professionals Alliance for Hong Kong
NPC member	1[a]	1
CPPCC members	4	6
Executive Council member	1	2
Legislative Council members	4 (elected from functional constituencies)	7 (from functional constituencies) 1 (from geographical constituencies)
District Council members	8	19

[a]Note: Originally the Liberal Party did not have any NPC member, but because of the death of Wong Man-kwong on March 11, 2019, LP member Chan Hiu-fung was the first member of substitution and replaced Wong

murder, would be extradited from Hong Kong to the PRC. Like the LP, the BPA also expressed its concern about the proposed extradition agreement, suggesting that white-collar crimes should be exempted from the list of offences that would be covered by any future extradition agreement between the HKSAR and the PRC.[9]

The largest pro-business political party in the HKSAR is now the BPA, which has eight members of the Legislative Council in 2019, seven of whom were elected from functional constituencies (Table 10.1). In March 2019, when the CPPCC and NPC meetings were held in Beijing, the BPA made an unprecedented step by holding its party's celebration of the Chinese New Year in the PRC capital, thereby demonstrating its political allegiance to the central government.[10] Two hundred guests attended the BPA's celebration, including the director of the HKMAO Zhang Xiaoming, Liaison Office director Wang Zhimin, former Chief Executive C. Y. Leung and current Chief Executive Carrie Lam. Clearly, the BPA distinguishes its political line from the LP under James Tien and adopts a

---

[9] Jeffie Lam, "Extradition agreement with mainland China would damage Hong Kong's 'safe reputation' for business, AmCham says," *South China Morning Post*, March 6, 2019, in https://www.scmp.com/news/hong-kong/politics/article/2188915/extradition-agreement-mainland-china-would-damage-hong-kongs, access date: March 16, 2019.

[10] See its website, https://www.bpahk.org/category/press/, access date: March 16, 2019.

politically loyal position toward both the Chief Executive and the central government. From Beijing's perspective, the BPA is politically useful and significant, for its members occupy important positions in Hong Kong's political arena. Andrew Leung is the Legislative Council President, Jeffrey Lam a member of the Executive Council and Priscilla Leung a member of the Basic Law Committee. Table 10.1 also shows that the BPA has more District Council members than the LP. The decline of the LP and the rapid rise of the BPA demonstrated not only the political path of James Tien but also the changing political opportunism of the business elites in Hong Kong. In the eyes of most business elites, mainland China offers tremendous business opportunities for them. Due to the supremacy of protecting their business interests, it is politically detrimental to oppose both the Chief Executive and the central government. Hence, the case of James Tien represented a rare political example in the political dynamics between the local business elites and Beijing. Tien's political autonomy illustrated his perception of the need to separate the political loyalty to the Chief Executive from Beijing. Yet, this separation was and is seen as politically unacceptable to PRC officials dealing with Hong Kong affairs.

Individual Business Elites: Contributions to China's Modernization

In August 2018, the HKSAR held a large-scale exhibition showing the economic contributions of many local business elites to the PRC's modernization. These business elites are the targets of co-optation mainly because they did and do contribute immensely to China's economic modernization. They include, for example, the late Henry Fok Ying-tung, who was depicted as the first Hong Kong businessman supportive of China's open-door policy in the late 1970s and early 1980s.[11] Fok accompanied the late PRC leader Deng Xiaoping to visit his Hong Kong-style White Swan Hotel in Guangzhou in 1984. His contributions to China could be traced back to the early 1950s, when the PRC was affected by the American and British economic embargo in the Korean war. Fok used his shipping fleet to transport iron plates, rubber, wheels and medical supplies from

[11] See the exhibition photos of the contributions of Hong Kong business sector to China's economic modernization, Hong Kong Convention and Exhibition Centre, August 10, 2018. The authors took 330 photos from this exhibition and the content of these photos provide the data for this section.

Hong Kong to mainland China at night time for at least a year so that the PRC could have a crucial outlet to receive logistical support from the outside world.[12] Fok's activities were labeled by some people as engaging in "smuggling" and he was regarded as pro-CCP by the British colonial rulers, thus affecting his business operation and development in Hong Kong.[13] Fok's investment and donations in Hong Kong under the British rule were adversely affected, like his properties lacking electricity and water supplies while public hospitals and universities refusing to accept his generous donations.[14] Yet, his patriotism was fully recognized by the PRC authorities. As the PRC underwent rapid economic reforms in the 1980s and 1990s, he contributed to its infrastructure development, including the building of hotels and the development of the tourist industry. Fok was determined to impart the knowledge of how to build up and manage modern hotels to the mainlanders, triggering the process of the modernization of China's tourism industry. He even spent billions to invest in Nansha's economic development in the 1990s, but the mainland bureaucratism and corruption did obstruct his investment, according to his adviser the late Ho Ming-sze.[15] Ho revealed in public that some local officials in Nansha were bureaucratic and corrupt, leading to wastage and delay in the supply of electricity and water to the areas where Fok invested heavily. As a patriot, Fok died in Beijing in 2006.

Apart from Henry Fok, Sir Yue-kong Pao was another crucial target of the PRC's co-optation. Y. K. Pao was a famous shipping magnet born in Ningbo in 1918 and he went to Hong Kong to develop his shipping industry quickly from the 1950s to the 1960s. Although he reduced his shipping fleet in the late 1970s in anticipation of the global downturn in shipping business, Pao was described by PRC authorities as a patriotic Chinese businessman who "led the overseas Chinese to participate in the development of new China."[16] He was also depicted as a bridge between

[12] *Ta Kung Pao*, December 18, 2018, pp. A11–A14.
[13] Ibid.
[14] Ibid.
[15] Ho died in 2018 at the age of 95. He joined the CCP in 1939 and later quit the party after the 1989 Tiananmen incident. See Gary Cheung, "Ho Ming-sze: influential Hongkonger who fought Japanese, and brought city's tycoons and China's Deng Xiaoping together dies, aged 95," *South China Morning Post*, September 6, 2018, in https://www.scmp.com/news/hong-kong/society/article/2163078/ho-ming-sze-influential-hongkonger-who-fought-japanese-and, access date: March 17, 2019.
[16] Posters on the display board describing Pao's contributions to China's economic reform and modernization, Hong Kong Convention and Exhibition Centre, August 10, 2018.

Britain and the PRC in the 1982–84 Sino-British agreement over Hong Kong's future, a deputy director of the Basic Law Drafting Committee from 1985 to 1990 and a member of the Ningbo economic development committee.[17] Pao died in 1991, but the way in which PRC authorities appointed him to the Basic Law Drafting Committee and the Ningbo economic development committee illustrated their united front finesse to deal with successful business elites in Hong Kong and to utilize their expertise to help China's modernization.

Like Fok and Pao, Robert Kuok Hock-nien is another Chinese contributing to China's modernization and has become a crucial target of business co-optation. Kuok was born in Malaysia in 1923 and his father had Fujianese heritage. In the 1950s, he set up his sugar company in Malaysia, becoming a successful business magnet and venturing into the hotel and property businesses in both Singapore and Hong Kong. In 1977, Kuok was invited by the PRC government to participate in the development of the hotel industry in Hangzhou and to help China tackle poverty from 2007 onwards.[18] In 1984, Kuok established the first Shangri-La Hotel in Hangzhou, thirteen years after he had founded the first Shangri-La Hotel in Singapore. Clearly, the PRC authorities made use of his expertise, knowledge and capital to assist the mainland's development of the tourism and hotel sectors. Kuok was also appointed by the PRC government as a Hong Kong affair advisor in the final transition period from British rule to the Chinese governance of Hong Kong. The pattern of co-option of Kuok was the same as Fok and Pao: successful business elites in Hong Kong were encouraged and invited to participate in China's economic modernization, thereby fully utilizing their expertise, knowledge and capital in the motherland's development.

Similar to Kuok, Fok and Pao, another pro-Beijing businessman was the late Tang Hsiang-chien, the father of the former Financial Secretary and Chief Secretary Henry Tang. Tang Hsiang-chien was born in Jiangsu province and studied in Shanghai, Manchester and Illinois. But he did not return to China after the CCP came to power in the mainland in 1949. Instead he chose to develop his business and career in Hong Kong, building up his textile industry successfully from the 1950s to the 1970s.

[17] Ibid.
[18] Posters on the display board describing Kuok's contributions to China's economic reform and modernization, Hong Kong Convention and Exhibition Centre, August 10, 2018.

During China's open-door policy in the mid-1970s, Tang returned to invest in the development of the textile industry in Xinjiang and Shanghai.[19] After the Tiananmen incident in 1989, some foreign investors withdrew from the PRC but Tang remained a Hong Kong businessman investing in China's newly developing electronic industry. From 2007 to 2012, Tang began to donate money to help the educational development in the mainland. His perseverance in investing heavily in China's economic reform was praised by PRC authorities.

The PRC also recognized the contributions of Gordon Wu Ying-sheung, a Hong Kong-born businessman and the chairman of the famous Hopewell Holdings Limited. Wu played a crucial role in giving advice to the PRC government to develop the infrastructure projects, such as highways, electricity stations and hotels, in the Guangdong province.[20] In a television interview, Wu publicly said that in the 1970s and 1980s he was surprised by the PRC socialist system and that he decided to use incentives to reward those workers and employees who worked diligently.[21] Wu hoped that the PRC policy of modernization could become more "flexible and alive."[22] By establishing an electricity factory in Shenzhen and investing in Guangzhou's China Hotel, Wu began to impart his knowledge of modernization to PRC officials in Guangdong. He also advised the Guangdong government to open six lanes rather than just four lanes in the new Guangzhou-Shenzhen highway, and invested in helping the Shenzhen government to build its cross-border inspection checkpoint and customs building so that 24-hour opening between Shenzhen and Hong Kong could be achieved.[23] The most important contribution of Wu to China's reform was perhaps his advice to Beijing as early as 1983 that a bridge linking Hong Kong with Macau and Zhuhai should be built. Yet, his ideas were opposed by some government officials in Hong Kong until 2002 when he raised this idea again to PRC authorities, who then decided to study and implement his plan. The completion of the Hong Kong-

---

[19] Posters on the display board of Hong Kong business people's contributions to China's economic reform and modernization, Hong Kong Convention and Exhibition Centre, August 10, 2018.
[20] Posters on the display board of Hong Kong business people's contributions to China's economic reform and modernization, Hong Kong Convention and Exhibition Centre, August 10, 2018.
[21] Hong Kong TVB interview with Gordon Wu, October 6, 2018.
[22] Ibid.
[23] Ibid.

Zhuhai-Macau bridge in 2018 was a testimony to the far-sightedness of Gordon Wu, whose ideas and efforts at helping the PRC modernize its infrastructure projects were pivotal. He advised the people of Hong Kong that "we should not look down upon the mainlanders but we should ask how much our young people improve themselves."[24] He concludes that the HKSAR has strengths in its rule of law and relatively free foreign exchange system and that the PRC's talents can and will help the mainland and Hong Kong develop the innovative technology and business sectors. Wu stands out as a pragmatic Hong Kong-born business elite who has been continuing to contribute his ideas and efforts at assisting China's economic modernization.

Another Hong Kong businessman, Tsang Hin-chi, was praised by the PRC government for his contributions to the motherland's economic modernization. Tsang was born in a poor family in Guangdong and moved to reside in Hong Kong in 1968 at the age of 34. He worked hard as a grassroots-level and self-employed worker repairing and making ties in the late 1960s and then his business under the brand name of Goldlion Group expanded rapidly in the early 1970s. From 1978 to 1986 he began to invest heavily in helping his hometown Meizhou develop the tie factory and many other schools.[25] In November 2016, his son Tsang Chi-ming set up an education foundation for youth development, focusing on how to inspire them to "love China and Hong Kong" and to "develop correct worldviews."[26] The cases of Tsang Hin-chi and his son showed how the PRC authorities embraced successful Hong Kong business people into the umbrella of united front and the motherland's modernization efforts.

In short, co-optation of Hong Kong's business elites has positive functions in the PRC's modernization. Their expertise, knowledge, ideas and capital can facilitate China's development and contribute to its infrastructure projects. The investment of Hong Kong business people in the PRC is a testimony to their confidence toward the mainland's economic development. It can and will stimulate more overseas Chinese to follow suit.

Table 10.2 sums up the major contributions of many other Hong Kong business people to China's modernization. From the perspective of united

---

[24] Ibid.
[25] Posters on the display board of Hong Kong business people's contributions to China's economic reform and modernization, Hong Kong Convention and Exhibition Centre, August 10, 2018.
[26] Ibid.

Table 10.2 The contributions of Hong Kong Business Elites to China's modernization

Name	The contributions to China's modernization
Annie Wu Suk-ching	Established an airline food company and assisted the development of China's airline food industry
Henry Fong Yun-wah	Donated money to improve China's development in science, education, medical systems after 1977
Lim Por-yen	Assisted the Shantou special economic zone to build up an exhibition center
Kwok Tak-seng	Built schools in Guangdong province and nurtured the development talented individuals
Tin Ka-ping	Established the Tin Ka-ping foundation and built many schools in different parts of China
Lui Che-woo	Promoted the development of Chinese culture and education and donated money to benefit 20 universities and 122 primary and secondary schools in the mainland
Sir Run Run Shaw	Donated money to run schools after 1985 and assisted China in the process of preserving national cultural relics
Stanley Ho Hung-sun	Established the Stanley Ho Hung-sun Aerospace Science and Technology Talent Training Foundation in 1990 and promoted the development of Chinese art and culture
Sir Gordon Wu	Assisted the development of private enterprises in the PRC and promoted the mainland's economic development by investing in the construction of various infrastructure projects

Source: This table is constructed from the posters and display boards in the Exhibition of the 40th Anniversary of China's Reform and Opening Up, Hall 3B, Hong Kong Convention and Exhibition Centre (New Wing) from August 10, 2018, to August 12, 2018, an event that was organized by Hong Kong Ta Kung Wen Wei Media Group Limited

front, the contributions of Hong Kong business elites to China's modernization can not only win the hearts and minds of more Hong Kong people but also attract other overseas Chinese to return and invest in the PRC.

Co-opting the Democrats

The PRC authorities have since July 1, 1997, been making extra efforts at co-opting some Hong Kong democrats for the sake of not only luring political foes to its side but also dividing the political opponents (Table 10.3). This strategy has been working smoothly, especially since the eruption of the 2014 Occupy Central Movement, because some moderate democrats, such as Ronny Tong of the Civic Party, and Tik Chi-yuen and

Table 10.3 Co-opting pro-democracy elites

Name (political party affiliation before co-optation)	Political position in Hong Kong and/or mainland China
Lau Kong-wah (United Democrats of Hong Kong)	1. The Secretary for Home Affairs (2015–present) 2. Undersecretary for Constitutional and Mainland Affairs (2012–2015) 3. Executive Council member (2008–2012) 4. Legislative Council member (1998–2012) 5. Provisional Legislative Council member (1997–1998) 6. District Council member (1985–2003 and 2011–2012)
Lau Nai-keung (Meeting Point)	1. Basic Law Committee member (2007–2018) 2. CPPCC Member (1987–2007)
Tik Chi-yuen (Democratic Party)	1. Legislative Council member (1991–1995)
Nelson Wong Sing-chi (Democratic Party)	1. Legislative Council member (2000–2004 and 2008–2012) 2. District Council member (1991–1994, 1999–2003 and 2007–2011)
Ronny Tong Ka-wah (Civic Party)	1. Executive Council member (2017–present) 2. Legislative Council member (2004–2015)
Anthony Cheung Bing-leung (Democratic Party)	1. Transport and Housing Bureau (2012–2017) 2. Executive Council member (2005–2017)

Sources: See https://www.post852.com/179322/, access date: March 5, 2019; https://www.hk01.com/, access date: March 5, 2019; https://thestandnews.com/politics/, access date: March 5, 2019; and https://www.hk01.com/, access date: March 5, 2019

Wong Sing-chi of the Democratic Party, disagreed with the ways in which the radical and confrontational democrats pushed for democratization in the HKSAR. Table 10.3 illustrates that while some Hong Kong democrats gradually changed their political allegiance from the pan-democratic camp to the pro-Beijing front, others withdrew from their previously affiliated parties and formed new groups. Ronny Tong was one of the Civic Party's barristers who rose up against the legislation on Article 23 of the Basic Law in July 2003. However, he felt that the Occupy Central Movement went too far to exert pressure on the central government in Beijing to make concessions on Hong Kong's democratization. Hence, shortly after the vote against the government's political reform plan in the summer of 2015, he decided to withdraw from the Civic Party and formed a political think tank named the Path of Democracy. Similarly, due to the divergent opinions among the democrats on the desirability of the 2014 Occupy Central Movement, Tik Chi-yuen and Wong Sing-chi left the Democratic

Party and formed the Third Force, a political group that has become relatively inactive since its failure in the 2016 Legislative Council direct election. Tik publicly supported the need for the national education in the HKSAR, while Wong criticized the democrats for their obstinacy in opposing the government's political reform plan in the summer of 2015.

Other democrats who changed sides include Lau Kong-wah, who was a founding member of the United Democrats of Hong Kong (UDHK) but who later quit the party and joined the pro-Beijing DAB. Lau was criticized by some democrats as a political opportunist when he left the UDHK and formed a political group named Civic Force in the New Territories East. The Civic Force evolved into a pro-government and pro-Beijing political group composed of district councilors and activists to participate in the local and legislative elections. Lau was directly elected as a legislative councilor, making his crucial transition to become a member of the top policy-making Executive Council in 2008. In 2012, Lau joined the HKSAR government as an undersecretary for constitutional and mainland affairs, thereby climbing his political ladder to the top echelon of the Hong Kong government.

Apart from Lau, the late Lau Nai-keung was a founding member of the pressure group named Meeting Point in the 1980s. He wrote a Chinese monograph in support of China's assertion of its sovereignty over Hong Kong at a time when the Sino-British negotiation over Hong Kong took place in 1982–84. The PRC authorities regarded his political view as patriotic and politically utilizable, thus co-opting him into the pro-Beijing side, grooming him to be a Hong Kong member of the CPPCC and later appointing him to the influential Basic Law Committee. Before Lau passed away in November 2018, he wrote many commentaries in public, staunchly supporting Beijing's policy toward Hong Kong and praising the Liaison Office for supporting the campaign of Carrie Lam in her 2017 Chief Executive election.

Finally, Anthony Cheung Bing-leung, who had been the chairman of the pro-democracy Meeting Point from 1989 to 1994, resigned from the Democratic Party vice-chairmanship in 2004 when factionalism erupted between his moderate Meeting Point members and the more pro-welfarist socialist democrats. In 2002, Cheung tried to participate in the Hong Kong NPC election, but he failed to get sufficient nominations to enter the preliminary election.[27] His gesture was that he portrayed himself as a political moderate to Beijing. After the ideological split within the

---

[27] *Apple Daily*, November 11, 2002.

Democratic Party, Cheung joined the HKSAR government in 2005 as a member of the Executive Council until 2017. Although Cheung was originally not explicitly pro-Beijing, his political moderation has become a relatively easy target of co-optation by the HKSAR government. After Cheung joined the HKSAR government, he has appeared to become more pro-Beijing than before. For instance, he publicly supported the co-location arrangement between the PRC and the HKSAR in having the high-speed railway station and custom checkpoints located inside Hong Kong.[28]

Co-opting Former Civil Servants and Attacking Pro-Democracy Former Bureaucrats

The PRC authorities have also paid special attention to woo the political support of civil servants, who are however expected to be politically neutral in the HKSAR. Given that civil servants possess their own political views, the PRC officials grasp this opportunity of the individual right to express their political views to identify suitable civil servants for political co-optation. After all, co-opting some civil servants is necessary for the PRC's new united front work because their expertise, knowledge and experiences in running the HKSAR government are cherished as assets from Beijing's standpoint.

Table 10.4 shows those civil servants who have been co-opted into the PRC political institutions as either CPPCC members or NPC members. They include the former security officials Ambrose Lee and Lai Tung-kwok; former anti-corruption commissioners Timothy Tong and Fanny Law; former police commissioners Andy Tsang and Tang King-shing; former secretaries for home affairs David Lan and Patrick Ho; former health officials Margaret Chan and Ko Wing-man; former Chief Secretaries Henry Tang and Rafael Hui; former constitutional affairs secretary Raymond Tam; and former education secretary Arthur Li. Obviously, these former senior civil servants whose portfolios ranged from police to anti-corruption work, from health to education, from constitutional affairs to security and from finance to administrative leadership, tended to be the crucial targets of political co-optation into the PRC institutions.

---

[28] Sum Lok-kei, "Call to explain co-location deal," *The Standard*, January 4, 2018, in http://www.thestandard.com.hk/section-news.php?id=191322&sid=4, access date: March 18, 2019.

Table 10.4 Co-opting Hong Kong civil servants

Name of civil servant	Position in the HKSAR government	Political position in China Chinese Politics
Ambrose Lee Siu-kwong	Secretary for Security (2003–2012) Commissioner for the Independent Commission Against Corruption (2002–2003)	Hong Kong member of the NPC (2012–2018)
Timothy Tong	Commissioner for the Independent Commission Against Corruption (2007–2012) Commissioner of Customs and Excise (2003–2007)	CPPCC Member (2013–2018)
Lai Tung-kwok	Secretary for Security (2002–2017) Undersecretary for Security (2009–2012) Director of Immigration (2002–2008)	CPPCC Member (2018–present)
Andy Tsang Wai Hung	Commissioner of the Hong Kong Police Force (2011–2015)	CPPCC Member (2018–)
Fanny Law Fan Chiu-fun	Executive Council member (2012–present) Commissioner for the Independent Commission Against Corruption (2006–2007) Permanent Secretary for Education and Manpower (2002–2006) Secretary for Education and Manpower (2000–2002)	Hong Kong member of the NPC (2008–2018)
Tang King-shing	Commissioner of the Hong Kong Police Force (2007–2011)	CPPCC Member (2013–2018)
Raymond Tam Chi-yuen	Secretary for Constitutional and Mainland Affairs (2011–2017) Director of the Chief Executive's Office (2009–2011) Undersecretary of the Constitutional and Mainland Affairs Bureau (2008–2009)	NPC Deputy (2018–)
Rafael Hui Si-yan	Unofficial Member of the Executive Council (2007–2009) Chief Secretary for Administration (2005–2007) Secretary for Financial Services (1995–2000)	CPPCC Member (2008–2013)
David Lan	Secretary for Home Affairs (1997–2000)	CPPCC Member (2003–2013)
Patrick Ho Chi-ping	Secretary for Home Affairs (2002–2007)	CPPCC Member (2008–2013)

(*continued*)

Table 10.4 (continued)

Name of civil servant	Position in the HKSAR government	Political position in China Chinese Politics
Ko Wing-man	Secretary for Food and Health (2012–2017)	CPPCC Member (2018–)
Margaret Chan Fung Fu-chun	Director of Health (1994–2003)	CPPCC Member (2018–)
Arthur Li Kwok-cheung	Secretary for Education and Manpower (2002–2007)	CPPCC Member (2013–)
Henry Tang Ying-yen	Chief Secretary for Administration (2007–2011) Financial Secretary of Hong Kong (2003–2007) Secretary for Commerce, Industry and Technology (2002–2003)	CPPCC Member (2013–)

Sources: *Sing Pao*, January 26, 2003, p. A10; *Ming Pao*, January 26, 2008, p. A04; *Metro Daily*, March 14, 2008, p. P8; *Apple Daily*, January 31, 2013, p. A2; *Ta Kung Pao*, February 3, 2013, p. A1; *Hong Kong Economic Journal*, January 24, 2018, p. A11; *Wen Wei Po*, March 3, 2018, p. A5

Another crucial target of political co-optation was the former Secretary for Security Regina Ip, who supported and initiated the controversial legislation on Article 23 in early half of 2003. After the mass protests against the Tung Chee-hwa government in July 2003, Ip resigned from the administration and went to Stanford University in the United States to pursue her studies. When she returned to Hong Kong, Ip has been participating actively in politics, forming the New People's Party, grooming young elites to participate in local elections and aspiring to run in the 2017 Chief Executive election. However, the PRC authorities did not support her to run in the 2017 Chief Executive election, mostly because of their concern about her negative political image left over from the debacle of the enactment of Article 23 legislation in mid-2003. Although Ip lost the full political support from Beijing, she has remained explicitly pro-Beijing, saying that all American goods are "dangerous" in the midst of the US-China trade war in late 2018 and vowing to use Huawei i-phone after the Sabrina Meng incident in Canada.[29]

Unlike Ip and other former senior civil servants who have been politically co-opted, Anson Chan Fang On-san, who was the former Chief

---

[29] *Ming Pao*, December 11, 2018, p. A18 and *Ming Pao*, December 10, 2018, p. A18.

Secretary of the HKSAR government from 1997 to 2002, is regarded as a pro-democracy and "pro-foreign" politician by Beijing. The pro-Beijing mass media in the HKSAR often criticizes Anson Chan as a Hong Kong person for "betraying Hong Kong interests" and "working in conformity with the United States to check and balance China."[30] Anson Chan is constantly seen by the pro-Beijing media as the "enemy" of the HKSAR administration and the PRC state for several reasons. First, she has been supporting the pro-democracy movement after she retired from the government in 2002. Second, during her term of office as the Chief Secretary, it was an open secret that she was at loggerheads with the former Chief Executive Tung Chee-hwa over policy issues, especially her opposition to any policy that would accelerate Hong Kong's economic integration with the mainland. Third, Chan has been often visiting foreign countries, especially the United States and United Kingdom, to talk about Hong Kong's political development. Since she is regarded as the "conscience for Hong Kong" and speaks her mind about the complexities and difficulties of the "one country, two systems," PRC authorities have seen her as a Hongkonger blemishing the image of Hong Kong and mainland China. In an era when many PRC authorities are anti-foreign, especially as China's rapid economic rise has aroused the suspicions and concerns of some Western and Asian states, Anson Chan's frequent interactions with foreign officials and politicians are labeled as a political "traitor." The political correctness of PRC authorities in Beijing, and their followers in the HKSAR, must view Chan as a political opponent whose activities have to be criticized and labeled as "incorrect."

Since the dominance of Beijing's hardline conservative nationalists on its policy toward Hong Kong in 2012,[31] there has been an obvious tendency of the pro-Beijing mass media in the HKSAR to label and severely criticize those democrats, including Anson Chan, Charles Mok and Civic Party members Dennis Kwok and Alvin Yeung who often interact with American, British and foreign officials on Hong Kong matters, as "traitors" of Hong Kong. It is crystal clear that the criterion of political correctness focuses on whether or not a local politician often contacts foreigners and complains to them about Hong Kong's political "underde-

---

[30] Editorial, "Working in conformity with the United States to check and balance China, Anson Chan is betraying the Hong Kong interests," *Wen Wei Po*, March 18, 2019, p. A4.

[31] Sonny Shiu-Hing Lo, "Ideologies and Factionalism in Beijing-Hong Kong Relations," *Asian Survey*, vol. 58, no. 3 (June 2018), pp. 392–415.

velopment" and "decay."[32] The boundaries between Beijing's friends and enemies have become very clear since the politicization of Hong Kong in 2014, when the Occupy Central Movement challenged the political bottom line of Beijing on Hong Kong's democratization.

Co-opting Individual Educators

Given that the educational sector is difficult for PRC authorities to influence and control, as the previous chapter has shown, they have been targeting at individual educators, especially the leaders at Hong Kong's universities, so that some indirect influences on universities can be exerted. PRC officials in the HKSAR have various opportunities and channels, both formal and informal, to contact and lobby the top leaders of local tertiary institutions. Table 10.5 shows how the academic leaders of ten universities in the HKSAR published a joint statement to not only condemn the "abuses" in the freedom of expression but also call for the abandonment of any advocacy of Hong Kong independence, which to them was and is "unconstitutional." The entire event was triggered in September 2017, when some banners and leaflets supporting Hong Kong "independence" appeared in the campuses of some universities. The irresponsible remarks made by a few students at the Education University of Hong Kong over the death of a son of a government official ignited the public outcry over the behavior of some university students. Eventually, the principals of ten universities issued a joint statement denouncing any call for "Hong Kong independence" and appealing to students not to violate the Hong Kong law. The entire incident illustrated that the top officials of local universities were united against the student call for "Hong Kong independence," although that there were rumors about the former president of the University of Hong Kong Professor Peter Mathieson harbored reservations over the content of the joint statement.[33] However, under the circumstances in which other university officials were eager to express their political stance, there was little choice for him except for following suit, especially as he was not very familiar with local politics.

---

[32] Jeff Loo, "A localist's critique of Hong Kong's political development: Political decay, legitimacy crisis and reverse democratization," *Asian Education and Development Studies*, vol. 7, no. 1 (2018), pp. 76–88.

[33] *Apple Daily*, November 8, 2017.

10 CO-OPTING INDIVIDUALS WITH EXTERNAL IMPLICATIONS: BUSINESS... 355

Table 10.5 Chronology of a joint statement of the principals of ten universities

Date	Event
September 5, 2017	The "Hong Kong independence" banner and leaflets appeared in the cultural square at the Chinese University of Hong Kong, whose officials reprimanded that such action violated the "rule of law" and that banner and leaflets would be demolished. About twenty students gathered in the evening to protect the guardian banners at the cultural square.
September 6, 2017	The slogan "Hong Kong independence" was posted on the City University's student union display board. The security guards at the City University removed the word "independence" and such action was recorded by some students. The students' representatives argued that such action intended to suppress their freedom of speech.
September 7, 2017	Some controversial slogans were posted by students at the Education University of Hong Kong, who went so far as to "congratulate" the death of a son of a principal secretary named Christine Choi Yuk-lin. Officials of the Education University reprimanded such student remarks and apologized to the affected government official.
September 8, 2017	Members of the pro-Beijing New Territories Different Sectors Concern Group and Defend Hong Kong Campaign went to the Education University of Hong Kong. They strongly condemned the cold-blooded youths who posted "slogans that annihilated humanity" and urged the university to investigate the incident. Chief Executive Carrie Lam and Education University's principal Stephen Cheung Yan-leung also criticized the students' behavior and they both said that "freedom of speech" had its own limits.
September 9, 2017	Some controversial slogans related to mainland dissident Liu Xiaobo and his wife Liu Xia were posted at the Education University's display board. The university issued a statement saying that it strongly condemned such malicious slogan at the student union display board.
September 11, 2017	A student at the Chinese University of Hong Kong started a signature campaign calling for a referendum within the university on the question of "independence."
September 13, 2017	The Hong Kong Polytechnic University demolished all slogans related to "independence" because it believed that such action would avoid students breaking the law.
September 15, 2017	The principals of eight public universities and also the principals of the Open University and the Shue Yan University issued a joint statement against any pro-independence behavior. They asserted that the call for "Hong Kong Independence" was unconstitutional and that it would violate Hong Kong law.

Sources: *Apply Daily*, September 6, 2017, p. A8; *Apply Daily*, September 7, 2017, p. A5; *Apply Daily*, September 8, 2017, p. A12; *Apply Daily*, September 9, 2017, p. A2; *Wen Wei Po*, September 9, 2017, p. A4; *Ta Kung Pao*, September 9, 2017, p. A; *Apply Daily*, September 10, 2017, p. A2; *Apply Daily*, September 13, 2017, p. A8; *Apply Daily*, September 14, 2017, p. A15; *Apply Daily*, September 16, 2017, p. A1

Coincidentally, after the September declaration against independence, Stephen Cheung of the Education University of Hong Kong was later appointed to be a Hong Kong member of the CPPCC in January 2018.[34] Similarly, Chan Cheuk-hay, the principal of the Hong Kong College of Technology, was appointed as a Hong Kong member of the CPPCC at the same time. Chan had decided to expel some defiant students who refused to stand up during the process of signing the PRC national anthem in the graduation ceremony in December 2017.[35] A member of the Board of Directors of the College, Lau Pui-king, said that teachers failed to educate the students to behave properly, and her remarks triggered the resignation and protest of six teachers. After the incident, Chief Executive Carrie Lam praised Chan's action and added that students should pay their respect to the national anthem. The appointment of Cheung into the CPPCC could perhaps be interpreted as an indication that the PRC authorities were satisfied with his handling of the deviant behavior of a few students immediately after the death of the son of an appointed official Christine Choi Yuk-lin. Chan Cheuk-hay's co-optation could be seen as a political reward to his seemingly hardline but politically "correct" attitude toward the defiant students who failed to respect the PRC national anthem. Political rewards have been extensively utilized by PRC authorities in their new united front work targeted at the people of Hong Kong.

Co-opting the Taiwanese: United Front Seen by Taiwanese as National Security and Espionage

The PRC co-optation of the Hong Kong elites has significant implications for Taiwan, because mainland Chinese officials have been targeting at various Taiwanese politicians and business people and wooing them to support Beijing's policy toward Taipei. The intention is clear: the PRC's new united front work toward Taiwanese aims at winning the hearts and minds of more Taiwan people so as to speed up the processes of economic interactions and integration between the mainland and Taiwan in the short run, and to achieve the long-term objective of reunification. Although the long-term objective of reunification is difficult to be achieved, especially as most Taiwan people see the Hong Kong version of the "one country, two systems" as unworkable and inapplicable to Taiwan, PRC officials have

---

[34] *Oriental Daily*, January 25, 2018.
[35] See https://www.hk01.com/, December 16, 2017, access date: March 19, 2019.

been reaching out to politicians from various parties in Taiwan. Table 10.6 illustrates some major Taiwan political figures who went to the mainland and met PRC officials, including Lien Chan, Eric Chu, Hung Hsiu-chu and Wu Poh-hsiung of the KMT, James Soong of the People First Party, Yok Mu-ming of the New Party and independent Ko Wen-je. The PRC authorities sent very high-ranking leaders to meet them, including the former PRC President Hu Jintao, current PRC President Xi Jinping, provincial party secretaries and CPPCC chairpersons. From Beijing's perspective, the more interactions with the Taiwanese politicians, the more vulnerable the Taiwanese to its united front work.

However, the Taiwan government under the Democratic Progressive Party (DPP) has seen the PRC's united front work as not only threatening Taiwan's national security but also representing espionage activities leading to the "betrayal" of some Taiwan people. In June 2018, New Party spokesman Wang Ping-chung and other members were arrested on the charge of spying and "violating" the national security law.[36] According to Taiwan's prosecutors, Wang cooperated with youth members, Ho Hanting and Lin Ming-cheng to organize a spy network with financial support from the PRC. The suspects allegedly worked with a convicted mainland Chinese spy named Zhou Hongxu, who set up a pro-reunification propaganda website. The Taiwan prosecution also claimed that the New Party members initiated the Association of New Chinese Sons and Daughters and the Chinese Culture Rejuvenation Association at the National Taiwan University in order to influence some Taiwan youths. Clearly, the national security apparatus in Taiwan has been conducting surveillance on not only those Taiwan people who interact with mainlanders but also the financial sources of pro-reunification websites.

As early as 2014, some Taiwanese people in Shanghai and Zhejiang became the target of the mainland's new united front work. In the city of Ningbo, mainland united front officials spent 110,000 yuan to buy life and traffic accident insurance for 137 Taiwanese business people.[37] Although holding CPPCC membership is a breach of the law in Taiwan as

---

[36] Jason Pan, "New Party arrests show China's deep infiltration: pundit," *Taipei Times*, June 15, 2018, p. 3, in http://www.taipeitimes.com/News/taiwan/archives/2018/06/15/2003694912, access date: March 20, 2019.

[37] Yimou Lee and Faith Hung, "Special Report: How China's Shadowy Agency is working to absorb Taiwan," Reuters, November 27, 2014, in https://www.reuters.com/article/us-taiwan-china-special-report/special-report-how-chinas-shadowy-agency-is-working-to-absorb-taiwan-idUSKCN0JB01T20141127, access date: March 20, 2019.

Table 10.6 Major Taiwan political figures who met mainland Chinese officials

Name (political party affiliation)	Time of the visit to the mainland	Purposes	Key Chinese officials who interacted with the Taiwan side
Lien Chan (Kuomintang)	April 26, 2005–May 3, 2005	1. Discover a new path of developing cross-strait relations 2. Find possible solutions to avoid conflicts between Taipei and Beijing	1. PRC President Hu Jintao 2. Party Secretary of Jiangsu Province, Li Yuanchao 3. Chairman of CPPCC, Jia Qinglin
James Soong Chu-yu (people first party)	May 5, 2005–May 13, 2005	1. Looking for the root of the common ancestry and building a bridge between the two sides in the future 2. Pursue stable cross-strait relations 3. Discover possible solutions for future Beijing-Taipei relations	1. PRC President Hu Jintao 2. Head of Taiwan Affairs Office of the State Council, Chen Yunlin 3. Chairman of CPPCC, Jia Qinglin
Yok Mu-ming (new party)	July 6, 2005–July 13, 2005	Build up the spirit of national unity	1. PRC President Hu Jintao 2. Party Secretary of Guangdong province, Zhang Dejiang 3. Chairman of CPPCC, Jia Qinglin
Wu Poh-hsiung (Kuomintang)	May 26, 2008–May 31, 2008	The two sides would shelve the dispute over sovereignty but would promote direct flights between the two places so as to benefit the mainland tourists visiting Taiwan	1. PRC President Hu Jintao 2. Chairman of CPPCC, Jia Qinglin 3. Head of the Taiwan Affairs Office of the State Council, Chen Yunlin
Eric Chu Li-luan (Kuomintang)	May 2, 2015–May 7, 2015	Under the 1992 consensus in which both sides agreed to disagree on the meaning of one China, both sides would deepen mutual consensus and build trust	1. PRC President Xi Jingping 2. Chairman of CPPCC, Yu Zhengsheng

(*continued*)

Table 10.6 (continued)

Name (political party affiliation)	Time of the visit to the mainland	Purposes	Key Chinese officials who interacted with the Taiwan side
Hung Hsiu-chu (Kuomintang)	October 30, 2016– November 3, 2016	The KMT acts as a bridge to benefit the people of Taiwan, to promote Taiwan's participation in international affairs, to minimize the mainland military threat and to defuse the time bomb in cross-strait relations	1. President of PRC, Xi Jingping 2. President of CPPCC, Yu Zhengsheng
Ko Wen-je (Independent)	July 1, 2017–July 3, 2017	Deepen the interactions between Shanghai and Taipei	1. Shanghai Mayor, Ying Yong 2. Head of the Taiwan Affairs Office of the State Council, Zhang Zhijun
Han Kuo-yu (Kuomintang mayor in Kaohsiung)	March 22 to March 28, 2019	Promote Kaohsiung's economy and enhance economic interactions between Kaohsiung and the cities of Hong Kong, Macao, Shenzhen and Xiamen	1. Director of Hong Kong Liaison Office, Wang Zhiman 2. Director of Macao Liaison Office, Fu Ziying 3. Director of the Taiwan Affairs Office, Liu Jieyi

Sources: *United Daily News*, April 27, 2005, p. 1; April 29, 2005, p. 1; May 6, 2005, p. 1; May 9, 2005, p. 1; July 7, 2005, p. 1; July 13, 2005, p. 1; May 22, 2005, p. 2; May 28, 2005, p. 4; May 3, 2015, p. 2; October 29, 2016, p. 2; July 2, 2017, p. 8; *Liberty Times*, October 30, 2016, p. 8; *Liberty Times*, March 23, 2019; *Liberty Times*, March 30, 2019

Taiwanese citizens cannot take political office in the mainland, the Association of Taiwan Investment Enterprises on the Mainland, which was composed of 130 Taiwanese business interest groups in the PRC, lobbied the Taiwan President Ma Ying-jeou in December 2012 to change the Taipei policy, but it failed to do so.[38]

Yet, the case of Lu Li-an in 2017 showed that the PRC's new united front work was aggressive to such an extent that a few Taiwanese began to shift their political allegiance from Taipei to Beijing. Born in Taiwan and educated in the United Kingdom for her doctorate in literature, Lu was

[38] Ibid.

Table 10.7 The chronology of the Lu Li-an incident

Year	Event
1997	Lu Li-an went to teach at Fudan University together with her husband
2002	Lu participated in the Taiwan hometown association work in Shanghai and served the Taiwanese people living there
2014	Applied to the CCP to be a member
2015	Became a preparatory member of the CCP
2016	She formally became a member of the CCP
2017	Lu used the title of "a representative from the Taiwan province" in public, meaning that she was co-opted as a member of the CPPCC in the mainland
2017	The DPP government quickly revoked her citizenship and household registration status in Taiwan
2017	Lu became one of the ten Chinese who were selected by the official China Central Television as the person who made other people feel emotional and sentimental

Source: *Yazhou Zhoukan,* August 19, 2018, no. 32, in https://www.yzzk.com/cfm/blogger3.cfm?id=1533785760789&author=%E5%BC%B5%E6%AE%BF%E6%96%87, access date: March 20, 2019

hired as a university teacher at Fudan University in 1997 (Table 10.7). She began to participate in Shanghai's Taiwanese hometown association in 2002, but then applied to the CCP to become a member in 2014. In 2015, she was allowed to be a preparatory member of the CCP and then became a full CCP member one year later. In 2017, Lu even used the title of a representative from the "Taiwan province" in public, meaning that she became a CPPCC member in the mainland. In response, the Taiwan government under the DPP leadership in 2017 decided to revoke her Taiwanese household registration status. Politically, Lu remarked that she joined the CCP not because of the attraction of fame and profit but because of her conviction that the Chinese nation should be reunited between the mainland and Taiwan. She said: "I feel honored to be a Taiwanese. I feel proud of being a Chinese. I love Taiwan and the mainland. Such love is the same as loving my father and mother."[39] As such, Lu's identity as a Chinese culturally and nationally prompted her move to join the CCP and act as a bridge between Beijing and Taipei. The case of Lu demonstrated how the PRC succeeded in co-opting a Taiwanese into the mainland political institution.

In response to the DPP government's cancelation of Lu's citizenship status, the former KMT President Ma Ying-jeou said that the governmen-

[39] Ibid.

tal reaction was excessive.[40] In the minds of the pro-reunification Taiwanese, Lu's application and action to join the CCP was nothing special but represented the natural outcome of a Taiwanese who has strong cultural and political identity in the mainland. Ma added that he saw Lu's action as the freedom of a Taiwan citizen. However, pro-independence Taiwanese criticized Lu as not only a "CCP member holding a Buddhist scripture to conduct united front work" but also an irony because her father was pro-Japanese in the past.[41] Clearly, the identity division between the pro-reunification and pro-independence Taiwanese shaped the varying responses to Lu's move. To put it in another way, the different responses were a testimony to the political divide between the blue and green camps in Taiwan.

The PRC government since February 2017 has implemented its thirty-one policy privileges toward the Taiwan business people and students who wish to invest, work and study in mainland China. When Beijing formulated the Greater Bay Area plan for Hong Kong and Macao in mid-2018, it also used the new residency permits for the people of Hong Kong, Macao and Taiwan to be an instrument of co-opting more Taiwanese people to work and reside in the PRC. In response to more Taiwanese who apply for the mainland residency permit, the DPP government even proposed in early 2019 that those Taiwanese who got mainland residency permits would perhaps be barred from entering the Taiwan civil service. Clearly, while the PRC's united front work targeting at the Taiwanese has been working smoothly since 2017, the DPP regime in Taiwan has been adopting counter-united front measures to minimize the national security threats to the island republic.

Another case of a Taiwanese who was appointed by the PRC as a CPPCC member is Ling Yau-sze. Born in Taiwan and migrating to Hong Kong at the age of 17, Ling became politically red later in 2019 as she was appointed to the CPPCC. Her father had been a KMT solider fighting against the PLA. After Ling migrated to Hong Kong, she studied at the University of Hong Kong and later joined the Central Policy Unit of the HKSAR government as a researcher. In 2019, Ling's bold remarks raised the eyebrows of some people in Taiwan. She said:

[40] Ibid.
[41] See https://newtalk.tw/news/view/2018-03-03/116009, access date: March 21, 2019.

There is only one China in the world. The whole China has one legitimate government and it is called the PRC government. I feel proud of being a honest Chinese who participate in the national political system. The PRC is the only legitimate government in China and it is also the legitimate regime. This status is the most important in the process of cross-strait reunification. In future peaceful negotiations, China as the legitimate government has to abide by the main principle of "one China, one constitution, one central government, and one military." If "Taiwan independence" occurs, then those Taiwanese have to shoulder the responsibility of citizens who commit crime.[42]

According to the Taiwan Interior Ministry, Ling's acceptance of the CPPCC appointment and her remarks violated the law concerning the relations between Taiwan and the mainland, and therefore she was penalized for NT500,000.[43] In response, Ling said that the Taiwan law violated her right and that the penalty on her was "unreasonable."[44] Interestingly, a mainland commentator Zhang Lifan said that since Ling harped on the same themes as what the CCP viewed, she showed "almost low-level redness."[45] Regardless of who was right or wrong, Ling's appointment as the CPPCC member and her provocative remarks illustrate not only the success of the PRC united front work in co-opting her but also a boomerang effect of arousing severe criticisms against her.

In March 2019, the Kaohsiung mayor Han Kuo-yu, who is a Kuomintang member, visited Hong Kong, Macao, Shenzhen and Xiamen. He met the directors of the Liaison Office in both Hong Kong and Macao and was the target of the PRC's united front work. Han's critics saw his direct contacts with PRC officials as problematic, but his visits highlighted how PRC officials grasped the golden opportunity to woo him to forge closer relations with the mainland, especially as the new Kaohsiung mayor was keen to enhance Kaohsiung's exports to the Greater China region. The PRC's united front work on the Taiwanese is in full swing as President Xi Jinping is eager to tackle the question of Taiwan's political future perhaps in his lifetime.

---

[42] Ibid.
[43] See https://www.bbc.com/zhongwen/trad/chinese-news-47621219, access date: March 31, 2019.
[44] Ibid.
[45] Ibid.

Table 10.8 Huang Xiangmo's donation to Australian political parties

Year	Declared donation amount to the Australia Labor Party (ALP) (AUS$)	Declared donation amount to the Liberal Party of Australia (LPA) (AUS$)	Declared donation amount to the National Party of Australia (NPA) (AUS$)
2012	300,000	0	0
2013	600,000	865,000	0
2014	60,000	200,000	0
2015	50,000	20,000	0
2016	80,000	12,200	15,000
Total	1,090,000	1,207,000	15,000

Source: See https://www.smh.com.au/politics/federal/a-man-of-many-dimensions-the-big-chinese-donor-now-in-canberra-s-sights-20190206-p50vzt.html, access date: March 6, 2019

THE CASE OF HUANG XIANGMO IN AUSTRALIA: UNITED FRONT AS VIOLATING DONATION LAW

The case of Huang Xiangmo showed that the PRC's united front work in Australia could violate the donation law there. Born in Guangdong and later migrating to Hong Kong and then Australia in 2011, Huang became an overseas Chinese businessman donating money to Australia's Labor Party, Liberal Party and National Party (Table 10.8). In 2015, Huang was the chairman of the Australian Council for the Promotion of the Peaceful Reunification of China, an interest group that could be seen as an arm of the PRC's united front work targeted at some overseas Chinese and foreigners. In 2017, an opposition Labor Party member Sam Dastyari was forced to withdraw politics when news reports revealed that his office received cash from Huang to pay legal bills.[46] After intensive investigation into Huang's activities and background, the Australian government in early 2019 revoked his Australian permanent residency and rejected his citizenship application.[47] Huang criticized the Australian government's decision saying that his action of promoting reunification of mainland China and Taiwan was in conformity with Australia's foreign policy toward cross-strait relations. Huang's experiences showed that the PRC's united front outreach could run the risk of being regarded as violating the domestic law of a foreign country, and in this case the donation law of Australia.

[46] "Australia cancels residency of CCP-linked billionaire," *Taipei Times*, February 7, 2019.
[47] Ibid.

Conclusion

Since the HKSAR sovereignty belongs to the PRC, Beijing's extensive and intensive united front activities, ranging from the business people to democrats, and from civil servants to educators, are by no means violating any law of Hong Kong. Nevertheless, united front activities in the form of using individuals and interest groups to lobby for the political support of foreigners and overseas Chinese could be potentially and legally problematic, as with the case of Huang Xiangmo in Australia. Even in Taiwan, united front activities conducted by the PRC on the Taiwanese can be seen as moves "violating" the Taiwan law, threatening Taipei's national security and operating espionage work. As such, the line between legality and illegality is in stark contrast once united front work is conducted in places outside mainland China, Macao and Hong Kong. Taiwan under the rule of the DPP is especially sensitive and resistant to the PRC's united front work, which is seen as politically subversive, legally problematic and socially destabilizing by those Taiwanese who have a very strong Taiwan identity and who harbor pro-Taiwan "independence" sentiments.

CHAPTER 11

Conclusion

The objectives of China's new united front work in the HKSAR are multiple: (1) winning the hearts and minds of more Hong Kong people than ever before, (2) securing most Hong Kong people's support of the central government's policies toward Hong Kong, (3) enhancing patriotism and the Chinese national and politico-cultural identity of the Hong Kong people, (4) achieving Beijing's dominant control or "comprehensive jurisdiction" over Hong Kong, (5) isolating and defeating political enemies and opposition, including the moderate democrats and radical ones, (6) strengthening a coalition of "patriotic" elites governing Hong Kong and (7) protecting Beijing's interest of maintaining the supremacy of "one country," specifically its national security interest. All these objectives have become prominent in the PRC policy toward Hong Kong since the beginning of the Xi Jinping era in March 2013 as he was elected as the PRC President.

Article 22 of the Basic Law says that "no department of the Central People's Government and no province, autonomous region, or municipality directly under the Central Government may intervene in the affairs which the HKSAR administers on its own in accordance with this law."[1] Nevertheless, by convention, the Liaison Office did and does intervene in

---

[1] *The Basic Law of the Hong Kong Special Administrative Region of the People's Republic of China* (Hong Kong: Hong Kong Special Administrative Region Government, April 2017), p. 8, in https://www.basiclaw.gov.hk/en/basiclawtext/images/basiclaw_full_text_en.pdf, access date: March 23, 2019.

the affairs of the HKSAR. It can be argued that, from Beijing's perspective and as the late PRC leader Deng Xiaoping asserted, the central government's intervention in the HKSAR affairs can be positive. The Liaison Office's intervention, or penetrative politics, in Hong Kong is only a matter of degree, as this book has shown.

The role of the Liaison Office in the PRC's new united front work in Hong Kong is significant. It plays the role of organizer, facilitator, coordinator and mobilizer in united front politics. The Liaison Office organizes pro-Beijing groups and the DAB, coordinates among themselves and mobilizes supporters to vote for candidates in the pro-PRC front in elections. It also facilitates the process of developing the patriotic front by holding study sessions immediately after the annual CPPCC and NPC meetings, interpreting the PRC leaders' remarks and policies, creating new pro-Beijing groups, interacting with more Hong Kong people so as to reduce the secrecy of the Liaison Office, encouraging its own staff members to learn Cantonese in order to be better local cadres and organizing daily and weekly meetings with all sectors of the society to deepen the depth and broaden the breath of penetrative politics. In recent years, the Liaison Office has opened its headquarters to the members of the public, conducting new united front work in a far more transparent and grassroots-based manner.

Under the authoritarian regime of President Xi Jinping, the Liaison Office has become a loyal implementation agent characterized by political correctness and positive reports on Hong Kong's "one country, two systems." Shortly after the July 1, 2003, mass protests, Beijing did reflect on its possible miscalculations of Hong Kong's political development. Nevertheless, the Liaison Office under Zhang Xiaoming and Wang Zhimin have shifted to a loyal implementator harping on the same themes with the central government in Beijing. This situation is understandable as the PRC under President Xi has shifted toward "hard" authoritarian by changing the Chinese constitution, terminating the limits on the term of office of both the president and vice-president and utilizing the Standing Committee of the National People's Congress to interpret the Basic Law in November 2016 for the sake of terminating and punishing the disrespectful behavior of two Hong Kong legislators-elect who dared challenging the PRC's legitimacy and authority.

In the context of increasingly "hard" authoritarian regime in the PRC, its united front work in the HKSAR has taken new forms. The tone of the 2014 White Paper on the implementation of the Basic Law emphasized

Beijing's "comprehensive jurisdiction" over Hong Kong. After the promulgation of the revised work regulation on the CCP's united front work in April 2015, and after the establishment of the Central Leading Small Group on United Front in Beijing in July the same year, the PRC's united front work on Hong Kong has taken a sharp turn to not only full mobilization of pro-Beijing forces but also aggressive attacks launched by local patriotic media against the democrats, especially the radical ones. From Article 29 to Article 32 of the revised united front regulations in 2015, united front work in Hong Kong would have to emphasize the support of HKSAR government policies, the consolidation of the national identity of Hong Kong people, the mobilization of Chinese to oppose Taiwan's "independence," and the co-optation of more people to such institutions as the NPC and CPPCC. The events from 2015 to the present prove that the PRC's new united front work has been revived, reactivated, rejuvenated and reorganized. Hence, when President Xi visited Hong Kong in October 2017 and emphasized Beijing's exercise of its "comprehensive jurisdiction" over Hong Kong, it was clear that its united front work in the HKSAR was in full swing. Even the People's Liberation Army that stations in Hong Kong has expanded its outreach to the community by not only visiting schools and opening military camps but also volunteering to clean fallen trees after typhoon attack on the HKSAR.

The PRC's attacks on its political enemies in the HKSAR has been conducted through the local pro-Beijing media. The visit to the United States by local democrats such as Anson Chan, Dennis Kwok and Charles Mok in March 2019 was severely criticized and labeled as "traitors." Their visit in late March coincided with the visit from the Kaohsiung mayor Han Kuo-yu to Hong Kong and Macao. Han was received by officials of the Liaison Office, including Wang Zhimin. The two visits showed how PRC authorities extended their united front hands to Han while denouncing the local democrats who visited the United States as those who "betrayed" the interest of Hong Kong people.

Attacks on political enemies have been accompanied by the utilization of economic incentives to win the hearts and minds of more Hong Kong people. This phenomenon can be seen in the formulation and implementation of the Greater Bay Area in late 2018 and early 2019, respectively. Hong Kong's business people and private sector have been encouraged and mobilized to form interest groups that can help the process of closer economic integration between the HKSAR and Southern China. Other interest groups, ranging from women to youth, have been either consolidated or established to foster linkages between Hong Kong and the other cities in the Greater Bay Area. The plan is reminiscent of the Maoist era in which "policy wind" occurred with central-level officials mobilizing the lower-level ones to implement new policies.[2] As the wind blows stronger, the local-level agents are expected to implement such policies more forcefully. The mobilization of pro-Beijing interest groups in support of the Greater Bay Area plan in early 2019 is the hallmark of such "policy wind" blowing from Beijing to Hong Kong. The "one country, two systems" in the HKSAR has displayed the mainland's political features as "one country" has been heavily emphasized.

In fact, since 2015, the breadth and depth of the PRC's united front work in the HKSAR have been increasing prominently. A new focus on the youth, ethnic minorities, women and scientists can be seen in the new united front campaign. Many new groups involving youth, women, clans and ethnic minorities have been created and encouraged to be volunteers helping the community. Through community work, a sense of belonging is cultivated among the volunteers and penetrative politics has become silently entrenched at the district level. A new pattern has been emerging: there are core interest groups in a particular societal sector so that women, youths, clans and kaifongs can strengthen their coherent social networks through which a stronger sense of Chinese national identity and a greater capability of electoral mobilization can be achieved.

The major continuities of China's united front work in the period before and after the Xi Jinping era are the cross-class nature of its outreach and the persistence of penetrative politics. While the former director of the New China News Agency, Xu Jiatun, emphasized the importance of united front work on the capitalist, middle and working classes, he was criticized for being too close to the capitalist class. The Xi Jinping era has witnessed a balanced approach adopted by the Liaison Office officials to reach out to as many members of the capitalist, middle and working classes as possible. On the other hand, penetrative politics has continued to be significant in China's united front work, because communist-style political dynamics are characterized by the ruling party's political infiltration into the civil society through the creation, utilization and mobilization of various kinds of interest groups to support the regime in power. Although the HKSAR does not have any ruling party, the DAB arguably represents a miniature

---

[2] David Zweig, *Agrarian Radicalism in China, 1968–1981* (Cambridge, Massachusetts: Harvard University Press, 1989), p. 38.

of the CCP in Hong Kong. Moreover, the Fujianese interest groups are like those pro-government clan groups in the mainland, staunchly supporting the ruling regime. The Hong Kong FTU is akin to the All-China Federation of Trade Unions, acting as a unifying agent to rally the members of the working class. The Hong Kong Federation of Women is comparable to the All-China Federation of Women, absorbing the local pro-Beijing women and acting as one of the core groups conducting united front work on other women. The DAB, FTU, Fujianese interest groups, women groups and other pro-Beijing religious groups constitute the transmission belts for the CCP to penetrate into the Hong Kong polity. Penetrative politics in Hong Kong are in many ways similar to that in the PRC. In Hong Kong, penetrative politics has dual purposes: supporting not only the HKSAR administration but also the central government in Beijing. What is new about the PRC penetrative politics in Hong Kong is that it is now openly, visibly and prominently conducted. Utilizing all the open sources, this book has proven the openness, visibility and prominence of the PRC's new united front campaign in the HKSAR.

Beijing has won the hearts and minds of more Hong Kong people than before, judging from the votes gained by the DAB and pro-Beijing forces in legislative direct elections and district elections. Nevertheless, the inroads of pro-Beijing forces have remained more impressive and successful in district-level elections than legislative direct elections. The pro-Beijing forces have captured around 55% of the votes in the direct elections of District Councils. However, they have gained roughly 45% of the votes in the direct elections of Legislative Council. These electoral results mean that many voters are still relatively politically autonomous and free from the influence of the propaganda, mobilization and appeals of pro-Beijing forces. Benny Tai has written: "We hope that the gained understanding of China's sharp power in Hong Kong will enable the international community to formulate an appropriate strategy to respond to the global advancement of authoritarianism by the Chinese Communist Regime."[3] "Sharp power" is characterized by "the use of manipulation to sap the integrity of independent institutions," the limitations on free expression, the distortion of the political environment and the penetration of information into

---

[3] Benny Tai, "Introduction: The Rise of China's Sharp Power in Hong Kong," in Benny Tai, ed., *China's Sharp Power in Hong Kong* (Hong Kong: Hong Kong Civil Hub, 2018), p. 11.

the environment of targeted countries.[4] Our book, however, has found that China's "sharp power" has increased in Hong Kong, but it is not really so sharp in the sense that the electoral votes gained by the pro-Beijing forces cannot completely reverse the so-called sixth-fourth golden rule, which referred to 60% of pro-democracy votes versus 40% of pro-Beijing votes in legislative direct elections from 1991 to 1997. Hence, the PRC's new united front work still needs more diligent efforts for the sake of catching up the popularity of the pro-democracy forces in the coming years.

Indeed, the post-1997 legislature has been artificially and politically manipulated because the existence and persistence of functional constituencies provide the necessary instrument for the pro-Beijing law-makers to veto, block and obstruct the pro-democracy legislators. The pro-democracy forces continue to call for the abolition of functional constituencies, but this demand has been vehemently opposed by the business elites. Given the triple alliance between the PRC, the Hong Kong government and the local capitalist class, it will be very difficult for the local democrats to push for the full democratization of the Hong Kong political system along the path of having a fully directly elected legislature and a Chief Executive directly elected by citizens through universal suffrage. From a realpolitik perspective, the local democrats have to make concessions and ponder how to bargain with PRC authorities in a more skilful manner.

On the other hand, it will take some years, or perhaps decades, for the pro-Beijing forces to turn their electoral support to an absolute majority in the legislative direct elections. It is true that the PRC has enhanced its political influence in Hong Kong, but it cannot easily control and dominate the entire Hong Kong polity in which some degree of pluralism persists, especially the resistance and opposition to China's new united front operations.

Of course, if the inward migration of mainlanders into the HKSAR continues, and the outward migration of some Hong Kong people to the Greater Bay Area persists, then the process of mainlandizing the HKSAR will hopefully be accelerated. Still, it is doubtful whether many Hongkongers would really move to work and reside in the mainland. It is also possible that many mainlanders who migrate to Hong Kong will soon be politically assimilated by the Hong Kong core values of human rights

---

[4] Christopher Walker, "What is 'Sharp Power?,'" *Journal of Democracy*, vol. 29, no. 3 (July 2018), pp. 12–13.

and the rule of law. Some of them may accept post-materialistic values of social justice, sustainable development and open government rather than the authoritarian and paternalistic style of governance in mainland China. On the other hand, newly landed migrants from mainland China tend to be more politically patriotic toward the PRC and they tend to provide a constant source of political target of united front work from the local pro-Beijing forces. But for the younger generation of mainland migrants, once they are assimilated into the Hong Kong society and values, their political mindset can be more autonomous than conventional wisdom assumed.[5] In short, generational change in Hong Kong can make China's new united front work difficult to be sustained in the long run, even though pro-Beijing forces can invest a huge amount of money and manpower to maintain the momentum of united front work.

To put it simply, China's penetrative politics in Hong Kong have their severe limitations. Although the mainstream media are easily under the mainland ownership and influence, the pro-democracy forces have shifted to the Internet media. Like a cat-and-mouse game, the battleground of winning the hearts and minds of the people of Hong Kong has shifted to other arenas not easily controlled by pro-Beijing forces and the Liaison Office in the HKSAR. The pro-Beijing media are still unattractive to many people, especially the youths who rely on the Internet and particularly social media to understand the developments of Hong Kong.

Another limitation on penetrative politics is that Hong Kong has a bitterly divided and internally heterogeneous civil society. This civil society is by no means dominated by pro-Beijing forces but is punctuated with a relatively strong voice independent and critical of both the HKSAR government and Beijing. The divided civil society is characterized by the fierce competition between two sectors: one pro-Beijing and the other pro-democracy. The pro-Beijing sector is composed of the DAB, Fujianese interest groups, FTU, district-level federations and four of the six main religious groups, namely the Buddhist, Taoist, Confucian and Islamic ones. Although many women groups are increasingly pro-Beijing, and although the religious sector is under the PRC's heavy united front influence, many Catholics and Christians are still imbued with the political value of upholding human rights because they understand how their

---

[5] A good example is Edward Leung, who was born in the mainland and who migrated to Hong Kong. See Lo and Loo, "An Anatomy of the Postmaterialistic Values of Hong Kong Youth: Opposition to China's Rising 'Sharp Power,'" pp. 95–126.

counterparts in the mainland are controlled by the CCP. Even in the working-class sector, it is bitterly divided into pro-Beijing and pro-democracy camps, while some workers prefer to be politically neutral. The educational sector of the civil society is far less pro-Beijing than conventional wisdom assumed. Given the weakness of pro-Beijing educational interest groups, PRC authorities dealing with Hong Kong matters have turned to focus on individual intellectuals, educators and academics in their new united front work. Still, the local intellectuals, educators and academics are politically diverse, making it difficult for PRC authorities to conduct penetrative politics easily, smoothly and successfully. The educational sector is the most troublesome segment of the civil society; the opposition to the national education policy in 2012 and the eruption of the 2014 Occupy Central Movement were the testimony to the failure of China's united front work in Hong Kong's educational stronghold. The ongoing encouragement of Hong Kong's scientists to go into the Greater Bay Area to conduct scientific research would likely politically co-opt some local academics, while some others will remain politically autonomous or indifferent. It will perhaps take decades for the PRC to penetrate the educational sector successfully and exert control on it effectively.

Related to the relatively autonomous educational sector is the presence of many politically defiant young people, who are imbued with strong post-materialistic values like human rights, democracy and the rule of law. Unlike the materialistic and opportunistic youths who are vulnerable to united front work, the post-materialistic young people of Hong Kong despise the PRC's united front work, old or new, and they yearn for a political system that is truly democratic along the line of selecting the chief executive through universal suffrage and without any prominent control from Beijing. In a sense, the debate over Hong Kong's democratization in the 2014 Occupy Central Movement illustrated the serious ideological differences between the politically paternalistic PRC authorities and the pro-democracy Hong Kong youth. Although PRC authorities have launched an extensive and intensive campaign to woo more local youths into the united front umbrella, the youth sector remains deeply divided. Even if the national education is implemented and accelerated in the HKSAR, it cannot easily capture the psyche of the relatively autonomous youths.

Arguably, the HKSAR has witnessed the birth of a new form of citizenship. Some intellectuals, notably Joshua Wong and Benny Tai, have seen peaceful resistance to China's united front work as their perception of citizenship in Hong Kong. This new form of citizenship entails a concept of rightful and peaceful resistance to the powerful overlord, the PRC, through the 2014 Occupy Central Movement and electoral participation. Citizenship, to many localists in Hong Kong, is composed of the determination of citizens to express themselves freely, to shape their political future through referendums, to select their political leaders democratically, to fight for the rule of law and to oppose authoritarianism. The ideas of Tai and some localists in attempting at capturing more directly elected seats in both Legislative Council and District Councils have constituted a national security threat to the psyche of PRC authorities responsible for Hong Kong affairs. The PRC version of citizenship is different; authoritarian regime cherishes political apathy and the materialistic orientations of citizens. Ironically, the increasingly post-materialistic values of many Hong Kong people are in direct conflict with the PRC vision of the ideal citizenship in the HKSAR. The clashes of two concepts of citizenship—the Hong Kong one that entails peaceful resistance and the mainland that stresses political obedience—are prominent in the local resistance to China's new united front politics. The resistant citizenship of many Hong Kong people could be seen in June 2019, when almost a million protestors succeeded in delaying the discussion of an extradition bill in the legislature. The Chief Executive Carrie Lam apologized to the public for her handling of the bill, although she claimed the bill was initiated by the Hong Kong government rather than by Beijing.

Revisiting the Twelve Perspectives on China's New United Front Work in Hong Kong

To understand China's new united front work in the HKSAR, we adopt a comprehensive approach to integrate the twelve perspectives: (1) enhancing the legitimacy of both the central and local governments; (2) co-opting the Hong Kong elites; (3) achieving politico-economic convergence and integration between the mainland and Hong Kong; (4) narrowing the elite-mass linkage; (5) creating a pro-Beijing civil society through the mobilization of social capital; (6) securitizing the HKSAR and the mainland CCP regime; (7) curbing the political opposition through electoral competition; (8) engaging in ideological struggles between China's paternalistic authoritarianism and Hong Kong's limited pluralism; (9) encountering the resistance from citizens and groups with relatively stronger local Hong Kong identity; (10) facing the tensions between materialistic values held by most pro-Beijing Hongkongers and post-materialistic values cherished by most pro-democracy Hongkongers; (11) distributing favors to Beijing's clients through patronage networks and (12) seeing Hong Kong as a potentially political threat to the mainland from a geopolitical perspective.

From the viewpoint of legitimacy, the PRC has to consolidate its own legitimacy over Hong Kong and that of the HKSAR government by backing up their related policies. The PRC's legitimacy is still questioned by some Hong Kong people, including those who remember the tragedy of the 1989 Tiananmen incident and those who are post-materialists upholding the values of human rights, social justice and the rule of law. Beijing's "comprehensive jurisdiction" over Hong Kong embraces its support and endorsement of the Chief Executive, its preference of maintaining an executive-led polity over a powerful legislature and its determination to wipe out any local element who advocate "Hong Kong independence." Authoritarian politics in China means that political separatism is disallowed and curbed. The case of Hong Kong is the same. As such, the mainlandization of Hong Kong politics has become obvious in the Xi Jinping era since 2013.

The politics of co-optation is critical to the success of united front work. From a deductive approach, there are four types of elites in Hong Kong (Table 11.1): (1) the loyalists who exhibit a high degree of politico-ideological affinity with the PRC regime and a high degree of materialism (the tendency to embrace status, influence and power); (2) the unstable loyalists who have a high degree of politico-ideological affinity but a low degree of materialism; (3) the opportunists who have a low degree of politico-ideological affinity and high degree of materialism; and (4) resistant oppositionists who have a low degree of politico-ideological affinity and low degree of materialism. Except for the resistant oppositionists, the other three types of elites are politically co-opted. The loyalists include many business elites who did and do contribute immensely to China's economic modernization and infrastructure development. But a minority of loyalists who do not have strong ideological affinity with the mainland can become unstable, like some previously loyal Hong Kong CCP members who openly quit the party after the 1989 Tiananmen incident. A minority of business elites have also been questioned about their loyalty when they were reportedly minimizing their investment in the mainland and moving their assets out of Hong Kong. The most prominent unstable loyalist was the late lawyer Liu Yiu-chu who stood up in the 1991 NPC meeting to pay tribute to those who died in the 1989 Tiananmen incident, and whose behavior

Table 11.1 Four types of elites

	Low (degree of materialism)	High (degree of materialism)
Low (degree of politico-ideological affinity)	Resistant oppositionists	Opportunists
High (degree of politico-ideological affinity)	Unstable loyalists	Loyalists

shocked the PRC authorities.[6] The opportunists who support the PRC are numerous in Hong Kong's political arena, especially those who are materialistic and yearning for political influence, status and power. Some of them are eager to be appointed as the CPPCC members and elected as the NPC members. Yet, for those Hong Kong people who are post-materialistic, they tend to be the oppositionists who resist China's united front work, who prefer to adopt an autonomous political line and who support Hong Kong to have a more transparent, pluralistic and democratic polity. Many post-materialistic Hongkongers are imbued with, as argued in this book, a new form of citizenship, adopting peaceful resistance to united front, participating in protests and rallies and exercising their right to vote for pro-democracy and like-minded party candidates in local elections (Table 11.1).

While Alfred Meyer argued in 1970 that the former Soviet Union would gradually converge with the United States economically and politically,[7] it still takes a long time for the PRC to converge with America. Given China's long authoritarian tradition, it is highly doubtful whether it would converge politically with the United States. Yet, from the comparative standpoint, China is economically more similar to Hong Kong than ever before as the mainland is adopting capitalist means to achieve its socialist modernization. If convergence signals a process in which institutions develop with a diversity of viewpoints and priorities, as Meyer argued, mainland China in the post-Mao era was moving toward political modernization with more diversified viewpoints. Yet, the Xi Jinping era has been marked by the tighter political control over dissidents, increased media and Internet censorship and clampdown on Hong Kong's radical democrats. The gradual return of "hard" authoritarianism in China means that Hong Kong has moved a bit closer to the PRC polity than ever before. In short, some degree of political convergence between Hong Kong and the mainland has taken place since the Xi Jinping era. If political integra-

[6] "Thinking of Liu Yiu-chu," December 3, 2018, in https://www.worldjournal.com/5999258/, access date: March 23, 2019.

[7] Alfred Meyer, "Theories of Convergence," in Chalmers Johnson, ed., *Change in Communist Systems* (Stanford: Stanford University Press, 1970), p. 337.

tion between the HKSAR and the PRC is a long-term objective of China's united front work, identity transformation from a very strong local Hong Kong identity to Chinese patriotism is bound to generate resistance and opposition from some Hong Kong people. If political integration, as Ake observes, aims at transforming the political culture of citizens, the political culture of the Hong Kong people will have to be changed from a mix of political apathy and activism to being mostly politically patriotic toward the PRC. This change has to be natural and evolutionary rather than a coercive process imposed by the PRC and HKSAR authorities. The failure of the national education policy in 2012 showed that changing the political culture of the youths encountered severe resistance. Hence, it will take a long time for China's new united front work to instill patriotism in the psyche of more Hong Kong people. Many Hong Kong people see themselves as culturally Chinese, but they still do not identify themselves as the loyal supporters of the CCP in the mainland. Identity politics continue to obstruct the PRC's new united front work in Hong Kong.

China's new united front work does narrow the elite-mass gap in the pro-Beijing circle, but not the pro-democracy portion of the civil society. Due to the intensity of penetrative politics, the local pro-Beijing forces have become increasingly solidified and constituted a powerful force in local elections. All the pro-Beijing interest groups, ranging from clans to women groups, from labor unions to religious groups and from district federations to kaifongs, are playing a crucial role in bridging the elite-mass gap, enhancing their social capital and generating a relatively strong politically patriotic segment in Hong Kong's civil society. Yet, the pro-Beijing segment of the civil society is in direct conflict, ideologically and electorally, with the pro-democracy sector. Therefore, politicization and continuous political struggle will mark the feature of the competition between these two sectors of Hong Kong's civil society.

From a broader securitization perspective, China's new united front work in the HKSAR is driven by a fear among PRC authorities that Hong Kong may become a base for foreign powers to subvert both the territory and the mainland. This security-oriented fear is particularly prominent in China under Xi Jinping, who has to ensure that domestic political opponents are silenced, that Hong Kong's democrats should not have close interactions with the Western states and that the local pro-independence elements have to be nipped in the bud. The remarks and actions of PRC authorities responsible for Hong Kong matters have since 2013 exhibited their real concern about national security. To them, the national security threat to both Hong Kong and mainland China has been and is real and existential. The local pro-Beijing media have been utilizing their editorials, commentaries and reports to rationalize and strengthen such perception of the national security threat. The national security concern of PRC authorities has been elevated to an alarming level, especially when some local democrats visit foreign states, like United States and United Kingdom, to "internationalize" Hong Kong's political development. As Chinese history was characterized by foreign intervention and anti-foreignism, it is understandable why the PRC authorities have to enhance united front work in Hong Kong so as to stop the democrats, who are perceived as the "agents" of foreign states, to capture not only the directly and indirectly elected seats in the Legislative Council but also the directly elected seats in District Councils. The political opposition in the HKSAR, in the eyes of PRC officials, is collaborating with foreign countries to "subvert" the regimes in Hong Kong and mainland.

The security hysteria of PRC authorities is intertwined with their geopolitical mindset. They see China as the political heartland and Hong Kong as a political borderland. The borderland, to them, should not challenge the heartland, not to mention threatening the heartland's authority and legitimacy. In particular, Hong Kong was governed by the British for so long that it is accustomed to receiving foreign influence and intervention. In response to foreign intervention and influence on Hong Kong, Beijing has to take decisive measures in its policies toward Hong Kong, including the swift response to the call for "Hong Kong independence" and the interpretation of the Basic Law in November 2016 over the disrespectful behavior of two legislators-elect.

Furthermore, the PRC's new united front work in Hong Kong has strong ideological overtones. The authoritarian Chinese politics are in conflict with the more pluralistic Hong Kong, where the civil society has a relatively strong pro-democracy and anti-PRC segment. If the Xi Jinping regime is marked by, as Tang Wenfang has argued, "populist authoritarianism," it naturally sees the Hong Kong democrats as populist enemies who try to instigate the local voters to challenge Beijing's legitimacy and its policies toward the HKSAR. Populist authoritarianism in China is characterized by the use of mass line. The Hong Kong case demonstrates the extensive use of mass line in the pro-Beijing camp, where interest groups are constantly mobilized to support the policies of both the HKSAR and central governments. Yet, Tang has raised the issue of whether populist authoritarianism in China can sustain itself because of the huge amount of resources and energies required. In the Hong Kong case, while the amount of resources and energies can be astronomical and incalculable, China's new united front work will find it difficult to sustain unless the state machinery continues to inject resources, manpower and capital ceaselessly. If the economy of China and Hong Kong is affluent, Beijing's united front work can and will be sustained. Yet, in economically bad times, we can anticipate a retrenchment in China's united front in the HKSAR.

To many Hong Kong people who are post-materialistic and who dislike authoritarian politics, they resort to peaceful resistance to united front work by voting for the democrats in local elections, by supporting the 2014 Occupy Central movement, by protesting on the streets and by participating in local pro-democracy activities. These Hong Kong people will continue to be the pillar of pro-democracy forces and the hindrance to China's penetrative politics. Unlike mainland migrants who have been educated and politically indoctrinated in the PRC, the pro-democracy Hongkongers hold relatively stronger post-materialistic values and provide the powerful support for those oppositionists resistant to united front work. Unlike the pro-Beijing local elites who can be regarded as the clients of Beijing, the pro-democracy elites in the HKSAR despise patron-client relations and see united front work as the "dirty" politics of buying the political support from some people of Hong Kong.

The Legality, Illegality and Future of United Front

Since the HKSAR's sovereignty belongs to the PRC, Beijing's extensive and intensive united front work does not appear to violate the local law, unlike the cases of Taiwan and Australia. In Taiwan, any local Taiwanese who are deemed to be too close to mainland authorities are vulnerable to being labeled as the enemies of the Taiwan state. In particular, the PRC focuses on its communications with more Taiwanese than ever before. As long as the DPP is in power in Taiwan, mainland China's united front work that targets at Taiwanese is seen as activities suspected of conducting espionage work. Similarly, foreign countries, like Australia, are alarmed at China's united front outreach, including its contacts with the overseas Chinese.[8] The case of Huang Xiangmo in Australia showed that his activi-

---

[8] Alexander Bowe, *China's Overseas United Front Work: Background and Implications for the United States* (United States: US-China Economic and Security Review Commission, August 24, 2018), in https://www.uscc.gov/sites/default/files/Research/China%27s%20

ties were regarded as violating the Australian law. As such, once the PRC's united front work extends to other countries beyond mainland China, Hong Kong and Macao, it is bound to be controversial, both politically and perhaps legally.

In conclusion, this book argues that penetrative politics as a hallmark of authoritarianism has seeped into the political system of Hong Kong. The infiltration of pro-Beijing groups is deep-rooted in the local society. However, given that Hong Kong's civil society has a relatively strong pro-democracy segment and that it remains politically divided, it is not easy for PRC authorities and agents to capture the entire society. Electorally, many Hong Kong voters exercise their independent judgment without easily being succumbed to the influence of the PRC's united front work. It will take a long time for China to really win the hearts and minds of most Hongkongers. Yet, the outreach of China's united front work to other places, including Taiwan and foreign countries, is destined to be controversial, especially as the rapid rise of the PRC has raised the alarm and fear of many foreign countries. China's new united front work in Hong Kong is certainly a feature of "hard" authoritarianism under the Xi Jinping leadership. It will likely have legacies and implications for Hong Kong's political development in the long run.

The Drift Toward Hong Kong's "One Country, Two Mixed Systems"

The ways in which China's penetrative politics is conducted in the HKSAR prove that, through the mobilization and coordination of Beijing's agents in the territory, Hong Kong's "one country, two systems" is actually "one country, two mixed systems" because the political dynamics of the PRC are interacting and mingling with the political development of the special administrative region. The DAB, FTU, women groups, youth groups, pro-Beijing religious groups, district federations and *kaifong* associations are the de facto transmission belts of the CCP in the HKSAR. As such, the two political systems of mainland China and Hong Kong are interacting with each other. It is practically impossible to separate the two systems, politically speaking. Although the official version from both Beijing and the HKSAR government is that "one country, two systems" is working

Overseas%20United%20Front%20Work%20-%20Background%20and%20Implications%20for%20US_final_0.pdf, access date: March 23, 2019.

well, the reality is that, judging from the PRC's new united front operations, "one country, two mixed systems" is the ongoing trend of Beijing-Hong Kong relations. Even economically, the PRC is moving toward a mixed system, selectively borrowing from some capitalistic elements of Hong Kong. Hence, while some degree of political convergence can be seen, a parallel move toward economic convergence is under way. However, this does not mean that eventually both mainland China and Hong Kong will reach a point of convergence. Instead, amidst the current drift toward some degree of politico-economic convergence, both places have divergent features. Politically, Hong Kong is still characterized by the rule of law, the strong civil society in which the pro-democracy and post-materialistic segment is strong, and some societal sectors, such as education and youth, which remain quite resistant to China's new united front work. Many Hong Kong people are yearning for the Western-style of democratic and open politics rather than the mainland Chinese-style of penetrative politics. As such, we will continue to see political struggles, conflicts, bickering and contradictions in Hong Kong's relations with the PRC in the coming decades.

Bibliography

1. Newspapers, Television News, Radio News and Foreign News Agencies

"Missing Hong Kong book editor Lee Bo returns home," March 24, 2016, in https://www.theguardian.com/world/2016/mar/24/hong-kong-book-editor-lee-bo-returns-home-disappear-missing, access date: March 3, 2019.

"Remembering the fifteenth anniversary of the death of lawyer Liu Yiu-chu who loved Hong Kong," April 7, 2012, in https://www.bnn.co/news/gb/pubvp/2012/04/201204072307.shtml, access date: March 5, 2019.

Apple Daily (Hong Kong Chinese newspaper, various years).

BBC Monitoring Asia Pacific, July 17, 2010.

Bernstein, Sharon, "Second U.S. University cuts ties with the Confucius Institute," Reuters, October 2, 2014, in https://www.reuters.com/article/us-usa-china-confucius-institute-pennsyl/second-u-s-university-cuts-ties-with-chinas-confucius-institute-idUSKCN0HQ4UZ20141001, access date: February 2, 2019.

China Economic Review (mainland Chinese newspaper, various years).

Hong Kong Commercial Daily (Hong Kong Chinese newspaper, various years).

Hong Kong Economic Times (Hong Kong Chinese newspaper, various years).

Hong Kong Daily News (Hong Kong Chinese newspaper, various years).

Hong Kong TVB interview with Gordon Wu, October 6, 2018.

Jinghua Shibao (mainland Chinese newspaper, various years).

Lee, Yimou and Hung, Faith, "Special Report: How China's Shadowy Agency is working to absorb Taiwan," Reuters, November 27, 2014, in https://www.

reuters.com/article/us-taiwan-china-special-report/special-report-how-chinas-shadowy-agency-is-working-to-absorb-taiwan-idUSKCN0JB01T2014 1127, access date: March 20, 2019.
Ming Pao (Hong Kong Chinese newspaper, various years).
New York Times (American newspaper, various years).
Oriental Daily News (Hong Kong Chinese newspaper, various years).
Radio Television Hong Kong, May 2018.
Sing Tao Daily (Hong Kong Chinese newspaper, various years).
South China Morning Post (Hong Kong English newspaper, various years).
Ta Kung Pao (Hong Kong Chinese newspaper, various years).
Taipei Times (Taiwan Chinese newspaper, various years).
The Hong Kong Free Press, in https://www.hongkongfp.com/, access date: March 3, 2019.
The People's Daily (mainland Chinese newspaper, various years).
The Standard (Hong Kong English newspaper, various years).
The Sun (Hong Kong Chinese newspaper, various years).
Tian Tian Daily (Hong Kong Chinese newspaper, various years).
United Daily News (Taiwan Chinese newspaper, various years).
Voice of America News, "Dissident Hong Kong Book Publisher Returns Home," March 24, 2016, in https://www.voanews.com/a/dissident-hong-kong-book-publisher-returns-home/3253265.html, access date: March 3, 2019.
Wen Wei Po (Hong Kong Chinese newspaper, various years).

2. Government Documents and Government Websites

"Buddhist Festival saw the participation of Liu Yandong in meeting the six Hong Kong religious leaders," CPPCC news bulletin, July 27, 2004, in http://cppcc.people.com.cn/GB/34961/65233/65239/65802/4450761.html, access date: February 2, 2019.
"Interpretation of Article 104 of the Basic Law of the HKSAR of the PRC by the SCNPC," November 7, 2016, in https://www.basiclaw.gov.hk/en/basiclawtext/images/basiclawtext_doc25.pdf, access date: January 27, 2019.
"Lo Man-tuen," in http://www.cppcc.gov.cn/CMS/wylibary/showJcwyxtInfoWylibary.action?tabJcwyxt.guid=11W001877, access date: April 24, 2018.
"Speech by the Chief Executive at Women's Commission International Women's Day 2018 reception," in https://www.info.gov.hk/gia/general/201803/08/P2018030800787.htm, access date: June 17, 2018.
"The 2016 Population By-Census," (Hong Kong: Census and Statistics Department, 2016), in https://www.bycensus2016.gov.hk/data/16bc-main-results.pdf, access date: April 22, 2018.
"Chief Executive Carrie Lam attends the 26th anniversary of the HKUYA and its inaugural ceremony," in https://www.info.gov.hk/gia/general/201808/27/P2018082700848.htm, access date: February 19, 2019.

"China's religious situation," in http://www.locpg.gov.cn/zggq/2014-01/04/c_125956454.htm, access date: February 4, 2019.

"The Chinese Communist Party's United Front Regulation," September 23, 2015 in http://cpc.people.com.cn/n/2015/0923/c64107-27622040.html, access date: January 26, 2019.

"The Liaison Office's announcement," in http://www.locpg.gov.cn/ldjl/zj/200701/t20070122_1153.asp, access date: January 22, 2019.

"The meeting between Premier Zhou and the teachers and students from the University of Hong Kong," *China's United Front Magazine*, April 8, 2018, in http://www.locpg.hk/jsdt/2018-04/08/c_129845662.htm, access date: March 5, 2019.

"The Practice of the 'One Country, Two Systems' Policy in the Hong Kong Special Administrative Region," June 10, 2014, in http://www.fmcoprc.gov.hk/eng/xwdt/gsxw/t1164057.htm, access date: January 26, 2019.

"Xi elected Chinese president, chairman of the PRC Central Military Commission," March 14, 2013, in http://www.npc.gov.cn/englishnpc/news/Appointments/2013-03/14/content_1783118.htm, access date: February 4, 2019.

The Basic Law of the Hong Kong Special Administrative Region of the People's Republic of China (Hong Kong: Hong Kong Special Administrative Region Government, April 2017), p. 8, in https://www.basiclaw.gov.hk/en/basiclawtext/images/basiclaw_full_text_en.pdf, access date: March 23, 2019.

3. BOOKS, ARTICLES, MAGAZINES, MONOGRAPHS AND DISSERTATIONS

A Special Commemoration of the 95th Anniversary of the Fukien Chamber of Commerce and Hong Kong's 15th Anniversary of its Return to the Motherland (in Chinese) (Hong Kong: The Fukien Chamber of Commerce, September 2012).

A Special Publication on the Establishment Meeting of the National Returned Overseas Chinese Association (*Zhonghua quan guo gui guo huaqiao lianhe hui*) (Beijing: Gaihui, 1957).

Ahlen, Kristina, "Swedish Collective Bargaining Under Pressure: Inter-Union Rivalry and Incomes Policies," *British Journal of Industrial Relations*, vol. 127, no. 3 (November 1989), pp. 330–370.

Annual Newsletter of the HKFW, no. 74 (2017), in http://www.hkfw.org/chi/activities/publication/issue-74.pdf, access date: June 16, 2018.

Ake, Claude, *A Theory of Political Integration* (Homewood, Illinois: The Dorsey Press, 1967).

Akkerman, Agnes, "Union Competition and Strikes: The Need for Analysis at the Sector Level," *Industrial and Labor Relations Review*, vol. 61, no. 4 (July 2008), pp. 445–459.

Balassa, Bela, *The Theory of Economic Integration* (Westport, Connecticut: Greenwood Press, 1961).

Beetham, David, *The Legitimation of Power* (Basingstoke: Macmillan, 1991).

Burns, John P., "The Structure of Communist Party Control in Hong Kong," *Asian Survey*, vol. 30, no. 8 (August 1990), pp. 748–765.

Bernards, Nick, "The International Labour Organization and African trade unions: tripartite fantasies and enduring struggles," *Review of African Political Economy*, vol. 44, no. 153 (2017), pp. 399–441.

Bowe, Alexander, *China's Overseas United Front Work: Background and Implications for the United States* (United States: US-China Economic and Security Review Commission, August 24, 2018), in https://www.uscc.gov/sites/default/files/Research/China%27s%20Overseas%20United%20Front%20Work%20-%20Background%20and%20Implications%20for%20US_final_0.pdf, access date: March 23, 2019.

Brunner, Georg, "Legitimacy Doctrines and Legitimation Procedures in East European Systems," in T. H. Rigby and Ferenc Feher, eds., *Political Legitimation in Communist States* (London: Macmillan, 1982).

Butenhoff, Linda, *Social Movements and Political Reform in Hong Kong* (Westport, Connecticut: Praeger, 1999).

Buzan, B., Waever, O., and de Wilde, J., *Security: A New Framework for Analysis* (Boulder, Colorado: Lynne Rienner, 1998).

Carola, Frege, Heery, Edmund, and Turner, Lowell, "The New Solidarity" Trade Union Coalition-Building in Five Countries," in Carola, Frege and Kelly, John, eds., *Varieties of Unionism: Strategies for Union Revitalization in a Globalizing Economy*. (Oxford: Oxford University Press, 2004), pp. 137–158.

Carnoy, Martin, *The State and Political Theory* (New Jersey: Princeton University Press, 1984).

Chakrabarti, Anjan and Dhar, Anup Kumar, "Labour, Class and Economy: rethinking Trade Union Struggle," *Economic and Political Weekly* (May 31, 2008), pp. 73–81.

Chan, Chris King-chi, Chan, Sophia Shuk-ying, and Tang, Lynn, "Reflecting on Social Movement Unionism in Hong Kong: The Case of the Dockworkers' Strike in 2013," *Journal of Contemporary Asia*, vol:49, issue:1 (2019), pp. 54–77.

Chan, Ming, "Hong Kong Workers Towards 1997: Unionization, Labor Activism and Political Participation under the China Factor," *Australian Journal of Politics and History*, vol. 47, no. 1 (2001), pp. 61–84.

Chen, Feng-lan, "Transnational Mobilization of Overseas Chinese Village Officials and Qiaoxiang Social Governance: A Case Study of Mingxi Village in Fujian Province," *Journal of Overseas Chinese History Studies* (in Chinese), no. 1 (March 2017), pp. 19–28.

Cheung, Tat-ming, *What is the Evidence? Revealing the Black Hand Behind the Scene of Hong Kong's Chaotic Situation* (in Chinese) (Hong Kong: San See Cultural and Commercial Information, 2018).

Cheung, Tommy, "'Father' of Hong Kong Nationalism: A Critical Review of Chin Wan's City-State Theory," *Asian Education and Development Studies*, vol. 4, no. 4 (2015), pp. 460–470.

Chin, Wan, *A Discussion of Hong Kong as a City-State* (Hong Kong: Enrich Publishing Company, 2011).

Chiu, Stephen Wing-kai, *Strikes in Hong Kong: A sociological study* (Hong Kong: University of Hong Kong, 1987).

Chiu, Stephen Wing-kai and Levin, David A., "Contestatory Unionism: Trade Unions in the Private Sector," in Stephen Chiu Wing Kai and Lui Tai Lok, eds., *The Dynamics of Social Movement in Hong Kong* (Hong Kong: Hong Kong University Press, 2000), pp. 91–138.

Choi, Sally, "Feminist and Labor Movements in Hong Kong: Critical and Co-Constructive (Perspective)," a presentation in San Paulo, Brazil, July 30, 2013, in www.solidaritycenter.org, access date: January 7, 2019.

Choi, Susanne Y. P., "Association Divided, Association United: The Social Organization of Chaozhou and Fujian Migrants in Hong Kong," in Khun Eng, Kuah-Pearce and Hu-Dehart, Evelyn, eds., *Voluntary Associations in the Chinese Diaspora* (Hong Kong: Hong Kong University Press, 2006).

Chow, King-fun, "The Origins, Reflections, Unity and Friendship of Hong Kong's Six Religious Groups," in *Religious Reflections* (in Chinese), no. 27 (November 1995), pp. 73–81, in http://archive.hsscol.org.hk/Archive/periodical/spirit/S027k.htm, access date: February 2, 2019.

Chow, Yick. *A History of the Struggles of Hong Kong Leftists* (in Chinese). (Hong Kong: Lee Man, 2002).

Chu, Cindy Yik-yi, *Chinese Communists and Hong Kong Capitalists* (London: Palgrave Macmillan, 2010).

Cigler, Allan and Loomis, Burdett A., *Interest Group Politics* (Washington, D.C.: CQ Press, 1998).

DeGolyer, Michael, "Local Elections, Long Term Effects? The Hong Kong District Council Elections of 2011," pp. 38–59, in http://hktp.org/list/district-council-elections.pdf, access date: April 8, 2018.

Democratic Alliance for the Betterment and Progress of Hong Kong, *25th Anniversary Commemoration of the Democratic Alliance for the Betterment and Progress of Hong Kong: Choices and Promises* (Hong Kong: Democratic Alliance for the Betterment and Progress of Hong Kong, 2017).

Engeman, C., "Social movement unionism in practice: organizational dimensions of union mobilization in the Los Angeles immigrant rights marches," *Work, Employment and Society*, vol. 29, no. 3 (2015), pp. 444–461.

England, Joe and Rear, John, *Chinese Labour under British Rule: A critical study of labour relations and law in Hong Kong* (Hong Kong: Oxford University Press, 1975).

Falkenheim, Victor, ed., *Citizens and Groups in Contemporary China* (Ann Arbor: Center of Chinese Studies, University of Michigan, 1987).

Federation of Labor Unions. *30th Anniversary of the Federation of Labor Unions* (in Chinese) (Hong Kong: Federation of Labor Unions, 2014).

Federation of Trade Unions. *Federation of Trade Unions Walking with You: 65th Anniversary of Historical Essays* (in Chinese). (Hong Kong: Federation of Trade Unions, 2013).

Fine, Janice, "Solving the Problem from Hell: Tripartism as a Strategy for Addressing Labour Standards Non-Compliance in the United States," *Osgoode Hall Law Journal*, vol. 50, no. 4 (2013), pp. 813–844.

Fuzhou city's United Front Department, "Consolidating the work on the representatives from Hong Kong, Macau, Taiwan and the overseas," *China's United Front Line* (a Chinese magazine named *Zhongguo Tongyi Zhanxin*), August 2010.

Groot, Gerry, "The Expansion of the United Front Under Xi Jinping," in Gloria Davies, Jeremy Goldkorn, and Luigi Tomba, eds., *China Story Yearbook 2015* (Canberra: ANU Press, 2016), pp. 166–177.

Groot, Gerry, *Managing Transitions: The Chinese Communist Party, United Front Work, Corporatism and Hegemony* (London: Routledge, 2004).

Guldin, Gregory Elliot, "'Overseas' at Home: The Fujianese of Hong Kong," unpublished PhD thesis, University of Wisconsin, Madison, 1977.

Hathaway, C. A., "On the Use of 'Transmission Belts' in Our Struggle for the Masses," *The Communist: A Magazine of the Theory and Practice of Marxism-Leninism*, vol. 10, no. 5 (May 1931), pp. 409–423.

Horrocks, Robert James, "The Guangzhou-Hong Kong Strike, 1925–1926: Hongkong Workers in an Anti-Imperialist Movement," PhD thesis, Department of East Asian Studies, University of Leeds, October 1994.

Hough, Jerry F. and Fainsod, Merle, *How the Soviet Union is Governed* (Cambridge, Massachusetts, 1979), Chapter 14, "The Distribution of Power," pp. 518–555.

Hung, Steven Chung-fun, "Professional Teachers' Union as interest group fighting for democracy," in Sonny Shiu-hing Lo, ed., *Interest Groups and the New Democracy Movement in Hong Kong* (London: Routledge, 2018a), pp. 86–110.

Hung, Steven Chung-fun, "Interest groups and democracy movement in Hong Kong: a historical perspective," in Sonny Lo, ed., *Interest Groups and the New Democracy Movement in Hong Kong* (London: Routledge, 2018b), pp. 14–33.

Hung, Steven Chung-fun, "Student Resistance to Mainlandization in Hong Kong," in Joseph Cheng, ed., *Mainlandization of Hong Kong: Pressure and Responses* (Hong Kong: City University Press, 2017), pp. 125–160.

Hung, Steven Chung-fun, "Political participation of students in Hong Kong: a historical account of transformation," in Joseph Cheng, ed., *New Trends of Political Participation in Hong Kong* (Hong Kong: City University Press, 2014), pp. 240–284.

Huntington, Samuel P., "Democracy's Third Wave," *Journal of Democracy*, vol. 2., no. 2 (Spring 1991), pp. 12–34.

Inglehart, Ronald, *Modernization and Postmordernization: Cultural, Economic, and Political Change in 43 Societies* (Princeton, New Jersey: Princeton University Press, 1990).

Inglehart, Ronald, "Post-Materialism in an Environment of Insecurity," *American Political Science Review*, vol. 75, no. 4 (December 1981), pp. 880–900.

Islam, Shafiqul, "Gender Difference: How Does It Affect Trade Union Struggle? A Qualitative Study of Female Workers of Bangladeshi RMG Industries," *Socioeconomica: The Scientific Journal for Theory and Practice of Socio-economic Development*, vol. 6, no. 12 (2017), pp. 165–178.

Kan, Aline Lai-Chung, *The Kaifong Associations in Hong Kong*, unpublished PhD dissertation, Department of Sociology, University of California at Berkeley, March 1970.

Kelly, D., "Towards Tripartism: Industrial Relations in the Steel Industry 1978 to 1987," *Journal of Industrial Relations*, vol. 30, no. 4 (1988), pp. 511–532.

Kwong, Bruce, *Patron-Client Politics and Elections in Hong Kong* (London: Routledge, 2009).

Lam, Wai-Fung and Perry, James, "The Role of Nonprofit Sector in Hong Kong's Development," *Voluntas: International Journal of Voluntary and Nonprofit Organizations*, vol. 11, no. 4 (2000), pp. 355–373.

Lam, Wai-man, *Understanding the Political Culture of Hong Kong: The Paradox of Activism and Depoliticization* (New York: M. E. Sharpe, 2004).

Lam, Wai-man and Lam, Kay Chi-yan, "China's United Front Work in Civil Society: The Case of Hong Kong," *International Journal of Chinese Studies*, vol. 4, no. 3 (December 2013), pp. 301–325.

Lam, Wai-man and Tong, Irene L. K., "Political Change and the Women's Movement in Hong Kong and Macau," *Asian Journal of Women Studies*, vol. 12, no. 1 (2006), pp. 7–35.

Lee, Eliza, "Gender and Political Participation in Hong Kong," *Asian Journal of Women Studies*, vol. 6, no. 3 (2000), pp. 93–114.

Leung, Benjamin and Chiu, Steven, *A Social History of Industrial Strikes and the Labor Movement in Hong Kong, 1946–1989* (Hong Kong: Social Sciences Research Center, University of Hong Kong, 1991).

Li, Qirong and Xu, Haoliang, "Tan Kah Kee's Spirit of Patriotism and the China Dream," *Overseas Chinese Journal of Bagui* (in Chinese), no. 2 (June 2016).

Linz, Juan J., *Totalitarian and Authoritarian Regimes* (Boulder, Colorado: Lynne Rienner, 2000).

Liu, Rumei, "Discussion on the Origins and development of the United Front Work," *Journal of the Academy of Guizhou Socialism* (in Chinese), Vol. 4 (2014), pp. 26–30.

Liu, Hong, "Old Linkages, New Networks: The Globalization of Overseas Chinese Voluntary Associations and its Implications," *The China Quarterly*, no. 155 (September 1998).

Lo, Sonny Shiu-Hing, "Ideologies and Factionalism in Beijing-Hong Kong Relations," *Asian Survey*, vol. 58, no. 3 (2018a), pp. 392–415.

Lo, Sonny Shiu-hing and Loo, Jeff Hai-chi, "An Anatomy of the Post-Materialistic Values of Hong Kong Youth: Opposition to China's Rising 'Sharp Power,'" in David Trotman and Stan Tucker, eds., *Youth: Global Challenges and Issues of the 21st Century* (New York: Nova Science, 2018), pp. 95–126.

Lo, Sonny Shiu-hing, ed., *Interest Groups and the New Democracy Movement in Hong Kong* (London: Routledge, 2018b).

Lo, Sonny Shiu-hing, *The Politics of Policing in Greater China* (London: Palgrave, 2016).

Lo, Sonny Shiu-hing, *Hong Kong's Indigenous Democracy: Origins, Evolution and Contentions* (London: Palgrave, 2015).

Lo, Sonny Shiu-Hing, *The Politics of Controlling Organized Crime in Greater China* (London: Routledge, 2013).

Lo, Sonny Shiu-hing, *Competing Chinese Political Visions: Hong Kong vs. Beijing on Democracy* (Westport: Praeger Security International, 2010).

Lo, Sonny Shiu-Hing, *The Dynamics of Beijing-Hong Kong Relations: A Model for Taiwan?* (Hong Kong: Hong Kong University Press, 2008).

Lo, Sonny, "'The Mainlandization and Recolonization of Hong Kong," in Joseph Cheng Yu-shek, ed., *The First Decade of the Hong Kong Special Administrative Region* (Hong Kong: The City University of Hong Kong Press, 2007), pp. 179–231.

Lo, Sonny, Yu, Eilo, Kwong, Bruce, Wong, Benson, "The 2004 Legislative Council Elections in Hong Kong: The Triumph of China's United Front Work After the 2003 and 2004 Protests," *Chinese Law and Government*, vol. 38, no. 1 (January/February 2005), pp. 3–29.

Lo, Sonny, "Hong Kong, 1 July 2003: Half a Million Protestors," *Behind the Headlines*, vol. 60, no. 4 (2004a), pp. 1–14.

Lo, Shiu Hing, "Party Penetration of Society in Hong Kong: The Role of Mutual Aid Committees and Political Parties," *Asian Journal of Political Science*, vol. 12, no. 1 (June 2004b), pp. 31–64.

Lo, Shiu-hing; Yu, Wing-yat and Wan, Kwok-fai, "The 1999 District Councils elections," in Chan, Ming and So, Alvin, eds., *Crisis and Transformation in China's Hong Kong* (London: M. E. Sharpe, 2002), pp. 139–165.

Lo, Shiu-hing, *The Politics of Democratization in Hong Kong* (London: Macmillan, 1997).

Lo, Shiu-hing, "Legislative Cliques, Political Parties, Political Groupings and Electoral System," in Joseph Cheng and Sonny Lo, eds., From Colony to SAR: Hong Kong's Challenges Ahead (Hong Kong: The Chinese University Press, 1995), pp. 51–70.

Lo, Sonny Shiu-Hing, "The Chinese Communist Party Elite's Conflicts over Hong Kong, 1983–1990," *China Information*, vol. 8, no. 4 (Spring 1994), pp. 1–14.

Lo, Shiu-hing, "Decolonization and Political Development in Hong Kong: Citizen Participation," *Asian Survey*, vol. 28, no. 6 (June 1988), pp. 613–629.

Loh, Christine, *Underground Front: The Chinese Communist Party in Hong Kong* (Hong Kong: Hong Kong University Press, 2010).

Loo, Jeff Hai-chi, "A localist's critique of Hong Kong's political development: Political decay, legitimacy crisis and reverse democratization," *Asian Education and Development Studies*, vol. 7, no. 1 (2018a), pp. 76–88.

Loo, Jeff Hai-chi, "Workers as interest groups: Are they fragmented or powerless?," in Sonny Shiu-hing Lo, ed., *Interest Groups and the New Democracy Movement in Hong Kong* (London: Routledge, 2018b), pp. 102–114.

Lucio, Miguel Martinez and Connolly, Heather, "Transformation and Continuities in Urban Struggles: Urban Politics, Trade Unions and Migration in Spain," *Urban Studies*, vol. 49, no. 3 (February 2012), pp. 669–684.

Luo, Hai, "Discussion of the Party-Building and United Front Work Under the New Circumstances," *Journal of the Academy of Guizhou Socialism* (in Chinese), Vol. 4 (2013), pp. 40–43.

Mackert, Jurgen and Turner, Bryan S., "Introduction: citizenship and political struggle," in Jurgen Mackert and Bryan S. Turner, eds., *The Transformation of Citizenship, Volume 3: Struggle, Resistance and Violence* (London: Routledge, 2017).

Mackinder, Harold J., "The geographical pivot of history," *The Geographical Journal*, vol. 23, no. 4 (April 1904), pp. 421–444.

Marsh, D. and Grant W., "Tripartism: Reality or Myth?," *Government and Opposition*, vol. 12, no. 2 (1977), pp. 194–211.

Masiya, Tyanai, "Social Movement Trade Unionism: Case of the Congress of South African Trade Unions," *Politikon*, vol. 41, no. 3 (2014).

Massey, Douglas S., "The Political Economy of Migration in an Era of Globalization," in Samuel Martinez, ed., *International Migration and Human Rights: The Global Repercussions of U.S. Policy* (Oakland: University of California Press, 2009), pp. 25–43.

Meyer, Alfred, "Theories of Convergence," in Chalmers Johnson, ed., *Change in Communist Systems* (Stanford: Stanford University Press, 1970).

Michels, Robert, *Political Parties: A Study of the Oligarchical Tendencies of Modern Democracy*. (Kitchener: Batoche Books, 2001).

Ming, Kenneth Wai-Kin, "Journalists as Interest Groups: Implications for Democracy Movement," in Sonny Shiu-Hing Lo, ed., *Interest Groups and the New Democracy Movement in Hong Kong* (London: Routledge, 2018).

Ming, Shifa and Li, Lin, "The United Front Path and Improvement in Developing the Religious Sector and Charity Organizations," *Journal of Yunnan Nationalities University (Social Science)* (in Chinese), Vol. 29, No. 5 (2012), pp. 66–72.

Mongkok Kaifong Association, 1951–2011 (Hong Kong: Monkok Kaifong Association, 2011).

Mok, Hing-luen, "A Study of women's political participation in Hong Kong," Master of Social Sciences thesis, Department of Social Work, University of Hong Kong, 1991.

Morris, Paul and Vickers, Edward, "Schooling, Politics and the Construction of Identity in Hong Kong: The 2012 'Moral and National Education' Crisis in Historical Context," *Comparative Education*, Vol. 51, No. 3 (2015), pp. 305–326.

Nelson, Daniel N., *Elite-Mass Relations in Communist Systems* (London: Macmillan, 1998).

Nelson, Daniel N., "Political Convergence: An Empirical Assessment," *World Politics*, vol. 30, no. 3 (April 1978), pp. 411–432.

Newsletter of the Fujian Members of the Chinese People's Political Consultative Conference (Zhengxue Tiandi), vol. 7 (2017).

Newsletter of the HKDWA, no. 52 (November 2017), p. 17, in https://drive.google.com/file/d/1EP86s3d7v4t-9otbSQem9q5S1S3eiy0w/view, access date: June 17, 2018.

Newsletter of the HKDWA, no. 53 (April 2018), in https://drive.google.com/file/d/17nUp8QFZAGXHqEVykC8AvuwrteYCRbgz/view, access date: June 17, 2018.

Ng, Sek-hong and Ip, Olivia, "Labour and Society," in Cheng, Joseph Y. S., ed., *The Hong Kong Special Administrative Region in Its First Decade* (Hong Kong: City University of Hong Kong Press, 2007), pp. 443–493.

Nordenstreng, Kaarle, "From Mass Media to Mass Consciousness," in George Gerbner, ed., *Mass Media Policies in Changing Cultures* (New York: John Wiley & Sons, 1977), pp. 269–283.

Pavlidis, Periklis, "Social consciousness, education and transformative activity," *Journal for Critical Education Policy Studies*, vol. 13, no. 2 (October 2015), pp. 1–37.

Pedersen, Axel West; Hippe, Jon M.; Grodem, Anne Skevik; and Sorensen, Ole Beier, "Trade unions and the politics of occupational pensions in Denmark and Norway," *Transfer*, vol. 24, no. 1 (2018), pp. 109–122.

Pohjola, Matti, "Union Rivalry and Economic Growth: A Differential Game Approach," *Scandinavian Journal of Economics*, vol. 86, no. 3 (1984), pp. 365–370.

Press, Robert M., *Peaceful Resistance: Advancing Human Rights and Democratic Freedoms* (Aldershot, Hampshire: Ashgate, 2006).
Pulignano, Valeria, "Union struggle and the crisis of industrial relations in Italy," *Capital & Class*, vol. 79 (2003), pp. 1–8.
Putnam, Robert D., *Making Democracy Work: Civic Traditions in Modern Italy* (Princeton: Princeton University Press, 1998).
Putnam, Robert D., *The Comparative Study of Political Elites* (New Jersey: Prentice-Hall, 1976).
Pye, Lucian W., *The Spirit of Chinese Politics* (Cambridge, Massachusetts: Harvard University Press, 1992).
Rodan, Garry, ed., *Political Oppositions in Industrializing Asia* (London: Routledge, 1996).
Scipes, Kim, "Social Movement Unionism or Social Justice Unionism? Disentangling Theoretical Confusion within the Global Labor Movement," *Class, Race and Corporate Power*: vol. 2, no. 3 (2014), DOI: https://doi.org/10.25148/CRCP.2.3.16092119, in http://digitalcommons.fiu.edu/classracecorporatepower/vol2/iss3/9, access date: May 2, 2018.
Scott, James C., "Patron-Client Politics and Political Change in Southeast Asia," *American Political Science Review*, vol. 66, no. 1 (March 1972).
Selznick, Philip, *TVA And the Grass Roots: A Study in the Sociology of Formal Organization* (New York: Harper& Row, 1966).
Seward, Michael, "Cooption and Power: Who Gets What From Formal Incorporation," *Political Studies*, vol. 38, no. 4 (December 1990), pp. 588–689.
Shambaugh, David, *China's Future* (Cambridge: Polity Press, 2016).
Shangguan, Xiao-hong, "A Study of the Returned Fujian Overseas Chinese Associations in the Republic of China," *Journal of Overseas Chinese History Studies* (in Chinese), no. 3 (September 2017), pp. 87–90.
Shih, Wen, "Political Parties in Communist China," *Asian Survey*, Vol. 3. No. 3 (1963), pp. 157–164.
Spencer, Sara, ed., *The Politics of Migration: Managing Opportunity, Conflict and Change* (Oxford: Blackwell, 2003).
Sun, Lizhen, "China's Private-Sector Business Groups and the Features of United Front," *Journal of Zhejiang Shuren University* (in Chinese), Vol. 17, No. 1 (2017), pp. 105–108.
Tai, Benny, "Introduction: The Rise of China's Sharp Power in Hong Kong," in Tai, Benny, ed., *China's Sharp Power in Hong Kong* (Hong Kong: Hong Kong Civil Hub, 2018).
Tan, Kah Kee, "Tan Kah Kee's speech criticizing the Fujian administration in the welcome ceremony of the Fujian *tongxianghui* (townspeople association)," November 24, 1940, in *Fujian Huaqiao Archival History* (In Chinese) (Fujian: Archive Publishing, 1990).

Tan, Yao Sua; Thock, Ker Pong; Ngah, Kamarudin; Goh, Soo Khoon, "Maintenance and propagation of Chinese culture in a Malay state: the roles of the Chinese associations in Kuala Terengganu," *Asian Ethnicity*, vol. 13. No. 4 (2012), pp. 441–467.

Tang, Ka-jiao, *A History of Hong Kong Buddhism* (Hong Kong: Chung Hwa Bookstore, 2015).

Tang, Ka-jiao, *The 20th Century Hong Kong Buddhism* (in Chinese) ((Hong Kong: Society of Hong Kong History, 2008).

Tang, Wenfang, *Populist Authoritarianism: Chinese Political Culture and Regime Sustainability* (New York: Oxford University Press, 2016).

The First Inauguration Ceremony and Office-Bearers of the New Territories Associations Fraternization (Hong Kong: New Territories Associations Fraternization, 1979).

The HKTFA Newsletter, in http://www.hktaoist.org.hk/usr/files/newsletter/2018/2018_11.pdf, November 11, 2018.

The Third National Returned Overseas Chinese Representative Conference (in Chinese) (Beijing: National Returned Overseas Chinese Association, August 1984).

Thirteen Lectures on the Spirit of the 19th Party Congress (in Chinese) (Guangzhou: New Democracy Publisher, 2017).

Tong, Clement Tze Ming, *The Hong Kong Week of 1967 and the Emergence of the Modern Hong Kong Identity*, unpublished MA thesis, Department of History, University of British Columbia, August 2008.

Tsang, Jasper, *Straight Talk* (in Chinese) (Hong Kong: Cosmo Books, 1995).

Turner, L. and Hurd, R. W., "Building social movement unionism: The transformation of the American labor movement," in Turner, L.; Katz, H. C. and Hurd, R. W., eds., *Rekindling the movement: Labor's quest for relevance in the twenty-first century.* (Ithaca, NY: Cornell University Press, 2001), pp. 9–16.

Tuccio, Michele; Wahba, Jackline; and Hamdouch, Bachir, "International Migration: Driver of Political and Social Change?," No. 9794 (Institute for the Study of Labor, Bonn, Germany, March 2016), in http://ftp.iza.org/dp9794.pdf, access date: March 8, 2019, pp. 1–42.

Van Slyke, Lyman P., "The United Front in China," *Journal of Contemporary History*, Vol. 5, No. 3 (1970), pp. 119–135.

Vandenberg, A., "Social-movement Unionism in Theory and in Sweden," *Social Movement Studies*, vol. 5, no. 2 (2006), pp. 171–191.

Viroli, Maurizio, For Love of Country: An Essay on Patriotism and Nationalism (New York: Oxford University Press, 1995).

Waever, O., "Securitization and De-securitization," in R. Lipschutz, ed., On Security (New York: Columbia University Press, 1995).

Wang, James C. F., *Contemporary Chinese Politics: An Introduction* (New Jersey: Pearson Education, 2002), pp. 15–19.

Wang, Klavier Jie Ying, "Mobilizing Resources to the Square: Hong Kong's Anti-Moral and National Education Movement as Precursor to the Umbrella Movement," *International Journal of Cultural Studies*, Vol. 20, No. 2 (2017), pp. 127–145.

Wang, Mingqian, "'Three-Three System' and 'Two Factions': Regime-Building and United Front in Anti-Japanese Bases in Central China," *Journal of Zhejiang Normal University* (in Chinese), Vol. 40, No. 6 (2015), pp. 34–42.

Wang, Ray and Groot, Gerry, "Who Represents? Xi Jinping's Grand United Front Work, Legitimation, Participation and Consultative Democracy," *Journal of Contemporary China* (2018), in https://doi.org/10.1080/10670564.2018.1 433573, access date: April 22, 2018.

Wang, Xiaojin, "The Evolution of the United Front Theory and Practices of the Chinese Communist Party," *Research on the Chinese Communist Party's History and Building* (in Chinese), Vol. 219, No. 2 (2013), pp. 99–103.

Waterman, P., "Social-movement Unionism: A New Model for a New World," no. 110 (The Hague Institute for Social Studies Working Paper Series, 1991).

Walker, Christopher, "What is 'Sharp Power'?," *Journal of Democracy*, vol. 29, no. 3 (July 2018), pp. 12–13.

Waller, Michael, "Communist Politics and the Group Process: Some Comparative Conclusions," in Goodman, David S. G., ed., *Groups and Politics in the People's Republic of China* (Bristol: University of Cardiff Press, 1984), pp. 196–215.

Wen, Qiaoshi, *Tongzhan Gongzuo (United Front Work)* (Beijing: Chinese Communist Party History Publisher, 2008).

Williams, Michael C., "Words, Images, Enemies: Securitization and International Politics," *International Studies Quarterly*, vol. 47, no. 4 (2003), pp. 511–531.

Wong, Aline K., *The Kaifong Associations and the Society of Hong Kong* (Taipei: The Orient Cultural Service, 1972).

Wong, Hoi, *An Analysis of Hong Kong's Social Strata* (in Chinese) (Hong Kong: Commercial Press, 2017).

Wong, Pik-wan and Lee, Eliza W. Y., "Gender and Political Participation in Hong Kong: Formal Participation and Community Participation," occasional paper series, Hong Kong Institute of Asia-Pacific Studies, The Chinese University of Hong Kong, 2006.

Wu, Bin, "Liao Chengzhi and New China's United Front on Hong Kong and Macao," *Journal of Fujian Institute of Socialism* (in Chinese), Vol. 89, No. 2 (2012), pp. 9–12.

Xia, Yuqing, "Between the Family and State: *Nanqiao* engineers and the *Nanyang Huaqiao* society during the war years," *Southeast Asian Affairs* (in Chinese), vol. 2, no. 166 (2016).

Xie, Ying; Tong, Yunping; and Yang, Fenggang, "Does Ideological Education in China Suppress Trust in Religion and Foster Trust in Government?," *Religions*, vol. 8, no. 94 (2017), pp. 1–11.

Xu, Zhongtao, "The Basic Viewpoints of the Democratic Parties in Publicizing Public Opinion and Maintaining Principles," *Journal of the Academy of Guizhou Socialism* (in Chinese), Vol. 4 (2013), pp. 26–28.

Yan, Qinghuang, *Overseas Chinese Tradition and Modernization* (in Chinese) (Singapore: World Scientific, 2010).

Yip, Tin-sang, *A Collection of Materials on Hong Kong's Elections, 1996–2000* (Hong Kong: Institute of Asia-Pacific Studies, the Chinese University of Hong Kong, 2001).

Yuen, Kei-wang, *Twenty Years of History of the Democratic Alliance for the Betterment and Progress of Hong Kong* (Hong Kong: Chong Hwa Book Company, 2012).

Yuen, Kei-wang, *Hong Kong Road and the Democratic Alliance for the Betterment and Progress of Hong Kong* (Hong Kong: Chong Hwa Book Company, 2011).

Zhang, Hongyan and Zhang Xiaomin, "The Content, Impact and Implications of Deng Xiaoping's United front Theory," *Journal of Huzhou Teachers College*, Vol. 27, No. 5 (2005), pp. 51–55.

Zhang, Jiaoxia, "Examining the Characteristics of Intellectuals in Private Tertiary Schools Outside the Party and United Front Work," *Science and Technology Innovation Herald* (in Chinese), No. 11 (2013), pp. 217–218.

Zhang, Suyun and Xu Jian, "The Anti-Japanese Ethnic Nationalities' United Front and War Victory," *Journal of Liaoning University (Philosophy and Social Sciences)* (in Chinese) Vol. 33, No. 5 (2005), pp. 1–6.

Zhongguo Zhongjiao (*China Religion*) (mainland Chinese magazine, various issues).

Zweig, David, *Agrarian Radicalism in China, 1968–1981* (Cambridge, Massachusetts: Harvard University Press, 1989).

4. Materials from Other Websites and Facebook

"A Fading Vatican-China Agreement in the Midst of United Front," May 20, 2018, in http://kkp.org.hk/node/16793, access date: February 4, 2019.

"A report of the visit of the Shenzhen united front department to Hong Kong," in http://www.tzb.sz.gov.cn/xwzx/gzdt/tzsx/mzgz/zjgz/201710/t20171011_9336722.htm, access date: February 3, 2019.

"A report on the financial chaos within the Po Lin Monastery and its 'close relationship' with the united front officials in the mainland," in http://www.epochtimes.com/b5/17/11/24/n9887395.htm, access date: January 15, 2019.

"About HKUYA," in http://www.hkuya.org.hk/web15/web/subpage.php?mid=8, access date: February 17, 2019.

"An Urgent Appeal from the Hong Kong Buddhist Association," October 5, 2014, in http://www.hkbuddhist.org/zh/page.php?p=preview_detail&epid=26&cid=1, access date: January 15, 2019.

"Analyzing the Making of a Republic," September 9, 2009, in https://hk.appledaily.com/entertainment/art/20090909/13188390, access date: March 3, 2019.

"Assist Sichuan after the 2008 Earthquake," no date indicated, in http://www.hkcccu.org.hk/news/Szechwan/index.htm, access date: February 3, 2019.

"Brainwashing the national situation," June 3, 2018, in http://apostlesmedia.com/20180603/7833, access date: February 3, 2019.

"Cardinal Parolin Comments on Holy See-People's Republic of China Agreement," September 22, 2018, in https://zenit.org/articles/cardinal-parolin-comments-on-holy-see-republic-of-china-agreement/, access date: February 4, 2019.

"Comment on Leung's visit to China," in https://www.chinaaid.net/2018/06/blog-post_27.html, access date: February 9, 2019.

"Confucius Institute closed at US university amid concerns about Chinese influences on campuses," August 15, 2018, in https://www.scmp.com/news/world/united-states-canada/article/2159888/confucius-institute-closed-us-university-amid, access date: February 2, 2019.

"From the Making of the Republic to the Making of an Army," July 16, 2017, in https://kknews.cc/zh-hk/entertainment/2mvjb8z.html, access date: March 3, 2019.

"Fujianese give money and support in the anti-Occupy Central Movement," in http://www.post852.com/, access date: April 25, 2018.

"Henan officials ordered the deletion of command one from the ten commandants," January 3, 2019, in https://www.christiantimes.org.hk/Common/Reader/News/ShowNews.jsp?Nid=156717&Pid=102&Version=0&Cid=2141&Charset=big5_hkscs, access date: February 3, 2019.

"History of Muslims in Hong Kong," in http://www.islam.org.hk/en/?p=13&a=view&r=27, access date: January 22, 2019.

Ho, Si-wing, "Hong Kong film commentary," October 30, 2010, in http://www.filmcritics.org.hk/film-review/node/2017/07/19/, access date: March 3, 2019.

"Hong Kong Press Freedom Index," July 11, 2018, in https://www.hkja.org.hk/en/survey-report/hong-kong-press-freedom-index/#more-3106, access date: March 3, 2019.

"Hong Kong: The Facts [on] Religion and Custom," May 2016, in https://www.gov.hk/en/about/abouthk/factsheets/docs/religion.pdf, access date: February, 2019.

"Interview with Kwok Nai-wang who appeal to the Hong Kong religious leaders and activists not to bow to those who are rich and powerful," October 10, 2018, in https://thestandnews.com/politics/, access date: February 3, 2019.

"Interview with Zhou Nan," June 19, 2017, in https://www.thestandnews.com/politics/, access date: February 5, 2019.

"Is the Liaison Office violating the two systems by possessing three publishers? Carrie Lam said we should not interfere as long as it was made in accordance with the law," May 29, 2018, in https://thestandnews.com/politics/, access date: March 3, 2019.

"Lei Chunmei meets Hong Kong's religious leaders," in www.hktaoist.org.hk/index.php?id=317, access date: February 3, 2019.

"Li Chuwen and the united front work on the Hong Kong religions," in http://medium.com/civic-faither/c-e6aa60fe81bs, access date: February 3, 2019.

"McMaster University severs ties with Confucius Institute," March 2013, in https://bulletin-archives.caut.ca/bulletin/articles/2013/03/mcmaster-university-severs-ties-with-confucius-institute, access date: February 2, 2019.

"Michael Yeung died and Joseph Ha is an temporary administrator dealing with religious affairs," January 4, 2019, in https://topock.kket.com/article/2243350, access date: February 4, 2019.

"Minister Ip visits the Confucian Academy," in http://blog.sina.com.cn/s/blog_4b32f63a01000741.html, access date: January 21, 2019.

"Pro-Beijing scholar Leung Yin-shing's remarks on the PRC protection of religious faith," in https://apostlesmedia.com/20180626/8195, access date: February 3, 2019.

"Reprimanding the PRC United Front Department, Joseph Zen appealed to the mainland Catholics not to abandon and betray the God," https://hkaboluowang.com/2009/0105/115369.html, access date: February 4, 2019.

"Sik Kin Chiu dies and he was involved in scandals with life insurance and a nun," https://www.hk01.com, July 6, 2018, access date: January 15, 2019.

"Six religious leaders issue a joint appeal in the new year, hoping the nation would be rich and Hong Kong having social harmony," February 15, 2018, in https://thestandnews.com/society/, access date: February 2, 2019.

"Six religious leaders issue a joint message in the Chinese New Year," January 27, 2017, in https://www.thestandnews.com/society/, access date: February 2, 2019.

"Submission by the Justice and Peace Commission of the Hong Kong Catholic Diocese to the United Nations Human Rights Council for its Universal Periodic Review Regarding Religious Freedom in the People's Republic of China," July 18, 2013, in http://www.hkjp.org/focus_en.php?id=55, access date: February 4, 2019.

"Taoist Festivals in the Two Straits and Four Places," in http://zytzb.gov.cn/zjswxw/70116.jhtml, access date: February 3, 2019.

"Thanks for your support at our New Territories region flagday on 11 Nov 2017," Independent Assurance Report, in http://ntascs.hk/flagdayreport/Flagdayreport20171111chi.pdf, access date: February 1, 2018.

"The 40th anniversary of the six religions' conference gathering," in http://www.hkcc.org.hk/acms/content.asp?site=hkccnew&op=showbyid&id=58427, access date: February 2, 2019.

"The confrontation after 1967: the period from red fire to transition," November 12, 2010, in https://www.inmediahk.net/, access date: March 5, 2019.

"The Doubtful Representation of the Hong Kong Buddhist Association: Loving the Nation and Loving the Religion," October 31, 2015, in https://thestandnews.com/, access date: January 15, 2019.

"The Forty-two years of linkage between the SRA and Shumshuipo," in https://kowloonpost.hk/2018/07/13/20180711p8/, access date: February 12, 2019.

"The late Ellen Li," in http://www.elicf.com/eng/Dr%20Ellen%20Li.htm, access date: June 16, 2018.

"The mystery of Jaime Sze becoming the ACYF vice-chairman," in https://hk.on.cc/hk/bkn/cnt/news/20150728/bkn-20150728222031319-0728_00822_001.html, access date: February 19, 2019.

"Thinking of Liu Yiu-chu," December 3, 2018, in https://www.worldjournal.com/5999258/, access date: March 23, 2019.

"Two Systems Under Siege," Release of the Hong Kong Journalist Association, July 2, 2017, in https://www.hkja.org.hk/en/press-release/two-systems-under-siege-hkja-releases-2017-annual-report/#more-1071, access date: March 3, 2019.

Cao, Erbao, "Governing Hong Kong under the conditions of 'one country, two systems," in *Study Times*, No. 422, January 29, 2008, translated into English, in https://www.civicparty.hk/cp/media/pdf/090506_cao_eng.pdf, access date: January 26, 2019.

Choi, Siu-kei, "How do Christians cope with the religious policy under Xi Jinping's era," June 6, 2015, in http://christiantimes.org.hk/, access date: February 3, 2019.

Dreher, Rod, "Rome Betrays Underground China Church," September 22. 2018, in https://www.theamericanconservative.com/dreher/vatican-betrays-underground-china-church/, access date: February 4, 2019.

Facebook of the Quanzhou Association, in https://www.facebook.com/Hong-Kong-Quanzhou-Associations-Youth-Committee-893683283997735/?ref=py_c, access date: April 22, 2018.

Huang, Zheping and Huang, Echo, "A brief history: Beijing's interpretations of Hong Kong's Basic Law, from 1999 to the present day," in https://qz.com/828713/a-brief-history-beijings-interpretations-of-hong-kongs-basic-law-from-1999-to-the-present-day/, access date: April 8, 2018.

Jiang, Tao, "Authorities remove church crosses on flimsy pretexts," April 9, 2018, in https://bitterwinter.org/authorities-remove-church-crosses-on-flimsy-pretexts/, access date: February 3, 2019.

Koo, Sun-wing, " Who says Hong Kong has only six major religions?," October 17, 2016, in https://www.inmediahk.net/node/1045215, access date: February 2, 2019.

Lau, Chi-wai, "Muslims in Hong Kong," in https://www.bbc.com/zhongwen/trad/chinese-news-39124578, access date: January 22, 2019a.

Lau, Chi-wai, "Islam in Hong Kong: Different Challenges in China and Hong Kong," March 1, 2017, in https://www.bbc.com/zhongwen/trad/chinese-news-39124578, access date: January 22, 2019b.

Lau Kwei-biu, "Confucius Temple or Confucius Institute? A Tool of Maintaining Political Stability?," in https://www.inmediahk.net/node/1018023, access date: January 21, 2019.

Lau, Shan-ching, "My first encounter with uncle Kan," June 23, 2016, in https://www.inmediahk.net/node/1043023, access date: March 5, 2019c.

Leung, Po-lung, "The Workers' Movement in Hong Kong before the Japanese Occupation, 1937–1941," 2017, in https://wknews.org/node/1362, access date: February 9, 2019a.

Leung, Po-lung, "Hong Kong's war relief associations and the Chinese Communist Party," February 10, 2017, in https://www.inmediahk.net/node/1047538, access date: March 5, 2019b.

News Bulletin, "Hong Kong Religious Sector in Celebration of the 68th Anniversary of the PRC," in http://www.hkbuddhist.org/zh/page.php?p=preview_detail&epid=39&cid=1, access date: January 15, 2019a.

News Bulletin, "Hong Kong Religious Sector in Celebration of the 69th Anniversary of the PRC," in http://www.hkbuddhist.org/zh/page.php?p=preview_detail&epid=39&cid=1, access date: January 15, 2019b.

Occupy Central Movement leaders' declaration in January 2013, see http://oclp.hk/index.php?route=occupy/book, access date: January 26, 2019.

Ramzy, Austin, "Toronto School District Cancels Plans for Confucius Institute," October 30, 2014, in https://sinosphere.blogs.nytimes.com/2014/10/30/toronto-school-district-cancels-plans-for-confucius-institute/, access date: February 2, 2019.

Rogers, Benedict, "China's war on Christianity," September 20, 2018, in https://catholicherald.co.uk/issues/sep-21st-2018/chinas-war-on-christianity/, access date: February 4, 2019.

"Severely condemning the remarks on the democracy wall of the Education University of Hong Kong, requesting the authorities that they should penalize the offenders," in http://www.ntas.org.hk/blog_post.jsp?rid=91&cate_id=2, access date: February 10, 2019.

The Facebook of the New Territories West's Residents Association, in https://www.facebook.com/, access date: February 10, 2019.

The HKIF website, in http://www.hk-if.org/special.php?id=10, access date: February 12, 2019.

The website of HKIWA, in http://www.hkiwa.org/web/, access date: June 17, 2018a.
The website of HKIWA, in http://www.hkiwa.org/web/album.php, access date: June 17, 2018b.
The HKUYA mission and vision, in http://www.hkuya.org.hk/web15/web/subpage.php?mid=9, access date: February 17, 2019.
The website of KWOF, in http://www.kwof.org.hk/web/index.php?option=com_content&view=article&id=53&Itemid=53, access date: June 17, 2018.
Woo Chun-loong, "A traitor of Confucius and Mencius," in https://www.inmediahk.net/node/1006169, February 14, 2010, access date: January 21, 2019.
Wooden, Cindy, "Vatican signs provisional agreement with China on naming bishops," September 22, 2018, in https://www.catholicnews.com/services/englishnews/2018/vatican-signs-provisional-agreement-with-china-on-naming-bishops.cfm, access date: February 4, 2019.
Ying, Fuk-tsang, "Using Facts to Convince Me: The Six Explanations in Defence of the Chinese Communist's Religious Policy," July 9, 2018, in http://faith100.org/, access date: February 3, 2019a.
Ying, Fuk-tsang, "Today we have to revisit a history of 'united front' work on Christians," January 28, 2019b, in http://faith100.org/, access date: February 3, 2019.
Zen, Joseph Ze-kiun, "The Pope Doesn't Understand China," October 24, 2018, in https://www.nytimes.com/2018/10/24/opinion/pope-china-vatican-church-catholics-bishops.html, access date: February 4, 2019.

Index[1]

A
Academics, 8n30, 9, 14, 15, 42, 77, 154, 197, 198, 201, 320, 324, 326–328, 330, 354, 372
Aircrew officers' strikes, 144
All-China Federation of Women Hong Kong Delegates Association (ACFWHKDA), 150, 160
All-China Women Federation (ACWF), 153, 157, 160, 182, 186
All-China Youth Federation (ACYF), 255–258, 260, 261, 263, 266, 267, 273, 287
Alliance, 1, 71–73, 100, 106, 110, 126, 130, 184, 190, 229, 238, 301, 370
America, 12, 198, 302, 375
Anglican Church, 207, 217
Anti-foreign, 353
Anti-national education movement, 3, 265
Anti-Occupy interest groups, 66, 105
Apathy, 24, 36, 373, 376
Apple Daily, 293, 295
Article 23, 6n26, 13, 212, 338, 348, 352
Association for the Advancement of Feminism (AAF), 150, 161, 185, 186
Association of Hong Kong Nursing Staff, 122
Attack, 5, 6, 11, 15, 136, 190, 206, 278, 287, 329, 367
Australia, 42, 111, 302, 363, 364, 378
Authoritarian, 25, 31–35, 40, 41, 200, 329, 366, 371, 373, 375, 377
politics, 26, 301, 312, 374, 378
Authoritarianism, 17, 33, 34, 109, 331, 369, 373, 375, 377, 379
Autonomous, 22, 30, 161, 209, 239, 305, 314, 330, 338, 365, 369, 371, 372, 375

---

[1] Note: Page numbers followed by 'n' refer to notes.

© The Author(s) 2019
S. S.-H. Lo et al., *China's New United Front Work in Hong Kong*,
https://doi.org/10.1007/978-981-13-8483-7

402 INDEX

Autonomy, 8–10, 13, 14, 28, 202, 205, 211, 304, 342

B

Ban, 6n26, 29, 30, 295
Basic Law, 4, 6n26, 9, 14, 14n42, 68n13, 98, 99n59, 169, 207, 212, 229, 244, 257, 265, 278, 311, 327, 338, 348, 365, 365n1, 366
  interpretation, 5, 14, 14n42, 29, 67, 68n13, 70, 99, 99n59, 244, 251, 283, 377
Basic Law Committee members, 98, 100, 342
Basic Law Consultative Committee, 46, 205, 207
Beijing, 4–8, 10, 13, 14, 17–19, 21, 22, 24–32, 36, 38–41, 44, 45, 47, 50, 61, 67, 68n13, 70, 74, 75, 78, 81, 93, 94, 154, 160, 182, 184, 190–192, 194–197, 199, 203, 204, 206–209, 211–219, 225, 230, 232, 233, 255, 256, 258, 267, 270, 272, 273, 275, 280, 283, 293, 295, 298, 301, 305, 306, 314, 320, 324, 326, 327, 331, 334, 338–343, 345, 348–350, 352–354, 356, 357, 359–361, 364–369, 371, 372, 374, 377–379
Bing-leung, Cheung Anthony, 349, 350
Bishops, 210–213, 210–211n77, 213n84
British, 5, 6n26, 23–25, 30, 39, 46, 113–117, 146, 150, 152, 189–191, 195, 203, 215, 222, 223, 225, 232, 277, 298, 310–312, 327, 342, 343, 353, 377

British colonial administration, 222, 223
Buddhist, 185, 189–195, 215–217, 217n94, 219, 361, 371
Business, 20, 21, 25, 44, 69, 79, 80, 83, 91, 94, 106, 111, 140, 142, 143, 150n3, 199, 205, 258, 334, 337–364
  elites, 6, 42, 92, 94, 106, 224, 258, 260, 263, 337–364, 370, 374
  people, 2, 3, 5, 8, 21, 37, 83, 94, 133, 143, 263, 272, 304, 340, 345n19, 345n20, 346, 346n25, 356, 361, 364, 367
Business and Professionals Alliance (BPA), 337, 339–342
Businessman, 92, 94, 266, 340, 342–346, 363
By-elections, 16, 51, 52, 65, 66, 70, 74, 91, 185n52, 244, 248, 249, 251, 280

C

Campaign, 4, 5, 16, 33, 64, 66, 100, 103, 110, 126, 160, 165, 169, 208, 218, 225, 229, 235, 238, 240, 249–252, 349, 368, 372
  expenditure, 248–250
Candidates, 9, 16, 19, 51–55, 57–59, 70, 84, 88–91, 93, 95, 97, 106, 108, 112, 126, 130–132, 146, 160, 161, 163–166, 168, 175, 184, 211, 221, 229, 230, 238, 242, 244, 249, 251–253, 270, 280, 315–317, 325, 327, 329, 338, 339, 366, 375
Capitalist, 1, 7, 32, 305, 368, 375
  class, 1, 6, 17, 368, 370
Catholic/Catholics, 139, 189, 190, 194, 210–215, 217, 219, 314, 371

INDEX 403

Cells, 11, 21, 230
Censorship, 375
Central government, 6, 9, 10, 12, 17, 19, 25, 29–31, 40, 67, 74, 93, 94n56, 154, 184, 197, 206, 275, 295, 326, 338–342, 348, 362, 365, 366, 369, 377
Chan, Anson, 352, 353, 353n30
Chee-hwa, Tung, 30, 90, 200, 238, 317, 327, 338, 352, 353
Chengzhi, Liao, 2, 3, 6
Cheuk-yan, Lee, 130, 131, 136, 249, 252
Chief Executive, 19, 27, 28, 30, 32, 37, 39, 49, 67, 68, 78, 96, 97, 106, 132, 141, 154, 157, 195, 199, 207, 208, 213, 215, 229, 266, 271, 276, 317, 322, 338–342, 370, 372, 374
  election, 19, 93, 94n56, 96, 97, 154, 338, 349, 352
China, 1–75, 78, 116, 169–178, 190, 222, 256, 301, 337, 342–347, 368, 373–378
Chinese Association of Hong Kong and Macao Studies (CAHKMS), 324, 326, 327
Chinese Communist Party (CCP), 1–7, 4n18, 11–13, 17, 18, 20–23, 31–35, 43, 78–80, 88, 108, 171, 179, 199, 200, 206, 207, 209, 210, 212, 219, 223, 230, 240, 256, 276, 293, 299, 301, 303, 305, 310, 312, 329, 333, 343n15, 344, 360–362, 367, 369, 372–374, 376, 379
Chinese dream, 17, 26, 198, 260, 303
Chinese General Chamber of Commerce, 45
Chinese identity, 4, 7, 13, 15, 23, 43, 360, 365, 376

The Chinese Muslim Cultural and Fraternal Association (CMCFA), 203, 204
Chinese national identity, 54, 159, 311, 368
Chinese Patriotic Catholic Association (CPCA), 210
Chinese People's Political Consultative Conference (CPPCC), 2, 11–14, 20, 49, 78, 84, 92, 98, 99, 106, 133, 146, 159, 169, 171–175, 177, 181, 191, 199, 200, 204, 208, 216, 217, 217n94, 230, 240, 247, 248, 258, 271, 305, 340, 340n4, 341, 349, 350, 356, 357, 360–362, 366, 367, 375
Chinese renaissance, 13, 17, 26, 196, 197, 247
Chi-wai, Sik, 191, 192
Christian, 189, 193, 194, 206–210, 215–217, 219, 276, 314, 371
Chun-hoi, Pang, 125
Citizenship, 17, 35–36, 109, 360, 363, 372, 373, 375
Civic Party, 278, 347, 348, 353
Civil servants, 14, 42, 49, 54, 122, 131, 251, 337–364
Civil servants' unions, 122, 124
Civil society, 17, 26–27, 30, 32, 40–42, 289–335, 368, 371–373, 376, 377, 379, 380
Clans, 14, 16, 54, 65–67, 103, 222, 231, 289, 334, 335, 368, 369, 376
Clansmen Association, 87
Coalition, 7, 108, 145, 219, 365
Collective bargaining bill, 112, 136, 146
Common interests, 78
Communist International, 1
Communist Youth League, 256, 310
Competitiveness, 57, 140, 273

Comprehensive jurisdiction, 7, 10, 13, 14, 365, 367, 374
Comrades, 3, 12, 13, 22, 30, 43, 44, 88
Confederation of Trade Unions, 107–147
Confront, 5
Confrontation, 311n32, 329, 330
Confrontational, 348
Confrontational approach, 113, 206
Confucian, 189, 193, 194, 199, 200, 215, 217, 219, 371
Confucian Academy, 198–202
Confucius Institute, 198–202
Conservative nationalists, 23n64, 32, 353
Constitution, 4, 10, 205, 265, 362, 366
Convention, 100, 190, 263, 365
Convergence, 17, 21–25, 375, 380
Cooperative Resources Center (CRC), 337, 338
Co-optation, 13, 15, 19–21, 42, 160, 169–174, 181, 189, 194, 205, 208, 214–219, 224, 225, 232, 263, 271, 274, 279, 301, 309, 320, 327, 337, 342–344, 346, 350, 352, 356, 367, 374
Co-opted, 7, 157, 158, 169, 171, 181, 182, 186, 187, 195, 199, 200, 206–209, 206n60, 216, 235, 258, 262, 299, 311, 326, 350, 352, 374
Co-optees, 327
Coordination, 14, 16, 34, 44, 61–73, 153, 197, 277, 314, 379
Co-production, 299
Core, 4, 10, 16, 20, 29, 153, 160–162, 186, 205, 230, 255–256, 258, 287, 292, 339, 368–370
Court, 13, 91, 169, 185, 251, 283

Critical Marxists, 280
Culturally Chinese, 22, 256, 376
Culturally patriotic, 256
Culture, 13, 23, 24, 31, 32, 79, 195, 196, 198, 200–202, 217, 239, 266, 271, 290, 293, 376

D
Democratic Alliance for the Betterment and Progress of Hong Kong (DAB), 14–16, 43–75, 78, 90–92, 94, 95, 106, 112, 126, 129, 130, 146, 160, 175, 177, 178, 182, 183, 224, 229, 230, 232, 235–239, 244, 245, 248–253, 263, 314, 325, 349, 366, 368, 369, 371, 379
Democratic centralism, 31, 48
Democratic parties, 2, 11–13, 43
Democratic Party, 21, 90, 108, 178, 179, 348–350
Democratic political reform, 185
Democratic Progressive Party (DPP), 357, 360, 361, 364, 378
Democratization, 4, 40, 75, 110, 213, 270, 295, 329, 348, 354, 354n32, 370, 372
Democrats, 3, 5, 7, 9, 18, 19, 31, 34, 42, 51, 66, 131, 160, 161, 179, 182, 207, 208, 213, 250, 252, 253, 270, 293, 312, 328, 333, 337–365, 367, 370, 375–377
Depoliticization, 24
Direct elections, 37n127, 46, 49, 51–53, 55, 65, 70, 84, 126, 130, 146, 161, 164, 169, 171, 207, 242, 246, 251–252, 334, 338, 349, 369, 370
Disrespect, 14, 29, 169
Disrespectful, 185, 251, 366, 377

District Councils, 31, 41, 44, 52–55, 54n11, 59, 74, 84, 89–91, 95, 100, 112, 130, 131, 146, 165, 168, 169, 175–179, 185, 236–240, 242, 265, 266, 272, 328, 342, 369, 373, 377
District federations, 221–253, 376, 379
District-based, 96, 152, 155, 156, 171–179, 184, 222, 233, 242, 244, 246
District-based federations, 39, 42, 178–184, 229–232, 246, 252, 253
Divergence, 348, 380
Dock workers' dispute, 144
Donation, 70, 87, 144, 152, 153, 157, 175, 176, 178, 184, 185, 199, 209, 238, 245, 249, 276, 310, 343, 363

E
Eastern District All-Sectors Association (EDAA), 246
East Kowloon District Residents' Committee (EKDRC), 242, 243
Economic integration, 22, 22n59, 244, 273, 292, 353, 367
Economic interactions, 356
Editorial position, 295–298
Editorials, 293, 295, 304, 306, 339, 377
Education, 3, 4, 6n26, 24, 61, 85, 151, 154, 176, 193, 201, 202, 216, 218, 223, 239, 244, 261, 265, 266, 272, 279, 289–335, 346, 349, 350, 372, 376, 380
Education functional constituency, 315

Education sector, 149n2, 289, 291, 309–327
Educators, 42, 45, 86, 138, 317, 322, 327, 337–364, 372
Election Committee, 19, 78, 91, 92, 96, 97, 132, 133, 199, 208, 214, 215, 266, 322, 325
Elections, 9, 44, 49–59, 84, 108, 154, 207, 221, 224, 311, 338, 366
Electoral affairs committee, 249
Electoral competition, 17, 30–32, 35, 74, 91, 130, 131, 225, 338, 373
Electoral engineering activities, 249
Electoral machine, 106, 253
Electoral mobilization, 31, 36, 38, 100, 165, 221–253, 368
Electoral performance, 55
Elite/elites, 5, 7, 17, 19, 32, 39–41, 44, 48, 91, 94–96, 152, 153, 156, 171, 177, 181, 182, 184, 207, 222, 224, 225, 232, 245, 246, 248, 252, 258, 262, 266, 272–274, 287, 309, 327, 330, 337–365, 373–375, 378
Elite-mass gap, 17, 25–26, 376
Elite-mass linkage, 26
Enemies, 5, 7, 15, 166, 206, 219, 301, 327–331, 340, 353, 354, 365, 367, 377, 378
Entrepreneurs, 45, 156, 271, 312
Erbao, Cao, 8, 8n31, 9
Espionage, 356–362, 364, 378
Ethnic minorities, 3, 11–13, 15, 43, 48, 85, 196, 205, 368
Executive Council (ExCo), 9, 49, 136, 140, 143, 144, 162, 169, 338, 339, 342, 349, 350
Executive Councilors, 49, 163
External, 2, 9, 42, 92, 272, 280, 337–364
Extradition arrangement, 340

F
Factionalism, 113, 349
Federation of Hong Kong and Kowloon Labour Unions (FLU), 118, 120, 121, 123, 125, 126, 132, 144, 320
Federation of Trade Unions (FTU), 14, 42, 52, 53, 64, 91, 107–147, 160, 200, 224, 233, 235, 238, 245, 252, 253, 317, 369, 371, 379
Federations, 14, 16, 42, 157, 178–184, 187, 221–253, 257, 262, 263, 371, 376, 379
Feminist, 150, 185
Fok Ying-tung, Henry, 342–344
Foreign countries, 42, 271, 295, 337, 353, 363, 377–379
Foreigners, 39, 202, 327, 328, 337, 353, 363, 364
Fragmentation, 107, 113, 139, 146
Freedom, 206, 207, 211, 214, 304–306, 354, 361
Freedom of speech, 36, 180, 329
Fujian, 79–81, 80n12, 83, 85, 88, 106, 150n3, 159, 196, 246, 263
Fujianese, 14, 42, 77–106, 246, 253, 344, 369, 371
Fujian Overseas Chinese Association, 80
The Fukienese Association, 81–85
Functional constituencies, 31, 91, 125, 128, 164, 169, 215, 251, 272, 315, 341, 370

G
Geopolitical, 18, 39–40, 374, 377
Globalization, 23, 267, 290
Government Employees Association, 121
Grassroots level, 55, 64, 65, 106, 122, 130, 155, 159, 225, 252, 339, 346
Greater Bay Area, 15, 22, 42, 84, 179, 194, 208, 244, 246, 267, 273, 291, 309, 334, 335, 367, 368, 370, 372
Greater Bay Area plan, 15, 291, 331, 335, 361, 368
Guanxi, 33, 83, 85, 160

H
Hakka, 250
Hardline, 143, 353, 356
Hin-chi, Tsang, 346
The Hong Kong Army Cadets Association (HKASTA), 273–277
Hong Kong Chinese Christian Churches Union, 209
The Hong Kong Chinese Women's Club (HKCWC), 150–153, 156, 185
Hong Kong Christian Industrial Committee (CIC), 161
Hong Kong Civil Servants General Union (CSGU), 122, 132
Hong Kong Commercial Daily, 46, 298
Hong Kong CPPCC Youth Association (CPPCCYA), 255, 271–273, 287
Hong Kong Federation of Buddhist Associations, 192
Hong Kong Federation of Civil Service Unions (FCSU), 132
Hong Kong Federation of Fujian Associations (HKFFA), 77, 78, 81, 83–85, 91, 92, 97, 100–106
Hong Kong Federation of Women (HKFW), 150, 153–160, 166, 169, 178, 183, 184, 186, 369

Hong Kong Fukien Chamber of
  Commerce, 81
Hong Kong identity, 15, 17, 23, 37,
  54, 223, 280, 330, 373, 376
Hong Kong Island Federation
  (HKIF), 53, 54, 64, 229–231,
  245–248
Hong Kong Island Women Association
  (HKIWA), 155, 182–184
Hong Kong National Party (HKNP),
  29, 280, 295, 297–298
Hong Kong Outlying Islands Women
  Association (OIWA), 171,
  174–177
Hong Kong Progressive Alliance
  (HKPA), 44, 45, 53, 91, 129
Hong Kong Public Relations
  Professionals' Association, 298
Hong Kong Special Administrative
  Region (HKSAR), 3, 17–18, 49,
  81, 109, 152, 190, 214–219,
  224, 256, 291, 305, 338, 365,
  376
Hong Kong Taoist Federation of
  Associations (HKTFA), 195–198
Hong Kong United Youth Association
  (HKUYA), 255–266, 287
Hong Kong Women Development
  Association (HKWDA), 150,
  150n3, 155, 159–162, 177
Hong-man, Ng, 45
Human rights, 37, 68, 75, 185, 202,
  214, 256, 304, 306, 370–372,
  374

I
Ideological, 17, 23, 28, 32, 112, 146,
  289, 290, 349, 372–374, 377
  conflicts, 31–35
  enemy, 113
  inclinations, 256
  indoctrination, 309
Ideology, 33, 108, 112, 118, 121,
  219, 225, 279, 290
Inaugural ceremony, 85, 177, 265,
  265n7, 266, 271
Independence, 3, 5, 6n26, 8, 13, 28,
  29, 43, 68, 93, 244, 280, 305,
  306, 320, 354, 356, 364, 367
Individual, 1, 2, 12, 14–16, 24, 27,
  30, 35, 36, 38, 43, 69, 111, 131,
  153, 171, 180, 185, 221, 233,
  236, 237, 257, 258, 320, 326,
  327, 337–364, 372
  academics, 324, 326
Indoctrination, 32
Industrialist, 45
Infiltrate, 17, 40, 80, 153
Infiltration, 17, 20, 310, 368, 379
Infrastructure projects, 345, 346
Intellectuals, 2, 3, 5, 11, 12, 14, 15,
  28, 138, 201, 290, 310, 324,
  328, 330, 372
Interest groups, 12, 14–17, 25–27,
  32, 35, 39, 42, 44, 67, 77–106,
  110, 149–187, 190, 200,
  203–205, 214, 221, 224, 225,
  229, 231, 233, 235–238,
  240–242, 244–246, 252, 253,
  255–287, 289, 309, 310, 314,
  317, 319, 324, 325, 334, 359,
  363, 364, 367–369, 371, 372,
  376, 377
International Labour Organization
  (ILO), 111–112
Internet, 293, 295, 371, 375
  media, 290, 306–309, 371
Inter-union rivalry, 107–147
Intervene, 8, 278, 365
Intervention, 8, 10, 36, 38, 39, 280,
  329, 366, 377
Investment, 85, 136, 190, 331, 343,
  346, 374

Islam, 203, 205
Islamic, 79, 189, 193, 194, 203–205, 219, 371

J
Japan, 41, 79, 85, 150, 154, 169, 191, 310, 311
Jiang Zemin, 3, 256
Judicial autonomy, 75
Judicial process, 67
Judiciary, 9
Justice and Peace Commission (JPC), 214, 214n88

K
kaifong, 224, 225
Kaifong associations (KA), 14, 15, 42, 221–229, 252, 379
Kin-chiu, Sik, 192
Kong-wah, Lau, 130, 276, 349
Kowloon City Residents Association (KCRA), 242, 244, 250
Kowloon Federation of Associations (KFA), 16, 53, 54, 64, 95, 158, 179, 229, 230, 233, 240–244, 251
Kowloon West New Dynamic (KWND), 241, 243, 250
Kowloon Women's Organization Federation (KWOF), 155, 179–182
Kuok Hock-nien, Robert, 344, 344n18
Kuomintang (KMT), 1, 223, 310, 337, 357, 360–362
Kuo-yu, Han, 362, 367
Kwok-kwong, Sik, 190
Kwun Tong Residents Association (KTRA), 242

L
Labor movement, 113, 118, 147
Labour Advisory Board, 117, 118, 131, 132, 136, 141, 143, 144
Lam, Carrie, 49, 132, 154, 215, 247, 265, 265n7, 271, 304, 304n17, 327, 334, 338, 341, 349, 356
Lee Wai-king, Starry, 46, 47, 183, 229, 244, 245, 248, 252
Legislative clique, 37, 338
Legislative Council (LegCo), 4, 14, 29, 31, 37, 37n127, 41, 44, 46, 49, 51, 52, 58, 65, 70, 73–75, 84, 91, 92, 95, 100, 106, 112, 125, 126, 128–130, 133, 136, 140, 141, 144, 146, 161, 162, 164, 167, 169, 207, 215, 218, 222, 229, 242, 244, 246, 248, 251, 252, 265, 272, 280, 282, 314, 315, 328, 337, 339, 341, 342, 349, 369, 373, 377
Legislative Council members, 92, 150n3, 169, 337
Legislative Councilors, 164, 236, 349
Legislature, 49, 126, 169, 215, 251, 338, 339, 370, 374
Legitimacy, 17–20, 25, 26, 28, 30, 31, 33, 34, 40, 212, 224n7, 301, 309, 330, 354n32, 366, 373, 374, 377
Leung, Baggio, 14, 15, 29, 99n59, 166, 169, 282, 283
Leung, C. Y., 28, 49, 195, 271, 276, 338–341
Liaison Office (LO), 7–9, 14–16, 61–73, 78, 83–85, 87, 100, 153, 156, 159, 166, 178, 179, 182, 183, 190, 193, 196, 197, 200, 204, 213, 228, 244–247, 253, 265, 267, 271, 272, 277–279, 303, 304, 304n17, 311, 317,

330, 334, 340, 341, 349, 362, 365–368, 371
Li-an, Lu, 359–361
Liberalization, 23
Liberalize, 30
Liberal Party (LP), 51, 53, 129, 142, 143, 252, 337–342, 340n8, 363
Lik, Ma, 46, 91
Livelihood, 140, 177, 306
  issues, 16, 61, 68, 229, 230, 244, 252
Localism, 61, 279
Localist groups, 255, 256, 276, 284–287
Localist/localists, 4, 14, 28, 29, 32, 36–38, 70, 239, 246, 251, 255, 275, 279–287, 292, 320, 373
Local politicians, 97, 106, 131, 353

M

Macao, 2–4, 2n9, 6, 11–14, 20, 22, 43, 44, 183, 191, 192, 197, 204, 219, 257, 267, 273, 278, 291, 302, 324, 326, 327, 331, 334, 335, 361, 362, 364, 367, 379
Mainland, 3, 4, 6, 8–16, 18, 20–22, 31, 35, 39, 40, 42, 59, 64, 67–70, 78, 83, 84, 87, 100, 116, 118, 121, 123, 132, 150, 151, 153, 154, 156, 157, 159, 169, 171, 177, 181, 189–192, 194–199, 201, 205–208, 210–214, 219, 221, 222, 225, 230, 239, 242, 244–246, 255–257, 262, 263, 266, 267, 271–273, 287, 291–293, 299–301, 303–310, 312, 324, 326, 327, 329–331, 333–335, 337, 340, 342–346, 349, 353, 356–364, 368–380, 371n5
Mainlandization, 292, 292n8, 305–308, 374
Maintain stability, 16, 33, 112, 146, 192, 199, 221, 222, 247
Maladministration, 289
Manifesto, 44, 67, 283, 286
Mao Zedong, 1, 33, 257
Mass/masses, 12, 13, 25, 25n76, 26, 30–34, 36, 37, 39–41, 64, 80, 184, 213, 225, 229, 238, 289–335, 352, 366, 377
Mass media, 19, 20, 32, 46, 78, 106, 179, 191, 192, 266, 274, 275, 278, 289–335, 353
Materialism, 36–38, 374
Materialistic, 17, 37, 37n127, 38, 40, 160, 221, 256, 287, 372, 373, 375
May 1967 riot, 116
Media, 5, 21, 28, 39, 42, 169, 179, 218, 266, 276, 277, 289–335, 353, 367, 371, 375, 377
  ownership, 293
Meeting Point, 349
Membership, 21, 48, 49, 53, 55, 57, 74, 78, 96, 98, 109, 113, 115–118, 120–123, 127, 159, 175, 209, 229, 230, 232–237, 240, 245, 258, 260, 263, 265, 266, 272, 277, 314, 317, 319, 321–322, 324, 340, 357
Middle class, 6, 17, 30, 251, 252
Migrants, 21, 77n2, 109, 222, 230, 242, 263, 267, 291, 331, 333, 334, 371, 378
Migrate, 45, 46, 79, 92, 151, 242, 263, 312, 331, 361, 370, 371n5
Migration, 42, 289–335, 370
Military, 5, 18, 27, 211, 274, 277–279, 287, 301, 309, 337, 362, 367
  camp, 278, 367

Minimum wage legislation, 141–143, 147
Mobilization strategy, 251
Moderate, 5–7, 111, 112, 118, 146, 152, 206, 208–210, 213, 251, 256, 280, 293, 295, 347, 349, 365
Modernization, 3, 21, 23, 30, 80, 209, 342–347, 374, 375
Mongkok Kaifong Association (MKA), 225, 228
Mongkok riot, 4, 36, 156, 265
Muslim, 79, 203–205, 215, 217, 219
Mutual Aid Committees (MACs), 224, 240

N
Nai-keung, Lau, 349
Nai-wang, Kwok, 207–209, 207n64, 219
National education, 3, 3n15, 4, 6n26, 85, 314, 349, 372
National education policy, 3, 193, 309, 314, 372, 376
National People's Congress (NPC), 5, 7, 20, 45, 49, 67, 78, 98, 106, 133, 135, 311, 366
National security, 10, 27, 30–32, 40, 266, 280, 330, 356–362, 364, 373, 376, 377
National security interest, 7, 246, 365
Neighborhood associations, 14, 15, 25, 42, 221–253
Neutrality, 26, 122
New China News Agency (NCNA), 5–7, 20, 190, 191, 207, 368
New Party, 337, 357, 357n36
New People's Party (NPP), 14, 51, 52, 129, 245, 246, 252, 352
Newspapers, 293–295, 303, 304, 339

New Territories Associations of Societies (NTAS), 53, 54, 229–240
Nomenklatura, 20, 21, 230, 240, 266
Non-governmental organizations, 161, 198, 205, 228, 279
North Point, 85, 88–91

O
Oath-taking, 5, 5n21, 14, 29, 70, 99n59, 169, 170, 185, 251, 282, 283
Occupy Central Movement, 4, 5, 6n26, 9, 35, 66, 67, 84, 100, 103, 131, 149, 154, 156, 160, 177, 179–182, 185, 193, 207, 213, 218, 225, 226, 229, 239, 244, 246, 263, 265, 267, 273, 274, 277, 287, 295–297, 301, 306, 340, 347, 348, 354, 372, 373, 378
Officials, 6–8, 15, 16, 18, 19, 27, 28, 34, 36–39, 47, 49, 52, 55, 67, 70, 74, 75, 78, 80, 81, 81n20, 83–85, 88, 93, 100–106, 153, 157, 159, 162, 166, 182, 183, 189, 190, 194, 196, 201, 204, 206, 208, 209n71, 210, 212, 213, 230, 231, 245–250, 253, 265–270, 272, 273, 276, 277, 310, 317, 333, 339, 342, 343, 345, 350, 353, 354, 356–359, 362, 367, 368, 377, 379
One country, two mixed systems, 379–380
One country, two systems, 3, 8–10, 8n31, 10n35, 21, 23, 42, 43, 61, 84, 88, 93, 154, 157, 193, 195, 217, 247, 265, 298, 304, 324, 329, 339, 353, 356, 366, 368, 379

One-way permit, 291, 331–333
Organization/organizations, 12, 14–16, 19, 20, 25, 26, 33, 39, 41, 44–49, 53, 54, 59–61, 64, 66, 77n2, 78–81, 83–85, 93–95, 103, 110, 122, 150, 153–156, 159, 160, 169, 174–179, 182, 184, 201, 203, 211, 221–223, 225, 228–233, 235, 239–242, 245, 250, 255, 257, 258, 265, 267, 271, 272, 293, 295–299, 304, 305, 317, 327
Oriental Daily News, 295, 340n4
Owners Corporations (OC), 224, 240
Ownership, 293–295, 304, 305, 371

P
Pao, Sir Yue-kong, 343, 344
Party, 1, 3, 11, 12, 13n41, 14, 16, 20, 21, 23, 26, 31, 37, 43, 44, 48, 49, 55, 57, 59, 61, 65–68, 78, 81, 88, 92, 94, 112, 121, 130, 175, 176, 199, 204, 212, 224n8, 230, 238, 240, 249, 278, 289–291, 295, 297–298, 301, 303, 309, 333, 339–341, 347–350, 357, 363, 368, 374, 375
  members, 59, 179, 252, 353, 357, 363
Paternalistic authoritarianism, 17, 373
Path of Democracy, 348
Patriotic, 4, 7, 11, 16, 22, 24, 27, 83, 106, 122, 212, 233, 239, 244, 246, 256, 258, 260, 271, 292, 311, 312, 339, 343, 349, 365–367, 371, 376
  forces, 4, 83
Patriotism, 88, 118, 200, 257, 271, 274, 287, 299n12, 343, 365, 376
Patron-client relations, 38, 179, 378

Peaceful, 100, 185, 193
Peaceful resistance, 36, 372, 373, 375, 378
Peaceful reunification, 43–44, 258, 266
Penetrate, 27, 41, 175, 201, 223, 224, 251, 290, 301, 304, 305, 309, 310, 320, 369, 372
Penetrative politics, 5–17, 42, 221–253, 255, 291, 305, 309–327, 335, 366, 368, 369, 371, 372, 376, 378–380
People First Party, 357
People's Liberation Army (PLA), 247, 265, 271, 278–279, 301, 367
People's Republic of China (PRC), 1, 43, 77, 107, 153, 189, 221, 255, 290, 337, 365
Peripheral, 16, 41, 161, 178, 256
Periphery, 41, 255
Pluralism, 17, 31, 32, 32n98, 78n6, 370, 373
Pluralistic, 26, 31–35, 32n99, 39–41, 291, 309, 330, 375, 377
Police, 4, 32, 100, 113, 116, 139, 154, 182, 222, 223, 239, 244, 251, 274, 277, 309, 350
Policies, 2, 3, 6–10, 6n26, 10n35, 13, 14, 18, 19, 23, 23n64, 26, 32, 34, 37, 40, 41, 43, 44, 48, 59, 61–74, 78, 80–83, 85, 88, 92, 94, 99, 106, 109–112, 133, 136, 146, 157–160, 162, 176, 182, 184, 185, 193, 194, 202, 206, 209, 213, 214, 217, 218, 223, 225, 239, 240, 247, 253, 255, 257, 267, 272, 273, 289, 291, 293, 303, 304, 320, 324, 327, 335, 340, 342, 345, 349, 353, 356, 359, 361, 363, 365–368, 374, 377
Policy suggestions, 68, 69

412 INDEX

Po Lin Monastery, 189–195
Politburo, 3, 11
Political
   appointment, 121, 217, 258, 309
   capture, 53, 221, 225, 228
   control, 19–21, 23, 31, 40, 375
   co-optation, 15, 208, 216, 224, 225, 232, 252, 263, 271, 274, 337, 350, 352
   divide, 295, 311, 361, 379
   enemies, 7, 365
   force, 9, 15, 44, 90, 91, 106, 225, 228, 258
   influence, 260, 287, 370, 375
   ingredient, 182
   legitimization, 290
   line, 341, 375
   mobilization, 26, 32, 54, 103, 123, 166–170, 181, 240
   opposition, 17, 30–31, 373, 377
   outlook, 298, 334
   participation, 33, 35, 61, 77–106, 162–166, 168, 263, 267, 317
   realities, 67
   representation, 49, 50, 78, 132, 134–135, 169, 171
   stance, 67, 354
   structure, 64
   struggle, 35n119, 113, 376, 380
   threat, 18, 374
   tolerance, 301, 340
Politically loyal position, 342
Politically neutral, 156–157, 317, 320, 340, 350, 372
Politically opportunistic, 256
Politico-economic convergence, 17, 21–25, 373, 380
Pope, 210–213
Popularity, 130, 306–308, 370
Populist authoritarianism, 32–34, 377
Positive synergy (PS), 241, 243

Post-materialistic, 17, 37, 38, 40, 256, 287, 371, 372, 374, 375, 378, 380
Post-materialist values, 36–38, 373
Po-yan, Wong, 99, 99n59
PRC Buddhist Association, 191, 194, 195
PRC Taoist Association, 195–198
Press, 4n18, 36, 280, 303, 304n19, 305, 306, 330
Principal officials, 9, 19, 34, 39, 49, 276
Pro-Beijing, 149–187
   forces, 34, 45, 51, 52, 54, 55, 74, 78, 95, 106, 161, 165, 166, 182, 225, 253, 315, 317, 320, 328, 334, 335, 367, 369–371, 376
   front, 52, 221, 255–287, 348
   schools, 274, 312–314
Pro-democracy, 9, 10, 17, 19, 30, 34, 37, 40–42, 50, 52, 54, 66, 70–75, 90, 93, 107–147, 150, 161, 162, 165, 166, 169, 170, 180, 185, 187, 207, 213, 214, 219, 224, 249, 251, 252, 256, 265, 276, 293, 295, 306, 309, 315–317, 320, 322, 328–330, 334, 348–354, 370–372, 374–380
   forces, 19, 31, 44, 50, 52, 55, 68, 70–75, 166, 175, 221, 238, 315, 320, 338, 370, 371, 378
Professionals, 16, 25, 43–45, 48, 61, 133, 146, 154, 155, 159, 160, 171, 258, 260, 271, 272, 287, 298, 306, 314
Professional Teachers' Union (PTU), 121, 316, 317, 320, 320n42, 322
Pro-independence, 361, 376
Propaganda, 159, 201, 280, 289, 310, 357, 369

Pro-Taiwan, 3, 5, 8, 113, 117, 118, 125, 231, 233, 364
Protest/protests, 7n28, 8, 8n29, 30, 35, 36, 45, 78, 90, 100, 116, 118, 141, 142, 175, 238, 239, 309, 310, 317, 329, 352, 356, 366, 375
Protestors, 4, 30, 100, 141, 154, 310
Provisional Legislative Council, 91, 112, 136, 146, 191
Public opinion, 2, 2n6, 8, 80, 106, 136, 205, 309

R
Radical/radicals, 5, 7, 14, 29, 36, 42, 112, 118, 133, 136, 160, 169, 218, 255–287, 348, 365, 367, 375
Rapprochement, 211
Regional Council, 163, 164, 166
Religion, 13, 35, 42, 189–219
Religious, 9, 12, 13, 189, 190, 194–196, 203–210, 213–219, 214n85, 371
  groups, 39, 197, 205, 219, 369, 371, 376, 379
  leaders, 190, 193, 194, 197, 206–209, 207n64, 214–219, 218n98
Religious and charity groups, 2
Religious-governmental partnership, 219
Resist, 36, 38, 40, 42, 210, 214, 255, 276, 287, 338, 375
Resistance, 17–19, 32, 35–36, 209, 212, 255–287, 370, 372, 373, 375, 376, 378
Resistant, 194, 210, 219, 276, 280, 364, 374, 378, 380
Reunification, 9, 13, 44, 257, 258, 266, 356, 362, 363
Rule of law, 32–34, 37, 41, 169, 274, 306, 329, 346, 371–374, 380

S
Scholarism, 180, 193
Schools, 80, 85–88, 151–153, 157, 180, 189, 190, 195, 199, 203, 205, 208, 245, 273, 274, 278–280, 287, 290, 309, 310, 312–314, 317, 320, 346, 367
SCNPC interpretation, 15, 251
Secession, 6n26, 212, 338
Securitization, 27–30, 40, 376
Security, 7, 10, 27–32, 40, 141, 223, 251, 266, 280, 280n52, 328, 330, 350, 356–362, 364, 365, 373, 376, 377
Sedition, 6n26, 212, 338
Self-determination, 280
Separatist, 280n52
Separatist activity, 43
Shumshuipo Residents Association (SRA), 242, 250
Sing Tao Daily, 298
Sinification, 205
Sino United Publishing, 303
Socialization, 59, 290
Socially materialistic, 256
Social movement, 35, 108, 110–112, 110n16, 306
  unionism, 108–112, 117, 118, 139, 146
Social stability, 16, 44, 171, 192, 247, 257
Socio-economic integration, 309, 335
Socio-political mobilization, 183
Socio-political recognition, 187
Southern District All-Sectors Association (SDAA), 246
So-yuk, Choy, 90–92
Spiritual development, 185

414 INDEX

State-party-military alliance, 301
Steel benders' dispute, 136
Strategies, 4, 21, 31, 50, 110–112, 139, 144, 146, 202, 204, 206, 224, 233, 251, 252, 335, 347, 369
Strikes, 109–111, 113, 116, 118, 136, 138–140, 144, 146, 222, 247, 309
Subjective feelings, 181, 187
Subversion, 6n26, 212, 338
Subversive, 280, 330, 364
Success rate, 54, 55, 57–59, 131, 163, 164, 166, 168
Sustainable development, 37, 176, 185, 256, 306, 327, 371
Szeto Wah, 315

T

Taiwan, 3, 11–13, 41, 43, 44, 80n18, 86, 93, 156, 190, 198, 212, 219, 231, 257, 299–302, 311, 337, 356–359, 361–364, 378, 379
Ta Kung Pao, 5, 232, 271, 295, 298, 339
Taiwanese, 8, 42, 159, 301, 337–364, 378
Tan Kah Kee, 79, 79n11, 80n12
Tang Ying-ren, Henry, 338, 339, 350
Taoist, 189, 193–198, 215, 217, 219, 371
Taoist Cultural Study Center (TCSC), 198
Taoist Festival Day, 195, 196, 198
Terrorists, 9–11, 223
Think tank, 14, 324, 327, 348
Third Force, 349
Tiananmen incident, 6, 343n15, 345, 374
Tiananmen tragedy, 311
Tien, James, 142, 252, 338–342, 340n4, 340n5, 340n8

Tongxiang, 80n12, 81, 85, 106
Trade Union Council (TUC), 113, 117, 118, 125, 145, 146
Trade union politics, 107, 110, 113–117
Trade unions, 20, 25, 42, 107–147, 233, 235, 289, 317–320, 323–324
Transmission belts, 12, 25–27, 64–65, 106, 108, 171–178, 184, 253, 258, 369, 379
Transmission Belts, 25n76
Treason, 6n26, 213, 338
Tripartism, 108–112, 117, 118, 139, 146
Tsang, Jasper, 45, 46, 183, 252, 314
Two governing forces, 8
Typhoon, 190, 278, 287, 367

U

Underground, 21, 179, 210, 210n77, 211, 211n79, 223, 230, 310
Uniformed cadet groups, 255, 271–273, 275, 277
United Democrats of Hong Kong (UDHK), 129, 349
United front, 5–17
  campaign, 368, 369
  work, 1–75, 78, 78n4, 80, 85, 88, 93, 106, 133, 149, 157, 159–161, 166, 171–180, 185, 187, 189–219, 221, 223, 225, 229, 232, 239, 247–249, 251–253, 255–258, 260, 263, 265, 273, 274, 277, 279–287, 291–293, 299, 301, 305, 309, 311, 312, 314, 315, 317, 320, 326, 327, 333, 335, 337, 338, 350, 356, 357, 359, 361–380
United Front Work Regulations, 11, 43, 43n1, 43n2

United Kingdom, 59, 302, 353, 359, 377
United States, 6, 21, 59, 111, 199, 201, 311n30, 352, 353, 353n30, 367, 375, 377
Universities, 8n30, 12, 198, 200–202, 206n60, 207, 218, 222n1, 223n5, 239, 258, 263, 266, 290, 309–311, 310n26, 320, 326, 327, 343, 352, 354–357, 360, 361
Urban Councilors, 165
Utilization, 16, 17, 33, 34, 186, 229–232, 252, 367, 368

V
Vatican, 210–213, 211n77, 213n84
Violate, 4, 169, 304, 354, 362, 363, 378
Violence, 29, 35, 36, 162, 185
Violent, 4, 5, 34, 113, 139, 270
Volunteer, 81, 84, 159, 183, 242, 273, 287, 334, 335, 367, 368
Voter registration, 84
Voters, 16, 48, 50, 54, 55, 64, 65, 68, 70, 74, 75, 161, 166, 175, 177, 182, 225, 246, 252, 329, 334, 369, 377, 379
Votes, 7, 15, 37, 49–55, 57, 65, 68, 70, 73–75, 90, 91, 106, 131–133, 161, 178, 184, 215, 221, 230, 238, 242, 244, 249, 251–253, 314, 315, 322, 325, 328, 339n3, 348, 366, 369, 370, 375

W
Wanchai, 245, 246, 277
Wen Wei Po, 5, 77n1, 136, 138, 250, 295, 298, 330n55, 353n30

White Paper, 10, 154, 366
Women
 activists, 156, 176, 186, 187
 participation, 157, 163–167, 176, 186
The Women's Welfare Club, 152–153, 185
Wong, Joshua, 180, 193, 265, 372
Workers, 1, 43, 45, 69, 79, 95, 110–112, 117, 121, 130, 133, 136, 138, 139, 141–143, 147, 162, 222, 222n3, 228, 233–235, 251, 305, 309n26, 312, 314, 317, 345, 372
Working class, 6, 7, 17, 108, 113, 116, 133, 142, 147, 162, 224, 238, 368, 369, 372
Working hours, 141
Wu, Gordon Ying-sheung, 345, 346

X
Xiangqing, 80, 81
Xiangmo, Huang, 363, 364, 378
Xi Jinping, 3, 3n14, 7, 7n27, 11–13, 13n41, 17, 23, 26, 27, 32, 40, 41, 78n4, 84, 88, 202, 208, 209, 267, 274–276, 278, 303, 338, 338n2, 357, 362, 365–368, 374–377, 379
Xu Jiatun, 6, 190, 368

Y
Yandong, Liu, 194, 217, 217n94
Yau-sze, Ling, 361, 362
The Y Elites Association (YEA), 255, 266–272, 287
Ying-jeou, Ma, 359–361
Yiu, Edward Chung-yim, 52, 70, 169, 249, 251, 252
Yiu-chung, Tam, 46, 125, 136

Yiu-ting, Benny Tai, 5, 328–330, 328n52, 329n53, 369, 369n3, 372, 373
Yiu-tong, Cheng, 138, 143, 245
Youngspiration, 29, 280
Youth, 4, 6n26, 15, 29, 30, 39, 42, 43, 48, 58, 61, 79, 84, 116, 151, 176, 177, 218, 230, 239, 242, 245, 252, 255–287, 289, 306, 334, 335, 346, 357, 367, 368, 371n5, 372, 380
groups, 14, 15, 39, 42, 255–256, 271, 277, 279, 280, 287, 306, 379
Yuen-han, Chan, 129, 130, 136
Yu-shek, Cheng Joseph, 328–331, 328n51

Z
Ze-kiun, Joseph Zen, 211–214, 211n80, 213n82, 219
Zhou Enlai, 5, 200, 310